Constructing National Interests

BORDERLINES

A BOOK SERIES CONCERNED WITH REVISIONING GLOBAL POLITICS
Edited by David Campbell and Michael J. Shapiro

For more books in the series, see p. vi.

Constructing National Interests

The United States and the Cuban Missile Crisis

JUTTA WELDES

BORDERLINES, VOLUME 12

University of Minnesota Press

Minneapolis

London

Portions of this book, especially the introduction and chapter 3, first appeared as "Constructing National Interests," *European Journal of International Relations* 2(3) (1996); copyright 1996, reprinted by permission of Sage Publications, Ltd. Some material, used especially in chapters 5 and 7, is drawn from "Making State Action Possible: The U.S. and the Discursive Construction of 'the Cuban Problem,' 1960–1994," *Millennium: Journal of International Studies* 25(2) (1996); copyright *Millennium: Journal of International Studies,* reproduced here by permission of the publisher.

Published by the University of Minnesota Press
111 Third Avenue South, Suite 290
Minneapolis, MN 55401-2520
http://www.upress.umn.edu

Library of Congress Cataloging-in-Publication Data

Weldes, Jutta.
    Constructing national interests : the United States and the Cuban missile crisis / Jutta Weldes.
        p.   cm. — (Borderlines ; v. 12)
    Includes bibliographical references and index.
    ISBN 0-8166-3110-7 (hardcover). — ISBN 0-8166-3111-5 (pbk.)
        1. Cuban Missile Crisis, 1962.   2. National security—United States—History—20th century.   I. Title.   II. Series: Borderlines (Minneapolis, Minn.) ; v. 12.
    E841.W45 1999
    973.922—dc21   99-17321

Printed in the United States of America on acid-free paper

The University of Minnesota is an equal-opportunity educator and employer.

10 09 08 07 06 05 04 03 02 01 00 99   10 9 8 7 6 5 4 3 2 1

Contents

BORDERLINES

Acknowledgments

No book is produced outside of a specific social context, and this one is no different. Many of the ideas that appear here were first conceived, aired, discussed, dissected, reconceived, and so on in discussions and conversations at the University of Minnesota with Monali Chowdhurie, Rhona Leibel, Jennifer Milliken, Himadeep Muppidi, and Alex Wendt. Thanks for the specific ideas and suggestions, general support, timely advice, and a stubborn unwillingness to take a sloppy argument for an answer. I am also grateful to Bud Duvall, David Sylvan, Martin Sampson, John Mowitt, and Ron Aminzade for their careful readings of and suggestions on an earlier version of this argument. My special thanks to Diana Saco, who read and reread most of the chapters of this book. I am hugely grateful for her generosity. Her suggestions and insights, as well as our collaborative work, have enriched this book immensely. At a late stage in the preparation of the manuscript, David Welch agreed to read the first three chapters, to which he applied his considerable expertise on the Cuban missile crisis. I am grateful for his comments and observations, and for saving me from saying some things I really did not mean to say.

Bashorat Usmanova and Jack Blanton carried out the tedious task of checking the many quotations and citations in this book with thoroughness and good humor. Ridge Bowman saved my sanity when, just before the manuscript was due at the press, the a: drive on my computer died.

viii · ACKNOWLEDGMENTS

It has been a real pleasure to work with the people at the University of Minnesota Press. I would like especially to acknowledge Carrie Mullen and Lisa Freeman, whose encouragement and enthusiasm for the project has meant a lot to me. I am also grateful for advice and support from the editors of the Borderlines series, David Campbell and Michael Shapiro. Thanks are also due to an anonymous reviewer. I am indebted to Kathy Delfosse for her outstanding copy editing.

Finally, I would like to thank Mark Laffey for his friendship, encouragement, support, and understanding as I have worked on this book. I could not have done it without him. I would like to dedicate this book to my daughter, Sadie, and my son, Finian, who give my life meaning.

Introduction:
The Problem of National Interests

The notion of the national interest permits the state to jettison its erstwhile concern with life to assert and pursue concerns higher than life.

— WENDY BROWN, MANHOOD AND POLITICS

When you're asking Americans to die, you have to be able to explain it in terms of the national interest.

— HENRY KISSINGER, QUOTED IN KELLY,
"'AMICABLE DIVORCE' COULD TURN NASTY, EXPERTS SAY"

MAKING THE MEANING OF MISSILES

For most Americans, at least, the so-called Cuban missile crisis of October 1962 plainly revolved around the Soviet deployment of nuclear-capable missiles in Cuba. But is this really so obvious? Though the Soviet installation of medium-range ballistic missiles in Cuba provided a referent to which the Kennedy administration and others could articulate the notion of a "crisis," of a severe threat to U.S. national interests, the mere fact of the missile installation does not, and cannot, determine that meaning. To be sure, the detonation of a nuclear warhead in a populated area will result in the loss of human life. This consequence derives from thermonuclear physics and human physiology. The U.S. objection to the missiles in Cuba, however, was not based on such general claims about the threat that any nuclear weapons pose because of their physical properties. After all, the maintenance and legitimacy of the U.S. nuclear arsenal,

1

located both in the United States and abroad, has depended upon avoiding precisely this connection between "all nuclear weapons" and concerns with threats to human life. Physical facts, then, do not alone determine what meanings will be attached to particular weapons and what the implications of those weapons are for particular national interests. Instead, the U.S. objection to the missiles, the perception that the United States faced a serious foreign policy crisis, and the U.S. national interest were all based upon a more elaborate set of meanings, which exceeded any physical facts about the detrimental effects of nuclear explosions, that came to be attached to the missiles in Cuba.

That the missile deployment signaled a serious crisis and that the U.S. national interest in that crisis required that, one way or another, the missiles had to go seems self-evident to most of us because, for U.S. policy makers and for the public they instructed alike, the missiles quickly became laden with a multiplicity of interconnected meanings. Central to these meanings was the assumption that the only purpose these "large, long-range, and clearly offensive weapons of mass destruction" (Kennedy, 1962c: 2) could possibly serve was "to provide [the Soviet Union with] a nuclear strike capability against the Western Hemisphere" (1). The missiles, that is, were understood to be offensive weapons targeted at the United States and its allies: They represented "a major [Soviet] military investment in Cuba with advanced weapons systems with substantial offensive capability" (Rusk, 1962c: 720). But the missiles signified more. They meant, for example, that, in direct contravention of the Monroe Doctrine, the U.S.S.R. was willing to act aggressively in the Western Hemisphere. They meant that Kremlin-inspired international communism was on the march in this prized U.S. sphere of influence. And they meant that the credibility of the U.S. claim to lead the defense of the free world was in jeopardy. Awash as they were in this particular sea of meanings, the missiles were understood to pose an intolerable danger to the United States.

The Soviet missiles, in short, had to be *made* to mean something before it was possible for U.S. state officials to know what to do about them, or, for that matter, before it was possible to know whether anything needed to be done about them at all. This observation leads us directly to the question that animates this book: How do we get from the Soviet missile deployment in Cuba to the Cuban missile crisis, with its attendant U.S. national interest in forcing the removal of those missiles? I address this question by examining the processes through which the so-called national interests of states— and specifically of the U.S. state—come to be constructed.

RESURRECTING THE NATIONAL INTEREST

The concept of the national interest has long been central to theories of international politics because of its role in the explanation of state action. Nonetheless, the analytical usefulness of the national interest has been as often contested as defended. On one side of this dispute stand critics who argue that the notion of the national interest, though seductive, also has grave flaws. According to Steve Smith, for example, the popularity of the concept is due not to its analytical power, which is suspect, but to the fact that "it can be used to mean whatever the user wishes" and to its "commonsensical appeal" (1986: 23–26). Others have pronounced the concept to be "over-simplified and wrongheadedly dogmatic" (Hoffmann, 1978: 133) and denounced it as "a weapon that saps democratic processes" (David Wood, in Clinton, 1986: 495) because it is often used to stifle debate over foreign policy decisions and state actions. For a variety of reasons, in short, the concept of the national interest has been dismissed by some scholars as a moribund analytical concept with "little future" (Rosenau, 1968: 39).[1] On the other side of this dispute are those who insist that the notion of the national interest should remain central to explanations of state action and thus of international politics. Most prominent among this latter group of scholars are the realists, who follow Hans Morgenthau in his assertion that the national interest is explicitly "the main signpost that helps political realism to find its way through the landscape of international politics" (1978: 5).

In this book, I side with those who have argued for the continued salience of the national interest to accounts of state action and hence to theories of international politics. The national interest is important to explanations of international politics and so requires adequate theorization quite simply because it is the language of state action. In the making of foreign policy, the "internal language of decision is the language of national interest" (Hollis and Smith, 1990: 166). As even one rather strong critic of the national interest has admitted:

[political] actors have found . . . the concept useful both as a way of thinking about their goals and as a means of mobilizing support for them. That is, not only do political actors tend to perceive and discuss their goals in terms of the national interest, but they are also inclined to claim that their goals *are* the national interest, a claim that often arouses the support necessary to move toward a realization of the goals. Consequently, even though it has lost some of its early appeal as an analytical tool, the national interest enjoys considerable favor as a basis for action and has won a prominent place in the dialogue of public affairs. (Rosenau, 1968: 34, emphasis in the original)

In other words, the national interest is important to international politics in two ways. First, it is through this concept that policy makers understand the goals to be pursued by a state's foreign policy. It thus in practice forms the basis for state action. Second, it functions as a rhetorical device that generates the legitimacy of and political support for state action. The national interest thus wields considerable power in that it helps to constitute as important and to legitimize the actions taken by states. As Henry Kissinger recently put it: "When you're asking Americans to die, you have to be able to explain it in terms of the national interest" (in Kelly, 1995: 12). Because the national interest in practice plays these vital roles in the making of foreign policy, and so in determining state actions, it clearly should occupy a prominent place in accounts of international politics.[2]

But how should the national interest be conceptualized? I argue that it is best understood as a social construction. Before state officials can act for the state, they engage in a process of interpretation in order to understand both what situation the state faces and how they should respond to it. This process of interpretation, in turn, presupposes a language shared, at least, by those state officials involved in determining state action and by the audience for whom state action must be legitimate. This shared language is that of the national interest. The content of the national interest, I then argue, is produced in or emerges out of a process of representation through which state officials (among others) make sense of both their domestic and their international contexts. The national interest, that is, is constructed, is created as a meaningful object, out of shared meanings through which the world, particularly the international system and the place of the state in it, is understood.

REALISM AND THE NATIONAL INTEREST

With realists, then, I agree that the national interest is crucial to our understanding of international politics. In both the classic and the structural, or "neo-," varieties of realism, the national interest—or what is sometimes called state interest or state preference—carries a considerable explanatory burden. However, the way in which realists have conceptualized the national interest is inadequate. Examining the realist conception of the national interest with an eye to its shortcomings provides a starting point for rethinking the national interest as a social construction.

In realist accounts, international politics differ from domestic politics primarily in their anarchic character. The absence of a suprastate Leviathan places states in inevitable and perpetual competition—the so-called security dilemma (e.g., Herz, 1951). As a result, states must necessarily be concerned with their survival. The general content of the national interest is thus determined deductively; it is inferred from the anarchic, self-help character of the international system.[3] For Hans Morgenthau this meant that the fundamental national interest of any state was to "protect [its] physical, political, and cultural identity against encroachments by other nations" (1952: 972). More specific threats to states are determined by their relative power in the international system. That is, the particular threats facing a state or challenging its national interest are (or should be) "calculated according to the situation in which the state finds itself" (Waltz, 1979: 134), specifically with reference to the structure of the system—the distribution of capabilities or the number of great powers. "To say that a country acts in its national interest," Kenneth Waltz argued, "means that, having examined its security requirements, it tries to meet them" (1979: 134). Power and wealth supply the means necessary for states to survive, to meet their security requirements, and thus to continue to compete in a system in which other states are necessarily either actual or potential threats. State officials and policy analysts are therefore advised realistically to assess the distribution of power; they should overcome their "aversion to seeing problems of international politics as they are" (Morgenthau, 1951: 7) in order objectively to assess the national interest in light of the distribution of power. Every state, that is, must pursue its national interest "defined in terms of power" (Morgenthau, 1952: 964) because this is the surest road to security and survival.

On this realist argument, then, the national interest clearly plays a pivotal role in accounts of international politics. Through the need for security, it connects the nature of the international system, specifically anarchy and the distribution of power, with the policies and actions of states. There are, however, two problems with this realist notion of the national interest that are important for my argument. First, its content—it defines national interest as the security and survival of the state—is so general as to be indeterminate. Second and more important, the notion rests on a questionable empiricist epistemology that ignores the centrality of processes of interpretation.

As many critics have noted, the deductive determination of national interests prevalent in realism has led to a conception of those interests that is "too broad, too general, too vague, too all-inclusive" to explain state action (Sondermann, 1987: 60). The reason is simple: Political realism "deals with the perennial conditions that attend the conduct of statecraft, not with the specific conditions that confront the statesman" (Tucker, 1961: 463).[4] It tells us that states pursue, or should pursue, security and, as a means to that end, power and wealth, but it does not tell us what exactly that means states will or should do, because the "dictates of power are never clearly manifest" (Rosenau, 1968: 37). As a result, realist analyses of the international system cannot "convincingly" be related "to specific choices in the world of action" (Rothstein, 1972: 353). The traditional realist conception of the national interest therefore cannot help us to explain the adoption by a state of particular policies over alternative means for achieving security. That is, it cannot tell us about the historically contingent content of the national interest as identified and pursued by state officials.[5] "The injunction to 'pursue the national interest,'" it seems, "has no substantive content" (Rosenberg, 1990: 291) and so is not very helpful for understanding the concrete actions of states in the international system.[6]

More important, the realist notion of national interest rests upon the assumption that an independent reality is directly accessible both to state officials and to analysts. It is assumed that the distribution of power in the system can be "realistically," or objectively, assessed and, consequently, that threats to a state's national interests can be accurately recognized. Morgenthau could therefore urge state officials to overcome their "aversion to seeing problems of international politics *as they are*" (1951: 7, emphasis added).[7] The difficulty, of course, is that objects and events do not present themselves unproblematically to the observer, however realistic he or she may be. Determining what the particular situation confronting a state is; what, if any, threat a state faces; and what the correct national interest with respect to that situation or threat is always requires interpretation. Rather than being self-evident, threats, and the corresponding national interest, are fundamentally matters of interpretation. For example, U.S. decision makers' statements to the contrary notwithstanding, the Soviet deployment of nuclear missiles in Cuba in 1962 was not self-evidently a threat to the United States. To see it as a threat to U.S. national interests—instead of, say, as the defense of Cuba—required significant interpretative labor. Realism, with its assumption that threats are self-evident, cannot explain why particular situations are understood to constitute threats to the state. It therefore also cannot explain why certain actions, ostensibly taken in response to these threats, are in the national interest in the first place.

NATIONAL INTERESTS AS SOCIAL CONSTRUCTIONS

Perhaps surprisingly, the beginning of a retheorization of the concept of the national interest that overcomes the indeterminacy and the empiricism of the realist conception can actually be found in the work of the father of realism, Hans Morgenthau. Morgenthau did, of course, argue that "[national] interest defined as power" is an "objective category" that is "universally valid" for all states. This is the troublesome notion of the national interest most often associated with Morgenthau as quintessential realist. But Morgenthau's understanding of the national interest was considerably more complex. He also claimed that analysts and statesmen should not assume a "meaning" or specific content for the national interest "that is fixed once and for all." Instead, though he believed that the "*idea* of interest is indeed of the essence of politics and is unaffected by circumstances of time and place," he also maintained that "the kind of interest determining political action in a particular period of history depends upon *the political and cultural context* within which foreign policy is formulated. The goals that might be pursued by nations in their foreign policy can run the whole gamut of objectives any nation has ever pursued or might possibly pursue" (1978: 8–9, emphasis added). This neglected insight suggests that the concept national interest could be reformulated so that it refers not to the abstract and indeterminate interest of realism but instead to a set of concrete interests, to the "whole gamut" of historically contingent and context-specific objectives that states—or, more accurately, state officials—claim to pursue. State officials' understandings of such goals, the methods for realizing these goals, and public and private debates surrounding both the goals and the methods are routinely structured around and in relation to the central notion of the national interest. As such, they together determine what national interests *are*. The outstanding problem, then, is to provide a retheorization of the concept of the national interest that can capture the historically and culturally specific content ascribed by state officials and others to the national interest.

Morgenthau did not pursue this contingent and contextual national interest, because he thought that science could make only limited contributions to specifying its content. Instead, he concentrated on the abstract, deductive notion of the national interest with which his name is usually associated (1952: 973). However, recent postpositivist and postbehavioralist analyses that contribute to what Jim George has called "the search for thinking space" (1989) in the study of international relations make it possible to overcome the difficulties that plague the realist conception of the national interest. Specifically, this work takes seriously the centrality of meaning in the conduct and analysis of world politics.[8] It thus allows us to pursue Morgenthau's neglected understanding of the concrete meaning of the national interest as both contingent and historically and culturally specific.

Alexander Wendt's (1987, 1992) recent criticism and reformulation of realism provides one such starting point. Wendt has convincingly argued, against realist orthodoxy, that self-interested, security-oriented conceptions of state interest are not unproblematically produced by or deducible from the systemic condition of anarchy;[9] instead, "anarchy is what states make of it" (1992: 395). This is the case because both the interests of states and the identities on which those interests depend rest not solely upon the structure of the system but also upon the "collective meanings that constitute the structures which organize" state action (397). In order to explain state interests and thus state action, Wendt reasons, we must account for the "intersubjectively constituted structure of identities and interests" of states (401). This can be done on the basis of the fundamen-

tal principle "that people act towards objects, including other actors, on the basis of the *meanings* that the objects have for them"
(396–397, emphasis added), meanings that are intersubjectively
constituted. Such a starting point allows us to pursue Morgenthau's
insight that interests are dependent upon political and cultural context by allowing us to examine the intersubjectively constituted
identities and interests of states and the collective meanings out of
which they are produced.

Wendt's argument thus provides some grounds for reconceptual-
izing the national interest as the product of intersubjective processes
of meaning creation. However, his own analysis does not itself provide an adequate account of national interests for at least one important reason. Wendt's "anthropomorphized"[10] understanding of
the state continues to treat states, in typical realist fashion, as unitary actors with a single identity and a single set of interests (Wendt,
1992: 397, note 21). The state itself is treated as a black box whose
internal workings are irrelevant to the construction of state identities and interests. In Wendt's argument, the meanings that objects
and actions have for these unitary states, and the identities and interests of states themselves, are therefore understood to be formed
through processes of *interstate* interaction (401, passim). But as
Wendt himself recognized,[11] the political and historical context in
which national interests are fashioned, the collective meanings that
define state identities and interests, cannot arbitrarily be restricted
to those meanings produced only in interstate relations. After all,
states are unitary actors only analytically, not in fact. The meanings
that objects, events, and actions have for states are necessarily the
meanings they have for those individuals who act in the name of the
state.[12] And these state officials do not approach international politics with a blank slate onto which meanings are only written as a
result of interactions among states. Instead, they approach international politics with an already quite comprehensive and elaborate
appreciation of the world, of international politics, and of the place
of their state within the international system. This appreciation, in
turn, is necessarily rooted in collective meanings already produced,
at least in part, in domestic political and cultural contexts. After all,
as Antonio Gramsci argued, "civil society is the sphere in which the
struggle to define the categories of common sense takes place"
(1971a: 112).[13]

SECURITY IMAGINARIES AND THE NATIONAL INTEREST

In contrast to the realist conception of the national interest as an objective category, I contend that national interests are social constructions created as meaningful objects out of the intersubjective and culturally established meanings within which the world, particularly the international system and the place of the state in it, is understood. The categories of common sense for foreign policy, the intersubjective and culturally established *meanings* on the basis of which state officials make decisions and act, are provided by the security imaginaries of states.[14] A security imaginary is, quite simply, a structure of well-established meanings and social relations out of which representations of the world of international relations are created. At the heart of what Cornelius Castoriadis has called the "social imaginary" we find "an original investment by society of the world and itself with meaning—meanings which are not 'dictated' by real factors since it is instead this meaning that attributes to these real factors a particular importance and a particular place in the universe constituted by a given society" (1987: 128). It is through the imaginary that "the total world given to a particular society is *grasped* in a way that is determined practically, affectively, and mentally, that an articulated meaning is imposed on it, that distinctions are made concerning what does and does not possess value . . . , and what should and should not be done" (145–146, emphasis in the original). The social imaginary of a society, and, in the case of foreign policy, the security imaginary in particular, provides answers to a variety of questions, including "Who are we as a collectivity? What are we for one another? Where and in what are we? What do we want; what do we desire; what are we lacking?" These questions must be answered, Castoriadis explains, because "society must define its 'identity,' its articulation, the world, its relation to the world and to the objects it contains, its needs and its desires. Without the 'answer' to these 'questions,' without these 'definitions,' there can be no human world, no society, no culture—for everything would be undifferentiated chaos" (146–147). Similarly, the security imaginary of a state provides what might be called the cultural raw materials out of which representations of states, of relations among states, and of the international system are constructed. National interests, in turn, emerge out of these representations.[15]

This claim immediately raises at least three questions: By whom are these representations, and thus the national interest, constructed? Why? And how? As to the first—the preeminent site for the construction of the national interest is, not surprisingly, the institution or bundle of practices that we know as the state. Because identifying and securing the national interest is, in the modern international system, considered to be quintessentially the business of the state, those individuals who inhabit offices in the state play a special role in constructing the meaning of the national interest. As Morgenthau argued, statesmen are the representatives of the state; they "speak for it, negotiate treaties in its name, define its objectives, choose the means of achieving them, and try to maintain, increase, and demonstrate power" (1978: 108). Exactly which state institutions and offices are involved in national interest construction will of course vary across states, but it is perhaps safe to say that the national interest is produced primarily, although not exclusively, by foreign policy decision makers.

The institutional location of processes of national interest construction in the state—that is, the allocation of authority and responsibility for the national interest to the state and the establishment of the power relations on which that allocation rests—is already prefigured in the security imaginary. As Castoriadis explained, the institutions of society, even the second-order institutions such as the bureaucracies of the state, are made possible by a particular imaginary (1987: 117–127). In the case of the United States, it is the postwar security imaginary that underpins the apparatuses of the "national security state" (Yergin, 1977). This imaginary has enabled the allocation of vast power over foreign and national security policy to the "imperial presidency" (Schlesinger, 1973; Koh, 1990) and to the institutions of the Office of the Presidency, such as the National Security Council, and the federal bureaucracy. The U.S. security imaginary makes possible the investment of these institutions with extensive authority both in defining the national interest and in identifying threats to it. As a result, they are recognized as the appropriate, responsible agents with respect to the definition and the protection of the U.S. national interest. State officials' responsibility for determining national interests is thus grounded in the security imaginary itself. State actors and their capabilities, then, are not themselves external to the security imaginary. Moreover, to speak of state officials as producing, reproducing, or transforming national interests is not to imply that national interests are wholly reducible to the conscious intentions of these state officials. Rather, as I argue in more detail later, the security imaginary preexists these state officials and is, in part, the condition of possibility for state actors, their practices, and their authority and, in part and conversely, the unintended outcome of state actors' representational practices. When state officials (and others) construct the national interest, they do so out of extant resources—including linguistic, cultural, and institutional resources—provided by the security imaginary and, in so doing, reproduce their own positions as those responsible for the national interest. State officials, then, are subjects in both senses of that term: They are, on the one hand, intentional actors actively engaged in the construction of meaning, and they are, on the other hand, always already subject to the repertoire of meanings offered by the security imaginary that produces them.

As to the "Why?": The answer is quite simply that for the state to act, it must have some understanding of its surroundings and some specification of its goals. In order to make sense of international relations, state officials necessarily create broad representations, both for themselves and for others, of the nature of the international system and the place of their state in that system. And to enable the state to make a decision or to act in a particular situation, state officials must describe to themselves the nature of the specific situation they face. After all, people "act in terms of their interpretations of, and intentions towards, their external conditions, rather than being governed directly by them" (Fay, 1975: 85). In the case of the Cuban missile crisis, for instance, U.S. officials functioned within the postwar U.S. security imaginary, which permitted the representation of the international system as one of "cold war." Within this representation, a narrower situation description, "the Cuban problem," defined the particular relations that obtained between the United States and Cuba and thus the narrower context of the missile crisis.[16] Even more specifically, the problem faced by the United States in October 1962 had then to be interpreted specifically as a Cuban missile *crisis* rather than, say, as a Cuban missile *nuisance* that, though annoying, demanded no U.S. action. These layers of interpretation, necessary for state officials to make decisions and to act, are grounded in and produced out of the security imaginary.

Finally, and most important, as to the "How?": The construction of national interests, I contend, works as follows: Drawing on and constrained by the array of cultural and linguistic resources already available within the security imaginary, state officials create representations that serve, first, to populate the world with a variety of objects, including both the self (that is, the state in question and its authorized officials) and others. These others include, prominently, other states, but they may encompass as well the decision makers of other states, nonstate actors, social movements, domestic publics, and the like. Each of these objects is simultaneously given an identity; it is endowed with characteristics that are sometimes precise and certain, at other times vague and unsettled. It might be endowed with leadership; it might be aggressive and hostile or peaceful and nonthreatening; it might be potentially but not actually dangerous; it might be weak, strong, or simply irritating. In the orthodox postwar U.S. representation of international politics, for example, the world was populated by a very particular United States, one understood to have a special global leadership role, as well as, among others, by aggressive totalitarians, duplicitous communists, puppets of the Kremlin, unstable underdeveloped states, friendly dictators, freedom-loving allies, and uncivilized terrorists.

Second, such representations posit well-defined relations among these diverse objects. These relations often appear in the form of quasi-causal arguments such as the Munich analogy and the domino theory.[17] I call them "quasi-causal" rather than "causal" arguments because the relations and causal chains they posit may or may not be empirically valid on their own terms. Their importance lies not in their accuracy but in their provision of "warranting conditions" that "make a particular action or belief more 'reasonable,' 'justified,' or 'appropriate,' given the desires, beliefs, and expectations of the actors" (Fay, 1975: 85).[18] In providing warranting conditions, they help to specify, among other things, which objects are to be protected and which constitute threats. The domino theory, for example, holds that when a small state falls victim to communism, surrounding small states will follow. Throughout the 1960s, the nature of "dominoes" and the (putative) progressive logic depicted by this theory were invoked to provide warrants for the United States to become and then to remain involved in the anticolonial and civil war in Vietnam. The situation was understood to be such that, had the (constructed, not to say mythical) object "South Vietnam" succumbed to "communist aggression" from (the equally constructed) "North Vietnam," the surrounding dominoes—Burma, Thailand, Indonesia, Formosa, the Philippines, New Zealand, Australia, and finally Japan—would ultimately and necessarily have tumbled as well.[19] It was therefore reasonable and appropriate for the United States, with its identity as the leader in the global battle with communism, to commit its troops to prevent the communist takeover of the independent state of South Vietnam.

Finally, in providing a vision of the world of international relations—in populating that world with objects and in supplying quasi-causal, or warranting, arguments—these representations have *already* defined the national interest. Because "identities are the basis of interests" (Wendt, 1992: 398), the interests of the state are already entailed within the representations in which the identities of and relations among the relevant actors or objects are established. Interests are entailed in these representations because they (seem to) follow from the specific identities of the objects represented and the relations posited to obtain among them. Once a situation has been described, that is, the national interest has already been determined; it *emerges* out of the representations of identities and relationships constructed by state officials. As Castoriadis has argued:

> problems can be problems, can be constituted as *these* specific problems, presenting themselves to a particular epoch or a particular society as a task to be completed, only in relation to an imaginary central to the given epoch or society. This does not mean that these problems are invented out of nothing, that they spring up out of nowhere. But what for each society poses a problem in general . . . is inseparable from its way of being in general, from the sense—a problematical sense, indeed—which it casts on the world and on its place in the world. (1987: 133, emphasis in the original)

It is thus out of the security imaginary that the problems—the threats to national interests—faced by states are ultimately constructed. To continue the example begun above, during the cold war, once a situation had successfully been represented as one in which one or more aggressive totalitarian states were threatening to cause the collapse of a domino, U.S. national interests had already been determined. The United States, with its identity as the leader of the free world, had an obligation—to itself, to its allies, and to its moral convictions—to act to forestall the toppling of that domino.

In short, the security imaginary makes possible representations that clarify both for state officials themselves and for others who and what "we" are, who and what "our enemies" are, in what ways we are threatened by them, and how we might best deal with those threats. The postwar U.S. security imaginary, for example, made possible a cold war representation of international politics that constructed a reality in which we (the United States) were the winners of World War II, in which the United States therefore bore the burden of leadership in the free world and was obliged to defend both democracy and freedom. It was a reality in which the United States was threatened—psychologically, politically, and militarily—by the expansion of and aggression from, among others, a totalitarian Soviet Union and the international communist movement it sponsored. As a result, it was a reality in which the United States had a national interest in maintaining a position of strength in order to fulfill its national interest in containing this deadly threat to its very way of life. In this way, the U.S. security imaginary and the prevailing representation of the U.S. cold war situation fleshed out the skeletal, abstract conception of the national interest in survival and power that is posited by realists, providing as it did a rather more detailed picture of who was to be protected, from what threat, and by what means. National interests, then, are social constructions that emerge out of a ubiquitous and unavoidable process of representation—itself grounded in and made possible by the state's security imaginary—through which meaning is created. In representing for themselves and others the situation in which the state finds itself, state officials have *already* constructed the national interest.

In examining a state's security imaginary and the representations through which a state's national interests are constructed, a particular type of question—a "how-possible" question—is being addressed. How-possible questions ask "how meanings are produced and attached to various social subjects/objects, thus constituting particular interpretive dispositions which create certain possibilities and preclude others" (Doty, 1993: 298). Such questions differ from the conventional questions of international relations and foreign policy analysis, which ask "*why* particular decisions resulting in specific courses of action were made" (298, emphasis in the original). These why questions, as Doty explains, are incomplete. In particular, "they generally take as unproblematic the possibility that a particular decision or course of action could happen. They presuppose a particular subjectivity (i.e., a mode of being), a background of social/discursive practices and meanings which make possible the practices as well as the social actors themselves" (298). In examining the social construction of national interests, the question being asked is not why a particular course of action was chosen but how it was possible, and indeed commonsensical, for the officials of the state to understand its national interest in one particular way rather than in some other way. The brief answer is that it is possible, and indeed commonsensical, because these national interests emerge out of representations enabled by and constructed from within the security imaginary.

CHAPTER OUTLINE

In order to illustrate this retheorization of the national interest as a social construction, I provide an empirical examination of the construction of the U.S. national interest in the Cuban missile crisis. The Cuban missile crisis offers a particularly useful example because that crisis has "assumed genuinely mythic significance" (Blight, Nye, and Welch, 1987: 170) in the conduct and analysis of U.S. foreign policy. It has come to be treated, at least in the U.S. practice and study of international relations and foreign policy, as the paradigmatic cold war crisis. It was "one of the few known nuclear crises in world history" (Thorson and Sylvan, 1982: 540) and one that starkly exposed the dangers of nuclear confrontation. As one analyst put it: During these days, "the American people lived under the threat of disaster" (Divine, 1971: 3), as, of course, did many others. The Cuban missile crisis has also achieved canonical status as a masterpiece of crisis management. According to the orthodox story of the events of October 1962, John F. Kennedy's "combination of toughness and restraint, of will, nerve and wisdom, so brilliantly controlled, so matchlessly calibrated . . . dazzled the world" (Schlesinger, 1965: 841).[20] Both the transformation of these events into a myth and the perception that this was a masterpiece of crisis management rest on the assumption that the U.S. national interest in the missile crisis—forcing the removal of the Soviet missiles from Cuba—was accurately divined. In fact, that national interest was considered at the time (and continues generally to be considered to have been) "obvious" (Douglas Dillon, in Blight and Welch, 1990: 49), or self-evident: The missiles simply had to go. If it can be shown, in the face of overwhelming consensus to the contrary, that the U.S. national interest in the Cuban missile crisis was a contestable social construction, then the argument that all national interests are social constructions is rendered that much more plausible.

To begin the analysis, I examine in more detail three stories purporting to describe the same events of October 1962: the orthodox U.S. narrative of the "Cuban missile crisis," the official Soviet story of the "Caribbean crisis," and the Cuban rendering of the "October crisis." These three narratives highlight a central puzzle: Why have the events of October 1962 been understood in the United States in one specific way—with the attendant and apparently unproblematic U.S. national interest in forcing the removal of the missiles—rather than in some other way. These alternative narratives and the first puzzle are laid out in chapter 1.

I then examine the U.S. national interest as it was defined by the members of the Executive Committee of the National Security Council (ExComm) during the crisis itself. I begin by investigating the representation of the events of October 1962 that emerged during and shaped the ExComm discussions of October 1962, paying particular attention to the objects of and threats to U.S. security, the understanding of the U.S. national interest entailed in this representation, and the policy options available to achieve that national interest. I then focus in more detail on a number of issues that, quite significantly, are absent both from those ExComm discussions and from subsequent analyses of the missile crisis. These absences or silences—the failure to understand Soviet motives in deploying the missiles to Cuba, the failure to acknowledge Cuban sovereignty, and the failure seriously to consider the strategic irrelevance of the missiles in Cuba—all provide important windows into the orthodox U.S. understanding of the Cuban missile crisis. In other words, they help to illuminate what was taken for granted in the apparently self-evident description of the Cuban missile crisis. In doing so, they bring into stark relief the generally unchallenged but nonetheless problematical determination that the U.S. national interest required the removal of these Soviet missiles from Cuba. Chapter 2 thus adds a second puzzle to be investigated: Why did U.S. decision makers (and much subsequent analysis) understand the crisis in this particular way and how did they come to define and to accept as self-evident a particular national interest?

The argument continues in chapter 3, in which I present a more detailed reconceptualization and retheorization of national interests as social constructions that can, in principle, solve the puzzles raised in chapters 1 and 2. Specifically, I examine how specific representations of international politics and the problems of foreign policy, entailing or making possible particular national interests, are constructed out of the security imaginary. I argue that the concepts of articulation and interpellation, in particular, provide useful tools that allow us to understand how specific representations and the attendant national interests are constructed out of the security imaginary and why those representations and the concomitant interests are persuasive to most of their audience most of the time.

Having provided a set of conceptual tools for the analysis of national interest construction, I then return to the Cuban missile crisis and examine how both the myth of the Cuban missile crisis and, more important, the U.S. national interest in that crisis were produced. Drawing on the theoretical material presented in chapter 3, I examine in some detail the actual process through which the U.S. national interest in the Cuban missile crisis was fashioned. I argue that both the orthodox story of the Cuban missile crisis and the U.S. national interest during it were constructed within the boundaries of, and using the discursive resources provided by, the postwar U.S. security imaginary. Central elements of this imaginary, based on historically contingent ideological articulations and interpellations, functioned as a template against which both the U.S. national interest and the accompanying story of the Cuban missile crisis were forged. The representation of the "cold war" was, of course, a pivotal element of the security imaginary and of central importance in constructing the crisis. The prevailing U.S. understanding both of U.S.-Soviet relations and of U.S.–Latin American relations in the cold war provided the setting for the orthodox U.S. understanding of the missile crisis and helped to define the deployment of the Soviet missiles as unacceptable to the United States. These cold war representations and their consequences for the U.S. national interest are examined in chapter 4. Representations of the "Cuban problem" and of the Castro regime, of course, provided the immediate context of the Cuban missile crisis. These constructions, also generated out of the postwar U.S. security imaginary, and their consequences for the U.S. national interest during the crisis are examined in chapter 5.

The analyses presented in chapters 4 and 5 highlight the centrality of the identity of the U.S. state to this process of national interest construction. In fact, it becomes clear through these analyses that U.S. state identity sits at the heart of the construction of U.S. national interests. In chapter 6, I examine the importance of U.S. state identity in more detail, arguing not only that that identity was central in the construction of the Cuban missile crisis and the attendant U.S. national interest, but, conversely, that the crisis was in part also an exercise in the reproduction and reinscription of a particular, and always precarious, U.S. state identity. Despite a major transformation in the structure of the international system with the collapse of the Soviet Union, U.S. identity and national interests continue to require a hostile and aggressive U.S. foreign policy toward Cuba. In chapter 7 I conclude the argument by briefly detailing continuities in U.S. policy toward Cuba after the cold war, noting where U.S. constructions of the Cuban problem have been rearticulated. Through the duel processes of articulation and interpellation, I argue, contingent and contestible representations of world politics are rendered apparently natural and commonsensical for diverse publics. The politics of representation thus prompt a critical engagement with common sense and its production.

1

Representing Missiles in Cuba

"Ever bought a fake picture? . . . The more you pay for it, the less inclined you are to doubt it. Silly, but there we are."
— GEORGE SMILEY, IN JOHN LE CARRÉ,
TINKER, TAILOR, SOLDIER, SPY

THREE REPRESENTATIONS OF THE MISSILES IN CUBA

Benedict Anderson has argued that what we know as the apparently self-evident event called the French Revolution is in fact a social construction. After it had occurred, he asserted,

> the overwhelming and bewildering concatenation of events experienced by its makers and its victims became a "thing"—and with its own name: The French Revolution. Like a vast shapeless rock worn to a rounded boulder by countless drops of water, the experience was shaped by millions of printed words into a "concept" on the printed page, and, in due course, into a model. Why "it" broke out, what "it" aimed for, why "it" succeeded or failed, became subjects for endless polemics on the part of friends and foes: but of its "it-ness," as it were, no one ever after had much doubt. (1991: 80–81)

The same can be said of the Cuban missile crisis. With even less dispute over its causes or its consequences, the essential character of the Cuban missile crisis as a thing—its "it-ness"—has not been in doubt. The self-evident nature of the crisis and of the U.S. national interest in it can nonetheless be challenged. In fact, the Cuban missile crisis is

21

far from a self-evident or natural thing; it is instead an ideological construction. Both the crisis and the U.S. national interest in that crisis were products of a ubiquitous process of representation.

The constructed nature of the Cuban missile crisis can nicely be illustrated through an examination of several quite distinct representations of the events of October 1962. In this chapter, I contrast the orthodox U.S. representation of "the Cuban missile crisis" with both the official Soviet story of "the Caribbean crisis" and the Cuban narrative of "the October crisis."[1] Other representations could, of course, be examined as well. As Len Scott and Steve Smith have recently reminded us, "there are also British, Italian, and Turkish stories" of these events (1994: 666). I focus here on the Soviet and Cuban representations for two main reasons. First, they are the official stories of the other principle states most directly involved in the events of October 1962 and thus provide a useful parallel to the official U.S. narrative. Second, in providing clear contrasts to the U.S. story, they function as a useful corrective to the assumption that the it-ness of the missile crisis can be taken for granted. Each of these three stories purports to describe and explain the events of October 1962—and each does so in notably different, and indeed in partially contradictory, ways. In fact, the Cuban missile crisis, the Caribbean crisis, and the October crisis are three different "things": They are distinct representations of the events of October 1962; of the deployment and discovery of, the crisis over, and the eventual removal of the Soviet missiles in Cuba; and of the national interest of the central state actors. That these events are labeled with three different names is not merely a rhetorical or literary flourish. Instead, it reflects the differential construction of these events—they are in fact different things—because of their construction within divergent security imaginaries.

The Cuban Missile Crisis

On Tuesday morning, October 16, 1962, shortly after 9:00 o'clock, President Kennedy called and asked me to come to the White House. He said only that we were facing great trouble. Shortly afterward, in his office, he told me that a U-2 had just finished a photographic mission and that the Intelligence Community had become convinced that Russia was placing missiles and atomic weapons in Cuba. (Kennedy, 1971: 1)

So began the Cuban missile crisis.[2]

President Kennedy's famous address, delivered at 7:00 P.M. on October 22, inaugurated the orthodox U.S. understanding of what was, for the United States at least, perhaps the outstanding crisis of the postwar era. In his speech, Kennedy began the public phase of the crisis by informing the American people that "unmistakable evidence" proved that the Soviet Union was deploying strategic missiles on Cuba. This deployment was unacceptable because "the purpose of these bases can be none other than to provide a nuclear strike capability against the Western Hemisphere" (Kennedy, 1962c: 1). The Kennedy administration was adamant that the missiles be removed for at least three reasons: The missiles were offensive rather than strictly defensive weapons, the installation of the missiles had been undertaken secretly, and the deployment directly contravened the integrity of the Western Hemisphere.

First, in contrast to other shipments of Soviet arms to Cuba, the missiles discovered in October 1962 were considered by U.S. policy makers to be offensive rather than defensive weapons. Despite repeated assurances by the Soviet Union that the arms buildup it was supporting in Cuba was defensive, that "there is no need for the Soviet Government to shift its weapons for a retaliatory blow to any other country, for instance Cuba" (Kennedy, 1962c: 3),[3] it was now deploying offensive nuclear weapons capable of striking targets in much of the United States and Latin America.[4] As Dean Rusk argued at the Organization of American States (OAS) meeting on October 23, "the U.S.S.R. is making a major military investment in Cuba with advanced weapons systems with substantial offensive capability" (1962c: 720).[5] This military investment, Kennedy insisted in a letter to Nikita Khrushchev on October 18, was "a hostile development to which we have an inescapable commitment to respond with military action" (in Blight and Welch, 1990: 115).

Second, as recent commentators have argued, Kennedy and his advisers "were deeply concerned to avoid setting a precedent whereby the Soviets believed they might deceive the United States and then escape unpunished when caught in the lie. . . . If the United States failed to stand up to Khrushchev in such a blatant case of deception, what gamble would he try next?" (Blight, Nye, and Welch, 1987: 176). Such Soviet duplicity was unacceptable to the United States. As Rusk charged in his speech to the OAS, the Cubans and the Soviet

Union were joined in a "partnership in deceit" and "the Communist regime in Cuba with the complicity of its Soviet mentors has deceived the hemisphere, under the cloak of secrecy and with loud protestations of arming for self-defense, in allowing an extracontinental power, bent on destruction of the national independence and democratic aspirations of all our peoples, to establish an offensive military foothold in the heart of the hemisphere" (Rusk, 1962c: 720; see also Stevenson, 1962b, 1962c).

Third, this "secret, swift, and extraordinary build-up of Communist missiles" (Kennedy, 1962c: 5) violated the integrity of the Western Hemisphere and the historical exclusion, codified in the Monroe Doctrine, of foreign interference from that hemisphere. The deployment of the missiles clearly constituted "intervention," and indeed "aggressive intervention," by the Soviet Union and by the "international Communist movement" into the Western Hemisphere (Rusk, 1962c: 721). It constituted, in fact, the "importation of the cold war into the heart of the Americas" (Stevenson, 1962a: 725). "The presence of these large, long-range, and clearly offensive weapons of sudden mass destruction," Kennedy asserted in his speech of October 22, "constitutes an explicit threat to the peace and security of all the Americas, in flagrant and deliberate defiance of the Rio Pact of 1947, the traditions of this nation and hemisphere, the Joint Resolution of the 87th Congress, the Charter of the United Nations, and my own public warnings to the Soviets on September 4 and 13" (Kennedy, 1962c: 2–3).[6] The missile crisis, as Douglas Dillon reiterated in 1989, "was something that they had started in our own backyard" (in Blight and Welch, 1990: 100).

For these three reasons, once the missiles had been discovered and the duplicity of the Soviets and the Cubans exposed, the primary objective of the United States naturally became the removal of the missiles from Cuba. The only outstanding question was how to achieve this result. After intense and exhaustive deliberations within the ExComm about possible U.S. actions, Kennedy ordered "a strict quarantine on all offensive military equipment under shipment to Cuba" (Kennedy, 1962c: 7). The quarantine was accompanied by a large-scale U.S. mobilization of military resources. The Strategic Air Command (SAC) moved from Defense Condition 3 to Defense Condition 2, the level just short of general war (May and Zelikow, 1997: 347), began dispersing its bombers, and "placed all aircraft on an upgraded alert—ready to take off, fully equipped, within 15 minutes." In addition, "fighter interceptors and HAWK and NIKE-HERCULES missile battalions were moved to the southeast to supplement local air defense forces"; marines "were loaded on amphibious ships and ordered to sea"; marine units were sent by air and by sea to reinforce Guantánamo; dependents were evacuated from Guantánamo; "Task Force 135, including the carrier *Enterprise,* was sent to the south of Cuba, ready to join in the defense of Guantánamo"; antisubmarine forces were deployed "to cover the quarantine operations"; and air support for ground forces was provided when "hundreds of tactical fighters, reconnaissance, and troop carrier aircraft" were moved to the southeast of the United States (U.S. Department of Defense, 1964: 5–6). As General William Smith (special assistant to the chairman of the Joint Chiefs of Staff in October 1962) explained in 1989, "the United States was doing everything within the military capability that it had at that time to be prepared to launch an air strike, and, if necessary, begin an invasion of Cuba" (in Allyn, Blight, and Welch, 1992: 95). Beyond initiating these concrete defensive measures, Kennedy also announced that the United States would "regard any nuclear missile launched from Cuba against any nation in the Western Hemisphere as an attack by the Soviet Union on the United States, requiring a full retaliatory response upon the Soviet Union" (Kennedy, 1962c: 7–8). "This latest Soviet threat," he declared, "must and will be met with determination. Any hostile move anywhere in the world against the safety and freedom of peoples to whom we are committed—including in particular the brave people of West Berlin—will be met by whatever action is needed" (10).

In the wake of Kennedy's speech, fear of nuclear war gripped the United States. The ExComm continued to meet. While conducting both public and private correspondence with Khrushchev in order to halt construction of the Soviet missile sites and secure the removal of all nuclear-capable weapons systems from Cuba, it continued to debate additional military options, including a limited air strike against the Soviet missile bases and an all-out invasion. By October 24, the threat that this superpower confrontation would escalate toward a nuclear war seemed to be abating. Although construction on the Soviet missile sites had not stopped, Soviet ships suspected of transporting military cargo to Cuba either slowed down or turned back toward the Soviet Union as they approached the quarantine zone.

On October 26, it appeared that the crisis might be resolved. The U.S.S. *Pierce* and the U.S.S. *Kennedy* stopped and boarded the Lebanese freighter *Marucla,* which was under charter to the Soviet Union. When no contraband was found, the ship was allowed to continue to Cuba. On the same day, a message arrived from Khrushchev in which he offered to remove the missiles in exchange for a U.S. pledge not to invade Cuba.

Then, on Black Saturday, as October 27 quickly became known, the crisis again threatened to escalate out of control. Throughout the twenty-seventh, "SAC bombers continued their round-the-clock circling in Arctic skies. Nearly 100 warships maintained the quarantine, and more ships readied for invasion. U.S. destroyers patrolled constantly over Soviet submarines in the Atlantic. The 5th Marine Expeditionary Brigade began boarding ships that would carry it to the invasion staging area" (May and Zelikow, 1997: 629). Under these tense conditions, a U.S. U-2 collecting atmospheric samples from Soviet nuclear tests near the North Pole strayed into Soviet airspace. The specter of U.S.-Soviet war again appeared as Soviet MiG fighters attempted to intercept the U-2 and American fighters based in Alaska were sent to protect it if and when it reentered U.S. airspace (519). At the same time, low-flying U.S. reconnaissance aircraft were greeted by Cuban antiaircraft fire, challenging the U.S. assumption that Cuban air defenses would not shoot at unarmed U.S. reconnaissance flights. Worse yet, a U.S. U-2 on a reconnaissance mission over Cuba was shot down by a surface-to-air missile and its pilot, Major Rudolph Anderson of the U.S. Air Force, was killed, becoming the only U.S. combat fatality of the Cuban missile crisis. As recent commentators have put it, "the Soviets had drawn first blood, and the tension rose to a crescendo" (Blight and Welch, 1990: 4). Under these increasingly complex and terrifying conditions, a second letter from Khrushchev reached the ExComm. In the letter, Khrushchev raised the stakes in the crisis by proposing that the missiles in Cuba be traded for U.S. Jupiter missiles in Turkey.

Fortunately, cool heads prevailed. Further correspondence between Khrushchev and Kennedy ultimately led to a successful resolution of the crisis. On October 28, after yet another exchange of letters, "word reached Washington that the Kremlin had accepted the U.S. terms" (Welch and Blight, 1987–88: 12).[7] In the face of the Kennedy administration's firmness and effective crisis management, including its efforts to allow Khrushchev to retreat without humiliation, the Soviet Union had backed down. The Cuban missile crisis was won when, "eyeball to eyeball" with the United States, the Soviet Union "blinked" (Rusk, in Abel, 1966: 153).[8] According to the story of the Cuban missile crisis, Kennedy's "combination of toughness and restraint, of will, nerve and wisdom, so brilliantly controlled, so matchlessly calibrated . . . dazzled the world" (Schlesinger, 1965: 841). A prominent U.S. analyst summarized the "missiles of October" as follows:

> For thirteen days in October 1962, the United States and the Soviet Union stood "eyeball to eyeball," each with the power of mutual annihilation in hand. The United States was firm but forebearing. The Soviet Union looked hard, blinked twice, and then withdrew without humiliation. Here is one of the finest examples of diplomatic prudence, and perhaps the finest hour of John F. Kennedy's Presidency. (Allison, 1971: 39)[9]

The Caribbean Crisis

The Caribbean crisis had its genesis in a long history of U.S. aggression against Cuba.[10] From the outset of the twentieth century, the United States, an imperialist and expansionist power, had been intent upon the global pursuit of a "counterrevolutionary politics of the 'big stick'" (Gromyko, 1970: 299).[11] This was particularly true in Latin America. Moreover, the United States feared that the socialist model offered by the Cuban Revolution might have nefarious effects on the policies or social movements of other Latin American states, and it therefore harbored particularly hostile and aggressive intentions toward the Cuban Revolution and the Castro government. As Andrei Gromyko argued in 1989, "the whole chain of events began with the very sharp, aggressive stand of the Washington administration concerning the new Cuba, and the new figure of the Cuban leadership, headed by Castro. Cuba was unacceptable. Cuban leadership was not suitable. . . . The personalities were not the point. The social regime was the main thing that was unsuitable" (in Allyn, Blight, and Welch, 1992: 147–148).

The Alliance for Progress was one method used by the United States to halt the spread of socialism and national liberation movements throughout Latin America. The alliance was proposed by the United States "because the revolution in Cuba, which shook the foundations of the domination of U.S. monopolies in Latin America, has forced them to think about how to dam up the inexorable advance of the national-liberation movement all over the continent" (Borovsky, 1961: 23). Moreover, just as with the military intervention by the United States (and its allies) into the Russian civil war and the U.S. intervention in Guatemala in 1954,[12] U.S. aggression against Cuba was ultimately "organized with a view to forcibly changing its [Cuba's] internal system" (Khrushchev, 1961a: 9). In 1960, in pursuit of this goal, the United States cut off Cuba's supply of oil, its main source of energy, by refusing to allow American-owned refineries to process Soviet crude oil. As a result, the Cubans turned to the Soviet Union for assistance. And U.S. aggression did not stop there. In January 1961, Kennedy severed diplomatic relations with Cuba. In March he eliminated the Cuban sugar quota, threatening the highly specialized and dependent Cuban economy with complete collapse. Then, in April 1961, the United States orchestrated the infamous counter-revolutionary invasion of Cuba at the Bay of Pigs. This attack by "foul mercenary gangs" ("Rooseveltian policies," 1961: 7) was designed to trigger an anti-Castro revolt that would, it was hoped, lead to the overthrow of the legitimate revolutionary government of Cuba.

In response to this long series of aggressive acts, the Soviet Union had already intensified its military and economic aid to Cuba. In the wake of the Bay of Pigs invasion, the Soviet government had become "quite certain that the . . . invasion was only the beginning and that the Americans would not let Cuba alone" (Khrushchev, 1970: 545). In a letter to President Kennedy on April 18, Khrushchev therefore wrote: "Let there be no misunderstanding of our position: We will give the Cuban people and their government every assistance necessary to repulse the armed attack on Cuba" (1961b: 5). The fear of a direct U.S. invasion of Cuba was then further intensified when Kennedy requested that Congress authorize the calling up of 150,000 reservists in September 1962 (see "TASS statement on aid to Cuba," 1962: 13).[13] In response to the continued threat of active U.S. military aggression, the Soviet Union and Cuba jointly agreed to install missiles in Cuba. As Khrushchev later explained, after the Bay of Pigs the Soviet leadership was certain that

> the Americans would never reconcile themselves to the existence of Castro's Cuba. They feared, as much as we hoped, that a Socialist

Cuba might become a magnet that would attract other Latin American countries to Socialism. Given the continual threat of American interference in the Caribbean, what should our own policy be? . . . Everyone agreed that America would not leave Cuba alone unless we did something. We had an obligation to do everything in our power to protect Cuba's existence as a Socialist country and as a working example to the other countries of Latin America. It was clear to me that we might very well lose Cuba if we didn't take some decisive steps in her defense. The fate of Cuba and the maintenance of Soviet prestige in that part of the world preoccupied me. . . . What will happen if we lose Cuba? I knew it would have been a terrible blow to Marxism-Leninism. It would gravely diminish our stature throughout the world, but especially in Latin America. If Cuba fell, other Latin American countries would reject us, claiming that for all our might the Soviet Union hadn't been able to do anything for Cuba except to make empty protests to the United Nations. We had to think up some way of confronting America with more than words. We had to establish a tangible and effective deterrent to American interference in the Caribbean. But what exactly? The logical answer was missiles. (1970: 545–546)

The installation of nuclear missiles in Cuba, undertaken in agreement with the Cuban government, was designed to "restrain the United States from precipitous military action against Castro's government" (547). An official government statement reported by TASS explained that

a certain amount of armament is . . . being sent to Cuba from the Soviet Union at the request of the Cuban government in connection with the threats by aggressive imperialist circles. . . . The arms and military equipment sent to Cuba are intended solely for defensive purposes. . . . If normal diplomatic and trade relations were established between the United States of America and Cuba, there would be no need for Cuba to strengthen her defense capacity, her armed forces. ("TASS statement on aid to Cuba," 1962: 14–15)

In sending arms, including nuclear missiles, to Cuba, the Soviet Union was assisting it in defending its sovereignty and independence in the face of external aggression. The basic goal was to "strengthen the situation for Cuba as a sovereign independent socialist state" (Andrei Gromyko, in Allyn, Blight, and Welch, 1992: 148). The missiles were installed secretly because "if the United States discovered the missiles were there after they were already poised and ready to strike, the Americans would think twice before trying to liquidate our installations by military means" (Khrushchev, 1970: 546–547). Contrary to U.S. propaganda, this secrecy did not indicate that the Soviet Union intended to use the missiles aggressively. Indeed, "only a fool would think that we wanted to invade the American continent from Cuba. Our goal was precisely the opposite: we wanted to keep the Americans from invading Cuba, and, to that end, we wanted to make them think twice by confronting them with our missiles" (549). The Caribbean crisis was thus the direct result both of the history of past U.S. aggression against Cuba and of the imminent threat of a U.S. invasion. As the Soviet ambassador to the United Nations declared in the Security Council on October 25, 1962: "The point here does not lie in what the United States Press and the President of the United States labeled 'the incontrovertible facts of offensive weapons being installed in Cuba,' but in the aggressive intentions of the United States with respect to Cuba. That is where the core of the matter lies" (Valerian Zorin, in Stevenson and Zorin, 1962: 79).

Furthermore, concern by the U.S. administration over the proximity to the United States of the Soviet missiles in Cuba was simply hypocritical in the light of the global military policy and nuclear missile–basing policy pursued by the United States. In addition to serving the primary goal of defending Cuba, the missiles would also "have equalized what the West likes to call 'the balance of power.' The Americans had surrounded our country with military bases and threatened us with nuclear weapons, and now they would learn just what it feels like to have enemy missiles pointing at you; we'd be doing nothing more than giving them a little of their own medicine" (Khrushchev, 1970: 547).[14] In a letter to Kennedy after the Bay of Pigs, Khrushchev wrote: "You allege that Cuba can make her territory available for actions against the United States." But, he went on to point out,

> in some countries directly bordering on the Soviet Union on land or sea, governments at present exist that follow a far from reasonable policy, governments that have concluded military treaties with the United States and have made their territory available for the estab-

lishment of American military bases. And your military say openly that these bases are directed against the Soviet Union, as if this were not self-evident. So if you consider yourself entitled to take such measures against Cuba as the U.S. government has been resorting to lately, you must admit that other countries have no lesser grounds for acting in the same way with respect to the states on whose territory preparations are actually being made that constitute a threat to the security of the Soviet Union. (Khrushchev, 1961a: 8)

The Soviet Union, Khrushchev asserted, had the same right as had the United States to protect itself. "If you do not want to sin against elementary logic, you must obviously concede this right to other states" (8; see also "Tass statement on aid to Cuba," 1962: 14).

Elementary logic notwithstanding, once the Kennedy administration had discovered the missiles, it aggressively set about generating a crisis. It did so, first of all, by mounting an extravagant press campaign, fanning the flames of U.S. hostility against the Soviet Union and Cuba. More important, the United States launched a belligerent and illegal show of military strength through its naval blockade, an act of war and tantamount to piracy on the high seas. The Soviet Union, for its part, responded with caution, maintaining its commitment to negotiation and to the peaceful coexistence of states. After conducting both official and unofficial correspondence with Kennedy and the U.S. administration, "we sent the Americans a note saying that we agreed to remove our missiles and bombers on the condition that the President give us his assurance that there would be no invasion of Cuba by the forces of the United States or anybody else. Finally Kennedy gave in and agreed to make a statement giving us such an assurance" (Khrushchev, 1970: 553). The crisis thus resulted in a satisfactory outcome for the Soviet Union. "The main point about the Caribbean crisis," Khrushchev wrote to Castro, "is that it has guaranteed the existence of a Socialist Cuba" (555–556).[15] As Khrushchev asked the Supreme Soviet rhetorically in December 1962: "One asks, in what respect have we retreated? Socialist Cuba exists. Cuba remains a beacon of Marxist-Leninist ideas in the Western Hemisphere. The power of its revolutionary example will grow. The government of the U.S. has pledged on behalf of its country not to invade Cuba; the menace of thermonuclear war has been averted. Is this retreat ours?" (1962b: 3). A Soviet commentator summarized the Caribbean crisis as follows:

An objective analysis of the military-political aspects of the events of the fall of 1962 . . . shows that the Soviet strategic rockets stationed in Cuba did not give rise to, but on the contrary prevented the further dangerous development of the Caribbean crisis and simultaneously averted the outbreak of a war in the region of the Caribbean sea which could have quickly grown from a local to a world war. They [the Soviet rockets] saved revolutionary Cuba. (Major General I. D. Statsenko, in Pope, 1982: 248, brackets in the original)

The October Crisis

The October crisis[16] was a direct outgrowth of the "neocolonialist methods of domination" (Castro, 1976: 87) pursued by the United States in the Western Hemisphere and of the hostile and aggressive attitude displayed by the United States toward Cuba in particular. The "so-called Cuban question," Cuba's President Osvaldo Dorticós argued before the U.N. General Assembly in 1962, was caused not by Cuba but by the United States. Indeed,

the tension which surrounds our country, the situation which exists between the United States and Cuba, began long before our revolution had taken on the socialist characteristics it now displays. It was enough for us to promulgate laws which affected the United States, monopolistic interests in our country, it was enough to promulgate the land reform act at a period when our revolutionary development was not yet shaped by socialist principles, for aggressive action against our homeland to be undertaken by the United States Government. (Dorticós, 1962: 370)

The United States pursued its hostile policies toward Cuba with a succession of "insolent diplomatic notes" as well as "piratical flights" over Cuban territory. It threatened to destroy the Cuban economy by eliminating the Cuban sugar quota from the U.S. market and by halting supplies of petroleum to Cuba. At the same time, it attempted to isolate Cuba diplomatically from the rest of Latin America. Most dramatically, the United States then added injury to insult by helping to stage an armed invasion of Cuba using "mercenary forces financed, trained in warfare, militarily protected and commanded by the Government of the United States: the invasion of Playa Girón" (Dorticós, 1962: 370).[17] After that "ridiculous fiasco,"

we immediately became the victims of further acts of aggression with the infiltration of agents landed on our coasts and trained by the

Central Intelligence Agency, new attempts at sabotage, the military training of groups to carry out the hitherto unsuccessful internal subversion of our country and the increase of economic pressure on our homeland—tenaciously and doggedly applied in the hope that it would undermine our revolution and that, as a result, their sole objective would be attained: the downfall of the Revolutionary Government of Cuba. (Dorticós, 1962: 370)

The Cubans were well aware of the continued hostility of and the aggressive plans laid by the United States. As Castro has repeatedly argued:

The United States government indubitably was very irritated, very dissatisfied with what had happened [at the Bay of Pigs], and the idea of solving through force, of liquidating through force, the Cuban Revolution was not abandoned. But it was not considered possible to go back and repeat the Girón experience, and the idea of a direct invasion of Cuba was being seriously considered and analyzed. And we, through various sources, had news of the plans being elaborated, and we had certainty of this danger. (Castro, in Szulc, 1986: 578)[18]

Despite the Cuban victory at the Bay of Pigs, the United States persisted in its aggressive policies because "the course taken by the Government of the United States . . . is a course dictated by arrogance, by a desire to dominate and by panic at the example of the Cuban revolution" (Dorticós, 1962: 374).[19] In short, "the main origin of the crisis was American aggression against Cuba" (Jorge Risquet, in Allyn, Blight, and Welch, 1992: 149) and the firm Cuban expectation that further direct U.S. military aggression was in the offing. After the failure of the Bay of Pigs and other U.S. plots against Cuba and Castro, Risquet has explained: "For us [Cubans] there was no doubt that if the United States wanted to destroy the Cuban revolution, the only formula they had left was direct military assault" (in Allyn, Blight, and Welch, 1992: 15).[20]

Because of this well-established pattern of U.S. aggression, Cuban-Soviet relations had grown increasingly close. As Castro put it, by 1962

the Soviets were already quite committed to us. They were giving us maximum help, they had responded with the purchase of Cuban sugar when [our] market in the United States was totally closed, they supplied petroleum when all the sources of petroleum supply were suspended, which would have annihilated the country. They, I say, had acquired a great degree of commitment toward us, and now we were discussing what measures should be taken. They asked our opinion, and we told them exactly—we did not speak of missiles— that it was necessary to make clear to the United States that an invasion of Cuba would imply a war with the Soviet Union. We told them: It is necessary to take steps that would imply, in a clear manner, that an aggression against Cuba is an aggression against the Soviet Union. (in Szulc, 1986: 579)[21]

Among the possible measures discussed for defending Cuba was "the installation of medium-range missiles." As Castro has described it: "We analyzed [the fact] that this, besides being convenient for us, could also be convenient to the Soviets from a military viewpoint. . . . We reached the conclusion that this [the missiles] was mutually beneficial." The Cubans therefore agreed to the missile deployment, which did not emerge "as the consequence of their coming over to us one day and saying to us, 'We want to install the missiles because it is convenient for this and for that.'" Rather, "the initiative of soliciting measures that would give Cuba an absolute guarantee against a conventional war and against an invasion by the United States was ours. The idea of the missiles, in a concrete way was Soviet" (in Szulc, 1986: 580). The missiles would have secured Cuba even against a conventional attack because "the United States' strategy was, and is, based on nuclear equilibrium." The presence of missiles in Cuba would have protected Cuba; it would have "insured us against the danger of a local war, of something similar to what the United States is doing in North Vietnam, a war that, for a small country, can mean almost as much destruction and death as that of a nuclear war" (in Lockwood, 1967: 201).[22] Although this strategy was undoubtedly somewhat risky, Castro later argued that "we preferred the risks, whatever they were, of great tension, a great crisis . . . to the risks of the impotence of having to wait, impotently, for a United States invasion of Cuba. . . . At least they gave us a nuclear umbrella, and we felt much more satisfied with the response we were giving to the policy of hostility and aggression toward our country" (in Szulc, 1986: 582).

The October crisis revolved, fundamentally, around the sovereignty and independence of Cuba. "From the moral point of view," Castro has argued:

I never had and I shall never have doubts that our attitude was correct. From a strictly moral as well as strictly legal viewpoint, as a sovereign country we had the right to make use of the type of arms we considered gave us a guarantee. And in the same way that the United States had missiles in Italy and Turkey, in the same way as the United States has bases in all parts of the world around the Soviet Union, we, as a sovereign nation, considered we had the absolutely legal right to make use of such measures in our own country. (in Szulc, 1986: 582)

For this reason as well, Castro recently pointed out that the Cuban government had refused to "go along with the game about the category of the weapons"—that is, to justify the missiles as being defensive rather than offensive:

We refused to go along with that game and, in public statements the government made and in the statements at the United Nations, we always said that Cuba considered that it had a sovereign right to have whatever kind of weapons it thought appropriate, and no one had any right to establish what kind of weapons our country could or could not have. We never went along with denying the strategic nature of the weapons. We never did. We did not agree to that game. We did not agree with that approach. Therefore, we never denied or confirmed the nature of the weapons; rather, we reaffirmed our right to have whatever type of weapons we thought appropriate for our defense. (1992: 337)[23]

The issue of Cuban sovereignty was raised in no uncertain terms in Castro's response to U.N. Acting Secretary General U Thant's appeal that Cuba stop the construction of the Soviet missile bases while the negotiations to end the crisis were underway. Castro wrote:

Cuba is prepared to discuss as fully as may be necessary, its differences with the United States and to do everything in its power, in cooperation with the United Nations, to resolve the present crisis. However, it flatly rejects the violation of the sovereignty of our country involved in the naval blockade, an act of force and war committed by the United States against Cuba.

In addition, it flatly rejects the presumption by the United States to determine what actions we are entitled to take within our country, what kind of arms we consider appropriate for our defense, what relations we are to have with the USSR, and what international policy steps we are entitled to take, within the rules and laws governing relations between the peoples of the world and the principles governing the United Nations, in order to guarantee our own security and sovereignty. (in "Texts of U.N.-Cuban notes," 1962: 31)

Because Cuban sovereignty lies at the heart of the October crisis, this story did not end happily on October 28, as did the Cuban missile crisis and, perhaps to a lesser extent, the Caribbean crisis. According to Castro, "it had really never crossed my mind that the option of withdrawing the missiles was conceivable" (in Szulc, 1986: 585). Thus, when the Soviet Union did agree to their withdrawal, the Cubans "were really very irritated over the fact that an agreement was reached without our participation, or without a consultation with us. . . . We were informed when the accord had already virtually been concluded" (586). In fact, as Castro put it in 1992, when news of the agreement arrived in Havana on October 28, 1962, "it provoked a great indignation because we realized that we had become some type of game token. We not only saw a unilateral decision; a series of steps had been taken without including us. They could have told us: there was the message on the 26th and on the 27th. There had been time, but we heard on the radio on the 28th that an agreement had taken place. We had to endure the humiliation" (1992: 339).

In response to the persistent and humiliating denial of Cuban sovereignty, Castro insisted on certain measures without which "the guarantees of which President Kennedy speaks against invasion of Cuba will not exist." In addition to the elimination of the naval blockade, he demanded (1) that the economic blockade of Cuba be ended, (2) that the United States cease all subversive activities in and against Cuba, (3) that "pirate attacks carried out from bases in the United States and Puerto Rico" be stopped, (4) that "all violations of air and naval space by North American military aircraft and ships" be halted, and (5) that the United States withdraw from the naval base at Guantánamo and return this territory to Cuba (Castro, 1962a: 19). Because none of these conditions was met, the eventual outcome of the October crisis was irretrievably marred. Furthermore, the United States then insisted not only that the missiles be removed, but that the Soviet IL-28s and Soviet troops be withdrawn from Cuba. In addition, the United States continued its surveillance overflights until well into November. In the Cuban view, in other words, the events of October 1962 were "a rather open attempt to disarm Cuba" (Lev Mendeleevitch, in Allyn, Blight, and Welch, 1992: 35) that persisted into November 1962. The October crisis thus did not end on October 28. Instead, the immediate crisis slowly wound down, as Castro put it, as things became "a little better" toward "the end of the year" (1992: 343). In a broader sense, this crisis has, for Cuba, still not been resolved. As Risquet argued in 1989: "Thirty years later Cuba has not been delivered, in that it still runs the same risks with conventional weapons. It still exists next to a neighbor many times more powerful and that neighbor maintains the same policy of aggression against it" (in Allyn, Blight, and Welch, 1992: 74).

Nonetheless, despite these significant drawbacks, the Soviet missile deployment had bought for Cuba a pledge of U.S. nonaggression. And Cuban sovereignty was partially reenacted through Castro's refusal to allow the United Nations or the International Red Cross to inspect the missile sites to ensure that Soviet missiles had been withdrawn. In a statement made on November 1, Castro pointed to what might be considered the crux of the Cuban position on both the issue of inspection and the entire resolution of the October crisis:

> The Secretary General [of the United Nations] centers his interest on the fact that the United States makes the public declaration, the compromise before the United Nations, that it will not invade Cuba.
>
> Regarding this I wish to say . . . that the United States does not have any right to invade Cuba and we cannot negotiate on a promise not to commit a crime. With only the promise of not committing a crime against the threat of that danger, we are more dependent on our decision to defend ourselves than on the words of the United States Government. (Castro, 1962b: 14)

In short, though Cuba was probably safe, in the meantime, from a direct U.S. military invasion, Castro "would have preferred a more satisfactory solution, with the participation of Cuba in the discussion" (Castro, in Lockwood, 1967: 200).

THE FIRST PUZZLE

These three narratives construct the events of October 1962 in strikingly different ways. Yet in the United States, a single representation—that of the Cuban missile crisis—has "assumed genuinely mythic significance" (Blight, Nye, and Welch, 1987: 170). Its status as a myth is due in part to the danger of the crisis: The superpowers are portrayed as having come terrifyingly close to, and then successfully avoiding, the nuclear abyss. "For six harrowing days in 1962," wrote Robert Divine, "the American people lived under the threat of disaster" (1971: 3). According to Theodore Sorensen, Kennedy believed "the odds that the Soviets would go all the way to war" in the Cuban missile crisis were "'somewhere between one out of three and even'" (1965: 705).[24] But as these conflicting representations indicate, this mythic incident, the "thing" that became the Cuban missile crisis, can be and has been understood quite differently. Furthermore, two of these representations implicitly deny that the crisis, and thus the approach to the brink of nuclear disaster, were necessary at all. Had a different narrative of the events of October 1962 taken root among U.S. state officials—for example, had the Soviet missiles been accepted as defensive—that (allegedly) perilous approach to the brink could perhaps have been avoided. The story of the Cuban missile crisis and the existence of alternative representations therefore reveal an important puzzle: Why did the events of October 1962 come to be understood in the United States in this, and not in some other, way?

One can ask, for example, why the central problem was the Soviet installation of missiles in Cuba. Why is the crisis defined by the Soviet missile deployment, which is treated as a bolt from the blue, as a threat that descended upon the United States without cause or provocation?[25] In the Soviet view, the missiles were deployed at least in part to defend Cuba because "U.S. policy with respect to Cuba was directed at secret preparation of new aggression" (Gromyko, 1971: 164). The Caribbean crisis was caused and defined both by the long-standing hostility and aggression of the United States and by its insistence, in violation of Cuba's right to self-defense, that the missiles be removed. In contrast to the Cuban missile crisis, the Caribbean crisis revolved around imperialist aggression—it was what might be called an imperialist crisis. For the Cubans, the October crisis was also caused and defined by U.S. aggression, by its hostility toward the Cuban Revolution, by its persistent attempts to overthrow the legitimate government of Cuba, and by its desire to dictate the means that Cuba could use to defend itself. In this view, it might well be called a "crisis of sovereignty." So why a *missile* crisis?

One can also ask why the elapsed time of the Cuban missile crisis

is perceived as so short, a mere thirteen days.[26] October 16, 1962—
the date on which the United States confirmed the deployment of
Soviet MRBMs in Cuba—conventionally marks the beginning of the
confrontation. October 28—the date on which the Soviet Union
agreed to remove those missiles—conventionally marks the end. The
Soviet and Cuban stories, on the other hand, significantly extend the
duration of their respective crises. Both stories begin much earlier
because the confrontation was understood to be the culmination of a
long-standing U.S. policy of harassment of and aggression against
Cuba. And for the Cubans, the crisis has never been satisfactorily
resolved. So why *thirteen* days?

One can ask as well why Cuba plays such an insignificant part in
the Cuban missile crisis. Only the United States and the Soviet Union
have important roles in this drama: The deployment of strategic missiles was a hostile and aggressive action by the Soviet Union against
the United States, which, in turn, was compelled to defend itself and
its hemisphere. Cuba as an actor scarcely appears in the U.S. story.
As I. F. Stone has pointed out, standard accounts of the Cuban missile crisis "are appallingly ethnocentric. Cuba's fate and interests are
simply ignored" (1966: 14). Instead, Cuba is primarily represented
as a physical space, one that is a too-close-for-comfort ninety miles
from the United States and is "under foreign domination" (Kennedy,
1962c: 10). In the Soviet and Cuban representations, on the other
hand, Cuba plays a more important part. In the Caribbean crisis, for
example, Cuba at least acts to request Soviet assistance in the face of
U.S. aggression. But it is, of course, in the October crisis that Cuba
plays the largest role. In this account Cuba is the central, and tragic,
actor, at first assisted by a friendly superpower to defend itself
against a hostile one but later unceremoniously pushed aside, its fate
decided by a superpower arrangement in which it played no part and
with which it did not agree. So why is *Cuba* marginalized?

One could, of course, argue that the U.S. representation is preferred over the others because it is, by and large, correct. The Soviet
missiles *were* a threat; the crisis *did* last thirteen days; Cuba *was*
insignificant. Such a response presupposes that an appeal to "the
facts" can arbitrate among competing interpretations of a historical
"event." But events and facts are themselves historically contingent
ideological constructions. As Graham Allison has written, "What we
see and judge to be important and accept as adequate depends not

only on the evidence but also on the 'conceptual lenses' through which we look at the evidence" (1971: 2).[27] What the facts are, what kind of event has occurred, which interpretation of an event makes sense and can therefore become a myth, and which facts are relevant to the understanding of an event are all in part determined by the narratives in which these facts and events are embedded and through which they take on meaning. As Erik Ringmar has recently argued, "The events of the past are nothing in themselves and only something when inserted into the context of a narrative; they are nothing but precursors awaiting future subsequents, just as the stories we tell about them are only temporary statements awaiting future revisions. History as that which 'actually happened' is nothing apart from history as 'our accounts' of these events" (1996: 28).[28] The competing U.S., Soviet, and Cuban narratives, which plot the facts and events of October 1962 in quite radically different ways, are, in turn, themselves made possible by the divergent security imaginaries of their narrators. What the central causes and issues of the crises of October 1962 were, when these crises began and ended, and which states played important roles in these crises are in each case scripted and positioned by the security imaginary within which these respective crises are constructed *as* particular crises to begin with. In chapters 4, 5, and 6, I demonstrate that the postwar U.S. security imaginary provided, and in large measure still provides, the conceptual and theoretical apparatus through which the Cuban missile crisis was constructed and continues, at least in the United States, generally to be understood. Before I turn to this explanatory task, however, a second and related puzzle remains to be considered.

2

The View from the ExComm

The dominant definition of the problem acquires, by repetition, and by the weight and credibility of those who propose or subscribe it, the warrant of "common sense."
— STUART HALL, "THE REDISCOVERY OF 'IDEOLOGY'"

ACTING IN THE NATIONAL INTEREST

The National Security Council's Executive Committee (ExComm), made up of the president and a select group of his advisers, debated U.S. policy options in the Cuban missile crisis under conditions of strict secrecy.[1] For the members of the ExComm, the situation faced by the United States in mid-October 1962 was in its essence quite simple. The Soviet Union had begun secretly to install missiles with offensive nuclear capabilities in Cuba. Because of these offensive capabilities, the missiles posed a "threat to peace" (Kennedy, October 27: 49) and their deployment was "intolerable and not acceptable" (Rusk, October 16: 172).[2] A clear U.S. national interest emerged from this simple situation description: The missiles had to be removed. As General Maxwell Taylor, chairman of the Joint Chiefs of Staff in October 1962, argued at the Hawk's Cay Conference[3] in 1987: "fortunately, there was no question about the problem. The president announced his objective within the hour after seeing the photographs of the missiles: it was to get the missiles out of Cuba" (in Blight and Welch, 1990: 77). Douglas Dillon, Kennedy's secretary of the treasury, put the matter even more strongly: "We had agreed at the very first meeting," on October 15, he said, "that the one thing we were all committed to was that the missiles must be removed." In a footnote to the transcript of this discussion he then added, "While everyone at our first ExComm meeting, specifically including the President, agreed that the emplacement of Soviet MRBMs and IRBMs in Cuba was totally unacceptable and that they had to be gotten out one way or another, *I do not recall any specific discussion then or at later meetings of the ExComm as to just why they were unacceptable. It just seemed obvious to all of us*" (in Blight and Welch, 1990: 49, emphasis added). The United States therefore had "an obligation to do what has to be done" (Rusk, October 16: 173).

The unacceptability of the missile deployment and the attendant U.S. national interest in securing their removal "one way or another" were simply taken for granted by U.S. state officials. The reason is simple: The Soviet missiles had, from the outset, come to signify a series of dangerous threats to the United States. As a result, the ExComm discussions revolved primarily around four issues: the causes of the Soviet deployment, the consequences of that deployment for U.S. national interests, the best policy option available to the United States for forcing the removal of the missiles from Cuba, and the day-to-day conduct of the crisis. Given the different narrative constructions of the events of October 1962 that were already then available to U.S. decision makers, however, it is worth asking just *why* it "seemed obvious" to U.S. decision makers that the missile deployment was beyond the proverbial pale and that the U.S. national interest required the removal of the missiles from Cuba. Exactly what threats had come to be attached to these missiles? That is, exactly what meanings had the missile deployment taken on that allowed it to function as the referent to which the notion of a crisis, of a severe threat to U.S. national interests, could be articulated?

Objects of and Threats to U.S. Interests

Although, as Dillon noted, there was no discussion "as to just why" the deployment was unacceptable, both the ExComm discussions and other complementary sources provide extensive evidence of the multiple meanings that came to be attached to those weapons. For U.S. state officials, the United States was being compelled to protect numerous objects of security because the Soviet missile deployment brought the United States face to face with multiple threats.[4] Although not extensively discussed in the ExComm meetings, concerns for the physical safety of both the United States and the Western Hemisphere hovered in the background. For the first time since the advent of nuclear weapons, much of the United States was within easy range of Soviet missiles. The medium-range ballistic missiles (MRBMs) already in place in Cuba had a range of approximately 1,200 miles, and the intermediate-range ballistic missiles (IRBMs) still to be deployed extended that range to about 2,000 miles. Together, these weapons gave the Soviet Union the capacity to strike all of the continental United States except the West Coast and the northwest corner.[5] And because Soviet MRBMs and IRBMs could strike much of Central and South America as well, these areas, it was claimed, had also become potential targets for nuclear devastation. As Secretary of State Dean Rusk explained in his speech to the OAS:

> This offensive capability is of such a nature that it can reach into the far corners of our hemisphere with its destructive force. . . . The missile sites in being for medium-range ballistic missiles are capable of carrying nuclear warheads as far west as Mexico City, as far south as the Panama Canal or Caracas, and as far north as Washington, D.C. The new sites for intermediate-range ballistic missiles in Cuba will be able to carry mass destruction to most of the major cities in the Western Hemisphere. In the face of this rapid buildup, no country of this hemisphere can feel secure, either from direct attack or from persistent blackmail. (1962c: 720–721)

U.S. Attorney General Robert Kennedy thus argued that "the bases in Cuba—uh—involve—uh—the security of the Western Hemisphere. This is not just a question of the United States. This is a question of all the Latin American countries" (October 27: 43). First and foremost, then, the Soviet missiles represented a physical danger to the United States and to Latin America that had to be removed.

A further object of U.S. security was the political integrity of the hemisphere. As Dillon explained to the Mexican finance minister, Ortiz Mena, on October 22, President Kennedy had to repel what he considered an "invasion of the hemisphere by a foreign power" (in Abel, 1966: 117). Later, on October 27, Rusk argued explicitly in ExComm that "the Cuba thing is a Western Hemisphere problem, an

intrusion in the Western Hemisphere" (October 27: 38). The threat
in this case was Soviet expansion into and political subversion of the
inter-American system, the traditional preserve of the United States.
As General Curtis LeMay, chief of staff of the Air Force, argued on
October 19: "But the big thing is, if we leave them [the missiles]
there, it's a blackmail threat against not only us but the other South
American countries that they [the Soviet Union] may decide to operate against" (October 19, in May and Zelikow, 1997: 182). And the
problem extended beyond the introduction of the missiles themselves. Early in the ExComm discussions, Rusk implicitly pointed to
a broader issue, the close relationship that existed between the government of Cuba, located in the Western Hemisphere, and the Soviet
Union: "It ought to be said to Castro that, uh, uh, this kind of base is
intolerable and not acceptable. The time has now come when he
must take the interests of the Cuban people, must now break clearly
with the Soviet Union, prevent this missile base from becoming operational" (October 16: 172). As inhabitants of the Western Hemisphere,
the Cuban people were assumed to have interests consonant with
those of the rest of the hemisphere. These interests, it was further implied, were being denied both by the close relationship of the Cuban
government with the Soviet Union and by the missile deployment itself. The Soviet missiles thus symbolized the close Soviet relationship
with Cuba, which in turn posed a threat to the integrity, the unity, of
the hemisphere.

Relatedly, the Soviet deployment represented a challenge to U.S.
power in Latin America. As Robert Kennedy bluntly put it, if the
missiles were to remain in Cuba, "the other problem is, uh, in South
America a year from now. And the fact that you got, uh, *these* things
in the hands of Cubans, here, and then you, say your, some problem
arises in Venezuela, er, you've got Castro saying, You move troops
down into that part of Venezuela, we're going to fire these missiles"
(October 16: 186, emphasis in the original). In other words, the Soviet
missiles might in the future constrain the ability of the United States
to use its own military forces in response to "some problem" in the
hemisphere. Such a constraint on U.S. action was not to be tolerated,
since, as had been established in the Monroe Doctrine and more recently formalized in the Rio Pact of 1947, Latin America fell within
the U.S. sphere of influence.

Though various objects of and putative threats to U.S. security were mentioned in the ExComm discussions, the threat to U.S. credibility ostensibly posed by the missile deployment received by far the most attention. This threat was itself multiple. That is, the Soviet missile deployment placed U.S. credibility in danger in a variety of ways: through the real or apparent change that it made in the strategic balance, through its challenge to U.S. commitments to its allies, and through its challenge to the commitments made by the Kennedy administration to its domestic public.

In the ExComm discussions considerable attention was given to the threat that the missiles posed to, and the consequent need to maintain, U.S. nuclear or strategic credibility. One serious concern was the change that the missile deployment brought about in the strategic relationship between the United States and the U.S.S.R. For example, in a discussion of possible U.S. military actions, President Kennedy answered his own question about the "advantage" that the Soviets might gain from the missile deployment with reference to this strategic relationship: It "must be that they're not satisfied with their ICBMs [intercontinental ballistic missiles]," he said (October 16: 176). This encapsulates one of the most prominent beliefs about Soviet motivations expressed in the ExComm. According to this view, Khrushchev was attempting to redress the Soviet missile gap. General Taylor agreed: "What it'd give 'em is primary, it makes the launching base, uh, for short range missiles against the United States to supplement their rather defective ICBM system" (October 16: 176). CIA director John McCone's view was the same and was raised at the ExComm by Dean Rusk. On October 16, Rusk reported to the meeting:

> About why the Soviets are doing this, uhm, Mr. McCone suggested some weeks ago that one thing Mr. Khrushchev may have in mind is that, uh, uh, he knows that we have a substantial nuclear superiority, but he also knows that we don't really live under fear of his nuclear weapons to the extent that, uh, he has to live under fear of ours. Also we have nuclear weapons nearby, in Turkey and places like that (October 16: 177).

Though the presence of forty or fifty Soviet missiles might not seem like a tremendous change, many of the members of the ExComm believed that it could in fact quite drastically alter the strategic balance. At the evening meeting on October 16, for example, Undersecretary of State George Ball reiterated the claim that the Soviet deployment was "an attempt to, to add to his [Khrushchev's] strategic capabilities" (October 16: 190). The reason was explained by Raymond Garthoff in a top secret State Department memorandum written during the crisis:

> The presence of 24 1,020 n.m. MRBM launchers and 12 or 16 2,200 n.m. IRBM launchers in Cuba provides a significant accretion to Soviet strategic capabilities for striking the continental United States. In view of the relatively limited numbers of Soviet operational ICBM launchers—at present an estimated 75—the missiles in the Caribbean will increase the first-strike missile salvo which the USSR could place on targets in the continental United States by over 40 percent. (1962: 202)[6]

The strategic threat posed by the missiles was twofold: In the event of a Soviet nuclear attack on the United States, they could decrease the warning time enjoyed by the United States and increase the number of U.S. launchers vulnerable to such a first strike. "The strategic significance of the Cuban missile complex," Garthoff therefore explained,

> is due not only to the substantial quantitative increase in megatons deliverable in a surprise first strike, but also by their effect on the U.S. deterrent striking force. . . . If the present base complex in Cuba is completed late in 1962, and taking into account the estimated Soviet ICBM force for the end of 1962, a Soviet attack without warning could destroy an appreciably larger proportion of over-all United States strategic capability than it could if the Cuban complex were not included. The number of US *weapons* surviving and ready to retaliate on targets in the USSR would be decreased by about 30 percent, and would thus leave only about 15 percent of the number in our pre-attack force. This force could still cause considerable destruction in a US retaliatory strike, the Soviets could not rely on the degree of surprise assumed in the above calculation, and it is very unlikely that the Soviets would be tempted toward resort to war by the change in the military balance. Nonetheless, this represents a serious dilution of US strategic deterrent capability. (202–203, emphasis in the original)

According to such worst-case calculations, the Soviet missile deployment threatened to undermine the existing U.S. nuclear deterrent. It therefore threatened U.S. strategic credibility.

At least as important to U.S. security as the actual change in the U.S.-Soviet strategic balance was the possibility that others might perceive a change in that relationship. Even if the nuclear balance were not significantly altered, a change in perceptions among, for example, U.S. allies would undermine the credibility of the U.S. nuclear umbrella and of its policy of extended deterrence. The importance of the appearance of an altered strategic balance was stressed by U.S. decision makers immediately after the resolution of the missile crisis. For example, President Kennedy argued that if the missiles had remained in Cuba, "it would have politically changed the balance of power. It would have appeared to, and appearances contribute to reality" (1962d: 898). This argument was later repeated by Arthur Schlesinger, who claimed that "the shift in the military balance of power would be less crucial than that in the political balance. Every country in the world, watching so audacious an action ninety miles from the United States, would wonder whether it could thereafter trust Washington's resolution and protection" (1965: 796–797). At Hawk's Cay, Garthoff concluded that "the main effect of the Cuban deployment was on perceptions" (in Blight and Welch, 1990: 31). Had the United States permitted the Soviet Union to redress (or even to appear to redress) their strategic inferiority, significant damage to U.S. credibility would have resulted. As President Kennedy said in his public address of October 22, the missile deployment was "a deliberately provocative and unjustified change in the *status quo* which cannot be accepted by this country if our courage and our commitments are ever to be trusted again by either friend or foe." And drawing on the ever-useful Munich analogy, he argued that "the 1930s taught us a clear lesson: Aggressive conduct, if allowed to grow unchecked and unchallenged, ultimately leads to war" (1962c: 5–6). The credibility of U.S. commitments in the face of aggression was thus at stake.

U.S. nuclear deterrence and U.S. strategic credibility, then, were clearly important reasons for the "obvious" need to secure the missiles' removal from Cuba. But concerns about U.S. credibility also surfaced with respect to three additional issues: the status and security of West Berlin, the Turkish missile trade, and domestic U.S. politics.

First, the missile deployment was seen as a direct challenge to the status of West Berlin within the Western bloc and the credibility of the United States as its guarantor. Aware that Khrushchev had been unhappy about the anomalous status of West Berlin and that he had long been searching for a way to rectify the anomaly, President

Kennedy believed that the missile deployment was designed, at least in part, as a remedy to Khrushchev's "Berlin problem." In fact, according to Secretary of Defense Robert McNamara's notes on a meeting held on October 21, Kennedy said

> that he could not help admiring the Soviet strategy. They offered this deliberate and provocative challenge to the United States in the knowledge that if the Americans reacted violently to it, the Russians would be given an ideal opportunity to move against West Berlin. If, on the other hand, he did nothing, the Latin Americans and the United States' other Allies would feel that the Americans had no real will to resist the encroachments of Communism and would hedge their bets accordingly. (in May and Zelikow, 1997: 207)

"If we attack Cuban missiles, or Cuba, in any way," President Kennedy argued on October 19, "it gives them [the Soviet Union] a clear line to go ahead and take Berlin, as they were able to do in Hungary under the Anglo war in Egypt. . . . We would be regarded as the trigger-happy Americans who lost Berlin" (October 19, in May and Zelikow, 1997: 175). A short while later, he returned to this theme, arguing: "You know, as I say, the problem is not really so much war against Cuba. But the problem is part of a worldwide struggle with the Soviet Communists, particularly, as I say, over Berlin. And the loss of Berlin, the effect of that and the responsibility we would bear. As I say, I think the Egyptian and the Hungary thing and the obvious parallels are what I'm concerned about" (October 19, in May and Zelikow, 1997: 183).[7] So, if the United States did act in Cuba, this action might threaten both West Berlin and U.S. credibility as its protector. The missile deployment, then, posed a direct threat to West Berlin because any military action by the United States might prompt, or allow, Khrushchev to respond there. On the other hand, however, as Taylor argued, U.S. credibility would also be jeopardized if the United States did not act: "I think we'd all be unanimous in saying that really our strength in Berlin, our strength anyplace in the world, is the credibility of our response under certain conditions. And if we don't respond here in Cuba, we think the credibility is sacrificed," to which President Kennedy replied, "That's right. That's right. So that's why we've got to respond" (177). The missile deployment thus presented a direct threat to the credibility of the United States as an alliance partner.

On October 18 Dean Rusk addressed this issue at length. He argued that taking "no action [against offensive weapons in Cuba] would undermine our alliances all over the world very promptly" (in May and Zelikow, 1997: 127). If the United States were to do nothing about the missiles, Rusk continued, "this would free their [Soviet] hands for almost any kind of intervention they might want to try in other parts of the world. If we are unable to face up to the situation in Cuba against this kind of threat, I think that they would be critically encouraged to go ahead and eventually feel like they've got it made as far as intimidating the United States is concerned." This, of course, would not do. After all, "We've got a major effort in the making in every continent. And it seems to me that inaction in this situation would undermine and undercut the long support that we need for the kind of foreign policy that will eventually ensure our survival" (127). Allowing the Soviet Union to complete the missile bases in Cuba and then announce their existence, according to Army Chief of Staff General Earle Wheeler, "would immediately have a profound effect in all of Latin America at least and probably worldwide because the question would arise: Is the United States incapable of doing something about it or unwilling to do something about it? In other words, it would attack our prestige" (October 19, in May and Zelikow, 1997: 180).

The Soviet missile deployment, it was also argued, indirectly challenged U.S. credibility because it raised the possibility of a trade between the Jupiter missiles deployed by the United States in Turkey and the Soviet missiles in Cuba. Although President Kennedy had already suggested "giving him [Khrushchev] some of our Turkey missiles" on October 18 (in May and Zelikow, 1997: 142), it became the centerpiece of discussion on October 27 subsequent to the receipt of Khrushchev's second letter, in which he apparently raised the stakes in the crisis by requiring such a trade.[8] Because the Jupiters were of little military importance, the problem that concerned U.S. decision makers was not whether or not such a trade would affect U.S. military strength. Their concern, instead, was to avoid *appearing* to trade the Jupiter missiles for the Soviet missiles in Cuba, as this might frighten U.S. allies and undermine U.S. credibility. Assistant Secretary of Defense Paul Nitze pointed to this fear when he argued that "everybody else is worried that they'll be included in this great big trade" (October 27: 37). In further discussions of the wisdom of calling an immediate NATO meeting to discuss the potential trade, George Ball argued that "the Turks feel very strongly about this. They—uh—we persuaded them that this [the basing of the Jupiter missiles] *was* an essential requirement, and they—they feel that it's a matter of prestige." McGeorge Bundy responded: "In their own terms it would already be clear that we were trying to sell our allies for our interests. That would be the view in all of NATO. It's irrational, and it's crazy, but it's a *terribly* powerful fact" (October 27: 39, emphasis in the original). U.S. credibility as an ally would receive a harsh blow if the United States undermined the prestige of Turkey or appeared to withdraw its nuclear support from its NATO allies in the face of a Soviet nuclear threat based in Cuba. Bundy reiterated this fear later in the discussion as well:

> I think that if we sound as if we wanted to make this trade, to our NATO people and to all the people that are tied to us by alliance, we are in *real* trouble. I think that—we'll all join in doing this if it's the decision, but I think we should tell you that that's the universal assessment of everyone in the government that's connected with these alliance problems. . . . if we appear to be trading our—the defense of Turkey for the threat to Cuba, we—we will—we just have to face a radical decline. (October 27: 49–50, emphasis in the original)

Although a Turkish missile trade was thus viewed as extremely undesirable because it would undermine U.S. credibility as an ally, it was simultaneously thought, especially by President Kennedy, that such a trade would be seen by others as rational. Referring to Khrushchev's second letter, he said, "We're going to be in an unsupportable position on this matter if this becomes his proposal. . . . to any man at the United Nations or any other rational man it will look like a very fair trade" (October 27: 36). A few minutes later he reiterated this point, arguing that Khrushchev has "got us in a pretty good spot here, because most people will regard this as not an unreasonable proposal. . . . I think you're going to find it difficult to explain why we are going to take hostile military action in Cuba, against these sites—what we've been thinking about—the thing that he's saying is, 'If you'll get yours out of Turkey, we'll get ours out of Cuba.' I think we've got a very tough one here" (October 27: 37; see also 39, 46, 49, 50). Later on the twenty-seventh, President Kennedy argued even more explicitly that "we can't very well invade Cuba . . .

when we could have gotten them out by making a deal on the same missiles in Turkey. If that's part of the record, *I don't see how we'll have a very good war*" (October 27: 83, emphasis added). For U.S. decision makers, then, the refusal to permit the appearance of a trade between the missiles in Turkey and those in Cuba would help to preserve U.S. credibility as a stalwart ally that honors its commitments. But precisely this course of action, required to maintain U.S. credibility, could undermine U.S. credibility in the event that the crisis escalated into a war. In that case the United States would begin to look both unreasonable and unbelievable as a world leader. As President Kennedy said at one point: "We all know how quickly everybody's courage goes when the blood starts to flow, and that's what's going to happen in NATO, when they—when we start these things, and they grab Berlin, and everybody's going to say, 'Well that [the trade] was a pretty good proposition.' . . . that's the difficulty. Today it sounds great to reject it, but its not going to, after we do something" (October 27: 58; see also 54). U.S. decision makers had truly constructed a dilemma for themselves: U.S. credibility was threatened whether they agreed to the missile exchange or not.

Finally, U.S. decision makers repeatedly voiced their concern that the administration would lose credibility in the eyes of the U.S. public if the Soviet missiles were not removed, because the word of the U.S. government and, more specifically, of the U.S. president was at stake. On September 4 and again on September 13 President Kennedy had expressly warned that the United States would not tolerate the introduction of offensive missiles, offensive Soviet capabilities, or offensive Soviet bases into Cuba. Under such conditions, he had warned, the United States would feel compelled to respond. After all, he had explicitly stated that "if Cuba should possess a capacity to carry out offensive actions against the United States . . . the United States would act" (1962b: 675). Moreover, the Joint Resolution passed by Congress on October 3 had made the same commitment (U.S. Congress, 1962). Because both the president and Congress had publicly committed themselves, in advance, to not tolerating Soviet missiles in Cuba, the president's credibility, the credibility of his administration, and the credibility of the U.S. government were at stake. During the meeting on October 16, President Kennedy referred back to these statements, arguing:

I said we weren't going to [allow the Soviets to deploy missiles in Cuba]. . . . Last month I said we weren't going to. Last month I should have said we're . . . that we don't care. But when we said we're *not* going to and then they go ahead and do it, and then we do nothing, then . . . I would think that our risks increase. Uh, I agree. What difference does it make? They've got enough to blow us up now anyway. I think it's just a question of . . . After all this is a political struggle as much as military. (October 16: 186–187, emphasis in the original)

A crucial issue, then, was the potential blow to the credibility of the U.S. government if the United States acquiesced to the Soviet missile deployment. In this context, Edwin Martin, assistant secretary of state for Latin America, suggested that the ExComm consider the "psychological factor" involved in the crisis. He argued that "it's a psychological factor that we have sat back and let 'em do it to us, that is more important than the direct threat" (October 16: 186). And these psychological consequences, McNamara added, would "reach the U.S. . . . This is the *point*" (October 16: 186, emphasis in the original). Later on, McNamara returned to the issue of the U.S. government's credibility with the American public:

I'll be quite frank. I don't think there *is* a military problem here. This is my answer to Mac's question [which was, "How gravely does this change the strategic balance?"] . . . and therefore, and I've gone through this today, and I asked myself, Well, what is it then if it isn't a military problem? Well, it's just exactly *this* problem, that, that, uh, if Cuba should possess a capacity to carry out offensive actions against the U.S., the U.S. would act. . . . this is a domestic, political problem. . . . we said we'd *act*. (October 16: 192, emphasis in the original)

McNamara then laid out a plan that he described as "a little package that meets the action requirement. . . . Because, as I suggested, I don't believe it's primarily a military problem. It's primarily a, a domestic, political problem" (October 16: 193). Ball responded by saying, "Yeah, well, as far as the American people are concerned, action means military action, period" (October 16: 193).[9] In the eyes of ExComm members, then, the credibility of the U.S. government in the face of its own public, its domestic political audience, was clearly an important stake in the Cuban missile crisis.

Although it has been ignored or underemphasized in many traditional accounts of the Cuban missile crisis, domestic politics played an extremely important role in setting the context for and defining the issues involved in the crisis because of the Kennedy administration's "sense of its own precarious electoral position, the coming of the November mid-term elections, and the place Cuba had occupied in public debate in recent years" (Nathan, 1975: 262).[10] As Roger Hilsman, assistant secretary of state for intelligence and research in October 1962, noted, "The United States might not be in mortal danger, but the administration most certainly was" (1967: 197).

The Kennedy administration was particularly vulnerable on the issue of Cuba for a number of reasons. First of all, in his 1960 presidential campaign against Richard Nixon, Kennedy had explicitly accused the Eisenhower administration and the Republicans of "losing Cuba" to communism. On October 6, 1960, for example, Kennedy had argued in a campaign speech that Cuba and Castro represented

> the most glaring failure of American foreign policy, . . . a disaster which threatens the security of the whole Western Hemisphere, . . . a Communist menace which has been permitted to arise only ninety miles from the shores of the United States. . . . The story of the transformation of Cuba from a friendly ally to a Communist state is in large measure the story of a Government in Washington which lacked imagination and compassion to understand the needs of the Cuban people; which lacked in vigor and leadership necessary to those needs, and which lacked the forthright [sic] and the vision to see the inevitable results of its own failures. (1960a: 20)

On October 20 Kennedy attacked again, charging that

> for six years before Castro came to power the Republicans did absolutely nothing to stop the rise of Communism in Cuba. . . . Now the Communists have been in power for two years. Yet we have done almost nothing to keep Castro from consolidating his regime and beginning subversive activities throughout Latin America. . . . The next Administration will have to do much better than Mr. Nixon has done, if it intends to wage a serious offensive against Communism on our very doorstep. (1960b: 18)

During the campaign, then, Kennedy had explicitly staked out a tough position with respect to Cuba.

Second, the disaster at the Bay of Pigs hung heavily over the administration. Kennedy thought that with that fiasco he had "handed his critics a stick with which they would forever beat him" (in Wyden,

1979: 310). Sorensen has also argued that "ever since the Bay of Pigs, Cuba had been the Kennedy administration's heaviest political cross" (1965: 669). Having failed once to deal adequately with "the problem" of Castro, the Kennedy administration could not afford to appear to fail again.

Finally, in the context of the congressional elections coming up in November 1962, numerous conservatives had been busily criticizing administration policy toward Cuba and pushing for a tougher stand against Castro. For example, Senators Kenneth Keating, Homer Capehart, and Barry Goldwater (Republicans from New York, Indiana, and Arizona, respectively) all participated in "an unrelenting attack against the Kennedy administration." For these Republicans, "the growing Soviet military presence in Cuba . . . provided an effective campaign issue that probed one of the administration's most vulnerable spots. Republicans thus strove to make Cuba . . . the leading topic of their congressional campaigns" (Paterson and Brophy, 1986: 94). In short, as Bundy explained at the Moscow Conference in 1989, "American public opinion would never have been able to accept a permanent installation, in the 1960s, of Soviet missiles in Cuba" (in Allyn, Blight, and Welch, 1992: 141).

The U.S. National Interest in the Cuban Missile Crisis

From this plethora of threatening meanings attached to the Soviet missile deployment, the national interest of the United States followed unproblematically: The missiles had to go. No other outcome was acceptable, or even conceivable. The October 16 transcript thus begins with the following statement by Rusk: "Now, uhm, I do think we have to set in motion a chain of events that will eliminate this base. I don't think we [can?] sit still" (171, brackets in the original). That the U.S. national interest in removing the missiles formed the starting point rather than the conclusion of analysis is also evident in a top secret memo that Charles Bohlen (special assistant to the secretary of state and then ambassador to France in October 1962) sent to Rusk on October 18 for transmission to the president. In this memo, he explained his views "as succinctly as possible." Point number one read: "The existence of Soviet MRBM bases in Cuba cannot be tolerated. The objective therefore is their elimination by whatever means may be necessary" (in Bohlen, 1973: 491). Similarly, John McCone, having briefed President Eisenhower on the crisis, reported Eisenhower's reactions and suggestions to the ExComm. According to McCone, "the thrust of his comments" indicated that "he felt first that the existence of [Soviet bases] in Cuba was intolerable from the standpoint of this country" (October 18, in May and Zelikow, 1997: 140, brackets in the original). And again, in offering the assessment of the Joint Chiefs of Staff to President Kennedy on October 19, Taylor reported that "from the outset I would say that we found we were united on the military requirement: we could not accept Cuba as a missile base; that we should either eliminate or neutralize the missiles there and prevent any others coming in" (October 18, in May and Zelikow, 1997: 174). From the very beginning, then, the deliberations of the ExComm and of other U.S. policy makers rested on the apparently self-evident assumption that the missiles must be removed. The "reality" of the situation was that "the missiles were the problem, and their removal was the solution" (Bundy, 1988: 398). President Kennedy reiterated the U.S. objective in his phone call with Prime Minister Harold Macmillan of Great Britain early on the evening of October 22: "What we want to do," he said, "is get these weapons out of Cuba" (in May and Zelikow, 1997: 284).

In order to secure this putatively self-evident national interest, the ExComm discussed a range of possible policy options. Most prominent among them were a naval blockade of Cuba and an air strike against the missile bases.[11] The proponents of these two solutions have come to be known as "doves" and "hawks," respectively.[12] A diplomatic or political solution was also mentioned, but it was discussed only briefly and then dismissed. General Taylor has picturesquely described these three options as the "squeeze the missiles out," "shoot the missiles out," and "talk the missiles out" strategies (in Blight and Welch, 1990: 77).[13]

The agenda for the ExComm discussions of policy options seems to have been set by the time the meeting on October 16 convened at 11:50 A.M. Dean Rusk started out with a summary of "two major, uh, courses of action as alternatives." These were either a "sudden, unannounced strike of some sort" or an approach whereby the United States would "build up the crisis to the point where the other side has to consider very seriously about giving in." This latter course of action would involve "a combination of things," including a decision "to alert our allies *and* Mr. Khrushchev that there is [an] utterly serious crisis in the making here" (October 16: 171–173, emphasis and brackets in the original). These two options then evolved into the three mentioned above. The third course of action, the "talk the missiles out" strategy, McNamara explained later on the sixteenth,

> is what I would call the political course of action, in which we, uh, follow some of the possibilities that Secretary Rusk mentioned this morning by approaching Castro, by approaching Khrushchev, by discussing with our allies. An overt and open approach politically to the problem [attempting, or in order?] to solve it. This seemed to me likely to lead to no satisfactory result, and it almost stops subsequent military action. (October 16: 182, brackets in the original)

As McNamara's statement indicates, a purely diplomatic course of action had little support from the outset. At best it would enable Khrushchev to seize the diplomatic initiative, "to break the story in his own way with his own spin" (Bundy, 1988: 409). At worst, the missiles would become operational during such diplomatic activities, giving Khrushchev the means with which to retaliate against any U.S. actions with a nuclear strike at the United States. Dillon aggressively argued this point of view, insisting that

> this alternative course of, of warning, getting, uh, public opinion, uh, OAS action and telling people in NATO and everything like that, would appear to me to have the danger of, uh, getting us wide out in the open and forcing the Russians to, uh, Soviets to take a, a position that if anything was done, uh, they would, uh, have to retaliate. Whereas uh, a, a quick action, uh, with a statement at the same time saying that this is all there is to it, might give them a chance to, uh, back off and not do anything. Meanwhile, I think that the chance of getting through this thing without a Russian reaction is greater under a quick, uh, strike than, uh, building the whole thing up to a, a climax. (October 16: 179; see also Kennedy, October 16: 179)

Furthermore, this diplomatic option would not in any case allow the president to fulfill his promise to *act*. As McNamara said, it did not meet "the action requirement" (October 16: 193). Moreover, Bundy has argued, "an overwhelming majority of Americans and their representatives in Congress would expect and demand the action that Kennedy had promised. If he were to begin by public diplomacy, he could expect an immediate clamor for deeds, not words, and a tumultuous babel of conflicting public advice as to what actions he should take, and how quickly" (1988: 394). A diplomatic solution thus neglected "a reality that could not possibly be neglected by the American administration in the five days after October 15—that the United States government had publicly pledged itself, in a manner wholly unambiguous to itself and its countrymen, not to accept any such deployment" (410). The fear that the missiles would become operational and concerns for the domestic credibility of the administration precluded a purely diplomatic solution, and this option disappeared from the agenda in short order.

Because a strictly diplomatic response was ruled out early on, the remaining ExComm deliberations demonstrate what one analyst has called a "peculiar search for the middle ground of a policy defined in terms of force" (Nathan, 1975: 270). Action was required and, as George Ball had said, that meant military action (October 16: 193). One possible military option, the "shoot the missiles out" strategy favored by the hawks, involved an air strike against the missile bases, possibly to be followed by an invasion of Cuba. McNamara described this option as "any one of [several] variants of military action directed against Cuba, starting with an air attack against the missiles. The Chiefs are strongly opposed to so limited an air strike. But even so limited an air attack is a very extensive attack" (October 16: 182). General Taylor forcefully advanced this option: "Our [the Joint Chiefs'] recommendation would be to get complete intelligence. . . . Then look at this target system. If it really threatens the United States, then take it right out with one hard crack" (October 16: 181–182). This option, though taken seriously and indeed favored in many of the ExComm discussions before October 20, ultimately lost out as the initial U.S. response for a number of reasons.[14] First, a "surgical" strike that could guarantee the removal of at least 90 percent of the missiles, as well as the Soviet MiGs and IL-28 bombers with which the Soviets could retaliate, would in fact be a major undertaking, requiring up to five hundred sorties. Such a large-scale strike might produce chaos and political collapse in Cuba, necessitating a U.S. invasion. Furthermore, it would undoubtedly kill both Russians and Cubans, in all likelihood provoking a military response from Khrushchev, either against the United States or against Berlin or Turkey. McNamara, for example, claimed that "it seems to me almost certain that any one of these forms of direct military action will lead to a Soviet military response of some type some place in the world. It may well be worth the price. Perhaps we should pay that. But I think we should recognize that possibility" (October 16: 183). In addition, the question of advance warning confounded the implementation of this option. If the United States gave advance warning of an impending attack, then the Soviets could prepare a response, perhaps even hiding the missiles. As Taylor said, "These are . . . really mobile missiles. . . . They can pull in under trees and forest and disappear almost at once" (October 16: 188). But if some warning were not given, Robert Kennedy pointed out, the United States would be perpetrating a "Pearl Harbor in reverse" (in Acheson, 1969b: 76). It was finally decided that an attack without warning would be unacceptable because "for 175 years we have not been that kind of country. Sunday-morning surprise blows on small nations were not in our tradition" (R. F. Kennedy, in Schlesinger, 1965: 806–807).[15]

The alternative course of action discussed, to "squeeze the missiles out," was the naval blockade favored by the so-called doves. Blockade, McNamara explained, was a course of action that "lies in between the military course we began discussing a moment ago and the political course of action." It "would involve declaration of open surveillance; a statement that we would immediately impose an, uh, a blockade against *offensive* weapons entering Cuba in the future; and an indication that with our open-surveillance reconnaissance which we would plan to maintain indefinitely for the future, [Deleted] . . ." (October 16: 182, emphasis and brackets in the original). After considerable debate about its shortcomings, including the fact that it could not by itself guarantee the removal of the missiles in the way that an air strike might,[16] President Kennedy decided on October 20 to implement a naval blockade of Cuba.

This alternative won out for a variety of reasons.[17] First, though it signaled U.S. commitment and the firmness of U.S. intentions, it was less extreme than a military strike and was less likely to provoke a military response from Khrushchev. Second, "because it was a limited, low-level action . . . the blockade had the advantage of permitting a more controlled escalation on our part, gradual or rapid as the situation required" (Sorensen, 1965: 688). It left the United States with further graduated options, including a tightening of the blockade, and it did not preclude further military actions, such as an air strike or an invasion, should these become necessary. As such, the blockade provided "a middle course between inaction and battle, a course which exploited our superiority in local conventional power and would permit subsequent movement either toward war or toward peace" (Schlesinger, 1965: 804–805). Third, the blockade had the advantage of placing the onus of the next move on Khrushchev; he could avoid a direct military clash with the United States by recalling his ships, or he could provoke a military clash by responding to the blockade with military action. The first move in a direct military engagement would then be Khrushchev's responsibility. These advantages led to the decision to respond to the Soviet missile deployment with a naval blockade against offensive weapons, which was announced by Kennedy on October 22.[18]

TELLTALE SILENCES

Though it has often been argued that the deliberations of Kennedy's advisers during the missile crisis were remarkable for their exhaustiveness, the scope of their discussions was in fact strangely limited.[19] There was extensive discussion of the possible consequences of a missile trade with Turkey, of an air strike against the missile bases, of an invasion of Cuba, and of a blockade, but numerous critical issues received no attention at all. Most notably, the content of the U.S. national interest, that is, the need to remove the missiles, was not itself discussed. As Dillon later noted, "I do not recall any specific discussion then or at later meetings of the ExComm as to just why they were unacceptable. It just seemed obvious to all of us" (in Blight and Welch, 1990: 49).[20] (Dillon's recollection is correct, as the recently released transcripts indicate [May and Zelikow, 1997].) This absence is all the more remarkable because on October 18 President Kennedy did recognize, if fleetingly, that others might not entertain the same view. In discussing the effect that a U.S. strike against Cuba would have on the NATO alliance, he noted that "most allies regard [Cuba] as a *fixation* of the United States and not a serious military threat. . . . they think we're *slightly demented* on this subject." He then added, "So there isn't any doubt that, whatever action we take against Cuba . . . a lot of people would regard this as a *mad act* by the United States" (in May and Zelikow, 1997: 134, emphasis added). Despite this implicit awareness that the U.S. construction of these events might be unique, the national interest remained clear and unquestioned. Sorensen put the matter bluntly in 1989: "It was the sense of the United States government that the missiles in Cuba were the source of the crisis" (in Allyn, Blight, and Welch, 1992: 91). As a result, as Bundy explained, "Our [the U.S. government's] principle concern at the time was simply with the elimination of the Soviet missiles from Cuba" (in Allyn, Blight, and Welch, 1992: 109).

In addition, several critical issues were basically ignored, including the possibility that the Soviet Union was in fact defending Cuba; the idea that Cuba, as a sovereign state, had a right to arm in self-defense; and the possibility that the Soviet missile deployment, because it was strategically irrelevant, required no response at all. An investigation of what the ExComm failed to discuss can shed some light on why, in the absence of any discussion of these issues, U.S. decision makers were so certain that the U.S. national interest required the removal of the missiles. Examining these telltale silences can help to explain how the missile crisis and the U.S. national interest were constructed by locating the boundaries, the "horizon of the taken-for-granted" (Hall, 1988: 44), of the security imaginary, beyond which "particular representations of the world seem 'unintelligible,' 'irrational,' 'meaningless,' or 'ungraspable'" (Muppidi, 1997: 8).

SPECULATING ON SOVIET MOTIVES

One might reasonably expect an understanding of Soviet motives to have been central to determining the U.S. national interest. After all, the stakes riding on the ExComm's assessment of Khrushchev's or Soviet motivations were quite high. Nonetheless, U.S. decision makers did not in fact understand what had moved Khrushchev, or the Soviet government, to deploy the missiles in the first place. Indeed, "President Kennedy and his closest advisors found the Soviets almost entirely inscrutable" and were "almost continuously mystified" by them (Blight, Nye, and Welch, 1987: 181, 183). In a discussion of Soviet behavior, including both the missile deployment itself and the means by which it was being implemented, the president bluntly confessed his puzzlement: "Well," he said, "it's a goddamn mystery to me" (October 16, in May and Zelikow, 1997: 107). At the Hawk's Cay Conference, while answering a question about Soviet motives, Sorensen acknowledged that "the only honest answer I have is: 'I don't know now and I didn't know then.' None of us knew." McNamara also admitted that "I don't know why the Soviets did what they did" (in Blight and Welch, 1990: 28–29). That the members of the ExComm did not understand Soviet motives is clear from the transcripts as well. Though they proceeded on the assumption that the missiles had to be removed, these deliberations were repeatedly interrupted to rehash, in one form or another, the same basic question: Why is the Soviet government, or why is Khrushchev, doing this? President Kennedy raised this question more often than anyone else. On October 16, for example, he asked, "What is the, uh, advant—. . . Must be some major reason for the Russians to, uh, set this up" (Kennedy, October 16: 176). Later he asked, "If the, uh, it [the missile deployment] doesn't increase very much their strategic, uh, strength, why is it, uh, can any Russian expert tell me why they . . . After all Khrushchev demonstrated a sense of caution" (189). And just a moment later, after some possible reasons had been given, he responded, "Why does he put these in there though?" and "What is the advantage of that?" (190).

Because U.S. decision makers were baffled by the Soviet missile deployment, they spent considerable time speculating about the objectives that might have animated Khrushchev and the Soviet government. The discussion revolved around a number of alternative hypotheses. Most prominent among them were that the missile deployment was an attempt to change the actual strategic balance between the United States and the U.S.S.R., that it was designed to change the appearance of the strategic balance, or that Khrushchev was trying to initiate a trade between the Soviet missiles in Cuba and a settlement of some other issue, perhaps involving the status of West Berlin. These motivations clearly parallel the threats that, for U.S. decision makers, had become attached to the missiles.

As discussed earlier, some members of the ExComm speculated that Khrushchev was attempting to alter the strategic balance in order to overcome the Soviet missile gap. On October 16, President Kennedy speculated that the Soviets weren't satisfied with their ICBM capabilities. General Taylor responded, "[Cuba] makes the launching base, uh, for short range missiles against the United States to supplement their rather defective ICBM system" (October 16: 176). He later added that these missiles "*can* become a, a very, a rather important adjunct and reinforcement to the, to the strike capability of the Soviet Union" (185, emphasis in the original). Because the Soviet Union did not have sufficient ICBMs to station inside the Soviet Union and because they could not produce them fast enough to rectify the shortfall, the argument went, they introduced the medium-

and intermediate-range SS-4s and SS-5s that they had in fact produced into Cuba—the only place to which they had access that was
close enough to the United States to make a difference. Furthermore,
Soviet delivery systems were typically unreliable, and basing the missiles in Cuba would help to overcome this deficiency as well. At
Hawk's Cay, Dillon argued that

> what we should really be paying attention to is the number [of nu-
> clear weapons] each could *deliver* on the other. Before the Soviets put
> missiles in Cuba, it was doubtful whether they could deliver any war-
> heads from Soviet territory at all. So while the Cuban installations
> didn't add very much to their numbers and didn't change the overall
> balance very much, my impression at the time was that they radically
> altered the numbers of *deliverable* warheads, and in that sense they
> significantly increased Soviet capability. (in Blight and Welch, 1990:
> 30–31, emphasis in the original)[21]

Some members of the ExComm, in turn, speculated that Khrushchev's goal was, rather, to alter the appearance of Soviet might,
thereby enhancing Soviet prestige. With the successful launching of
Sputnik in 1957 and the U.S. claims of an actual or potential missile
gap favoring the Soviet Union had come "a campaign of Soviet 'rocket
rattling'" (Powaski, 1987: 70). Khrushchev had already threatened
the possibility of nuclear war during the Suez crisis of 1956, and he
repeated these warnings on the occasions of the Taiwan Straits and
Berlin crises of 1958. In February 1961, however, it became public
knowledge that defense studies conducted by the Kennedy administration had found "no evidence that Russia has embarked on a
'crash' program of building intercontinental ballistic missiles or that
any 'missile gap' exists today" (Norris, 1961: 1). Instead of lagging
behind the Soviet Union, it turned out that the United States enjoyed
indisputable nuclear superiority. In exposing the missile gap as a
myth and thus deflating Soviet nuclear strategic pretensions, the U.S.
administration had in effect issued a direct challenge to Soviet credibility (see Kahan and Long, 1972: 564–568). On October 16, Deputy
Undersecretary of State Alexis Johnson therefore suggested that, in
view of Khrushchev's deficiency in ICBMs, perhaps he needed "a PR
[public relations] capacity. . . . He's got a lot of MRBMs and this is a
way to balance it out a bit?" (October 16: 190). Rusk also pointed
out that "one thing Khrushchev may have in mind is that, uh, uh, he

knows that we have a substantial nuclear superiority, but he also knows that we don't really live under fear of his nuclear weapons to the extent that, uh, he has to live under fear of ours. . . . we have nuclear weapons nearby, in Turkey and places like that" (October 16: 177). On this argument, the increased nuclear capability lent by the missiles themselves was less important to Khrushchev than was the change in the perceived strategic balance between the United States and the U.S.S.R. The deployment was designed to challenge the perception of U.S. nuclear superiority and to recapture lost Soviet prestige. It was in this way that the Soviet deployment was "upsetting the status quo" (Dillon, October 27: 40).

Still other U.S. decision makers suggested that Khrushchev had installed the missiles in Cuba for the express purpose of creating a bargaining chip with which to force a settlement in West Berlin and in Germany as a whole. West Berlin had come to symbolize the cold war in Europe and had been the site of repeated postwar crises, particularly the 1948 blockade and airlift, Khrushchev's nuclear "rocket rattling" in 1958, and the construction of the Berlin Wall in 1961. For Khrushchev, a satisfactory settlement of the Berlin and German issues was extremely important for a variety of reasons, including

> the growing military power of West Germany, its strengthened ties with the West, its attractiveness to technicians and other experts living in East Germany, the very weak position of the East German communist regime, the position of West Berlin as an espionage and propaganda center within the communist bloc, the growing fear of the Soviet peoples over West Germany's power, and, finally, Khrushchev's realization that with his ICBM braggadocio punctured as only myth, he needed a major strategic victory. (LaFeber, 1985: 218)

Because Khrushchev was adamant that Western power be eliminated from West Berlin, the idea of a trading ploy seemed reasonable. And by October 22, President Kennedy seems to have accepted the settlement of the Berlin issue as the most likely explanation of the Soviet deployment: "Whatever we do in regard to Cuba, it gives him the chance to do the same with regard to Berlin." Kennedy and his advisers should therefore "keep our eye on the main site, which would be Berlin" (Kennedy, in May and Zelikow, 1997: 256). On October 25 he reiterated this position, asserting that what "caused him [Khrushchev] to do this" was "his frustration over Berlin" (438). Rusk also thought that Berlin was

> very much involved in this. Uhm, for the first time, I'm beginning really to wonder whether maybe Mr. Khrushchev is entirely rational about Berlin. We've [hardly?] talked about his obsession with it. And I think we have to, uh, keep our eye on that element. But, uh, they may be thinking that they can either bargain Berlin and Cuba against each other, or that they could provoke us into a kind of action in Cuba which would give an umbrella for them to take action with respect to Berlin. In other words, like the Suez-Hungary combination. (October 27: 177–178, brackets in the original)

Later in the same conversation, another speaker argued that Khrushchev may be setting up "a ploy" to use against the United States. Khrushchev could "possibly use it [the missile deployment] to try to trade something in Berlin, saying he'll disarm Cuba if, uh, if we'll, uh, yield some of our interests in Berlin and some arrangement for it. I mean, that this is a, it's a trading ploy" (October 27: 190).[22]

Additional motives have also been posited by both participants in and analysts of the crisis.[23] Three of the motives suggested invoked international considerations. One suggestion is that Khrushchev was attempting to initiate a trade against U.S. missiles in Turkey. A second is that Khrushchev was playing cold war politics by seizing an opportunity to put the West, and especially the United States, on the defensive. Alternatively, it has also been suggested that Khrushchev was concerned, in the face of the Sino-Soviet split and Soviet competition with China for the leadership of the international socialist movement, to enhance the stature of the Soviet Union in the eyes of the socialist world. Two additional hypotheses have stressed the importance of Soviet domestic politics. One suggests that Khrushchev was thought to be engaged in a power struggle with hard-line opponents in the Kremlin. The missile deployment was thus an attempt by Khrushchev to maintain or enhance his political power. The other argued that Khrushchev needed a foreign policy victory to offset his persistent domestic policy failures.

The question of Soviet motivations has preoccupied analyses of the Cuban missile crisis since 1962. It is interesting to note, in this context, that the very first question asked at the Moscow Conference in 1989, which was put by Robert McNamara, was "What was the purpose of the deployment of the nuclear-tipped missiles into Cuba by the Soviet Union?" (in Allyn, Blight, and Welch, 1992: 7). The same question has been prominent in scholarly treatments of the Cuban missile crisis as well. For Graham Allison, for example, the Cuban missile crisis raised four central questions, the first of which was "Why did the Soviet Union place strategic offensive missiles in Cuba?" (1971: 1). In 1982, Ronald Pope argued that the analysis of newly available Soviet materials could shed light on several important issues, including, prominently, "why the missiles were sent to Cuba" (Pope, 1982: 3). And the question of Soviet motivations has remained important in the U.S. study of the Cuban missile crisis. In their 1990 study, Blight and Welch raise a large set of issues about that crisis. Early in their list are the questions "How did it happen? . . . Why did Khrushchev attempt to deploy missiles surreptitiously in America's backyard?" According to these authors, "the most glaring gap in our understanding of the event concerns Soviet motives and actions" (1990: 4, 8).

Ignoring the Defense of Cuba

What these oft-repeated discussions of and questions about Soviet motives reveal is that Khrushchev's explicit claim to have been defending Cuba against U.S. aggression was dismissed from the outset. As Barton Bernstein has pointed out, "neither Kennedy nor most of his advisors ever seriously considered that Khrushchev might be responding to American provocations" (1990: 236). Rather, the president and the members of the ExComm "were generally sure that the Soviets were acting aggressively, not out of defensiveness" (237). The notion that Khrushchev was defending Cuba thus scarcely arose during the discussions. When it did, it was essentially dismissed as nonsense. On October 16, for example, Bundy clearly rejected this interpretation of Soviet motives. After reading a quote from the TASS statement of September 12 in which the Soviet government had insisted that it had sent to Cuba only "harmless military equipment" that was "designed exclusively for . . . defensive purposes," Bundy asserted, "Now there, it's very hard to reconcile *that* with what has happened" (October 16: 178, emphasis added). Though nuclear weapons clearly are not harmless, it is equally clear that they can be deployed for defensive purposes. After all, the United States had itself installed nuclear missiles around the Soviet Union for the express purpose of defending the West. It is therefore difficult to reconcile this Soviet claim with subsequent Soviet actions only if the missiles are understood as unambiguously offensive. However, since missiles can be used both to deter and to attack, it cannot be demonstrated that they are necessarily offensive without knowledge of Soviet motives or intent. Without direct evidence of Soviet motives, however, their intentions were consistently inferred from the allegedly offensive character of the missiles themselves. In short, the offensive character both of the missiles and of Soviet intentions was assumed, and the Soviet claim to be acting defensively to protect Cuba from U.S. aggression was automatically ruled out.

On October 27, the members of the ExComm discussed at length Khrushchev's conflicting letters of October 26 and 27, in which he proposed an exchange of the Soviet missiles, respectively, for a U.S. pledge of nonaggression against Cuba and for the missiles in Turkey. The relative merits of the Trollope ploy, of striking a deal on the basis of the first Soviet proposal while ignoring the second, was a major source of debate. In this context, McNamara at one point declared:

> When I read that message of last night [October 26] this morning, I thought, *My God* I'd never sell—I'd never base a transaction on *that contract*. Hell, that's no offer. There's not a damned thing in it that's an offer. You read that message carefully. He didn't propose to take the missiles out. Not once—there isn't a single word in it that proposes to take the missiles out. It's twelve pages of—of fluff. (October 27: 79, emphasis in the original)

Since Khrushchev in fact did settle the crisis on the basis of that letter—since the Trollope ploy was successful—it was clearly something more than merely fluff. Nonetheless, McNamara simply could not believe that the Soviet Union might be willing to trade the missiles for a U.S. guarantee not to invade Cuba. Since the Soviet claim to be defending Cuba had already been dismissed from the outset, a U.S. promise not to invade Cuba did not seem a likely means for settling the conflict.

Not only did the members of the ExComm ignore the Soviet claim to be defending Cuba, but that claim has, until recently, been flatly rejected in most scholarly analyses of the Cuban missile crisis.[24] For example, Elie Abel described Khrushchev's public letter ending the crisis as including "six paragraphs of *tortured self-justification* having to do with Castro's fears that his country was about to be invaded" (1966: 202–203, emphasis added).[25] Arnold Horelick argued that Khrushchev's claim to be defending Cuba was simply a post hoc rationalization of what was in fact a major foreign policy failure. "To regard the outcome of the Cuban missile crisis as coinciding in any substantial way with Soviet intentions or motives," he wrote in 1964, "is to mistake skillful salvage of a shipwreck for brilliant navigation" (1964: 365). Adam Ulam simply dismissed Khrushchev's claim to be defending Cuba as "laughable." According to Ulam, Khrushchev made this argument only after the fact in order to avoid complete humiliation (1971: 332). The same claim has been made by Bundy: "The Soviet leader had certainly not made his enormous secret gamble for the purpose of pulling back so quickly, with or without an undertaking by Kennedy not to invade Cuba, with or without the dismantling of fifteen obsolete missiles in Turkey. Both of Khrushchev's letters were attempts to put a decent face on failure" (1988: 440). Even as late as 1990, Blight and Welch asserted, without evidence or explanation, that "the few Soviet accounts that have been written are difficult to take seriously" and concluded that "the Soviet side of the crisis, therefore, has been almost entirely opaque" (1990: 5).[26]

An Alternative Understanding

As recently as 1987, Graham Allison again refused to allow that the Soviets had any grounds for their claim to have been defending Cuba when he flatly denied the possibility that the United States had offensive objectives in Cuba. He asserted outright that "the United States had no such plans or intentions" (in Hershberg, 1990: 165). However, recently declassified U.S. documents have brought to light new information that does lend considerable credence to the Soviet and Cuban representations of the missile deployment as defensive.[27] As James Hershberg has pointed out,

> it is now clear that throughout the first ten months of 1962, Operation Mongoose, the Kennedy administration's secret program of covert operations against Cuba, was closely coordinated with enhanced Pentagon contingency planning *for possible U.S. military intervention to bring about Fidel Castro's downfall.* . . . Although the ultimate purpose of these intensified military operations remains unclear, I argue that one can no longer breezily dismiss, as have some commentators

and former officials, the possibility that, under domestic political pressure and even before they learned in mid-October that Soviet nuclear-capable missiles were in Cuba, *top U.S. policy makers seriously considered conventional military action—including, if necessary, a full-scale invasion*—to overthrow the Castro regime. (1990, 163–164, emphasis added)

Moreover, as Hershberg also notes, this more recent evidence "has implications for interpretations of Nikita Khrushchev's original decision to send nuclear missiles to Cuba." Specifically,

it suggests that *Moscow and Havana were justified in suspecting that Washington was considering an invasion of Cuba*, although it does not confirm that a decision to order an invasion was, in fact, ever made. And it raises the possibility that in addition to previously disclosed covert operations and assassination plots against Havana, large-scale U.S. conventional military maneuvers in the Caribbean in the spring of 1962, heretofore ignored in most analyses of the crisis, may have influenced the Soviet leader's perception that an American invasion was in the offing. (164, emphasis added)

The explicit goal of Operation Mongoose was "eventual revolution within Cuba" ("Minutes of the first Operation Mongoose meeting," 1961: 20). More specifically, its objective, developed "in keeping with the spirit of the Presidential memorandum of 30 November 1961," was for the United States to "help the people of Cuba overthrow the Communist regime from within Cuba and institute a new government with which the United States can live in peace" (Lansdale, 1962: 23). Perhaps not coincidentally, the "course of action" set forth for Operation Mongoose "aim[ed] for a revolt which can take place in Cuba *by October 1962*" (Lansdale, 1962: 23, emphasis added). Direct U.S. military intervention played an important role in this plan. It was assumed that "in undertaking to cause the overthrow of the target government, the U.S. will make maximum use of indigenous resources, internal and external" but that "final success will require decisive U.S. military intervention." Furthermore, it was argued, "Such indigenous resources as are developed will be used to prepare for and justify this intervention, and thereafter to facilitate and support it" (U.S. Special Group [Augmented], 1962: 38). The "thereafter" referred to U.S. plans for a "sustained occupation" of Cuba (U.S. Department of Defense Joint Chiefs of Staff, 1962: 48).

As Hershberg has argued, the plans for Operation Mongoose "show clearly that a U.S. invasion was central to hopes for Mongoose's success and that the covert program was intended to have the capacity to produce a pretext for direct U.S. intervention." In short, the members of the ExComm ignored, and the Cuban missile crisis myth continues to ignore, significant measures undertaken by the United States "to prepare for possible military action against Cuba and the personal interest taken by President Kennedy in those plans" (1990: 171; see also Paterson, 1990). In addition, they of course ignore the extensive history both of U.S. hostility toward and aggression against Cuba, which were part of the public record, and of U.S. attempts to assassinate Castro, which were then known only to U.S. decision makers.

Soviet fears of a U.S. invasion of Cuba, and thus the legitimacy of the defense-of-Cuba narrative, were reiterated at the Cambridge Conference.[28] The Soviet participants—Fyodor Burlatsky (Khrushchev's speech writer and political adviser for socialist countries of Eastern Europe), Sergo Mikoyan (son of Anastas I. Mikoyan, who had been first deputy premier under Khrushchev), and Georgy Shakhnazarov (an associate of several of the major Soviet decision makers during the Caribbean crisis)—agreed that the defense of Cuba was a significant reason for the Soviet missile deployment, although they disagreed on whether it was the most important reason or only second to the rectification of the strategic balance. At the conference, Mikoyan argued in no uncertain terms for the primacy of Cuban defense: "The main idea was the defense of Fidel's regime," he asserted.

> Khrushchev had some reasons to think the United States would repeat the Bay of Pigs, but not make mistakes anymore. . . . In 1962, at Punte del Este, Cuba was excluded from the Organization of American States. Khrushchev regarded this exclusion as a diplomatic isolation and a preparation for an invasion. And then the propagandistic preparation was the accusation of exporting revolution. So he thought an invasion was inevitable, that it would be massive, and that it would use all American force. (in Blight and Welch, 1990: 238)

Mikoyan made the same argument in an interview with Berndt Greiner on October 13, 1987. He asserted that "in the spring of 1962 we in Moscow were absolutely convinced that a second Bay of Pigs was at hand, that a new military invasion of Cuba was at hand, but this time with all American military might, not only with proxy troops." He later reiterated that

> I think that the first and most important reason to ship the missiles over was to defend Cuba. Other ideas certainly had a certain impact, but they were only secondary. Most important was to prevent an all-out invasion. You must understand: our intelligence and Cuban intelligence knew what was going on in the United States. The Americans called up reserves, had a CIA program called "Mongoose" to topple Castro, concentrated military power in the Caribbean, and so on and so forth. That's why we thought an invasion was imminent. (in Greiner, 1990: 209, 210)

One of the reasons for the intense Soviet interest in the fate of the Cuban revolution was described by Anastas Mikoyan in a memo written in November 1992. In this memo he explained that "a defeat of the Cuban revolution would mean a two or three times larger defeat of the whole socialist camp. Such a defeat would throw back the revolutionary movement in many countries. Such a defeat would bear witness to the supremacy of imperialist forces in the entire world. That would be an incredible blow which would change the correlation of forces between the two systems" (quoted in May and Zelikow, 1997: 710, note 23). As May and Zelikow note, the Soviets seemed to have their own version of the domino theory.

In their analysis of the Cambridge Conference, Blight and Welch acknowledge that "Sergo Mikoyan told the tale in a way which made the defense-of-Cuba hypothesis appear both plausible and persuasive." They contrast this "persuasive" account to those of Khrushchev and Gromyko, which "read more like polemics than analyses." It is because of this polemical tone, Blight and Welch maintain, that "American (and Soviet) audiences can be forgiven for being skeptical" about these accounts (1990: 294). The substance of the arguments offered by Burlatsky, Mikoyan, and Shakhnazarov, however, does not differ significantly from that provided by Khrushchev and Gromyko. The latter could as easily have been evaluated as at least plausible, despite their somewhat polemical character. Instead, these accounts have systematically been dismissed by policy makers and academics alike.[29]

By 1989, however, McNamara agreed that "if I was a Cuban and read the evidence of covert American action against their government, I would be quite ready to believe that the U.S. intended to mount an invasion" (in Blight and Welch, 1990: 329).[30] General William Smith (then special assistant to the chairman of the Joint Chiefs of Staff) also acknowledged that "I am becoming more and more convinced that the United States military forces were seen as destabilizing by the Cubans and the Soviets as they looked at what they saw about the United States view on Cuba and the possibility of the use of military force in that connection" (in Allyn, Blight, and Welch, 1992: 186). Similarly, Bundy has recently admitted that "Khrushchev certainly knew of our program of covert action against Cuba, and he could hardly be expected to understand that to us this program was not a prelude to stronger action but a substitute for it" (1988: 416). He is therefore now willing to allow that "in retrospect it seems likely that Khrushchev was also trying, although clumsily, to take account of our warnings [against an offensive weapons deployment] by offering assurances that all his deployments, of whatever sort, were *defensive*. Since we found it impossible to accept this reading, we assumed too easily that his assurances reflected *only* a vicious deception" (414, emphasis in the original). The question, then, is why it was impossible to accept this reading. All of the U.S. decision makers were aware of the history of U.S. hostility toward and actions against Cuba, especially the Bay of Pigs invasion. In addition, at least some of them, including the president, Taylor, Bundy, Alexis Johnson, Gilpatric, McCone, and Robert Kennedy,[31] were aware of Operation Mongoose. Yet they did not consider that their own actions might justify Soviet and Cuban fears or help to explain Soviet and Cuban actions. As Bundy points out, U.S. decision makers "did not understand that Khrushchev might take our hostile words about Cuba, and the very attitudes of our own people that we understood so well on October 16, as meaning that all we had learned from the Bay of Pigs was that we should do it right next time." What was most interesting about the defense-of-Cuba motive, he says, "is that it simply did not occur to us in Washington before October 15" (Bundy, 1988: 416).[32] And, as the transcripts of the ExComm deliberations indicate, even after October 15 it was neither seriously considered as a motive for the Soviet missile deployment nor understood to be of significance in defining the U.S. national interest.

While U.S. decision makers have struggled to discern Khrushchev's motives or those of his advisers, the resolution of the crisis itself could have provided subsequent analysts with at least some prima facie, if circumstantial, evidence that what the Soviet Union desired was, after all, the defense of Cuba. During the discussions of October 27, after the receipt of the second Soviet letter, Kennedy seemed quite convinced that "we're going to have to take our weapons out of Turkey" in order to get the Soviet missiles out of Cuba. Llewellyn Thompson (special adviser for Soviet affairs) disagreed, however, and the following exchange took place:

> THOMPSON: I don't agree, Mr. President, I think there's still a chance that we can get this line [the first Khrushchev offer] going.
>
> JFK: He'll back down?
>
> THOMPSON: Well, because he's already got this other proposal which he put forward. . . . The important thing for Khrushchev, it seems to me, is to be able to say "I saved Cuba, I stopped an invasion," and he can get *away* with this, if he wants to, and he's had a go at this Turkey thing, and that we'll discuss later. (October 27: 59, emphasis in the original)

A few minutes later Kennedy said, "I think it's a substantive question, because it really depends on whether we believe that we can get a deal on just the Cuban—or whether we have to agree to his position of tying [the Cuban to the Turkish missiles]. Tommy doesn't think we do. I think that having made it public how can he take these missiles out of Cuba. . . . if we just do nothing about Turkey." To which Thompson responded, "The position, even in the public statement, is that this is all started by our threat to Cuba. Now he's removed that threat" (October 27: 59–60). Stevenson had argued the day before that "what they [the Soviets] will want in return [for a halt to the missile base construction] is, I anticipate, a new guarantee of the territorial integrity of Cuba. They need that; it's what they said these weapons were for" (October 26, in May and Zelikow, 1997: 463). And as it turned out, of course, an explicit, public trade of the Jupiter missiles for the missiles in Cuba was not required because the Trollope ploy, returning the negotiations to the possibility of trading Soviet missiles for a U.S. pledge of nonaggression, worked. The resolution to the Cuban missile crisis thus provides significant evidence that Khrushchev might well have deployed the missiles to defend Cuba. Although no one pursued the suggestion, Thomas Schelling argued at Hawk's Cay that this might have been exactly what Khrushchev wanted:

> Take Khrushchev's profession of his desire to prevent the invasion of Cuba at face value, for a moment. If that is what he wanted to do, then he would have preferred that he secure Cuba against invasion without having his missiles there if he could. As things turned out, he emerged better off than when he went in. He got his assurances and he didn't even have to leave his nuclear missiles in. He also got his piece of cake, because the Turkish Jupiters were going to be coming out as well. (in Blight and Welch, 1990: 104)

Bundy also noted at Hawk's Cay the interesting point that "the missile crisis did not spread into any of the areas we expected it to. We had a respectable, but, as it turns out, wrong fear of a third Berlin crisis. It doesn't seem that the Soviets were thinking in terms of escalating the crisis to Berlin" (in Blight and Welch, 1990: 98–99). This additional negative evidence, even if again circumstantial, lends some plausibility to the Soviet defense-of-Cuba claim.

Although information about the resolution of the crisis was not, of course, available to the decision makers during the crisis, it has been available to subsequent analysts and propounders of the Cuban missile crisis myth. It is therefore astonishing that even scholarly analyses in the United States generally have not allowed for the defensive motivations claimed by Khrushchev and Castro. Though such information came too late to answer the questions about Khrushchev's and Soviet motives raised at the ExComm meetings, it could surely provide some answers, or alternative interpretations, for both analysts of and participants in the crisis after its resolution.

Silencing the Defensive Narrative

The ExComm discussion of Soviet motives and the neglect of the defense-of-Cuba argument both by U.S. decision makers and in the missile crisis myth raise a set of important questions. Why were Khrushchev's and Castro's claims that the missiles were installed to defend Cuba never accepted, or even seriously entertained, by U.S. decision makers as a plausible explanation of the Soviet missile deployment? Why, even in the face of a history of U.S. aggression and the existence of plans for renewed U.S. intervention, of which at least some U.S. decision makers in the ExComm were aware, was this suggestion rejected out of hand? Why, once the crisis was resolved through the expedient of a U.S. promise not to invade Cuba (and a private deal to remove obsolete U.S. missiles from Turkey), did it not seem reasonable to infer that Cuban defense had after all been at least one of Khrushchev's objectives in deploying the missiles? Why is the defense-of-Cuba argument absent from the orthodox U.S. representation of the missile crisis? Because one of the main reasons that the missiles in Cuba were understood to threaten the United States, and therefore to require removal, was their allegedly offensive character, it is possible that, had the Soviet deployment been interpreted as defensive, the U.S. national interest might not have been defined in terms of the missiles' removal. That is, with a different understanding of Soviet motives, the U.S. national interest might have been constructed differently and this (putatively) dangerous nuclear showdown avoided.

THE ROLE OF CUBA

Although in the United States these events are referred to as the *Cuban* missile crisis, Cuba, Castro, and the Cuban government are almost wholly absent as actors, as active players in this drama, both from the ExComm discussions and from the official myth.[33] Cuba is mentioned quite sparingly in the ExComm meetings. On October 16, Rusk did claim that the Soviets had "grossly misunderstood the importance of Cuba to this country," but he did not explain just what its importance was (October 16: 178). Later, President Kennedy expressed his concern that if the missiles were to remain in Cuba, "it makes [the Cubans] look like they're coequal with us." Douglas Dillon responded that it would look as though "we're scared of the Cubans" (October 16: 186). It would certainly not do to allow a state as small as Cuba to appear to frighten the United States. But in neither of these comments is Cuba being treated seriously as an agent whose actions are important for understanding or resolving the crisis. When Cuba did appear as an actor, it was sometimes in the guise of a Soviet client or puppet. Rusk was making such an assumption when he asserted on October 16 that the Soviet missile deployment "is no longer [Soviet] support for Cuba." Instead, "Cuba is being victimized here" and "the Soviets are preparing Cuba for destruction or betrayal." Castro must therefore "break clearly with the Soviet Union" (October 16: 172). When President Kennedy referred to "Soviet-Cuban aggression" (October 27: 40), he was also conflating Cuba with the Soviet Union and assuming that the real, the significant, agent was the Soviet Union.

Castro also makes only rare appearances in the ExComm discussions, generally in one of three contexts. First, brief mention is made of a possible negotiated settlement with Castro. On October 16, for example, Rusk suggested that "we are very much interested in the possibility of a direct message to Castro" because "if he knew that he were in deadly jeopardy" he might "elect to break with Moscow" (in May and Zelikow, 1997: 82). This line of argument quickly disappeared, although it was again briefly resurrected on October 26 (427, 440). Second, some concern was expressed over Castro's potential responses to U.S. military action against Cuba, including the possibility that he might order the retaking of Guantánamo (J. F. Kennedy, October 18, in May and Zelikow, 1997: 152–153). Finally, there are repeated references to the opportunity afforded by the missile crisis to take Castro out or bring Castro down (e.g., Thompson, October 18: 140; Alexis Johnson, October 18: 147, 163; Bundy and Taylor, October 18, 165, all in May and Zelikow, 1997).

In general, however, U.S. state officials did not treat Cuba or Castro as active or significant agents of world politics. Cuba does, of course, appear in these discussions, but with these few exceptions, it appears merely as a place, and a "little pipsqueak of a place" at that (Marine Corps Commandant David Shoup, October 19, in May and Zelikow, 1997: 181). Cuba is the place *in which* missiles are deployed and *from which* they must be removed. It is a place that requires continuous, even if increasingly dangerous, U.S. surveillance. It is a place that the United States, for its own national interest, must blockade, bomb, or invade. And it is a place in which, if the United States did choose to invade, it ran the risk of getting its "feet" stuck in "deep mud" (Taylor, October 16: 176).

The absence of Cuba and Castro as actors was not peculiar to the ExComm discussions; rather, they were missing from the actual conduct of the missile crisis, as well. As Castro has repeatedly stressed, the resolution to the crisis was arranged between the two superpowers alone. Castro and the Cuban government were excluded from the negotiations, a slight that left the Cubans "really very irritated"

(Castro, in Szulc, 1986: 586). Furthermore, whereas President Kennedy is typically (and problematically)[34] credited with having made a concerted effort to leave Khrushchev a face-saving way out of the crisis, and thus to avoid humiliating him, no such effort was made on behalf of the Cubans or of Castro. Instead of being treated as an active participant, Cuba was treated as "some type of game token" (Castro, 1992: 339).

Castro and Cuba have been omitted from the standard accounts of the Cuban missile crisis as well. As was mentioned in chapter 1, Cuba played no significant role in the conventional Cuban missile crisis narrative, and this neglect has persisted. In a recent text on U.S. defense policy, for example, the Cuban missile crisis is summarized as follows:

> In the summer of 1962, the Soviets attempted to install some 75 [sic] intermediate-range nuclear missiles *in Cuba.* In effect, this would have tripled their number of missile warheads targeted at the US in a very short period of time. In spite of US forward bases surrounding the USSR, the Kennedy administration refused to accept such an alteration in the balance of power in the Western Hemisphere. The confrontation escalated, and Khrushchev finally withdrew the missiles. US conventional options, notably the naval blockade, had contributed materially to resolving the issue without recourse to general war. (Sullivan, 1990: 175, emphasis added)

Cuba appears only once, as the place in which the Soviet missiles have been installed. The same is true of Bundy's summary of the crisis. Cuba is mentioned three times, always only as a physical space. He notes that "two American U-2 aircraft . . . took pictures *over Cuba,*" that "the Soviet Union was installing *in Cuba* nuclear missiles," and that offensive weapons were being delivered *to Cuba* (1988: 391, emphasis added). In Bundy's representation, again, the Cuban missile crisis quite clearly took place between two actors: the United States and the Soviet Union. Bundy could therefore unproblematically summarize the missile crisis in the following terms:

> There is some tendency for participants to tell war stories of these great events, but it remains a reasonable judgment that the conduct of *both sides* at the height of the crisis, and especially of the *two leaders,* was marked by prudence and skill. *Both governments* had made serious mistakes before the crisis broke *on them,* but in the days of imme-

diate alarm—thirteen for Kennedy and six for Khrushchev—*the two governments and their leaders* did well, and it is not easy even now to construct *for either side* a clearly better result than the one that was reached on October 28. (407, emphasis added)

Cuba might not have been involved at all. Castro also makes only rare appearances in Bundy's extensive discussion of the missile crisis. When he does, he is "a hostile pawn, to be captured, threatened, or spared as the central purpose [of the U.S. administration] might dictate" (398).[35] For Bundy, as for U.S. decision makers during the crisis, Castro was merely an unpleasant "third party" whose actions were those of a satellite or puppet and whose views thus did not merit serious attention (427).

Not only are Cuba and Castro absent as actors in the ExComm discussions and the missile crisis myth, but Cuba's views of those events have rarely received any attention.[36] In contemporary *New York Times* accounts of the Cuban missile crisis, for example, very little appears on the official Cuban view of these events. On October 28, 1962, the Week in Review was devoted to the missile crisis. Though it contained articles on reactions both to the Soviet missile deployment and to the U.S. response from Britain, France, Germany, Italy, Brazil, Chile, the United Arab Republic (U.A.R.), India, and Japan, it did not include a single article providing a Cuban interpretation or reaction. Cuban views were clearly considered irrelevant. Cuba was also almost invisible in Blight and Welch's *On the Brink* (1990) and in the two conferences associated with that book. The Hawk's Cay Conference involved only U.S. scholars and U.S. policy makers, and the Cambridge Conference, which provided some fascinating insights into the Soviet position, included three Soviet representatives. Although the subject matter of these conferences was the *Cuban* missile crisis, Cuba was not represented at either of them. Other standard treatments also fail to provide any Cuban account. Robert Divine's edited collection, *The Cuban Missile Crisis* (1971), is a case in point. The section of his book called "Initial Reactions to the Crisis" is devoted only to U.S. reactions. The section "The Problem of Soviet Motivation" includes a fleeting excerpt from a speech by Khrushchev, while the remainder is speculation by various Americans, including President Kennedy, on Soviet motives. Again, no Cuban view is included. Finally, in the last section, entitled "The Continuing Debate," the only Cuban view-point on the Cuban missile crisis is presented by "American-born Mario Lazo, who practiced law in Havana for many years under the Batista regime and then fled to the United States to escape a Castro firing squad." Lazo's contribution is an excerpt from the conclusion of his *Dagger in the Heart* (1968), which provides a "persuasive indictment of American policy in Cuba" by tracing "the shifting U.S. policy from the Spanish-American war through the advent of Castro" and blames "American liberals for the triumph of communism in Cuba" (Divine, 1971: 191).[37] Lazo's discussion of the Cuban missile crisis is consistent with this line of analysis and emphatically does not reflect Castro's view or that of the Cuban government at the time of the crisis; instead, it reproduces the orthodox U.S. cold war narrative of the Cuban problem. In short, the Cuban story, as well as Cuban interests and perceptions, have not warranted even a fraction of the attention lavished on the United States and even to some extent on the Soviet narratives.

Denying Cuban Sovereignty

The absence of Cuba from the ExComm discussions and from most standard U.S. accounts of the events of October 1962 implicitly denies Cuban sovereignty.[38] By constructing the confrontation as between the United States and the Soviet Union exclusively, both the ExComm discussions and the missile crisis myth effectively deny Cuba agency. They implicitly deny that Cuba was a sovereign state, at least at the time of the missile installation and the subsequent crisis. Cuba was instead represented as a state "under foreign domination" (Kennedy, 1962c: 10) that therefore was not in control of its own actions. As Adlai Stevenson argued in the United Nations, Castro had transformed Cuba into a "Communist satellite" and the "Castro regime" had submitted "to the will of an aggressive foreign power" (Stevenson, 1962a: 730). U.S. decision makers and other analysts of the Cuban missile crisis have implicitly assumed that the sovereignty of Cuba had been dissolved by its close relationship with the Soviet Union, that is, by its supposed status as a satellite state.

Conversely, U.S. decision makers themselves compromised Cuban sovereignty. On October 16, for example, Rusk argued that, in order to ensure its security and attain its national interest, the United States should first "announce that, uh, we are conducting a surveillance of Cuba, over Cuba, and we will enforce *our right* to do so" (October 16: 172, emphasis added). On October 27, after Major Anderson's U-2 was reportedly shot down by a SAM missile and low-flying U.S. reconnaissance aircraft were met with antiaircraft fire, Rusk reiterated this point, asserting that "we have to enforce *our right* to overfly and to have a look" (October 27: 86, emphasis added). Since it entailed a violation of Cuban airspace, this U.S. "right," of course, came at the expense of Cuban sovereignty. More important, the U.S. national interest constructed during the missile crisis—securing the removal of the missiles from Cuba—itself denied Cuban sovereignty. That U.S. policy contravened Cuban sovereignty was not then, and has since not typically been, of much concern. Instead, this important consequence of U.S. policy has been systematically ignored, downplayed, and even ridiculed. Castro's attempt toward the end of the crisis to reaffirm Cuban sovereignty by insisting that the United States meet certain conditions to ensure Cuba against invasion were described by Elie Abel as "an *interminable Castro harangue* directed against the Russians no less than the Americans" (1966: 210, emphasis added). Castro's claims were treated not as those of the representative of a sovereign state but as an annoying, even if insignificant, tirade. Moreover, Abel then described Castro's reaction to the U.S. failure to meet these conditions as "sulking" (211). Castro's anger was not the righteous indignation of outraged sovereignty but was instead a childish tantrum. In arrogating to themselves the right to determine which means were appropriate or inappropriate for Cuban self-defense, U.S. decision makers once again abrogated Cuban sovereignty for the sake of the U.S. national interest.

In the Cuban missile crisis, then, Cuba had no significant role to play. In fact, not only are Cuba and Castro conspicuous by their absence from the ExComm discussions and the tale of the Cuban missile crisis, but in two ways U.S. decision makers implicitly denied that Cuba was capable of playing any active, purposive role: By treating Cuba as an adjunct of the Soviet Union, authorship of and responsibility for any Cuban action could be transferred from Cuba to the Soviet Union. By insisting both on the right of the United States to maintain surveillance over Cuba and on its need to remove the missiles, Cuba's sovereignty was repudiated in practice by the United States.

An Alternative Understanding

The situation in October 1962 could, of course, have been understood differently. According to both the original Havana Charter of 1948 and the amended charter of 1967, "the principle of state sovereignty and its corollary of non-intervention" were important legal underpinnings for inter-American relations (Atkins, 1989: 215). In accordance with these principles, U.S. decision makers could have assumed that even though the deployment of Soviet missiles in Cuba was indeed threatening and even repugnant, Cuba nonetheless had the right, as a sovereign state, to arm itself as it saw fit. On this assumption, the issue of Cuban sovereignty would have played a more central role in the crisis, and the Soviet missile deployment might have been understood as a manifestation, however unpleasant, of Cuba's right to self-defense.

This alternative understanding was, of course, available to U.S. decision makers, as it has been to subsequent analysts. After all, it follows quite simply from Cuba's status as a member state of the United Nations. As Castro argued on October 28, 1962, "within the rules and laws governing relations between the peoples of the world and the principles governing the United Nations," Cubans were entitled to defend "our own security and sovereignty" ("Texts of U.N.-Cuban notes," 1962: 31). As these are principles to which the United States has formally declared its adherence, U.S. decision makers could have understood the Cuban missile crisis as a formal, legal issue of Cuban self-defense and sovereignty.

Moreover, this alternative understanding was available in both Cuban and Soviet statements, which continually stressed this aspect of the crisis. As Castro repeatedly argued, "as a sovereign country" Cuba "had the right to make use of the type of arms we considered gave us a guarantee" against U.S. aggression (in Szulc, 1986: 582). On this basis, Castro asserted on October 28, 1962, that Cuba "flatly rejects the violation of the sovereignty of our country involved in the naval blockade, an act of force and war committed by the United States against Cuba" ("Texts of U.N.-Cuban notes," 1962: 31). Cuban sovereignty and its legitimate right to defense were emphasized as well by Cuban President Osvaldo Dorticós. In his speech to the U.N. General Assembly, he responded to U.S. criticism of the Cuban military buildup by arguing that "Cuba has indeed armed itself; . . . it has the right to arm and to defend itself." He went on to explain that "we have armed ourselves because the people of Cuba have a legitimate right, sanctioned by history, to defend their sovereign decisions and to steer their country on the historic course which, in the exercise of their sovereignty, they have chosen." Furthermore, as a sovereign state, Cuba could do so without U.S. approval. Dorticós continued his argument, asserting that "we are in no way obligated to account to the United States Congress for what we are doing to defend our territorial integrity. We are arming ourselves as we think best for the defense of our nation . . . and, I repeat, we do not have to account for this to any Power or to any foreign congress" (1962: 373). The issue of Cuban sovereignty was also foregrounded in Soviet policy toward Cuba and in the Soviet story of the Caribbean crisis. In reference to the Bay of Pigs, for example, a Soviet government statement of April 19, 1961, had insisted that

> there can be no justification for this criminal invasion. The organizers of the aggression against Cuba are infringing the Cuban people's inalienable right to live free and independent; they are violating the elementary norms of international relations and the principles of the peaceful coexistence of states. . . . In an hour when the sovereignty and independence of Cuba—a sovereign state and a member of the U.N.—is being endangered, it is the duty of all member countries of the U.N. to give it all the necessary aid and support. ("U.S.S.R. government statement," 1961a: 3–4)

This particular understanding of the situation was systematically held up to U.S. decision makers by both Cuba and the Soviet Union. It was just as systematically ignored.

The absence of Cuba and Castro from the Cuban missile crisis is also called into question by the fact that Castro did play some role in these events. When asked by Sorensen at the Cambridge Conference "what outside influences were brought to bear on the Kremlin's decisionmaking during this period of time," Burlatsky responded, "The first influence was from Castro. We had to research his view and accept something of his advice." Sorensen seemed quite surprised: "But Castro always complained that no one listened to him," he responded.

MIKOYAN: That is not correct.

BURLATSKY: We did not *agree*—[Laughter]

MIKOYAN:	On some points we did not agree, on some we did.
BURLATSKY:	—But we had close contacts with Castro throughout.
MIKOYAN:	Without his approval, for example, we could not get those missiles physically out of Cuba.

. . . .

SHAKHNAZAROV:	. . . Castro thought that after the withdrawal there would be an invasion. He only agreed after he got assurances.
MIKOYAN:	And one condition was that one Soviet brigade would remain on the island as a guarantee.
GARTHOFF:	That was the brigade that caused all the embarrassment in the Carter Administration, which didn't realize it had been in Cuba all along. (in Blight and Welch, 1990: 266–267, emphasis and brackets in the original)

Though Sorensen may have been surprised that Castro or the Cuban government played any role at all, it seems quite obvious that the Soviets, at the very least, needed Cuban approval for the deployment of the missiles and, as Mikoyan points out, for their removal. A recognition of these factors might have made the role played by Cuba more prominent in U.S. accounts. It might therefore have raised questions about Cuban, rather than merely Soviet, motives and about Cuban rights to self-defense and sovereignty. But it did not. The first and second omissions—that is, the failure seriously to consider Soviet claims to be defending Cuba and the failure to treat Cuba as a serious actor—are thus interconnected. Recognizing Cuba as an actor and recognizing Cuban sovereignty might have entailed recognizing both past and contemporary U.S. policy toward Cuba as aggressive, which would, in turn, have helped to legitimize Soviet claims that it was acting in defense of Cuba.

That the blockade could have been interpreted as an act of aggression by the United States against a sovereign state was, of course, understood by the members of the ExComm. As Sorensen explains, the term "quarantine" was deliberately chosen to describe U.S. actions precisely in the attempt to circumvent this difficulty. "Without obtaining a two-thirds vote in the OAS," he said, a possibility "which appeared dubious at best—allies and neutrals as well as adversaries might well regard it as an illegal blockade, in violation of the U.N. Charter and international law. If so, they might feel free to defy it" (1965: 687). The term "quarantine" seemed a better option than "blockade" because it was "less belligerent and more applicable to an act of peaceful self-preservation" (694). (Rusk also apparently argued that the term "quarantine" was preferable because it elided any unpleasant comparisons between this U.S. action and the Soviet blockade of Berlin in 1948 [in May and Zelikow, 1997: 209].) Though this concern over the choice of terminology indicates some implicit recognition of Cuba's sovereignty, the recognition was never translated into a recognition of Cuba's right to defend itself, nor did it alter U.S. decision makers' determination to force the removal of the Soviet missiles.

Silencing Cuba

The absence of Cuba as an actor or as a sovereign state both from U.S. decision makers' deliberations and from the narrative of the Cuban missile crisis raises important issues concerning the construction of that crisis. Why was the confrontation viewed in the ExComm as a conflict that essentially involved only the United States and the Soviet Union? Why does the orthodox drama cast only the two superpowers in leading roles? Why has it been unproblematical to exclude Cuba from the *Cuban* missile crisis? In particular, given the declared commitment by the United States to the principle of national self-determination, why have Cuba, the issue of Cuban sovereignty, and the legitimacy of the Cuban right to self-defense been excluded from the U.S. understanding of these events? After all, Sorensen has claimed that in Latin America "nonintervention by the US was a religion" (Sorensen, 1965: 681). (I return briefly to this remarkable claim in chapter 4.) Whether or not the United States was willing to recognize the need for the Cuban state to defend itself against U.S. aggression, and despite U.S. anger at the Soviet missile deployment, U.S. decision makers and subsequent analysts could have recognized the legal right of the Castro government to arm in its own defense. Had they done so, Cuba would have appeared as a more autonomous actor in the Cuban missile crisis. Had Cuba, its sovereignty, or its right to self-defense been acknowledged, the U.S. national interest might have been constructed differently.

THE STRATEGIC BALANCE

As was discussed earlier, a central issue for U.S. decision makers was the change that the Soviet missile deployment would make either in the reality or in the appearance of the strategic balance. Two views on this issue emerged in the meetings on October 16. On the first view, the missiles substantially altered the strategic balance. Taylor argued, for example, that the missiles in Cuba would give the Soviets a "launching base" from which short-range missiles could be targeted at the United States (October 16: 176). This would give the Soviet Union a "pistol-pointed-at-the-head situation" in Cuba, just as the United States already had with respect to the Soviet Union (185). As also noted earlier, Garthoff believed that the missiles would constitute "a serious dilution of US strategic deterrent capability" (1962: 203). General Thomas Power, head of the Strategic Air Command during the missile crisis, also argued that the missiles in Cuba "could have hit us with virtually no warning." Because they could circumvent the U.S. early warning system, they were a significant threat "to the preservation of our deterrent." This was "the main reason why we had to get these missiles taken out" (in Bundy, 1988: 451–452). Similarly, for Rusk the missiles would "create a special threat for the United States" because they "increase the threat to a country [the United States] which is a principle nuclear support of 41 allies all over the world. . . . It seems to me that it ought to be pointed out that missiles of this magnitude are not something that we can brush aside, simply because the Soviets have some other missiles that can also reach the United States" (October 22, in May and Zelikow, 1997: 236).

The second view was that though the deployment did not substantially affect the military aspects of the strategic balance, it would nonetheless significantly affect the strategic relationship between the United States and the Soviet Union. At one point during the discussions of October 16, Bundy asked, "What is the strategic impact on the position of the United States of MRBMs in *Cuba*? How gravely does this change the strategic balance?" McNamara responded, "Mac, I asked the Chiefs that this afternoon, in effect. And they said substantially. My own personal view is, not at all" (October 16: 184, emphasis in the original). McNamara reiterated this view quite forcefully at the Hawk's Cay Conference. "As far as I am concerned," he said, it made *no* difference. Now, I don't recall that we had any hard evidence that there were Soviet warheads in Cuba, though I suppose that it is likely that they were there; but what difference would the extra forty have made to the overall balance? If my memory serves me correctly, we had some five thousand strategic nuclear warheads as against their three hundred. Can anyone seriously tell me that their having 340 would have made any difference? The military balance wasn't changed. I didn't believe it then, and I don't believe it now. (in Blight and Welch, 1990: 23, emphasis in the original)

According to Bundy, "most of us agreed with McNamara's summary judgment at the outset, that the Cuban missiles did not change the strategic balance—'not at all,' and I do not recall any serious discussion of the question in the ExCom" (1988: 452).[39] On this view, though the missiles were irrelevant to the strictly military aspects of the strategic balance, they still had to be removed. As argued earlier in this chapter, the basic reason was U.S. credibility. Allowing the missiles to remain in Cuba "would have politically changed the balance of power. It would have appeared to, and appearances contribute to reality" (Kennedy, 1962d: 898). As Schlesinger explained it three years later, if the Soviet missiles installed in Cuba had remained there, this would "still leave the United States with a 2 to 1 superiority in nuclear power targeted against the Soviet Union" (1965: 796). (According to McNamara, the ratio of strategic nuclear warheads was actually on the order of 17 to 1 in favor of the United States [in Allyn, Blight, and Welch, 1992: 23].) However, Schlesinger continued, "the shift in the military balance would be less crucial than that in the political balance. Every country in the world, watching so audacious an action ninety miles from the United States, would wonder whether it could ever thereafter trust Washington's resolution and protection" (1965: 796–797). Sorensen also argued that the president was "concerned less about the missiles' military implications than with their effect on the global political balance" (683). According to this argument, then, though the actual military balance had not been altered, the Soviet deployment challenged U.S. resolve and U.S. willingness to protect its allies; it threatened the United States with the appearance of a situation of appeasement in which, if a small step by the aggressor were permitted to pass without challenge, further aggression was sure to follow; and it undermined the credibility of the Kennedy administration by directly challenging explicit presidential promises not to tolerate such a deployment. I. F. Stone summarized these issues nicely when he stated that "the real stake was prestige" (1966: 12).[40]

Neglecting U.S. Superiority

Despite the importance of the strategic balance in these discussions, two crucial and interrelated issues were rarely addressed. First, it was only rarely mentioned that, even with the missiles in Cuba, the strategic balance overwhelmingly favored the United States. More important, conclusions that could have been drawn from the awareness of U.S. nuclear superiority and that might have affected the understanding of the U.S. national interest were never discussed. Second, it was rarely mentioned that there existed a severe imbalance in the extraterritorial basing capabilities of the United States and the U.S.S.R., and that this imbalance strongly favored the United States. Again, possible consequences of this imbalance for the U.S. national interest were systematically neglected.

On October 16, in speculating on Soviet motives, Rusk pointed out that Khrushchev may have been attempting to create a situation in which the United States had to live in fear of Soviet nuclear armaments just as the Soviets already lived in fear of U.S. nuclear weapons. After all, Rusk acknowledged, Khrushchev "knows that we have a substantial nuclear superiority" (October 16: 177). Similarly, at Hawk's Cay Garthoff pointed out that "the balance was changed greatly by the Cuban missiles, but the end result was still the same. The United States in either case had a considerable nuclear advantage" (in Blight and Welch, 1990: 32). U.S. nuclear superiority was not a secret known only to U.S. decision makers. The Soviets were painfully aware of it as well. Given Rusk's February 1961 announcement that there was not, and never had been, a missile gap—at least, not one that favored the Soviet Union—U.S. nuclear superiority was common knowledge. Nonetheless, important possible implications of the recognition of U.S. superiority were never pursued. In particular, the possibility was not considered that U.S. credibility, a central object of U.S. concern in the Cuban missile crisis, was not in fact at risk because its nuclear superiority remained intact.

Moreover, the imbalance between U.S. missile bases and submarine deployments surrounding the Soviet Union and the lack of corresponding Soviet capabilities was recognized at various points during the ExComm meetings. As noted earlier, Rusk recognized this imbalance when he acknowledged that "we don't really live under fear of [Khrushchev's] nuclear weapons to the extent that, uh, he has to live under fear of ours" (October 16: 177). A few moments later Bundy argued that though Soviet deployments clearly were not defensive in character, there were "many comparisons between Cuba and Italy, Turkey, and Japan. We have other evidence that Khrushchev is, honestly believes, or, at least affects to believe that we have nuclear weapons in, in Japan" (178). Despite the recognition that "there was indeed a compelling *superficial* symmetry" (Welch and Blight, 1987–88: 13, emphasis added) between the established extraterritorial nuclear deployments of the United States and the more recent Soviet deployment in Cuba, the superior strategic position that U.S. bases conferred on the United States was ignored. Furthermore, even a "superficial symmetry" between these resources was not regarded by U.S. decision makers as legitimate or acceptable. On October 16, in considering the possibility that Khrushchev was trying to force a favorable outcome in Berlin, the following fascinating exchange took place:

JFK:	Why does he put these [missiles] in there though? . . . What is the advantage of that? It's just as if we suddenly began to put a major number of MRBMs in Turkey. Now that'd be goddamn dangerous, I would think.
BUNDY?:[41]	Well, we *did,* Mr. President.
A. JOHNSON?:	We *did* it. We . . .
JFK:	Yeah, but that was five years ago.
A. JOHNSON?:	. . . did it in England; that's why we were short.
JFK:	What?
A. JOHNSON?:	We gave England two when we were short of ICBMs.
JFK:	Yeah, but that's, uh . . . that was during a different period then. (October 16: 190, emphasis in the original; brackets added)

When the United States deployed military forces, including nuclear weapons, outside of its own territory and on the borders of the Soviet Union, such actions were regarded as necessary, legitimate, and hence quite unproblematic. On the one occasion when the Soviet Union did the same, in contrast, it precipitated a political and military crisis of global proportions, despite the recognition that the installation of the missiles in Cuba produced a certain symmetry in the positions of the two countries. Moreover, the fact that the Soviet Union might legitimately want to rectify the strategic imbalance between the two states was never discussed. The Soviet deployment was instead defined as aggression.

Traditional scholarly analyses of the Cuban missile crisis have reinforced the neglect of these two strategic issues. As did the ExComm discussions, they tend to focus on the challenge posed to the strategic balance by the Soviet missiles and systematically ignore possible implications of the nuclear superiority enjoyed by the United States. For example, in their analysis of the missile crisis, Arnold Horelick and Myron Rush repeatedly mention U.S. "strategic superiority," to which, in conjunction with U.S. conventional superiority in the Caribbean area, they attribute U.S. success in the missile crisis:

> It is useless to debate whether conventional military superiority in the Caribbean area or over-all strategic superiority won the day for the United States. The United States possessed superiority in both types of military force and brought both to bear in the crisis; each reinforced the effectiveness of the other. The immediate military threat confronting the Soviet leaders, of course, was that posed locally to Soviet forces in Cuba and to the Castro regime. But this threat was amplified by American strategic superiority, which made credible the announced determination of the United States government to employ force locally if other measures, such as the quarantine, proved inadequate and to retaliate against the Soviet Union if Cuba-based weapons were launched against targets anywhere in the Western Hemisphere. (Horelick and Rush, 1966: 153)

However, despite their recognition of U.S. superiority as a major reason for the U.S. "victory," Horelick and Rush do not pursue the idea that this same U.S. superiority might bring into question the very understanding of the U.S. national interest that precipitated the crisis to begin with. Traditional analyses of the Cuban missile crisis also ignore the inequality in strategic capabilities revealed by comparing the far-flung basing system available to the United States with the limited Soviet extraterritorial resources.

Alternative Understandings

The failure to draw any conclusions for U.S. national interests in the missile crisis either from the overall nuclear superiority of the United States or from the imbalance between the extraterritorial military and nuclear resources of the United States and the Soviet Union again points to a set of possible alternative understandings of events in October 1962. The prevailing arguments about the U.S.-Soviet strategic balance in 1962 ignored both the strategic context within which the missile crisis took place and the right of the Soviet Union to defend itself. In so doing they ignore three critical issues: the possible irrelevance of the Soviet missiles to U.S. nuclear superiority, the possible irrelevance of nuclear superiority in an age of mutual nuclear competition, and the legal and moral right of the Soviet Union to self-defense. Had attention been directed at these issues, alternative understandings of the situation in October 1962 might have developed, leading perhaps to alternative understandings of U.S. national interests.

In one possible alternative interpretation, U.S. nuclear superiority rendered any reaction to the Soviet deployment unnecessary from the outset. As Horelick and Rush argued, "the immediate military threat confronting the Soviet leaders . . . was amplified by American strategic superiority." This enhanced the credibility of the U.S. threat to use its local conventional forces "if other measures, such as the quarantine, proved inadequate and to retaliate against the Soviet Union if Cuba-based weapons were launched at targets anywhere in the Western Hemisphere" (1966: 153). But with U.S. nuclear superiority, this ability would have persisted, even if the missiles had remained in Cuba. U.S.-theater nuclear superiority would still have been amplified by the overall U.S. strategic superiority. Any limited missile attack that the Soviet leadership might contemplate launching at the U.S. mainland from Cuba would run the risk of prompting a U.S. strategic response against the Soviet Union. This would, of course, have deterred the Soviets from launching any such attack just as effectively as it (allegedly) helped to resolve the missile crisis itself. Forcing the removal of the missiles from Cuba could thus have been understood to be completely unnecessary to U.S. security.

A second possible understanding was that the issue of nuclear superiority and inferiority was itself irrelevant in an era of mutual assured destruction. In an interview in 1987, Dean Rusk argued precisely this:

> There is that saving thought that when people look down the cannon's mouth of nuclear war, they cannot like what they see. We've now put behind us forty-one years since a nuclear weapon has been fired in anger, and those who really understand nuclear weapons understand that nuclear war is simply that war which must not be fought, because it not only eliminates all the answers, it eliminates all the questions. . . . And so the truth is that if these weapons begin to fly, that's the end. And that simple fact has prevented the firing of these weapons so far. (in Blight and Welch, 1990: 180–181)

Rusk's argument has become known as the "crystal ball effect." According to this argument, the utter destruction that the use of nuclear weapons might produce provides decision makers with what is in essence a crystal ball. They can see into the future to predict that a nuclear war would bring in its wake unacceptable devastation both to the aggressor and to the aggressed upon. The foresight provided by the crystal ball thus helps to prevent the outbreak of nuclear war by helping "to give the nuclear world at least some measure of stability" (Harvard Nuclear Study Group, in Blight, 1989: 3). As Bundy has since argued, even during the events of October 1962, "at the nuclear level it was not superiority but the fact of reciprocal mortal peril that was decisive. . . . At the nuclear level all that we needed was the strength to ensure that a nuclear war would never be attractive" to Khrushchev. Furthermore, he continued,

> what we knew about Soviet nuclear forces at the time was simply that they were large enough to make any nuclear exchange an obvious catastrophe for Americans too. Without counting the missiles in Cuba, the Soviets had a deployed strength of 50 on land (at the time we estimated 75) and 100 on submarines. They also had about 150 strategic bombers. We had to assume that in any nuclear exchange, no matter who started it, some of these missiles and bombers would get through with multimegaton bombs. Even one would be a disaster. We had no interest in any nuclear exchange other than to avoid it. The fact that our own strategic forces were very much larger gave us no comfort. (1988: 446–448)

The point, of course, is that the devastation that would follow upon the use of even a small number of nuclear weapons had prevented their use during the Cuban missile crisis and would continue to do so. Nuclear or strategic superiority was therefore simply irrelevant. Nuclear sufficiency, the ability to inflict unacceptable damage, was all that was needed. According to this view, the Soviet missile deployment in Cuba could have been dismissed as irrelevant to the global nuclear balance, which was a situation of mutual assured destruction whether or not the missiles remained in Cuba. Given the assumption that Khrushchev and the Soviet government were even minimally rational, so that they also wished to avoid a nuclear war, the Soviet missile deployment could have been understood to require no U.S. response at all.

A final alternative understanding parallels the focus on Cuban sovereignty. Given the status of the Soviet Union as a sovereign state, it had the right to deploy weapons to defend itself against the U.S. nuclear arsenal and the potential of nuclear war. As the United States had placed nuclear weapons on the territory of its allies, so the Soviet Union could deploy weapons on the territory of a state to which it was closely tied (e.g., Reston, 1960). As Shakhnazarov argued at the Cambridge Conference, the Soviet Union had the same right as the United States to defend itself. He argued that

> the deep cause [of the Caribbean crisis] was American policy toward the U.S.S.R., socialist Cuba, and other socialist countries. The United States did not want to recognize others' rights to equal security. It desired to keep its superiority. I have already asked Bundy and others why the U.S. thought it was okay to surround the U.S.S.R. with bases, and why the U.S.S.R. had no such right. I have no good answer, and according to international law, both sides have equal rights to make arrangements with third parties to protect their security. (in Blight and Welch, 1990: 257)

Terminological tricks about "offensive" and "defensive" weapons notwithstanding, the imbalance in the extraterritorial military resources of the United States and the U.S.S.R., and the persistent reliance by the United States on military and nuclear bases overseas, could have been recognized as a legitimate Soviet defensive concern. The Soviet missile deployment in Cuba could therefore have been interpreted as a regrettable but nonetheless legitimate attempt to respond in kind. Furthermore, it was not necessary to interpret the secrecy of the deployment as indicating aggressive intent. "You speak of deception, and so on," Mikoyan maintained. "But according to international law, we had *no reason* to inform you beforehand" (in Blight and Welch, 1990: 247, emphasis in the original). In short, an alternative understanding of these events that recognized the basic legal equality of states, and therefore the Soviet right to self-defense, might have generated an alternative understanding of U.S. interests. Even if the missile deployment had been deplored as threatening, deceptive, and as upsetting to the status quo, it might have been understood as a legitimate, if unnecessary, Soviet defensive move. In such a view, the U.S. national interest might have allowed a grudging toleration of the Soviet missile deployment.

Silencing Superiority, Symmetry, and Self-Defense

Concern in the Cuban missile crisis with the U.S.-Soviet strategic balance ignored U.S. nuclear superiority, it overlooked the irrelevance of nuclear superiority in an era of mutual assured destruction, and it denied to the Soviet Union a fundamental right that it granted to the United States: to use the territory of friendly states as a military and strategic asset. The absence of these issues from the ExComm discussions and the missile crisis myth raises a final set of questions about both the orthodox U.S. missile crisis narrative and the attendant U.S. national interest. Why were no consequences for the U.S. national interest drawn from the U.S. position of nuclear superiority? Why were no implications drawn for the U.S. national interest from the argument that nuclear superiority was irrelevant when states were faced with mutual assured destruction? Why was it illegitimate aggression for the Soviet Union to station nuclear forces overseas but legitimate defense for the United States to do so? Had any of these questions been addressed directly, possible alternative understandings of the situation in October 1962 might have taken root among U.S. decision makers, with correspondingly different definitions of the U.S. national interest.

THE SECOND PUZZLE

In the typical Cuban missile crisis narrative, the ExComm discussions and policy choices are depicted as a marvel of crisis management in which all options were discussed and in which a rational solution was masterfully crafted.[42] It has been described, for example, as "a feat whose technical elegance compelled the professionals' admiration" (Henry Pachter, in George, Hall, and Simons, 1971: 132). Similarly, according to Hans Morgenthau, Kennedy's decision in the missile crisis was "the distillation of a collective intellectual effort of a high order, the like of which must be rare in history" (1970: 158).[43] Irving Janis, who was quite critical of the "groupthink" dynamics that contributed to the Bay of Pigs disaster, has argued that Kennedy and the ExComm successfully avoided this problem during the Cuban missile crisis. "This policy making group," Janis has maintained, "met all the major criteria of sound decision making" (1972: 142). As the silences discussed above indicate, however, issues that could readily have been understood as of central significance to U.S. national interests and to U.S. policy simply did not appear in these deliberations. The most important absence, of course, was the failure to examine, or even to question, the supposedly obvious and overwhelming need for the United States to secure the removal of the missiles from Cuba. Despite the expressed fear by U.S. decision makers that a U.S. response to the deployment might provoke a significant U.S.-Soviet military engagement or even a nuclear war, the missiles had to go. Contrary to the image of "exceedingly vigorous and intensive debate" (Schlesinger, 1973: 173), the deliberations by U.S. decision makers did not consider crucial issues, including, most important, the U.S. national interest itself.[44] It just seemed obvious, and therefore required neither discussion nor justification. The clear alternative, tolerating the Soviet missile deployment, lay outside of the horizon of the taken-for-granted of the U.S. security imaginary.

To explain why ExComm members so quickly decided—or, more appropriately, simply assumed—that the Soviet missiles deployed in Cuba were a threat to U.S. national security and that U.S. national interests demanded their removal, it helps to ask a number of related questions. (These are basically the same issues that I raised in the first puzzle discussed, in chapter 1, after the comparison of the myth of the Cuban missile crisis with the stories of the Caribbean and October crises.) Why was (and is) Khrushchev's explanation of the deployment of missiles in Cuba as defensive dismissed as "laughable"? Why was (and is) the prior history of U.S. actions against Cuba ignored? Why was (and is) the Cuban role in, and understanding of, these events essentially irrelevant? Why did U.S. decision makers assume that the Soviet missiles were of strategic importance? Why did U.S. decision makers narrate the situation, and thus define U.S.

national interests, in such a way that, on their own estimation, led the world to the brink of nuclear war? Why, in short, was the Soviet missile deployment emplotted as a "clear and present danger" to U.S. national interests? (Kennedy, 1962c: 5).

In *Danger and Survival*, McGeorge Bundy asks the same question. "Just what was it," he asks, "that made it so clear to Kennedy and to Congress in September and October that they should take a firm and flat stand against Soviet nuclear weapons in Cuba?" Bundy's answer is quite interesting. It was, he argued,

> *a visceral feeling* that it was intolerable for the United States to accept on nearby land of the Western Hemisphere Soviet warheads that could wreak instant havoc on the American homeland. *In ways which Americans did not bother to explain to themselves,* the prospect of Soviet thermonuclear weapons on a next-door island was simply insupportable. . . . *it was not possible* in September 1962 to say that Soviet thermonuclear missiles in Cuba were acceptable. . . . When the matter became a public question at the end of the summer, the answer was self-evident and quickly given. (1988: 412–413, emphasis added)

According to Bundy then, the real reason that the United States unflaggingly pursued the removal of the missiles from Cuba was "the strong national conviction" (413) that such missiles could not be accepted; they were an "intolerable affront" to the United States (452). Just as the U.S. public thought such deployments were intolerable, Bundy reiterates that "all of us at the White House took it for granted . . . that Soviet nuclear weapons in Cuba were unacceptable" (413). But surely this begs the question. Why were they unacceptable? Why was it "not possible . . . to say that Soviet thermonuclear weapons in Cuba were acceptable"? What was the source of this "strong national conviction," this "visceral feeling," shared by the U.S. public and decision makers, that Soviet missiles in Cuba were not to be tolerated?

As I have argued here, the issues *not* discussed in the ExComm meetings and in most subsequent analyses of the missile crisis—those issues that, in Bundy's telling phrase, "Americans did not bother to explain to themselves"—can provide useful clues to the U.S. understanding of its national interest. These silences are important because they mark the horizon of the taken-for-granted for U.S. foreign policy. They thus provide insight into the security imaginary through which the Cuban missile crisis, and the U.S. national interest in that crisis, were produced. The most important puzzle raised by the ExComm transcripts is therefore not what the real relationship between hawks and doves was, who initially suggested the Trollope ploy, or whether the discussions on October 27 were or were not acrimonious.[45] Instead, the transcripts provide a starting point for examining the security imaginary out of which the Cuban missile crisis and the U.S. national interest were constructed.

3

Constructing National Interests

Social facts are not things. In truth, what is to be said is that social things are not "things"; they are social things and these particular things only inasmuch as they "incarnate" or, better, figure and presentify, social significations. Social things are what they are depending on the significations they figure.
— CORNELIUS CASTORIADIS,
THE IMAGINARY INSTITUTION OF SOCIETY

TOWARD A THEORY OF NATIONAL INTEREST CONSTRUCTION

To explain the historically contingent and culturally specific meaning of the national interest is to show how concrete elements of the security imaginary come together to produce representations of the state, the international system, the particular situation or threat faced by the state, and plausible courses of state action. In the case of the Cuban missile crisis, this means explaining how, that is, through what concrete processes or mechanisms, the missiles came to mean an intolerable threat to the United States such that there emerged an unquestioned national interest in their removal. It is through particular practices of representation, grounded in the security imaginary, that a set of threatening meanings came to be attached to the Soviet missiles in Cuba and the U.S. national interest in removing the missiles "came to be regarded as the only viable course of action" (Doty, 1996: 30). The myth of the Cuban missile crisis discussed in chapter 1 and the U.S. national interest discussed in chapter 2, then, are the ideological effects of the U.S. security imaginary. In this chapter, I discuss in more detail the mechanisms—the twin processes of articulation and inter-pellation—through which such meanings are produced.

Articulating National Interests

The term "articulation" refers to the process through which meaning is produced out of extant cultural raw materials or linguistic re-sources. Meaning is created and temporarily fixed by establishing chains of connotations among different linguistic elements (e.g., Laclau, 1979; Hall, 1985, 1986c, 1988). In this way, different terms and ideas come to connote or to "summon" one another (Hall, 1985: 104), to be welded into associative chains that make up an identifi-able, if not a logically consistent, whole. Most of these terms and ideas already make sense within a particular society. In the postwar United States, for example, these linguistic elements included nouns like "terrorist" and "puppets"; adjectives like "totalitarian," "expan-sionary," and "defensive"; metaphors like "the market" or "domi-nos"; and analogies such as those to "Munich" or "Pearl Harbor." In the process of articulation such extant linguistic resources are combined and recombined to produce contingent and contextually specific representations of the world. The security imaginary fur-nishes the rules according to which these articulations are forged. In the construction of the Cuban problem, for example, references to Castro and his revolutionary associates were persistently articulated to the adjective "bearded" (see chapter 5). This articulation estab-lished a particular set of meanings in U.S. representations of the Cuban problem: It connoted that these revolutionaries lacked re-sponsibility, were uncivilized, and constituted a threat to private property and thus ultimately to the American way of life. When Castro's beardedness was invoked, that is, it simultaneously carried with it (among other things) the connotation that Castro was irre-sponsible, uncivilized, and a danger to the United States. The articu-lation of these linguistic elements (i.e., "Castro," "revolutionaries," and "beards") came to constitute a partial representation of the Cuban problem as one in which uncivilized revolutionaries threat-ened the liberal American way of life. In the process of articulation, that is, particular phenomena are represented in very specific ways and given very particular meanings on which action is then based. With their successful repeated articulation, these linguistic elements come to seem as though they are inherently or necessarily connected, and the meanings they produce come to seem natural, come to seem an accurate description of reality.

Despite this apparent naturalness, however, the chains of association established between such linguistic elements are in fact conventional; that is, they are socially constructed and historically contingent rather than logically or structurally necessary. The contingent or nonnecessary character of such articulations is captured well in the term "articulation" itself. As Stuart Hall has argued,

> the term has a nice double meaning because "articulate" means to utter, to speak forth, to be articulate. It carries that sense of language-ing, of expressing, etc. But we also speak of an "articulated" lorry (truck): a lorry where the front (cab) and back (trailer) can, but need not necessarily, be connected to one another. The two parts are connected to each other, but through a specific linkage, that can be broken. (1986c: 53)

The nonnecessary character of any particular articulation means, of course, that these connections can be contested, with two important consequences. First, specific articulations are never simply produced once and for all. Instead, to prevent them from coming unglued, or from being forcibly pried apart, they must always be reproduced, and sometimes quite vigorously. Second, any articulation can be uncoupled, and the resulting component parts can be rearticulated in different, and perhaps novel, ways.

Put differently, alternative representations are always possible. An articulation, therefore, provides

> a connection or link which is not necessarily given in all cases, as a law or a fact of life, but which requires particular conditions of existence to appear at all, which has to be positively sustained by specific processes, which is not "eternal" but has constantly to be renewed, which can under some circumstances disappear or be overthrown, leading to the old linkages being dissolved and new connections— re-articulations—being forged. (Hall, 1985: 113, note 2)

It is not necessary, for instance, that "beardedness" be associated with the negative characteristics of irresponsibility, uncivilized behavior, and danger mentioned above. In Cuban revolutionary discourse (again, see chapter 5), beardedness was articulated differently: The "beard," in this context, was a positive symbol of the revolution. It connoted the hardships endured by the Cuban guerrillas during the revolution, and it conferred revolutionary status and legitimacy onto the *barbudos,* or "bearded ones." The manifest meanings of such notions, the actual articulations or chains of connotation that define them, are rooted in particular historical and social contexts and are therefore neither necessary nor inevitable. That articulations are contingent does not, however, mean that they are completely arbitrary. Instead, they are better conceptualized as conventional. As Raymond Williams has cogently argued,

> The notion [of arbitrariness] was introduced in opposition to the idea that the sign was an icon, and it is certainly true that there is in general no necessary relation of an abstract kind between word and thing in language. But to describe the sign as arbitrary or unmotivated prejudges the whole theoretical issue. I say it is not arbitrary but conventional, and that the convention is the result of a social process. If it has a history, then it is not arbitrary—it is the specific product of the people who have developed the language in question. (1979: 330; see also Eagleton, 1991: chapter 7)

All articulations are social constructions, then, but they are nonetheless precisely not arbitrary. Instead, they are the product of concrete social practices in concrete historical circumstances.

The nonnecessary and conventional character of such articulations can also be seen in the connection that was forged between the U.S. conception of its national uniqueness and greatness, on the one hand, and its global and expansionary vision of its national mission, on the other. As Michael Hunt has pointed out, there were other possible connotations of, or articulations that could have been formed to, U.S. national greatness. In particular, an alternative articulation could have been made to an introverted understanding of the U.S. mission, an understanding that focused on the development of democracy and liberty within the United States itself. Just such an introverted vision of national greatness has often been associated with Thomas Jefferson.[1] Hunt argues that

> the Jefferson who entered the Washington administration in 1790 carried with him a preoccupation with liberty that suffused his notion of a good society, of national mission, and of an appropriate foreign policy. . . . In foreign affairs a policy of aloofness was calculated to be the best way of preserving the liberties Americans had achieved and

of allowing them to develop still further as a free people. Geographic distance from a rapacious and turmoil-prone Europe already promised peace. That promise could be made secure if Americans could bring themselves "to abandon the ocean altogether . . . [and] to leave to others to bring in what we shall want, and to carry what we can spare." (1987: 22, emphasis added. The internal quotation is from Jefferson.)

Instead of an association between U.S. greatness and introversion, the articulation that was finally forged linked the vision of U.S. national greatness with an extroverted, missionary, and ultimately global U.S. foreign policy. This articulation has often been associated with Alexander Hamilton, who believed that "men are ambitious, vindictive, and rapacious" and that "conflict was the law of life" (in Hunt, 1987: 23). As Hunt says,

> These hard truths in turn dictated that Americans recognize the dominant role of power, self-interest, and passion in international affairs. The still-vulnerable country should move warily until it acquired the strength essential to assert its interests and influence. The first step [according to Hamilton] was the creation of "a vigorous national government" under the direction of an elite. . . . That step was to be followed at once by the construction of a strong navy to protect commerce from jealous European powers. Given time to develop and mature, Americans could become strong, stave off demands that they serve as "the instruments of European greatness," and eventually establish their own greatness. As a force in its own right, the United States would be "ascendent in the system of American affairs . . . and able to dictate the terms of the connection between the old and the new world!" (24. The internal quotations are from Hamilton.)

The articulation of U.S. national uniqueness to this particular extroverted understanding of the U.S. role in international affairs was produced through specific, historically contingent processes, not the least of which was the increasingly global expansion of U.S. capitalism (e.g., Williams, 1962). In particular, the connection was suggested, reiterated, and finally solidified during at least three major U.S. foreign policy debates: over the 1795 Jay Treaty initiating the U.S. alliance with Britain, over the proper role of the United States in the Mexican War of the 1840s, and over the peace terms of the Spanish-American War of the 1890s (see Hunt, 1987: chapter 2). In the end, a durable vision of a liberal and "dynamic republic" that would pursue "commercial prosperity, territorial expansion, and military security" had been constructed (38). In short, the world of international politics, the place of a particular state within it, and the consequent national interests attributed to that state are not objective facts to be discovered; instead, they are the products of contingent, historically forged articulations of linguistic and symbolic elements already present within the security imaginary of the state.

This discussion of articulation raises an important question often asked of constructivist analyses, namely, what degree of freedom exists in the forging of articulations, or, more concretely, what degree of freedom do state officials enjoy in constructing representations of international relations and thus in constructing the national interest? There is no simple or abstract answer to this question; rather, it is an empirical issue that requires a response grounded in extensive empirical analyses. Such analyses would demand an elaborate investigation of, among other things, the range of interpretive possibilities permitted by the security imaginary within a particular situation at a particular historical juncture and the constraints placed on possible articulations by extant power relations.[2] The larger question, however, concerns the "reality constraints" that face both state officials and analysts in the construction of their representations of international politics and so of the national interest. Recognizing the social construction of national interests does not deny that such constraints exist. Criticizing the orthodox U.S. construction of its national interest in the so-called Cuban missile crisis, for example, does not mean that one has to deny that the Soviets placed missiles in Cuba. Indeed, any interpretation of the missile crisis, to be plausible, must recognize and account for these missiles. In this sense, the existence of the missiles functions as a reality constraint on the construction of plausible narratives. The meanings articulated to those missiles, however, are contingent and contested. The reality constraint, then, is quite loose and allows a wide range of sometimes quite dramatically different representations, as the discussion in chapter 1 of the three different narratives of the events of October 1962 indicates. The meanings produced out of a state's security imaginary are therefore "not 'dictated' by real factors since it is instead this meaning that attributes to these real factors a particular importance and a particular place in the universe constituted by a given society" (Castoriadis, 1987: 128). What is at issue in the claim that national interests are socially constructed is *meaning* and its social effects, not physical existence. As Trevor Purvis and Alan Hunt have put it, "Of course earthquakes occur, and their occurrence is independent of consciousness; but it is their construction in discourse that determines whether they are 'movements of tectonic plates' or manifestations of 'the wrath of the gods'" (1993: 492).

Interpellating the Subjects of the National Interest

The articulation of linguistic elements of the security imaginary into connotative chains, into webs of association, is one part of the process of fixing meaning and so is one part of the process of constructing national interests. Another part of this constructive process involves the interpellation of subjects (e.g., Althusser, 1971; Hall, 1985; Laclau, 1979; Laclau and Mouffe, 1985). "Interpellation" refers to a dual process whereby subject positions or identities are created and concrete individuals are interpellated by, or "hailed" into (Althusser, 1971: 174), those subject positions.

Interpellation means, first, that specific subject positions are created when social relations are depicted. Different imaginaries and their representations of the world entail different identities. Hall described this process with respect to different representations of "the market":

> The same process—capitalist production and exchange—can be expressed within a different ideological framework, by the use of different "systems of representation." There is the discourse of "the market," the discourse of "production," the discourse of the "circuits": each produces a different definition of the system. Each also locates us differently—as worker, capitalist, wage worker, wage slave, producer, consumer, etc. Each thus *situates us* as social actors or as a member of a social group in a particular relation to the process and prescribes certain social identities for us. The ideological categories in use, in other words, *position us* in relation to the account of the process as depicted in the discourse. The worker who relates to his or her condition of existence in the capitalist process as "consumer"— who enters into the system, so to speak, through that gateway— participates in the process by way of a different practice from those who are inscribed in the system as "skilled laborer"—or not inscribed in it at all, as "housewife." All these inscriptions have effects which are real. They make a material difference, since how we act in certain situations depends on what our definitions of the situation are. (1986a: 39, emphasis in the original)

Specific subject positions are created when social phenomena are depicted; different descriptions entail different subject positions. Each subject position or identity carries with it particular ways of functioning in the world, is located within specific power relations, and is characterized by particular interests.

Within a state's security imaginary, a variety of subject positions are created, including those of various states—both "our state" and "their state," or "us" and "them" (in fact, typically a variety of "thems")—and other subjects. The central subject position created in any discussion of a state's national interest is, of course, that of the relevant state itself. Within the U.S. security imaginary, then, the central or nodal subject position is "the United States." Most fundamentally, the security imaginary establishes the existence of the United States *as* a subject. Out of an abstraction designating a territory, a population, and a set of governing principles and apparatuses is created an anthropomorphization, the fiction[3] of an apparently acting subject with motives and interests.[4] Moreover, it establishes that this fictional United States is a particular *kind* of subject, with a specific identity and the specific interests attendant upon that identity.[5] As a result of the interpellation of this subject position, "the United States" becomes the central object of discussions of U.S. foreign policy and national interests; it—rather than, say, individual American citizens—becomes the primary object of security that the security imaginary strives to protect. At the same time, "the United States" becomes the central subject of such discussions; it is not only the most important object to be protected, but it is also the subject charged with doing the protecting. "The United States," then, is the nodal position from which the imaginary is spoken, around which all other subject positions revolve, and into which individuals may (or may not) be interpellated. The interests articulated in this imaginary are the interests of the fictional subject "the United States" and the central warrants for action it generates justify and legitimize actions taken by that subject.[6]

In addition to highlighting the creation of subject positions, the notion of interpellation simultaneously points to the fact that concrete individuals recognize themselves in these representations of the world insofar as the subject positions or identities provided adequately account for their experiences. That is, these subject positions accord with individuals' self-understandings. Quite simply, people subscribe to, that is, are drawn into or successfully hailed by, specific representations because these make sense of at least part of their experience. Imaginaries and the representations they enable describe to individuals in a recognizable way the manner in which they live their lives; they construct and entail subject positions or identities from which both perceptions of the world and perceptions of the self make sense. As a result, the representations appear to be common sense, to reflect "the way the world really is."[7] As a result, individuals can speak from the identities—the subject positions—entailed in the imaginary. That is, subjects "recognize themselves in the discourse" and as a result they can "speak it spontaneously as its author" (Hall, 1985: 107). It comes naturally because it accords with their (already constructed) self-understandings.[8]

The U.S. security imaginary accomplished the task of interpellation, of generating recognition and identification, in part by representing "the United States" not only as *a* subject but as a subject that represents an "imagined" national "community" (Anderson, 1991). The subject position "the United States" constitutes a "representation . . . of belonging" (Tomlinson, 1991: 81) through which people are interpellated as members of this imagined U.S. community. The success and strength of the interpellations forged are highlighted, in the case of the United States, in the ubiquitous use of the term "we" by Americans in discussing U.S. foreign policy and state actions. Americans persistently and strikingly identify with the policies and actions, especially with the foreign polices and actions, of the U.S. state, asserting quite unself-consciously that "*we* had to show the Communists that they couldn't interfere in Vietnam," that "*we* should retaliate against the Japanese for their unfair trade practices," and that "*we* kicked Saddam's butt." Part of the strength, common-sense status, and legitimacy of orthodox postwar representations of U.S. national interests has resulted precisely from the often unproblematical identification of Americans with "we, the United States"— the imagined U.S. subject of the security imaginary.[9]

This "we" is of particular importance. The process of interpellation, at least in the United States, is facilitated by this "we," which functions as what Cathy Schwichtenberg has dubbed a "shifty shifter." A "shifter" is "a context-sensitive personal pronoun," such as "you" or "we." With such pronouns, "the 'person' designated by the message is always determined by the message itself." Shifters thus are named for their "referential ambiguity which can only be defined within, not only the context of the message itself, but the situation (the moment) in which the message is uttered" (1984: 305). The referential ambiguity of this "we" is central to its shiftiness and thus to its importance in the interpellation of subjects. When "we" are hailed into a statement about U.S. foreign policy and U.S. national interests—for example, when Kennedy argued during the Cuban missile crisis that "*we* have no desire to dominate or conquer any other nation or impose our system upon its people" (1962c: 5, emphasis added)—the referent of "we" is often deliberately ambiguous. It might, for example, refer to "we, the U.S. state," to "we, U.S. state officials," to "we, the American people," or to all of these at once. It might also, depending on the specific context, refer more broadly to "we, the Americans of the Western Hemisphere," to "we of the advanced West," or even to "we human beings." The shifty shifter's ambiguity serves a variety of functions simultaneously: It helps to define the subject position that the audience is asked to assume; it helps to weld potentially disparate members of its audience into a single, unified identity; as a result, it helps to create common sense by rendering the argument being offered intelligible to that audience; and, because it helps to create common sense, it also helps to legitimize that argument.

Not only does an imaginary entail subject positions from which to make sense of the world, but subject positions are also locations from which particular representations become sensible. For example, Stuart Hall has argued that Thatcherism "has been able to constitute new subject positions from which its [Thatcherism's] discourses about the world make sense" (1988: 49). It has done so in part by appropriating to itself "existing, already formed interpellations." The entire discourse of Thatcherism, Hall argued,

> combines ideological elements into a discursive chain in such a way that the logic or unity of the discourse depends on the subject addressed assuming a number of specific subject positions. The discourse can only be read or spoken unproblematically if it is enunciated from the imaginary position of knowledge of the self-reliant, self-interested, self-sufficient taxpayer—Possessive Individual Man (sic); or the "concerned patriot"; or the subject passionately attached to individual liberty and passionately opposed to the incursion of liberty that occurs through the state; or the respectable housewife; or the native Briton. . . . these imaginary positions . . . trigger off and con-

note one another in a chain of linked interpretations . . . as well as connecting one site of articulation with another: the liberty-loving citizen is *also* the worried parent, the respectable housewife, the careful manager of the household budget, the solid English citizen "proud to be British." (emphasis in the original)

Similarly, the postwar U.S. national interest constituted through the security imaginary made sense to many Americans to the extent that they were successfully hailed into an array of already familiar subject positions. As noted above, they were hailed, with the aid of the ubiquitous and shifty "we," into the position of "the United States," into the imagined community of Americanness. In addition, they were simultaneously hailed into other familiar subject positions of the security imaginary, including such comfortable identities as the "freedom-loving democrat" who abhors communism, the "concerned American patriot" who believes that "we" must protect Americans abroad, and the "civilized Westerner" appalled by the excesses of Middle Eastern terrorism. These identities help to make sense of the claims, the representations and quasi-causal arguments, articulated in the security imaginary. For example, since "we" Americans are freedom-loving democrats and civilized Westerners, it makes sense to claim that "our" U.S. actions abroad are designed to promote liberty and freedom, not self-interest or tyranny. Since "we" are concerned American patriots, the United States clearly has a right to do all that it deems necessary to protect the American free way of life. It is from these and other interconnected subject positions that the security imaginary could be read or spoken unproblematically; it is from these and associated identities that it made sense.

In summary, then, through processes of articulation and interpellation, a security imaginary enables the production of representations of the world. These representations, in turn, interpellate identities or subject positions that *already* entail particular interests. National interests are thus social constructions that *emerge* out of the representations enabled by and produced out of the security imaginary of the state. National interests, that is, are an ideological effect of the security imaginary and its representations.

Authoring the National Interest

As I argued in the introduction, the most important site for the construction of the national interest—for these processes of articulation and interpellation—is the institution, or bundle of practices, that we know as the state. The state plays a special role in constructing the meaning of national interests quite simply because identifying and securing the national interest is its business. Because the U.S. social imaginary has formally invested the state with the authority to conduct foreign relations, and thus with the concomitant responsibility for "discovering" the national interest, the central role of the state in the production of representations of international relations, and thus in the construction of the national interest, is generally treated as unproblematical.

In the postwar era, the concrete organizations of the U.S. state centrally involved in the construction of the U.S. national interest included, most prominently, those of the national security state (e.g., Koh, 1990; Yergin, 1990), such as the presidency, the National Security Council, the Joint Chiefs of Staff, the Department of Defense, the Department of State, and the Central Intelligence Agency. These various institutional sites, though of different relative importance at different times, were all involved in the construction of the national interest. In large measure the national interest was created in both the day-to-day and the extraordinary operations of these institutions. In formulating and implementing foreign policies, whether routinely or during crises, situations were defined, alternative situation descriptions were tested, and so on, and in these activities specific representations of the world, enabled by the security imaginary, were constructed.

In addition to the foreign policy or national security apparatuses of the state itself, a set of "ideological state apparatuses" (Althusser, 1971: 142–143, passim) are also involved in the (re)production of the security imaginary and thus in the construction of the national interest. These apparatuses include other institutions or bundles of practices, such as schools, religious institutions, the media, cultural institutions, and the family, that are less obviously or directly connected to the conduct and the justification of foreign policy. All of these institutions, however, contribute to the construction of the national interest. In the case of the United States, for example, the media has played a critical role in disseminating and reproducing, and only occasionally in contesting, the representations produced by state officials and so the commonsense understanding of the U.S. national interest. In a democratic society such as the United States, as many analysts have pointed out, "large numbers of journalists, consulting only their 'freedom' to publish and be damned, do tend to reproduce, quite spontaneously, without compulsion, again and again, accounts of the world constructed within fundamentally the same ideological categories" (Hall, 1985: 101; see also Herman and Chomsky, 1988; Hitchens, 1996). Schools also played an important role, socializing American children into U.S. nationalism, not the least through such rituals as the Pledge of Allegiance and the singing of the national anthem, but also through the dissemination of a particular interpretation of U.S. and world history.

The ideological state apparatuses include as well a subset that might be called the "intellectual apparatuses." These include think tanks like the quasi-governmental Rand Corporation and the American Heritage Foundation; private organizations designed both to study and to lobby for particular foreign policies, such as the Council on Foreign Relations, the Trilateral Commission, and the Committee on the Present Danger; private research centers like the Brookings and Hoover Institutions; and both public and private universities.[10] Such institutions house what Gramsci called the "traditional intellectuals" (1971b: 5–23, passim),[11] the official or unofficial ideologues of the dominant security imaginary. The traditional intellectuals are those academics and other writers, researchers, and scholars who provide the intellectual support and the rationale for the activities of the state. In the United States, academic institutions in particular have supported the broader institutional apparatus of the national security state by providing the trained personnel necessary to staff these institutions and by supplying both the information and the analytical and technical tools needed to formulate and implement its policies.[12] In the postwar era, analysis in all of these institutions proceeded primarily within the horizon of the taken-for-granted, functioning within the common sense of the U.S. security imaginary.

THE ROLE OF NONLINGUISTIC PRACTICES

Although the discussion thus far has directed attention to the linguistic aspect of national interest construction, it is, of course, by no means exclusively a linguistic process. Nonlinguistic practices are inextricably intertwined in the creation of the national interest as well. It does not follow from the constitutive nature of language and its role in producing national interests that national interests are *only* linguistic constructs. Instead, articulations, including the construction of the national interest, are always "materialized in concrete practices and rituals and operate through specific [state and other] apparatuses" (Hall, 1988: 46). They are produced and reproduced through nonlinguistic social practices as well as through linguistic practices. Though the security imaginary is extremely important in explaining social phenomena and "has its own specificity, its own kind of effects, its own mechanisms," it nonetheless does not "operate outside the play of other determinations; it has social, political, economic conditions of existence" (63; see also Castoriadis, 1987: 355–356).

Linguistic and nonlinguistic practices, in other words, are inextricably connected. In producing specific representations of the world, linguistic practices contribute to the production and reproduction of the nonlinguistic practices associated with and required by those representations. At the same time, the nonlinguistic practices are themselves part of the process of meaning construction. Michel Foucault's (1977) analysis of the development of criminality and the prison provides a clear example.[13] As he demonstrates, the categories "the criminal" and "the delinquent" were in part the product of a set of linguistic practices that established the categories' meaning by specifying the rules that determined which individuals were to be included and which were to be excluded. This linguistic process of definition was necessary to the creation of a disciplinary society. But it was not by itself sufficient to establish the meaning of these categories. Instead, their meaning was also, simultaneously, established through concrete material practices such as the organization of space in the prison and the processes of surveillance through which the lives of prison inmates were regulated. Both the linguistic delineation of the categories "the criminal" and "the delinquent" and the nonlinguistic, material practices of the prison were necessary to establish the discourse of criminality. The relationship between linguistic and nonlinguistic practices is thus reciprocal: They are mutually constitutive and jointly productive of the meanings of the social world.

The "we" of the imagined U.S. community, for instance, is the product of both linguistic and nonlinguistic practices. It is constructed not only out of words and ideas about the imagined U.S. community, about its uniqueness and its greatness, but also out of nonlinguistic practices such as the waving of U.S. flags at parades, the singing of the national anthem at sporting events, the establishment and patrolling of borders around the territory of the United States to distinguish it from other national territories, the establishment of bureaucratic procedures for granting or denying U.S. citizenship, the surveillance of other states from U-2 aircraft, and the global deployment of U.S. military forces. Nonlinguistic practices, including citizenship rites, border patrols, visa procedures, airborne surveillance, and the like, also contribute to the creation of the meaning of the U.S. community by placing boundaries on the meaning of "nation." As the examples of the Pledge of Allegiance and the singing of the national anthem make particularly clear, all practices are simultaneously both linguistic and nonlinguistic. Both of these activities include clearly linguistic components (in the form of the words spoken or sung) that contribute to the construction of U.S. identity and nonlinguistic components (the acts of standing and raising one's hand to one's heart) that are also part of what "being American" means. Similarly, the U.S. security imaginary offered a fundamentally racist vision of the United States, of the Third World, and of the relations between the two. This racist vision was constructed, in part, out of such linguistic elements as the terms "backward" and "advanced" (e.g., Doty, 1996). But U.S.–Third World relations were constructed not only in linguistic articulations of racism and ethnocentrism but also in routine, interventionary activities through which the United States could "set the limits of diversity" (Henry Kissinger, in Morris, 1977: 241). These practices include, for instance, the covert activities of the CIA, which in the case of Chile in the early 1970s were designed to bring down the Allende government. It was this complex of linguistic and nonlinguistic practices that helped to make sense of Kissinger's otherwise astounding claim, in discussing the democratic election of Salvador Allende in Chile, that "I don't see why we have to let a country go Marxist . . . just because its people are irresponsible" (240–241) and that allowed the United States to intervene in Chilean politics. As these few examples can only indicate, it is the complex of linguistic and nonlinguistic practices that both contributes to the construction of meaning and further reproduces the social relations entailed in particular representations. Nationalism just *is* (in part) the waving of U.S. flags and the securing of U.S. borders against undesirables; "backward" societies just *are* (in part) those subject to the interventionary practices of the "advanced" societies.

Despite the undeniable importance of nonlinguistic practices, the objective in this book is to demonstrate that linguistic practices *also* have real and independent effects. They are not reducible to non-linguistic practices, and they therefore deserve independent examination. These linguistic practices deserve attention not because they are the only relevant or important practices but because, despite their importance, they are typically given short shrift in explanations of U.S. foreign policy and of international politics more generally. It is thus my intention not to show that national interests are only linguistic products but, instead, to show that the policies and practices of states, including those of the United States, have linguistic conditions of existence as well.

ANALYZING NATIONAL INTERESTS

I have argued thus far that the national interest is socially constructed. It is enabled by the security imaginary and emerges out of representations that are themselves constructed, in part, through processes of articulation and interpellation. Through the articulation of meaning and the interpellation of subjects, a particular meaning of the national interest emerges and comes to be commonsensical and legitimate. The final, outstanding question to be addressed is this: How does one investigate the linguistic aspects of the construction of the national interest?

An obvious place to begin is with descriptions of the national interest. In the case of the United States, such descriptions appear in discussions, debates, and pronouncements about the U.S. national interest, U.S. national security, and U.S. foreign policy in general. Since the state is the central site at which the national interest is defined, the most important language is that of state officials. The primary locus of analysis is therefore statements in which foreign policy decision makers explain the goals of U.S. foreign policy, discuss the means deemed possible or necessary for accomplishing those goals, and offer arguments to explain and defend both the goals and the means. These statements about the national interest should be taken seriously in explaining U.S. foreign policy because they provide clues to the content of U.S. national interests, to the commonsense appeal of these national interests, and to the legitimacy that the national interest confers. Statements made by individuals who are members of the ideological state and intellectual apparatuses are important as well, since these individuals often take part in the reproduction of the security imaginary and thus in the construction of the national interest. Finally, popular statements about foreign policy that appear in the mass media cannot be neglected, since these generally reproduce, and only rarely contest, the orthodox meaning of the national interest, and in either case, they reveal the meaning attributed to the U.S. national interest and to U.S. foreign policy.

These different forms of communication take place both in public and in private. Public statements are those to which access is not restricted, such as statements made by U.S. state officials to, among others, the media, the public, other officials and representatives of the U.S. state, and sometimes foreign leaders. These statements include speeches and press conferences, open public hearings, government or semigovernment (for example, Rand Corporation) publications, and even leaks of information to the press. Private communications are those for which the audience is more restricted. These include closed congressional hearings; private discussions in the White House, such as the meetings of the ExComm during the Cuban missile crisis, in the National Security Council, or among the Joint Chiefs of Staff; classified documents such as NSC 68 (U.S. National Security Council, 1950); Policy Planning staff documents; war plans; and the like. All of these linguistic artifacts, whether public or private, reveal the process of national interest construction. By investigating statements about the U.S. national interest, one can identify the objects of security that the United States was determined to defend as well as the characteristic features assigned to those objects. One can identify the different subject positions entailed in the security imaginary and the characteristic features assigned to them as well. One can also identify the different quasi-causal arguments that both define the relations among the various subjects and objects and provide warrants for possible foreign policies and actions. In short, by revealing the way in which the world is understood, these linguistic artifacts can show how the national interest is constructed and what specific content or meaning is attributed to the national interest at a particular historical moment. Examining such linguistic artifacts for the Cuban missile crisis can help us to understand both how and what the Soviet missiles in Cuba were made to mean, such that the U.S. national interest required their removal.

AS REGARDS "MERE RHETORIC"

This explicit focus on the language used by decision makers and others in discussing the national interest is apt to provoke at least one indignant response: that such language does not represent real national interests but is instead merely rhetoric designed to persuade various audiences to support particular state policies and actions. Because such a criticism, if true, would vitiate the entire argument presented here, I want to respond to this charge before turning to a detailed account of the construction of U.S. national interests in the Cuban missile crisis.

The public rhetoric of national interests, it will surely be argued, is expressly intended to persuade and thus stands in an uneasy and indeed dubious relationship to the actual national interests pursued by state officials. In commenting on the Truman Doctrine speech (Truman, 1947), for instance, John Lewis Gaddis has argued that the "gaps between rhetoric and reality in U.S. foreign policy have often been large; indeed, such gaps might be said to constitute a defining characteristic of this country's diplomacy" (1974: 386). George Kennan also thought that the language of the Truman Doctrine misrepresented the true interests of the United States and that the same sort of misrepresentation plagued U.S. foreign policy throughout the cold war (1967: 321–322). According to political realists, there is a ubiquitous tendency for a gap to exist between rhetoric and reality. It is therefore considered to be "a characteristic aspect of all politics, domestic as well as international, that frequently its basic manifestations do not appear as what they actually are—manifestations of a struggle for power. . . . That is to say: the true nature of the policy is concealed by ideological justifications and rationalizations" (Morgenthau, 1978: 92). In response to the charge that the language of the national interest is merely rhetoric designed to justify policies made for reasons of state and that examining such language can tell us little or nothing about "real" national interests, I offer three counterarguments.

First, examining the language of the national interest, whether found in speeches, policy documents, memoirs, or other sources, helps to explain why claims about the national interest are believed. Even the most outrageously cynical statements are powerful because they make sense to at least some in their audiences. They accord with implicit understandings of the world, of the objects that populate that world, and of accepted forms of reasoning. Even exaggerated "rhetoric" thus provides a good indication of what makes sense in a particular political environment at a particular time. It provides us with insight into what Morgenthau called the "political and cultural context" (1978: 9) out of which the national interest is constructed. As Michael Hunt has argued,

> Public rhetoric is not merely a screen, tool, or ornament. It is also, perhaps even primarily, a form of communication, rich in symbols and mythology and closely constrained by certain rules. To be effective, public rhetoric must draw on values and concerns widely shared and easily understood by its audience. A rhetoric that ignores or eschews the language of common discourse on the central problems of the day closes itself off as a matter of course from any sizeable audience, limiting its own influence. If a rhetoric fails to reflect the speaker's genuine views on fundamental issues, it runs the risk over time of creating false public expectations and lays the basis for politically dangerous misunderstanding. If it indulges in blatant inconsistency, it eventually pays the price of diminished force and credibility. (1987: 15)

For all of these reasons, as Hunt continues, "Public rhetoric is tainted evidence for the historian seeking a widely shared ideology only when it violates these rules and falls unpersuasively on the ears of its ostensible audience." If we want to understand the structures of meaning on which concrete national interests depend, we can find ample evidence in the rhetoric that state officials and others employ to describe foreign policies and state actions.

Second, it is undeniably true that at least some statements about national interests are intended, perhaps even primarily, to persuade and to mobilize a particular audience or set of audiences. The Truman Doctrine speech provides an obvious example. It was explicitly intended to persuade a war-weary U.S. public and a skeptical, isolationist U.S. Congress of the need for the United States to take over Britain's role of supporting friendly governments in southern Europe, specifically in Greece and Turkey. In his memoirs, Dean Acheson described the prevailing attitude within the State Department toward the role of such speeches:

> In the State Department we used to discuss how much time the mythical "average American citizen" put in each day listening, reading, and arguing about the world outside his own country. Assuming a man or

woman with a fair education, a family, and a job in or out of the house, it seemed to us that ten minutes a day would be a high average. If this were anywhere near right, points to be understandable had to be clear. If we made our points clearer than truth, we did not differ from most other educators and could hardly do otherwise. (1969a: 375)

And such rhetoric is targeted not only at domestic constituencies. Kennedy's speech of October 22 during the Cuban missile crisis, for instance, was designed not only to influence the U.S. public and the U.S. Congress but also to persuade the Soviet leadership, and especially Khrushchev, of the folly of the Soviet deployment of nuclear missiles in Cuba and to rally OAS members in support of the U.S. quarantine. Statements such as the Truman Doctrine speech and Kennedy's missile crisis speech (1962c) are thus clearly rhetorical in the sense that they expressly aspire to entice their audiences, whether domestic or international, into one belief or another. However, the linguistic content of these avowedly rhetorical statements about the national interest is not unique to such public utterances. Precisely the same language and arguments—in short, the same rhetoric— appear in documents not intended for public consumption. The transcripts of the meetings of the ExComm during the Cuban missile crisis provide a case in point. Both Kennedy's public speech and these private discussions about the U.S. national interest in, and the suitable response to be made to, the Soviet missile deployment exhibit strikingly similar language and arguments. NSC 68 provides another telling example. As Gaddis has pointed out, "Portions of it sounded as though they had been intended for the floor of Congress, or some other conspicuous public platform. . . . This is not what one would expect in a top secret document destined not to be made public for a quarter of a century" (1982: 107). Finally, precisely the same language, the same arguments, and the same understandings of U.S. national interests are also reproduced in many ostensibly objective scholarly interpretations of the cold war and of U.S. foreign policy.[14] In all of these different venues—in public speeches, in private discussions among state officials and other decision makers, and in academic treatises—the same metaphorical and analogical, that is, explicitly rhetorical rather than merely literal, language is used to describe U.S. national interests. Central arguments about those interests have routinely been made on the basis both of metaphors, such as falling dominoes, spreading malignancies, and rotting apples, and of analogies, such as those to Munich, and the attendant dangers of appeasement, or to Pearl Harbor, with the attendant fear of a bolt from the blue. Thus, although certain statements, conventionally understood as rhetorical, may cynically be designed to manipulate particular listeners or readers, the same language is found in sources to which the cynical intent to manipulate is less easily attributed. Such rhetorical flourishes, in other words, are ubiquitous in the construction of the postwar U.S. vision of the world, of the place of the United States in that world, and thus of U.S. national interests.

Third and finally, the criticism that the language of national interests is "mere rhetoric" and so cannot help us to understand state action rests upon an unsustainable distinction between rhetoric, on the one hand, and truth or objectivity, on the other. Gaddis's surprise at the language deployed by the authors of NSC 68 is a function precisely of this common but ultimately untenable distinction. The term "rhetoric" is typically used to refer either to simple decoration (i.e., "mere rhetoric") or to "strategies and tactics" deployed "to assure persuasion of another in the pursuit of narrowly self-interested goals" (LaCapra, 1985: 36). That is, rhetoric is viewed, most commonly, either as ornamental or as intentionally and self-interestedly manipulative. But all language, whether it is intended to express the truth or to persuade and manipulate, is in fact rhetorical. As Dominick LaCapra has explained, "Rhetoric is a dimension of all language use rather than a separable set of uses or a realm of discourse" (17).[15] The reason is simple: All language use is in fact an attempt to persuade, that is, to provide "good reasons," "warrantable beliefs," and "plausible conclusions" (McCloskey, 1985: 29). The distinction between rhetoric and truth is thus essentially misconceived. Both the public and the private statements in which national interests are constructed are parts of a process of defining and constituting a world. They are part of a process of communication and persuasion in which state officials, in particular, define for their relevant publics, for other policy makers, and for themselves the nature of the world and the character of the objects in that world. And they are part of a process of providing good reasons, warrantable claims, and plausible conclusions about the national interests and state actions that are possible, or sometimes even necessary, within that world.

For all of these reasons, then, examining the languag e through which national interests are constructed is not the grave problem that might be expected. Instead, it is precisely the language of national interest that provides the specific, historically contingent content of those national interests that, according even to Morgenthau, determine state policy and action. The language of the national interest *is* the content and meaning of the national interest. It is in this language that objects, threats, and relations are understood and persuasively presented as real and that warrants for drawing political conclusions from that reality are provided. Maintaining a rigid distinction between rhetoric and reality, far from helping us to understand the content of the national interest and thus state action, actually precludes the systematic examination of the construction of national interests. National interests truly are saturated with rhetoric, but, as I have tried to argue here, there is nothing "mere" about their rhetorical character.

The next three chapters provide a detailed analysis of the construction of the U.S. national interest in the Cuban missile crisis. These chapters together demonstrate how representations of the Soviet missiles in Cuba, representations grounded in the postwar U.S. security imaginary, were constructed through the twin processes of articulation and interpellation in such a way that the missiles took on a particular set of meanings; as a result, a particular national interest in forcing the removal of those missiles emerged as both commonsensical and legitimate. In these chapters I examine the language, or "rhetoric," of U.S. national interests in order to determine how the situation faced by U.S. decision makers was defined, what elements of the postwar U.S. security imaginary were invoked and mobilized in the definition of the U.S. national interest, and why the policies adopted seemed reasonable and even necessary. Chapter 4 focuses on cold war U.S. representations both of the Soviet Union and the threats it posed to U.S. national interests and of Latin America as a central object of cold war U.S. national interests. Chapter 5 narrows the focus to the immediate context of the missile crisis, examining U.S. representation of the Cuban problem and of the Castro regime in particular. Chapter 6 then investigates in more detail the construction of "the United States," the central subject of the U.S. security imaginary and its attendant representations. Taken together, these chapters argue, on the one hand, that the myth of the Cuban missile crisis discussed in chapter 1 could have been constructed differently and that the obviously self-evident threat to the U.S. national interest discussed in chapter 2 could have been understood differently. They also attempt to show, on the other hand, how the dominant constructions were produced and why alternatives, which were theoretically or logically possible, were easily marginalized.

4

Constructing the Cuban Missile Crisis: Cold War Representations

Language precedes and exceeds material events, serving in turn as an interpretive framework for those events.
— VIRGINIA CARMICHAEL, FRAMING HISTORY

THE U.S. SECURITY IMAGINARY

Both the missile crisis myth and the description of the situation that emerged in the ExComm discussions issued from the postwar U.S. security imaginary. The orthodox story of the missile crisis became and has remained dominant because it represents events as occurring in a world of familiar objects and familiar threats, themselves forged out of conventional, already familiar articulations. Its commonsense character was and is secured by interpellating most Americans into familiar and acceptable subject positions. In the same way, the members of the ExComm represented the events of October 1962 so as to generate the "obvious" U.S. national interest in securing the removal of the missiles by drawing on linguistic resources—the same imaginary, made up of the same articulations and interpellations—that defined what they observed and what they deemed important.

In the production of the Cuban missile crisis, the U.S. security imaginary populated the international system with a set of objects and specified the quasi-causal relations that were purported to obtain among them. The resulting representation defined the cold war and U.S.-Soviet relations, the Western Hemisphere and U.S.–Latin

American relations, the problem of Cuba and U.S.-Cuban relations, and, most important, the identity of the United States itself. Taken together, as a vision of the world of international politics and the U.S. place in it, they defined the objects of U.S. security concerns (for example, Latin America and the Western Hemisphere), threats to U.S. national interests (such as Soviet aggressiveness and duplicity, international communism, and the Cuban revolution), and the specific relations among these objects and threats (including the dangers of appeasement, the creeping subversion instigated by international communism, and the validity of the Monroe Doctrine).[1] Tying these objects, threats, and quasi-causal arguments together and creating a coherent understanding of the U.S. national interest was the pivotal element of the security imaginary, the identity of the United States. The U.S. national interest during the Cuban missile crisis emerged from the articulation of these various components of the security imaginary into a more or less coherent representation of the situation faced by U.S. decision makers in October 1962. These objects, threats, and quasi-causal arguments, in conjunction with the identity of the United States, provided the warrants for the U.S. national interest in forcing the removal of the missiles and thus for the naval blockade of Cuba. In this chapter, I focus on the construction of the representations of the cold war context of the missile crisis and the way in which these events were situated in both the global U.S.-Soviet conflict and U.S. relations with the other American states.

THE COLD WAR AND THE SOVIET THREAT

For those former members of the ExComm who participated in the Hawks Cay Conference in 1987, questioning the intolerableness of Soviet missiles in Cuba was "an abstract, ahistorical, and naive exercise" that disregarded "the realities they faced in October 1962." Most prominent among these "realities" was "a bitter Cold War" (Blight and Welch, 1990: 121). As Robert McNamara later admitted, "the underlying cause of the crisis wasn't the deployment of missiles in Cuba but the basic tension—partly ideological—between the two blocs" (in Blight and Welch, 1990: 260). Not surprisingly, then, the cold war and U.S.-Soviet relations formed the primary context within which the Cuban missile crisis (both the policy problem and the subsequent myth) was situated.

As James Blight recalled in 1987, the cold war context of the crisis was explicitly stressed by U.S. decision makers: "I remember speaking to Mac Bundy about this, and the decision to define it as a U.S.-Soviet problem that happens to be occurring in Cuba was very significant to him, and also, he believes, the right decision to make. It was not a Cuban problem, it was a problem of U.S.-Soviet relations" (in Blight and Welch, 1990: 142). Moreover, the U.S. policy response to the Cuban missile crisis received a great deal of support around the world because of a "world-wide recognition that this was an East-West nuclear confrontation, not a U.S. quarrel with Cuba" (Sorensen, 1965: 706). By defining the crisis as a dangerous cold war confrontation between the superpowers, U.S. decision makers were attempting to generate widespread legitimacy for U.S. foreign policy. But the cold war setting of the missile crisis was not simply intentionally invoked by U.S. decision makers to legitimize the U.S. quarantine. That the cold war was the primary setting of U.S. foreign relations, and so of the events of October 1962, was already axiomatic within the U.S. security imaginary.

Totalitarian Aggressiveness

U.S. foreign policy was understood, within that imaginary, to be concerned primarily with "the Soviet threat" and with the containment of Soviet aggression and expansion.[2] During the ExComm discussions themselves, little was said explicitly about Soviet aggression, although President Kennedy did blame Khrushchev for the crisis when he asked, "He's initiated the danger, really, hasn't he? He's the one that's playing [his card, or God?], not us" (Kennedy, October 16: 184, brackets in the original transcription). Nonetheless, Soviet aggressiveness formed the taken-for-granted background to these discussions. Axiomatic within the postwar U.S. security imaginary was a representation of the Soviet Union as both "the inheritor of Russian imperialism" and a "world-wide revolutionary movement" (U.S. National Security Council, 1950: 395, passim). As a result, it was assumed within that security imaginary that "since 1918 the imperialistic and aggressive policies of Russian communism have resulted in the creation of a vast empire which poses a dire threat to the security of the United States and of all the free peoples of the world" (U.S. Congress, 1959: 206). The fundamental problem of the cold war was thus "Soviet expansion and empire" (Kirkpatrick, 1989–90: 14).

On the basis of this assumption, Soviet aggressiveness was easily invoked in describing the missile deployment in Cuba. For example, on October 22, Douglas Dillon had characterized the Soviet missile deployment as an "invasion of the hemisphere by a foreign power" (in Abel, 1966: 117). In his speech to the OAS, Dean Rusk called it "intervention" and then "aggressive intervention" into the Western Hemisphere (1962c: 721). Adlai Stevenson argued in the United Nations that "the issue of Cuba" was not one of revolution, socialism, or dictatorship. "The foremost objection of the states of the Americas to the Castro regime is . . . not even because Dr. Castro perverted a noble revolution in the interests of a squalid totalitarianism." Rather, he continued, Cuba was an "issue" because Castro "has aided and abetted an invasion of this hemisphere" (1962a: 730). In the ExComm meeting of October 27 Rusk also reiterated that "the Cuba thing is . . . an intrusion in the Western Hemisphere" (October 27: 38). This Soviet "invasion," "intervention," or "intrusion"— in short, this Soviet "aggression"—was problematic for two reasons. First, the so-called Western Hemisphere had traditionally been the preserve of the United States: Since the enunciation of the Monroe Doctrine in 1832, foreign powers had been warned to keep out. (I return to the issue of the Western Hemisphere and the Monroe Doctrine as social constructions later in this chapter). Second, this intrusion was thought to be but the first in a series of Soviet moves: Subsequent aggression would assuredly follow.

In the aftermath of the Cuban missile crisis, the quasi-causal argument justifying this assumption was embodied, among other places, in the metaphor of "salami slicing."[3] According to McGeorge Bundy, the Soviet Union had busily been implementing the "technique called salami slicing," first in Berlin and then in Cuba. That is, it had been pursuing a series of "little encroachments not easily resisted by democratic governments because each one in itself seems trivial" (1988: 364). In 1987 McNamara also argued that the Soviet missile deployment had taken a slice off the salami: "There was a slicing of the salami; slice by slice they were moving ahead, or trying to. That is why it was absolutely essential, Kennedy believed, and others believed, that we not convey to the Soviets the impression that we either were weak or would behave in a weak fashion. All these things added up to one unequivocal conclusion: We had to get the missiles out of Cuba" (in Blight and Welch, 1990: 191). McNamara's claim nicely illustrates the warrant for action entailed in the salami-slicing metaphor. The United States, faced with Soviet aggression, must respond firmly even if the immediate threat is small. This follows necessarily, since aggression will not be stopped if it receives only a weak response. As Sorensen argued in his discussion of the missile crisis, "Such a step [the installation of Soviet missiles in Cuba], if accepted, would be followed by more" (1965: 683). Because each small slice not vigorously opposed is necessarily followed by another, in the end, the whole salami will have been devoured.

Salami slicing is but one variant of the logic of appeasement embedded in the Munich analogy. The analogy to Munich and the attendant fear of appeasement provided a quasi-causal argument warranting immediate and decisive measures both to oppose aggression and to maintain U.S. credibility. The dangers of appeasement were a staple of the postwar U.S. security imaginary. In 1948, for example, William Bullitt, former U.S. ambassador to the Soviet Union, argued that the "high tide of appeasement" had already come with Roosevelt's concessions to Stalin at Yalta and was the fundamental reason that the United States had "won the war" but "lost the peace" (1948). Truman, in turn, invoked the Munich analogy in 1950 in response to "the forces of Communist imperialism" in Korea. We "will not engage in appeasement," he insisted. "The world learned from Munich that security cannot be bought by appeasement" (1950b: 16). That is why the "best time to meet the threat is in the beginning. It is easier to put out a fire in the beginning when it is small than after it has become a roaring blaze. . . . If [peace-loving nations] had followed the right policies in the 1930's—if the free countries had acted together to crush the aggression of the dictators, and if they had acted in the beginning when the aggression was small—there probably would have been no World War II" (1951: 223–224). In 1958, in defense of the deployment of U.S. troops to Lebanon, Eisenhower also drew on the logic of appeasement for support, claiming that "the action taken was essential to the welfare of the United States. . . . In the 1930's the members of the League of Nations became indifferent to direct and indirect aggression in Europe, Asia, and Africa. The result was to strengthen and stimulate aggressive forces that made World War II inevitable. The United States is determined that history shall not now be repeated" (1958: 556–557).

As was to be expected, the Munich analogy and the fearful

consequences of appeasement were repeatedly invoked during the missile crisis. Since Munich and appeasement had become "synonymous for failure to stand firm in the face of aggression" (May and Zelikow, 1997: 1), in his speech on October 22, for instance, Kennedy argued that the Soviet deployment "cannot be accepted by this country" because "the 1930s taught us a clear lesson: Aggressive conduct, if allowed to go unchecked and unchallenged, ultimately leads to war" (1962c: 6). In accordance with the axioms of the U.S. security imaginary, for Kennedy Soviet aggression could only be halted with firm resistance. Echoing Truman's bellicose claim that "unless Russia is faced with an iron fist and strong language another war is in the making. Only one language do they understand—'how many divisions have you?'" (1955: 552), Kennedy angrily asserted in 1961 that Khrushchev, "that son of a bitch, won't pay any attention to words. He has to see you move" (in Detzer, 1979: 33). The same quasi-causal argument for opposing Soviet aggression and maintaining U.S. credibility, this time with reference to the (alleged) Soviet and "communist" aggression against South Korea in 1950, played a prominent role in Stevenson's speech to the United Nations on October 23. He assured the U.N. delegates that the cold war

> isn't a private struggle; it is a world civil war. . . . Every nation that is now independent and wants to remain independent is involved, whether they know it or not. . . . We all recognized this in 1950, when the Communists decided to test how far they could go by direct military action and unleashed the invasion of South Korea. The response of the United Nations taught them that overt aggression would produce not appeasement but resistance. This remains the essential lesson. . . . We have . . . to make it absolutely clear that aggression will be met with resistance and force with force. (1962a: 729)

Stevenson hammered away at this critical point, insisting that, in the case of the Soviet missile deployment in Cuba,

> if the United States and the other nations of the Western Hemisphere should accept this basic disturbance of the world's structure of power, we would invite a new surge of Communist aggression at every point along the frontier which divides the Communist world from the democratic world. *If we do not stand firm here, our adversaries may think that we will stand firm nowhere—and we guarantee a heighten-*

ing of the world civil war to new levels of intensity and danger. (733 emphasis added)[4]

After the U.S. U-2 was shot down on October 27 and the members of the ExComm were debating the Turkish missile trade, Vice President Lyndon Johnson drew on the same logic of totalitarian unappeasability in sketching out the following cautionary scenario: "Look," Johnson warned his colleagues, "the whole thing is they [the Soviets] shot down one plane, and they [the Americans] gave up Turkey. Then they [the Soviets] shoot down another, and they [the Americans] give up Berlin. You know, like a mad dog—he tastes a little blood and he . . ." (October 27, in May and Zelikow, 1997: 592).

The metaphor of salami slicing and the analogy to Munich, both standard fare in the U.S. security imaginary, invoke the dangers of appeasement because they entail the argument that any aggressive step, however small, that is taken by a totalitarian state will, in the absence of resistance, be followed by further aggression. If this aggression is not stopped at once, the credibility of the United States and of the free or democratic world will be undermined. This, in turn, will lead to the inevitable escalation of aggressive actions by the adversary. The danger to the democracies will eventually become so great that they will be forced, for their own preservation, to respond. By then, however, the magnitude of the threat will have increased significantly, and the resulting war will be that much more ferocious. Better, therefore, to respond with force rather than weakness and sooner rather than later. According to this argument, then, it was not possible, in October 1962, for the United States to tolerate the Soviet missile deployment in Cuba. Such a policy would have been interpreted by the adversary as weakness, which would therefore have undermined U.S. credibility, which in turn would have prompted further Soviet or communist aggression. The United States was thus compelled to act promptly and forcefully, since one cannot successfully appease a totalitarian aggressor.

The quasi-causal argument provided by the Munich analogy and its variants, and the warrant for action they entailed, hinged on a prefabricated representation of the Soviet Union, drawn from the U.S. security imaginary, as a particular kind of object: a totalitarian state bent on ever-expanding aggression. Despite the importance of this assumption to the validity of the quasi-causal argument against appeasement, evidence that the Soviet Union actually planned further aggression was unnecessary. The characteristics of "Red Fascism" (Paterson, 1988: 5) or "Red totalitarianism" (Kennedy, 1946, in May and Zelikow, 1997: 7), an articulation that lumped the Soviet Union together with Nazi Germany as instances of "totalitarianism," were well known and widely accepted. Through the constructions "Red Fascism" and "totalitarianism," the Munich analogy and arguments against appeasement could readily be transferred from Hitler's Germany to the postwar Soviet Union. In addition, the prevailing understanding of the Soviet Union took for granted that its aggressiveness had been amply demonstrated by the lowering of the "iron curtain" (Churchill, 1946: 4) across what became "Eastern Europe." The resulting image of the Soviet Union as totalitarian, and hence as relentlessly aggressive, contributed to one particular understanding of the missile crisis. In this representation, Soviet missiles were necessarily offensive and the Soviet deployment of these offensive missiles was necessarily aggression. At the same time, this representation precluded an understanding either of the missiles themselves as defensive weapons or of the missile deployment as a defensive act.

These arguments simultaneously implied that the United States and the West in general did not share the aggressive features of "Red Fascism" or totalitarianism. Sorensen could therefore claim—even in the face of the long history of U.S. interventions in Latin America— that "the history of Soviet intentions toward smaller nations *was very different from our own*" (1965: 683, emphasis added). What the difference consists of is implicit in Kennedy's reference to Munich and the 1930s: Totalitarian states are aggressive and must be stopped by force; democratic states only apply force when compelled to respond to totalitarian aggression. The distinction between the two types of objects was explicit in Adlai Stevenson's speech to the United Nations. Stevenson drew on a series of oppositions that defined the basic character of these adversaries: The "pluralistic world" was contrasted to the "monolithic world," the "world of the U.N. Charter" to the "world of Communist conformity," and "moderation and peaceful competition" to "aggression" (1962a: 729). The characteristics of pluralism, moderation, and peaceful competition were firmly articulated to the democratic states, including, and indeed exemplified by, the United States, whereas the "world of Communism," exemplified by the Soviet Union, was defined as monolithic, as aggressive, and as both characterized by and in pursuit of further global conformity. These characteristic features, axiomatic within the U.S. security imaginary, represented the world in 1962 as one in which democratic diversity and toleration, embodied in the United States, was faced with a threat from totalitarian conformity, embodied in the Soviet Union. Furthermore, according to this view, the United States was committed to the defense of the so-called free way of life. As Kennedy said in 1961, "our nation is on the side of man's desire to be free, and the desire of nations to be independent" (1961e: 369). By assumption, then, in October 1962 the Soviet Union was acting aggressively, whereas the United States was merely acting to defend freedom and independence from totalitarian aggression. Since the Soviet Union was an aggressive totalitarian state and the United States was a state that defends freedom and independence, an understanding of the Soviet missile deployment as the defense of Cuba against U.S. aggression, such as that provided in the stories of the Caribbean and October crises, was unintelligible from within the U.S. security imaginary: It lay beyond the horizon of the taken-for-granted.

The Secrecy and Duplicity of Oriental Despotism

In the construction of the Cuban missile crisis and the U.S. national interest, aggressiveness was not the only important characteristic of the totalitarian Soviet state. Of equal significance was the "atmosphere of oriental secretiveness and conspiracy" (Kennan, 1946: 55) that marked this aggressive Soviet state. Not only was the Soviet Union acting aggressively by invading the Western Hemisphere with its missile bases, but it did so in a manner that betrayed the secretive and duplicitous nature of totalitarianism.

The secrecy surrounding the Soviet installation of the missiles in Cuba was, and continues to be, heavily emphasized. It was highlighted by the U.S. administration during the missile crisis and has also come to play a central role in the myth of that crisis. In fact, the secrecy of the weapons installation, rather than the existence of the missiles themselves, sometimes appears to have been the major cause for the crisis. In his speech on October 22, for example, Kennedy argued that "this *secret*, swift, and extraordinary buildup of Communist missiles . . . this sudden, *clandestine* decision to station strategic weapons for the first time outside of Soviet soil" was "a deliberately provocative and unjustified change in the status quo" (1962c: 5–6, emphasis added). The text of the OAS Resolution on the missile deployment, adopted on October 23, echoed Kennedy's speech. It charged that "the Government of Cuba" had "*secretly* endangered the peace of the Continent by permitting the Sino-Soviet powers to have intermediate and middle-range missiles on its territory capable of carrying nuclear warheads" (OAS, 1962: 723, emphasis added). Highlighting the "cloak of secrecy" (Rusk, 1962c: 720; Kennedy, 1962c: 5) under which the missiles were deployed was again an intentional strategy on the part of U.S. decision makers. As Sorensen has since explained, President Kennedy

> worried that the world would say, "What's the difference between Soviet missiles ninety miles away from Florida and American missiles right next door to the Soviet Union in Turkey?" It was precisely for that reason that there was so much emphasis on the *sudden* and *deceptive* deployment. Look at that speech [of October 22] very carefully; we relied very heavily on words such as those to make sure the world didn't focus on the question of symmetry. We felt that helped justify the American response. (in Blight and Welch, 1990: 246, emphasis in the original)

This emphasis on the secrecy surrounding the missile deployment helped to obscure the possible parallel between the missiles in Cuba and those that the United States had installed on the borders of Soviet territory and elsewhere. It was part of a conscious attempt to generate support for U.S. policy in the United States, among U.S. allies, and in world opinion in general while avoiding the thorny issue of the "superficial symmetry" (Welch and Blight, 1987–88: 13) between the Soviet missiles in Cuba and U.S. missile deployments abroad. After all, as Sorensen pointed out to the Soviet representatives at the Cambridge Conference, "all of our [U.S.] missiles in Europe were deployed openly" (in Blight and Welch, 1990: 240). As such, they were simply not to be compared to the secret Soviet deployment in Cuba.

During the missile crisis, the outrage produced by the secrecy with which the Soviet missiles had been deployed was rivaled only by the affront caused by Soviet duplicity.[5] In his October 22 speech, Kennedy explicitly stressed this Soviet duplicity, arguing that the Soviet deployment "contradicts the repeated assurances of Soviet spokesmen, both publicly and privately delivered, that the arms buildup in Cuba would retain its original defensive character and that the Soviet Union had no need or desire to station strategic missiles on the territory of any other nation." He then quoted a Soviet claim that its arms in Cuba were defensive and concluded: "That statement was false." He then quoted a similar assurance made privately by Foreign Minister Andrei Gromyko of the Soviet Union and again concluded that "that statement also was false" (1962c: 3–4). In his speech to the OAS, Rusk also emphasized Soviet deception, arguing that the Cubans and the Soviet Union were engaged in a "partnership in deceit." "The Communist regime in Cuba," he charged, "with the *complicity* of its Soviet mentors has *deceived* the hemisphere, under the *cloak of secrecy* and with loud protestations of arming for self-defense, in allowing an extracontinental power, bent on destruction of the national independence and democratic aspirations of all our peoples, to establish an offensive military foothold in the heart of the hemisphere" (1962c: 720, emphasis added). Like the focus on Soviet secrecy, this emphasis on Soviet duplicity or "treachery" (Stebbins, 1963: 100) was also used to legitimize the U.S. response. It again obscured the "superficial symmetry" of U.S. and Soviet extraterritorial missile deployments by directing attention to their (alleged) asymmetry.

Again, however, the construction of the Cuban missile crisis and, more specifically, the understanding of the threat as in part residing in the secrecy and duplicity of the missile deployment did not rest simply on intentional propaganda. The legitimation strategy pursued by U.S. decision makers was successful precisely because it drew on the already familiar representations provided in the U.S. security imaginary. In particular, it drew heavily on the already established reputation, or better, representation, of totalitarian regimes as secretive and duplicitous.

From the outset of the cold war, the Soviet Union had been represented, through the construction "Red Fascism," as embodying—and indeed exemplifying—both of these characteristics. That all totalitarian regimes, whether fascist or communist, share these features was considered to have been amply demonstrated by the Nazi-Soviet Nonaggression Pact of 1939. Throughout the postwar era, this contemptible agreement served as a constant reminder of totalitarian secrecy and treachery. It indicated that the Soviet leadership, like its

Nazi counterpart, would do anything to further its aggressive and expansionist aims, including entering into a treacherous treaty with its putative mortal enemy and secretly conspiring with that enemy to dismember a hapless victim. As Kennan explained in his memoirs, Stalin had concluded the Nonaggression Pact in order further to pursue the traditional Russian program of "territorial and political expansion" (Kennan, 1967: 519).[6] In 1961 Kennedy also emphasized the secrecy and duplicity with which despotic or totalitarian states pursue their aggressive goals. "Our adversaries," he asserted,

> use the *secrecy* of the totalitarian state and the discipline *to mask* the effective use of guerilla forces *secretly* undermining independent states, and *to hide* a wide international network of agents and activities which threaten the fabric of democratic government everywhere in the world. And their single-minded effort to destroy freedom is strengthened by the discipline, *the secrecy,* and the swiftness with which an efficient *despotism* can move. (1961e: 368)

The Soviet Union, in short, had already been constructed as a state that would use, and in fact relied extensively on, secrecy and duplicity in the pursuit of expansion. Paul Nitze summarized this understanding in a 1987 interview with Blight and Welch: "I was frankly annoyed at Gromyko having outrageously lied about this. It was a question of the character of the opposition, *so typical of the way in which the Soviets handle themselves*; I thought that to knuckle under to this kind of thing was unacceptable" (in Blight and Welch, 1990: 141, emphasis added).

The image of totalitarian treachery was further articulated to a racist vision of oriental despotism. This articulation welded together two representations that long predated the missile crisis: an image of the Russian national character as prone to despotic government and an image of despotism itself as oriental. At the time of the 1905 Revolution in Russia, for example, Theodore Roosevelt had expressed fears that the Russian movement toward "self-government and orderly liberty" would give way to "a despotism resting upon a corrupt and to a large extent incapable bureaucracy" (in Hunt, 1987: 112). Russians, it was presumed, suffered from a tendency toward despotic forms of government. During the Russian Revolution of 1917, the *Saturday Evening Post* characterized Bolshevism as "despotism by the dregs," and in 1919 the *New York Times* asked rhetorically, "Shall we wait for the Bolsheviks to conquer Europe and then carry their despotism elsewhere?" (in Hunt, 1987: 113, 115). It had, in short, long been established both that Russia was prone to despotism and that Bolshevism was a despotic form of government.

This image of Russian despotism was simultaneously articulated to a specifically racist image of the oriental. On this construction, the oriental is "a disturbing, even dangerous, bundle of contradictions—subhuman yet cunning, unfeeling yet boiling inwardly with rage, cowardly and decadent yet capable of great conquests" (Hunt, 1987: 69).[7] This vision of the oriental is part of the European cultural heritage of the United States. As Miquel Lopez de Legazpi, King Philip of Spain's representative in the Philippines in the later 1500s, wrote of the natives: "Face to face, they agree to anything—never saying 'no' to any proposal. The moment they turn their backs, however, they never keep a promise *nor have they any concept of honesty or sincerity*. Accordingly, it will be difficult to make durable arrangements with them on the basis of friendship, rather than through coercion and fear" (in Karnow, 1989: 45, emphasis added). The "unscrupulous oriental," a well-established type in U.S. racism, was articulated to the Russians because, as Hunt has argued, within the U.S. hierarchy of races, "the Slavs" are only "half European"; their other half is "Asiatic" (1987: 79). They thus display both a tendency toward despotic forms of government and the unscrupulousness of the oriental. In accordance with this image, military strategist Alfred Thayer Mahan, for example, argued in the late 1800s that Slavs were "cruel and barbarous" and that the Russians in particular combined "remorseless energy" with the "unscrupulous craft of the Asiatic" (80). Echoing this image, the *New York Times* characterized Bolshevism in 1917 as "our malignant and unscrupulous enemies" (in Hunt, 1987: 113). When these images were welded into a single representation, the Russians became a people prone both to despotic forms of government and to the unscrupulousness of the Asiatic.

After 1945, the idea of Russian oriental despotism was unhitched from "the Bolsheviks" (the revolutionary movement) and attached to "the Kremlin" (the governing regime). Indeed, the leadership of the Soviet Union was rarely referred to as "the Soviet government" or "the Soviet leadership," descriptions that might have lent the Soviet regime a modicum of respectability. Instead, it was typically dubbed "the Kremlin." This usage reinforced the image of an oriental and dangerous enemy, in part through the ubiquitous reproduction of photographic and other images of the exotic and alien onion domes of the Kremlin, which came for Americans to symbolize Moscow and, more specifically, the Soviet regime ensconced there. These exotic onion domes further reinforced the image of oriental despotism in which "opulence" was inextricably linked to "barbaric cruelty" (Kabbani, 1986: 75–77). It is the implicit appeal to this familiar conception of oriental despotism and its applicability to the Russians that allowed Kennan intelligibly to refer to "the atmosphere of oriental secretiveness and conspiracy" (1946: 55) within which Soviet policy was formed.[8]

Within the U.S. security imaginary, the image of the Asiatic unscrupulousness and duplicity of the Kremlin were reinforced as well by U.S. interpretations of Leninist doctrine. As Roy Rubottom, then assistant secretary for inter-American affairs, asserted in 1958, "Communist parties all over the world" follow Lenin in combining "the strictest loyalty to the ideas of communism with an ability to make all the necessary practical compromises." In the 1930s, for example, the "popular fronts" allowed Communists to hide behind "objectives or appeals which appear to coincide with the legitimate aspirations of a group" and so to turn those groups into "the innocent tools of the Communist conspiracy" (Rubottom, 1958: 2). In this view, Leninist doctrine or strategy was characterized by the "use of deception and violence" (Rusk, 1962a: 893). The secrecy and the duplicity of the oriental despot were, in the security imaginary, directly articulated to the operating principles of Marxist-Leninist politics. This interpretation of Leninist doctrine further strengthened the link forged between the Soviet Union and the secrecy and treachery of oriental despotism.

The articulation of an aggressive totalitarian Soviet state to the secrecy and duplicity of oriental despots helped to flesh out the nature of the situation faced by the United States during the Cuban missile crisis. That is, the secrecy and deception displayed by the Soviet missile deployment provided more detailed information about the nature of the danger that the missiles presented to the United States and to the Western Hemisphere. The focus on Soviet secrecy and treachery and implicitly on its oriental character illuminated the totalitarian and despotic character of the Soviet regime and by implication, the dangers posed by the encroachment of such an alien regime into Latin America. An alien, despotic regime threatened the very foundations of the Western free way of life characteristic of "the Americas." (I return to the "way of life" characteristic of "the Americas" later.) At the same time, this construction of the Soviet Union emphasized the vast difference between totalitarian states and democracies such as the United States. The not-so-subtle contrast constituted the United States, already defined as democratic in opposition to its totalitarian adversary, in more detail as a subject that was neither secretive nor treacherous and certainly not in the pursuit of aggressive, expansionary goals. Instead, it was implied, the United States is a subject that pursues "open covenants of peace, openly arrived at" (Wilson, 1918: 333). As Kennedy said in his October 22 speech, "Our own strategic missiles have never been transferred to any other nation under a cloak of secrecy and deception; and our history, unlike that of the Soviets since the end of World War II, demonstrates that we have no desire to dominate or conquer any other nation or impose our system upon its people" (1962c: 5). Stevenson reiterated this point on October 23, arguing that "the North Atlantic Treaty Organization, without concealment or deceit, as a consequence of agreements freely negotiated and publicly declared, placed intermediate-range ballistic missiles in the NATO area" in response to the threat posed to NATO by Soviet long-range missiles (1962a: 729). The State Department explained as well that "the distinction between Soviet missiles in Cuba and U.S. missiles in NATO countries" hinged on the fact that

> our missiles abroad were established under *open and announced agreements* with sovereign states. They serve to strengthen the independence of those countries. Soviet missiles were placed in Cuba *in secret, without any public statements and without an alliance.* Soviet bases in Cuba symbolize that country's subjection to alien control and domination; they were established without the knowledge of the Cuban people and were manned by Soviet personnel. (U.S. Department of State Bureau of Public Affairs, 1962: 7–8, emphasis added)[9]

Because the Soviet missiles in Cuba both belonged to and had been secretly and treacherously installed in despotic, totalitarian states, they were necessarily offensive. Furthermore, through such representations the Soviet missiles were rendered incommensurable with the U.S. missiles openly stationed on the territory of its NATO allies. The "symmetry" between U.S. and Soviet extraterritorial missile deployments was thus conclusively shown to be "superficial." Finally, the U.S. subject position entailed in these descriptions, analogies, and arguments confers on the United States an identity that uses force only defensively, that engages in open rather than secret diplomacy, and that is forthright and trustworthy rather than treacherous. These characterizations both of the Soviet Union and its missile deployment and of the United States entail a call to action: Because the United States is trustworthy, it must live up to its openly established commitments to protect its friends and allies, especially those of the Western Hemisphere, from totalitarian aggression and despotism.

Again, this construction of the cold war enemy and of the U.S.-Soviet relationship relegated a number of alternative understandings to the margins of possibility. In particular, it rendered it unthinkable that the Soviet Union, an aggressive, secretive, and duplicitous totalitarian state, could be acting to defend Cuba, a smaller, weaker, and more vulnerable state. Despots, after all, do not protect the weak; rather, they enslave and exploit them. That is why Soviet missile bases could be argued to "symbolize" Cuba's "subjection to alien control and domination" (U.S. Department of State Bureau of Public Affairs, 1962: 8). It also precluded an understanding of the crisis as the result of U.S. aggression against Cuba. "We" who are democratic and open, who "stand for freedom" and for "the independence and equality of all nations" (Kennedy, 1961f: 396, 397), do not engage in aggression against our smaller, weaker neighbors.

The Trojan Horse of International Communism

As the preceding discussion has already indicated, the cold war context of the missile crisis brought with it another familiar object: communism, or the international communist movement. In his speech to the United Nations on October 23, for example, Stevenson spoke not only of the Soviet threat but more broadly of "the Communist world," "Communist conformity," and "Communist aggression" (1962a: 733, 729, 733, respectively).[10] This "Communist world" sought to impose conformity on the pluralistic and democratic worlds at the expense of their free way of life. The same features out of which totalitarian and democratic states were constructed were used in this case to represent the contrasting worlds of communism generally (rather than of the Soviet Union specifically) and of freedom:

> Against the idea of diversity, communism asserts the idea of uniformity; against freedom, inevitability; against choice, compulsion; against democracy, dogma; against independence, ideology; against tolerance, conformity. Its faith is that the iron laws of history will require every nation to traverse the same predestined path to the same predestined conclusion. Given this faith in a monolithic world, the very existence of diversity is a threat to the Communist future. (726)

The threat from communism resided ultimately in its goal of world conquest. As had been affirmed in NSC 7, the "ultimate objective of Soviet-directed world communism is the domination of the world" (U.S. National Security Council, 1948: 165). Furthermore, its "insistence on extending its totalitarianism over the whole world" was "unappeasable" (Jessup, 1961: 38). This unappeasable threat extended quite explicitly to Latin America as well. A 1957 State Department pamphlet on the "communist penetration" of Guatemala, for example, reasserted that the "ultimate goal" of the Soviet Union "remains unchanged: a world molded in the image of the Soviet Communist state and under its domination" (U.S. Department of State, 1957: 1). This assumption, central to the U.S. security imaginary, was explicitly invoked by Stevenson during the Cuban missile crisis. Although he admitted that Khrushchev had modified some aspects of Stalin's rule, he nevertheless maintained that "there is one thing he has not altered, and that is the basic drive to abolish the world of the [U.N.] charter, to destroy the hope of a pluralistic world order. He has not altered the basic drive to fulfill the prophecies of Marx and Lenin and make all the world Communist" (1962a: 728).

The United States thus found itself engaged in a global battle with an international communist enemy pursuing world domination. This forced the United States to join "in a world-wide struggle in which we [the United States] bear a heavy burden to preserve and promote the ideals that we share with all mankind" (Kennedy, 1961f: 399). As Rusk argued in January 1962, the cold war in which the Cuban missile crisis would be set was not simply "a contest between the Soviet Union and the United States which the United States is pursuing for national ends." After all, "if every nation were genuinely independent, and left alone to work out its relations with its neighbors by common agreement, the tensions between Washington and Moscow would vanish overnight." Instead, "the cold war is simply the effort by communism to extend its power beyond the confines of the Communist bloc and the effort of free men to defend themselves against this systematic aggression." Indeed, it was "a struggle in the long story of freedom, between those who would destroy it and those who are determined to preserve it" (Rusk, 1962a: 894).

This standard element of the security imaginary—an international communist movement bent on world domination—was an important part of the conceptual apparatus with which U.S. decision makers and the U.S. public confronted the Soviet missile deployment. It was in the context of the global battle between international communism and freedom that the Cuban problem could explicitly be defined as the "Communist infiltration of Cuba" (Kennedy, 1960a: 20). Cuba was, quite simply, one site in the global battle not only with the Soviet Union but with communism in general. "The Castro regime," Rusk therefore argued in 1962, "has extended the global battle to Latin America" (1962a: 892). As a result, "the most urgent problem confronting the hemisphere" was "the efforts of the Sino-Soviet bloc to convert the island of Cuba into an armed base for Communist penetration of the Americas" (Rusk, 1962c: 720).

Claims of "Communist penetration" into Cuba made sense, even though it was the Soviet Union specifically that had deployed the missiles, because the object "Communism" or "international Communism" was understood to be a tool of the oriental despots residing in the Kremlin. As Kennan had explained in his famous "long telegram," the "inner central core" of all Communist Parties function together "as an underground operating directorate of world communism, a concealed Comintern tightly coordinated and directed by Moscow" (1946: 58). Eisenhower vividly described this phenomenon in 1959:

> There is loose in the world a fanatic conspiracy, international communism, whose leaders have in two score years seized control of all or parts of 17 countries, with nearly 1 billion people, over a third of the total population of the earth. The center of this conspiracy, Soviet Russia, has by the grimmest determination and harshest of means raised itself to be the second military and economic power in the world today. (1959a: 95)

In discussing communist "popular front" organizations in Latin America, Roy Rubottom presented a similar conspiratorial vision, arguing that "the Soviets now control 13 major international front organizations, each with dozens of subsidiary organizations all over the world. Each is a huge 'interlocking directorate' linking the Kremlin to a vast network of national organizations operated by local Communists or dupes" (Rubottom, 1958: 2). In other words, all Communists the world over, including those in Latin American and in Cuba, were linked to the Kremlin in a massive and monstrous conspiracy. Schlesinger could therefore argue that "it was idle to suppose that communism in Latin America was no more than the expression of an indigenous desire for social reform." After all, Latin Americans were "regularly summoned to training schools in Moscow or Prague," where they learned "everything from political doctrine to paramilitary warfare" and then "carried their lessons back to their homelands" (1965: 773–774). The same conspiratorial vision underlay the testimony of the Reverend Father Joseph F. Thorning to the Senate Judiciary Committee's Subcommittee on Internal Security in 1961. Thorning provided a vivid description of this conspiratorial communist threat to Latin America when he described the Latin American Conference for National Sovereignty, Economic Emancipation, and Peace, held in Mexico City in March 1961, as

> a propaganda show to promote political enslavement of all the American Republics under a Soviet regime, economic thralldom as a part of the Soviet economic juggernaut and internecine warfare throughout the Western Hemisphere, by means of Fidel Castro type revolutions against the lives, property, and democratic ideals of Western Hemisphere peoples, all this aided and abetted by active Soviet intervention. (U.S. Senate Committee on the Judiciary, 1961a: 3)[11]

Depicting communist movements as a Trojan horse captured the alleged conspiratorial nature of international communism and its links to the Kremlin. In a discussion of the "communist penetration" of Guatemala in the early 1950s, for example, a State Department pamphlet asserted that "the Communist Trojan horse strategy" was aimed at "penetrating and subverting independent Latin American countries" (U.S. Department of State, 1957: 6). In particular, the nationalist sentiments of Latin American peoples and the corresponding nationalist movements were portrayed as a favorite Soviet or communist Trojan horse. Rubottom could therefore argue that "the Communist use of nationalism" was a "Trojan horse of political penetration" and as such was "a most despicable betrayal of one of our most precious American heritages," the "love of one's country" (1958: 13). It therefore followed that "America's most important interests in the Caribbean are facing ultimate extinction at the hands of the international Communist conspiracy and its running mate, ignorant supernationalism" (Willauer, 1961: 882). After all, as John Foster Dulles argued in 1954, "If world communism captured any American state, however small, a new and perilous front is established which will increase the dangers of the entire free world and require even greater sacrifices from the American people" (591).

The Trojan horse metaphor implies, of course, that many, if not all, nationalist and reform movements are not, in fact, indigenous movements grounded in "love of one's country" or the pursuit of legitimate local aspirations. Nor are they spontaneous indigenous responses to structures of oppression. Through the Trojan horse metaphor they are instead represented as weapons wielded by an external, alien enemy secretively and deceitfully to infiltrate the Western Hemisphere. The notion of an international communist movement central to the postwar U.S. security imaginary, particularly a movement cast as a Trojan horse for alien infiltration into the Americas, undermined the legitimacy of what "Khrushchev somewhat hypocritically called 'wars of [national] liberation'" (Sorensen, 1965: 634). By depicting these movements as part of an international communist conspiracy, they were constructed as directed from and controlled by the Kremlin. In 1957, for example, the State Department asserted that

> in Latin America, as in other parts of the world, most national Communist parties *masquerade as* normal, patriotic political parties, *purporting* to reflect indigenous political impulses and to be led by indigenous elements. Communists in Latin America and elsewhere often *claim* to be interested in the problems of the common man, in his struggles for a better life against poverty and poor working conditions, in his hope for peace, and in his pride in national independence from foreign rule. *By appearing to support* the interests of the common man, Communists endeavor to direct his energies along lines which serve their basic purpose: to discredit the established society and ultimately *to seize power on behalf of the Kremlin*. (U.S. Department of State, 1957: 8–9, emphasis added)

And as General C. P. Cabell told the Subcommittee on Internal Security in 1961, "The so-called national liberation strategy seeks to offset Communist numerical and political weakness through international organizational support and clandestine techniques of infiltration and coordination." It does so by "surround[ing] its own Communist efforts by this aura of nationalism" (U.S. Senate Committee on the Judiciary, 1959: 142, 150). Such constructions, of course, undermine the legitimacy of these movements in the eyes of the "free world" by denying their claim to represent a "nation." It also denies that these movements might represent the wishes of the people and implies instead that their followers are duped or manipulated by the alien forces of a global conspiracy. When these movements are associated with "communist" aims such as radical economic reform, they become the design of the international communist movement and its masters in the Kremlin. It is in this context that the "lesson of Guatemala" can be said to have "exploded the myth of 'native' communism in Latin America. More than ever before it has now become apparent that what was mistakenly considered in some quarters as a 'local Guatemalan Communist orientation' was in truth a coldly calculated, armed conspiracy of international communism to extend the system of the Soviets to a small and strategically located country in the hemisphere" (U.S. Department of State, 1957: 70). In short, and as a result of this particular understanding of the workings of international communism, McNamara could argue early in 1962 that "what Chairman Khrushchev describes as wars of liberation and popular uprisings, I prefer to describe as subversion and covert aggression. We have learned to recognize the pattern of this attack. It feeds on conditions of poverty and unequal opportunity, and it distorts the legitimate aspirations of peoples just beginning to realize the reach of the human potential" (1962: 297).

It is in the context of the global battle between "the free world" and "the international communist conspiracy" that the Cuban problem (to be discussed more extensively in chapter 5) was defined explicitly as the "Communist infiltration" of Cuba (Stebbins, 1961: 292) or as "the establishment of a regime dominated by international Communism in the Western Hemisphere" (Eisenhower, 1960e: 568). The threat posed by the Cuban problem to the rest of the Western Hemisphere was embedded in this larger understanding of the U.S. goal of containing international communism. As Rusk had argued,

Castro's revolution was a problem because it was a piece of "the powerful offensive" consciously "launched by the Sino-Soviet Bloc . . . around the world to outflank the centers of power in the Free World" (in LaFeber, 1984: 150).

This context for the Cuban missile crisis was especially important because the Soviets had deployed the missiles in Cuba during a time when the United States faced "continuing crises"[12] in its attempt to contain this global "international communist" and "Sino-Soviet" offensive. It was a time when the Soviet Union, "eager to build a power base in the heart of Africa," was "rushing in to fill [the] gaping power vacuum" that had developed in the Congo after its independence from Belgium in 1960. The aim of U.S. policy in the Congo was therefore "the restoration of stability and order to a reunited, independent and viable Congo, free from Communist domination and free from both civil war and cold war conflicts" (Sorensen, 1965: 635–636). It was also a time when the United States was faced with a related series of communist threats in Asia, including a potential "Communist conquest" of Laos, a "Communist-sponsored guerilla war" in Vietnam, and "the larger menace of Communist China" (639, 649, 661). In each case, the "dilemma" facing the U.S. president was "how to disengage the Russians from the 'liberation' movement and prevent a Communist military conquest without precipitating a major Soviet-American military confrontation" (635). The global U.S. battle against aggression and subversion by an international communist conspiracy masterminded in the Kremlin thus formed an important part of the background for the understanding of the Cuban missile crisis. As Senator Kennedy had asked in 1960, in the fourth of his famous debates with Richard Nixon, "Which system, communism or freedom, will triumph in the next five or ten years? That's what should concern us. . . . I think the Communists have been moving with vigor—Laos, Africa, Cuba—all around the world they're on the move" (1960c: 8). As the defender of the free world, the United States was of course compelled to respond to these moves. As McNamara argued, these "wars of liberation . . . are often not wars at all." They are instead "conflicts" in which "the force of world communism operates in the twilight zone between political subversion and quasi-military action. Their military tactics are those of the sniper, the ambush, and the raid. Their political tactics are terror, extortion, and assassination." It therefore follows that "we [the

U.S.] must help the people of threatened nations to resist these tactics by appropriate means" (1962: 298). After all, as we have already seen, weakness in the face of totalitarian aggression or subversion was thought merely to invite further aggression, and the United States, which stood for "freedom" and "national independence," had an obligation to support and defend these values.

The United States and the Soviet Union

By defining the context of the events of October 1962 for U.S. decision makers, the U.S. security imaginary's representation of the cold war and of U.S.-Soviet relations contributed to the production of the crisis itself. The invocation of well-established objects such as an "aggressive totalitarian" state and a monolithic "international communist movement" directed from "the Kremlin" and of quasi-causal arguments, including the metaphor of salami slicing and the Munich analogy, provided a more detailed representation of the context in which the events of October 1962 took place. This representation conferred a specific and ominous meaning onto the bare fact of the Soviet missile deployment: The deployment constituted an aggressive intrusion by the international communist movement run from the Kremlin into the free world. This meaning, in turn, implied a particular U.S. national interest. Because the Soviet and communist threats, emanating ultimately from the Kremlin, would, in the absence of a forceful and active response, merely be the first in a series of similar encroachments, the United States was compelled, for its own future security and that of the democratic world, to respond vigorously to deny the Soviets a successful slice off the Latin American salami. It required that the United States, as the defender of freedom, democracy, diversity, and national independence, act firmly and without delay to prevent further communist expansion by securing the removal of the missiles. In short, out of the security imaginary was produced a representation of the situation facing the United States in October 1962 as a particular kind of cold war crisis, as a particular kind of Soviet threat. This representation, in turn, both entailed the U.S. national interest and legitimized U.S. actions.

At the same time, the Soviet claim to be defending Cuba, and specifically to be defending Cuba against further aggression by the United States, was rendered unintelligible. When faced with the orthodox U.S. representation, the Soviet claim simply did not make sense and could be dismissed as "laughable" (Ulam, 1971: 332). Having imagined the situation as one of totalitarian aggression, that is, it was no longer possible to argue sensibly that the Soviet missile deployment was a limited action, designed only to defend Cuba. Nor was it possible to hope that the Soviet missile deployment did not presage further Soviet aggression. Khrushchev's claims to be defending Cuba did not, and could not, make sense in a situation in which the United States, as a representative of democracy, diversity, openness, and trust, was confronted with an aggressive Kremlin action that signaled probable further incursions into the democratic world for the purpose of expanding the political and military domination of an alien and totalitarian communist conspiracy.

THE INTER-AMERICAN SYSTEM

The cold war and U.S.-Soviet relations were by no means the only elements of the U.S. security imaginary relevant for defining the Cuban missile crisis. Within the wider representation of the cold war and U.S.-Soviet relations, the Cuban missile crisis was also explicitly situated as a problem of the Western Hemisphere. As Rusk said on October 27, 1962, "The Cuban thing is a Western Hemisphere problem, an intrusion in the Western Hemisphere" (Rusk, October 27: 38). The prevailing representation of the Western Hemisphere, of Latin America, and of U.S. relations with the other American states provides more detailed pieces out of which the Cuban missile crisis and the U.S. national interest were constructed. With one exception, these representations were not directly addressed by U.S. decision makers during the missile crisis, nor have they been discussed in later representations of it. The meaning of the Western Hemisphere as the narrower context of the missile crisis must therefore be gleaned primarily from other sources.

The one exception concerns the strenuous efforts made by U.S. decision makers from the outset of the public phase of the crisis expressly to define it as a problem of the Western Hemisphere. The definition of the crisis as hemispheric in scope stood in contrast to two alternatives: that the conflict was a bilateral U.S.-Soviet confrontation or that it was a bilateral dispute between the United States and Cuba. Establishing the hemispheric boundaries of the crisis was crucial to U.S. decision makers because, in precluding these two alternatives, it helped to establish the legitimacy of the U.S. policy response.

Although, as just discussed, the crisis was understood as a cold war conflict between the United States and the U.S.S.R. (together with its international communist movement), the scope of this particular manifestation of cold war conflict was expressly limited to the Western Hemisphere. Had the conflict instead been delimited globally, certain unfortunate parallels might have arisen. In particular, setting the crisis in a global context might have highlighted the symmetry between the missiles installed by the United States on the territory of Turkey and the Soviet missiles in Cuba. Recognizing, or allowing others to infer, such symmetry might in turn have led to calls either for the removal of U.S. missiles from NATO territories or for the toleration of the Soviet missiles in Cuba. After all, the removal of U.S. missiles from Europe might have seemed a reasonable price to pay for defusing a potential nuclear war between the superpowers. As Kennedy had said at the ExComm meeting of October 27, "We're going to be in an unsupportable position on this matter if this [Turkish missile trade] becomes his proposal. . . . to any man at the United Nations or to any other rational man it will look like a very fair trade" (October 27: 36). Since such a course of action was anathema to U.S. decision makers and contradicted the "obvious" U.S. national interest in securing the removal of the Soviet missiles from Cuba, this definition of the crisis had to be avoided. The link between the Soviet missiles and U.S. missiles targeting the Soviet Union—the "superficial symmetry"—was severed by defining the missile crisis as a problem of the Western Hemisphere. This representation effectively limited the scope of the crisis and set the boundaries for what could appropriately be considered related issues. In this way, the Cuban missile crisis, though understood as an instantiation of Soviet and communist aggression within the broad confines of the cold war, could simultaneously be viewed as distinct from the European aspects of superpower and cold war rivalries. U.S. and NATO missile deployments were thus rendered irrelevant to the missile crisis.

Conversely, an understanding of the conflict as a dispute between the United States and Cuba was also precluded by defining it from the outset as hemispheric rather than bilateral in scope. In this case, U.S. decision makers strove to avoid potential condemnation in world opinion. In particular, they were concerned to avoid being left open to the charge of subjecting the world to a possible major war, or even a nuclear war, between the superpowers over a private U.S. dispute with Cuba. As Schlesinger later lamented, there had been an unfortunate "tendency" among the Latin American members of the OAS "to regard the Cuban matter as a private quarrel between Washington and Havana rather than as an inter-American responsibility" (1965: 780). In order to involve the states of the OAS in the U.S. attempt to secure the removal of the missiles, and thus to pre-empt possible hostile reactions to what might be interpreted as a unilateral and confrontational U.S. policy response, the Kennedy administration explicitly defined the crisis as hemispheric in scope.[13] Both during and after the missile crisis, U.S. decision makers took great pains to establish that the crisis, though limited to the Western Hemisphere, did indeed involve the entire Western Hemisphere and that the quarantine was a multilateral rather than a unilateral policy response.

In short, the precise construction of the setting of the missile crisis was of explicit political concern and was consciously manipulated by U.S. decision makers to legitimate U.S. policy decisions and actions. The U.S. administration was faced with the delicate task of defining the appropriate scope within which the crisis could most advantageously be set, and they managed this task quite successfully. In the construction of the crisis, U.S. decision makers thus consciously raised one particular interpretation of the situation to preeminence while marginalizing others. Again, however, this manipulation occurred using, and was made possible by, the discursive resources already well established within the U.S. security imaginary. The Western Hemisphere and Latin America had already been defined as specific kinds of objects, and particular relations were assumed to exist between and among its member states. The associations that the hemispheric definition of the crisis brought with it, while not explicitly addressed either by U.S. decision makers or in the subsequent myth of the missile crisis, are thus nonetheless significant in explaining the U.S. construction of the events of October 1962 and the attendant U.S. national interest.

The Western Hemisphere

Within the U.S. security imaginary, the "Western Hemisphere" exists as an unproblematic object. That is, the term is used as if it had a self-evident geographic referent. This impression is reinforced by the tendency to capitalize the terms "Western" and "Hemisphere," as I have done in this book, thus implying that it is the proper name of an objectively real entity. However, as Richard van Alstyne has pointed out, the idea of a "Western Hemisphere" could as easily be viewed as a fiction. After all,

> There are only two identifiable hemispheres on the globe, the northern and the southern, divided by the equator. The "western hemisphere" is an imaginary area, a figure of speech used, as Monroe used it, to identify the two American continents. But this is of course a geographical absurdity. . . . To be sure, any cartographer can depict any hemisphere and give it any label he wishes; but when we reflect that a scientifically drawn "western hemisphere" depends upon fictitious boundaries and that these boundaries can be changed at will, the concept opens itself to ridicule. (van Alstyne, 1978: 588)[14]

The "Western Hemisphere," invoked as though it had an unproblematic geographic referent, is a discursive construct. It is one way, but only one among others, in which the world could be carved up into identifiable regions. (It is interesting to note that there is no corresponding Eastern Hemisphere within the U.S. security imaginary.) The Western Hemisphere is the result of a politics of naming with significant political effects. The invocation of a Western Hemisphere helps to legitimize the need for, and the exclusive right of, the United States to intervene in this area by providing a referent for the Monroe Doctrine and its successors. (Perhaps, then, no corresponding Eastern Hemisphere appears in the U.S. security imaginary precisely because the existence of such an object might help to legitimate a corresponding "Monroe Doctrine" for some unsavory eastern "oriental despot.") As the following discussion indicates, the construct "the Western Hemisphere" predates the cold war. It is a sedimentation from an earlier period that has been absorbed into the postwar U.S. security imaginary. In this process of absorption, however, it was rearticulated in a way that gave it a specific meaning and thus specific implications for the construction of U.S. national interests in the missile crisis.

The Monroe Doctrine

The Western Hemisphere—encompassing all the "the Americas"—is the focus of the Monroe Doctrine. As explained by the *New York*

Times in mid-1960, the Monroe Doctrine, announced on December 2, 1823, declared "that there would be no colonization and no intervention by European states in the Americas." It was promulgated in response to two specific threats. The first emanated from "the Holy Alliance of Czarist Russia, Austria, and Prussia, an alliance that was supported by France. They sought to conquer and colonize Latin-American countries that had recently won their freedom from Spain and had been recognized by the United States as independent nations." The second threat came from Russia in particular, which had claimed "the northwest coast of North America" and had "issued an imperial order prohibiting non-Russians from navigating or fishing within 100 miles of that coast." In response, President Monroe had proclaimed that the United States would oppose both "the foreign seizure of territory" and foreign "political interference" in "the Western Hemisphere" ("Monroe Doctrine guards West," 1960: 3). In 1904, the Roosevelt Corollary extended the Monroe Doctrine. In this corollary, President Theodore Roosevelt announced that "continued misconduct or disturbance in a Latin American country might force the United States to intervene to prevent European intervention" (3).[15]

The notions of the Monroe Doctrine and of the Western Hemisphere were amended in the postwar era in at least two significant ways. First, the unilateral right of the United States to intervene in the hemisphere embodied in the Monroe Doctrine and the Roosevelt Corollary was replaced with the multilateralism of the Inter-American System. In the aftermath of World War II, the existence of an Inter-American System, the integrity of the Western Hemisphere, and the exclusion of extracontinental powers from that hemisphere were formalized in the Inter-American Treaty of Reciprocal Assistance of 1947 (the Rio Pact) and the Charter of Bogotá of 1948, which established the Organization of American States. As a result, the State Department explained in 1962, "The original purpose of the Monroe Doctrine, which was to prevent any extension to the Americas of a despotic political system contrary to the independent status of the countries of this hemisphere, has been adopted and supported by the Organization of American States as a multilateral safeguard for the American Republics" (U.S. Department of State Bureau of Public Affairs, 1962: 6). (It is in the context of these organizations and the declared policy of multilateralism that Sorensen could claim, quite remarkably in the face of the large number of U.S. interventions in and military occupations of various Latin American countries in the twentieth century, that Latin America was a region in which "nonintervention by the U.S. was a religion" [1965: 681].)

Second, these notions were rearticulated; that is, they were uncoupled from European, and specifically Russian, colonial threats and reattached to the Soviet and international communist threats. The Caracas Resolution of 1954, proposed by the United States in response to the supposed communist victimization of Guatemala, transformed the OAS into an explicitly anticommunist alliance. It specified that

> the domination or control of the political institution of any American state by the international communist movement extending to this hemisphere the political system of an extracontinental power would constitute a threat to the sovereignty and political independence of the American states, endangering the peace of America, and would call for a Meeting of Consultation to consider the adoption of appropriate action in accordance with existing treaties. (in Atkins, 1989: 223)

In the postwar era, then, Latin American states were to be protected not from European colonialism but from the menace of the Kremlin and its international communist movement. As the State Department explained, the principle embodied in the Monroe Doctrine "is just as valid in 1962 as it was in 1823, though the old imperialism of Western Europe has been replaced by the new and far more menacing political and ideological imperialism of international communism" (U.S. Department of State Bureau of Public Affairs, 1962: 6).[16] At the Tenth Inter-American Conference in Caracas in 1954, John Foster Dulles put it this way:

> Traditions of liberty have been established in this hemisphere under the leadership of many great patriots. They fought for individual human rights and dignity. They lighted the guiding beacons along freedom's road, which have burned brightly in the healthy air of patriotic fervor. These beacons must not be stifled by the poisonous air of despotism now being fanned toward our shores from Moscow. (quoted in U.S. Department of State, 1957: epigraph)

After all, the "intrusion of Soviet despotism" into Guatemala or any other country in the Western Hemisphere was nothing short of "a direct challenge to the Monroe Doctrine, the first and most fundamental of our [U.S.] foreign policies" (Dulles, 1954: 591).

In the late 1950s and early 1960s, U.S. relations with Latin America and, specifically, with Cuba were understood in this dual context of multilateralism and international communist aggression.[17] Focusing on the principle of multilateralism, Kennedy said during his 1960 presidential campaign, "I think that in the problem of Cuba we have to work with the other—the Organization of the American States, and I am most concerned, not only that we isolate Cuba, but that we attempt to isolate the Cuban revolution from the rest of South America. I think that is the big danger, that from Cuba as a base they will expand their power. I think we should use our influence to prevent it" (1960d: 81). Also in 1960, Senator Mike Mansfield argued that "if the need arises, we should seek common hemispheric action of whatever kind and degree may be necessary to prevent the establishment of military bases by nations not of this hemisphere in any American Republic" (1960: 95). In dealing with the security of the Western Hemisphere, U.S. unilateralism had apparently given way to a commitment to regional multilateralism. The U.S. desire for common, multilateral OAS action against Cuba was fulfilled in January 1962 at Punte del Este when the member states agreed to impose sanctions against Cuba. The meeting also produced a resolution entitled "Exclusion of the present government of Cuba from participation in the Inter-American system" in which it was declared that "as a consequence of repeated acts, the present government of Cuba has voluntarily placed itself outside the Inter-American system" (in Atkins, 1989: 223). It resolved, furthermore, that "adherence by any member of the Organization of American States to Marxism-Leninism is incompatible with the Inter-American System and the alignment of such a government with the communist bloc breaks the unity and solidarity of the hemisphere" (223–224). The existence of the Western Hemisphere—composed of multiple "American" states, characterized by "unity" and "solidarity," and requiring defense against the intrusion of "communism"—was thus explicitly ratified by the other American states. It was this declaratory commitment to a multilateral approach to the defense against communist penetration of the hemisphere that was invoked by the U.S. during the Cuban missile crisis both to create and to legitimize its hemispheric scope.

Nonetheless, while multilateralism was the ideal for inter-American relations, it was also clear that this ideal would be sacrificed by the United States to the yet higher good of preventing or fighting communist incursions. Mansfield therefore continued his argument to assert:

> I do not believe that the doctrine of non-intervention, as it now stands, is adequate to the present and future needs of the Americas. There are acts which can be committed by a government which grossly outrage the conscience of the Americas. There are policies which can be pursued by one nation in this hemisphere which gravely jeopardize the security of all the American nations. When these acts occur, when these policies are pursued, the doctrine of non-intervention in my opinion is not adequate to the need. (1960: 99)

Eisenhower made the same distinction, in fact reserving the right for the United States to intervene in Latin America unilaterally. When asked if the Monroe Doctrine had been supplanted by the principle of nonintervention embedded in the Rio Pact and other treaties, Eisenhower responded, "the Monroe Doctrine has by no means been supplanted. It has been merely extended. . . . Now, the OAS is an organization that, for a long, long time we have been supporting, just as strongly as we can. . . . But that does not, as I see it, inhibit any government, when it comes down to—when the chips are finally down, to looking after its own interests" (1960g: 651). In 1961, immediately after the Bay of Pigs, Kennedy also reasserted the U.S. right to intervene unilaterally in Latin America. Following his famous claim that, in the face of communist aggression or subversion, U.S. "restraint is not inexhaustible," Kennedy continued, "Should it ever appear that the inter-American doctrine of non-interference merely conceals or excuses a policy of nonaction—if the nations of this Hemisphere should fail to meet their commitments against outside Communist penetration—then I want it clearly understood that this Government will not hesitate in meeting its primary obligations which are to the security of our Nation! Should that time ever come," he insisted, "we do not intend to be lectured on 'intervention' by those whose character was stamped for all time on the bloody streets of Budapest!" (1961d: 304). "Communism," as Lincoln White, a State Department spokesman, succinctly put it, "is not negotiable in this hemisphere" (in "We must win the cold war," 1961: 64). During the missile crisis the United States acted consistently with its reserved right to intervene unilaterally in the hemisphere should its obligations require it: The United States sought multilateral OAS support for its quarantine of Cuba only after that policy had been decided upon and publicly announced and its implementation had begun.

While the members of the ExComm did not discuss the Monroe Doctrine and its successors during their meetings on October 16 and 27, that doctrine and the rearticulated postwar notion of hemispheric solidarity in the face of communist penetration are nonetheless salient to the construction of the Cuban missile crisis. The importance of these notions can be seen in the dispute that arose between the United States and the Soviet Union in 1960 (a dispute that continued through 1962) over the continued validity of the Monroe Doctrine, particularly with respect to Cuba. This dispute was first occasioned by Khrushchev's pledge to support the Cuban government, with arms if necessary. On July 9, 1960, Khrushchev explained that

> the United States is apparently contemplating perfidious and criminal steps against the Cuban people. President Eisenhower has stated that the United States will not purchase sugar and certain other goods from Cuba. This is a threat of economic pressure, an attempt to smother the economy of Cuba in order to impose on the Cuban people the will of the monopolists, so that they might lord it over other countries in Latin America, undermining their economy. . . . But the time of U.S. dictatorship has passed. The Soviet Union is raising its voice and extends the hand of assistance to the people of Cuba who are struggling for their independence. (1960a: 215–216)

To underscore Soviet support of Cuba, Khrushchev went on to point out that

> it must not be forgotten that now the United States is not at such an unattainable distance from the Soviet Union as in the past. Figuratively speaking, Soviet artillerists, in the event of necessity, can with their rocket firepower support the Cuban people if the aggressive forces in the Pentagon dare begin intervention against Cuba. And let it not be forgotten in the Pentagon that, as recent tests have shown, we have rockets capable of striking accurately in a set square at a distance of 30,000 kilometers. That is, if you like, a warning to those who would like to settle international issues by force and not by reason. (217)

In response to Khrushchev's "warning," Eisenhower avowed that

> the Inter-American system has declared itself, on more than one occasion, beginning with the Rio Treaty, as opposed to any such interference. We are committed to uphold those agreements. I affirm in the most emphatic terms that the United States will not be deterred from its responsibilities by the threats Mr. Khrushchev is making. Nor will the United States, in conformity with its treaty obligations, permit the establishment of a regime dominated by international Communism in the Western Hemisphere. (1960e: 568)

Khrushchev pursued the issue at a news conference held on July 12, at which he again challenged the validity of the Monroe Doctrine, this time quite explicitly. He announced to the world that "we [the Soviet Union] consider that the Monroe Doctrine has outlived its time, has outlived itself, has died, so to say, a natural death. Now the remains of this doctrine should best be buried as every dead body is so that it should not poison the air by its decay" (1960b: 6). Khrushchev's challenge was front-page news in the United States, eliciting vigorous defenses of the Monroe Doctrine and of the U.S. role in the Western Hemisphere. One reporter, for example, charged that Khrushchev's proclamation of the death of the Monroe Doctrine failed to take note of "the Rio Treaty of 1947, the Bogotá Charter of 1948, or the Caracas Resolution of 1954 in which American nations pledged that outside interference would not be tolerated in the affairs of nations of the Western Hemisphere" (Topping, 1960: 1). In response to Khrushchev's challenge, the *New York Times* also reported that

> State Department officials said today that Premier Khrushchev's report of the death of the Monroe Doctrine was premature. In fact, they said, the doctrine is very much alive and supported by similar recent commitments by all of the twenty republics of the American hemisphere. . . . As United States officials see it, the main idea of President Monroe's declaration was incorporated into the Rio Treaty, which said in Article 3 that the contracting parties agree "that an armed attack by any state against an American state shall be considered as an attack against all." ("Doctrine alive, U.S. says," 1960: 3)

In short, "it was for the United States rather than the Soviet Union to say whether the Monroe Doctrine barred the Western Hemisphere as a sphere of Soviet influence" ("White House upholds tenet," 1960:

3), and both the U.S. government and U.S. media maintained that it did.

The issue of the validity of the Monroe Doctrine arose again shortly before the Cuban missile crisis following reports of increased Soviet-Cuban cooperation. On September 4, 1962, the *New York Times* reported that "the increasingly close relationship between the Soviet Union and Premier Fidel Castro's regime in Cuba poses the most serious challenge to the [Monroe] doctrine since Emperor Napoleon III took advantage of the Civil War in the United States to set up a puppet monarchy in Mexico" (Olsen, 1962: 9). Adlai Stevenson also stressed the importance of the Monroe Doctrine to U.S.–Latin American relations during the missile crisis itself. In his October 23 speech to the United Nations he asserted,

> For 150 years the nations of the Americas have painfully labored to construct a hemisphere of independent and cooperating nations, free from foreign threats. An international system far older than this one [the United Nations]—the Inter-American system—has been erected on this principle. The principle of the territorial integrity of the Western Hemisphere has been woven into the history, the life, and the thought of all the people of the Americas. In striking at that principle the Soviet Union is striking at the strongest and most enduring strain in the policy of this hemisphere. (1962a: 731)

During the Cambridge Conference in 1987, the significance of the Monroe Doctrine to the Cuban missile crisis was reiterated. When Georgy Shakhnazarov asked, "Did anyone in the discussions with President Kennedy ever say that the Soviet Union had rights according to international law to deploy missiles in Cuba?" Bundy replied,

> Not very many people were saying that Khrushchev had the same right to deploy missiles in Cuba as we had in Turkey, though of course it is perfectly possible to make the international legal case. The basic problem for us was that we had repeatedly taken the public position that the presence of offensive missiles in Cuba was unacceptable. *Ever since the Monroe Doctrine,* the United States has perceived a special interest in excluding European military power from the Western Hemisphere. *This was a powerful fact of our political consciousness,* regardless of the international legal question. (in Blight and Welch, 1990: 244, emphasis added)

Shakhnazarov again raised the legal issue a few minutes later, saying, "You speak of deception, and so on. But according to international law, we had *no reason* to inform you before hand." In response, Bundy again invoked the Monroe Doctrine, saying, "Now, I realize that this is not terribly relevant to international law, but it was how we perceived our national interest—consistently with the Monroe Doctrine" (in Blight and Welch, 1990: 247, emphasis in the original).

The object "the Western Hemisphere" and the relations and responsibilities embodied in the Monroe Doctrine and its successors were central to the construction of the missile crisis and the attendant U.S. national interest. Within the broader context of the cold war, these elements of the U.S. security imaginary provide a more detailed representation of both the objects to be secured and the U.S. role in securing them. First, and most fundamentally, they together reproduced and reinforced the self-evident or commonsensical existence of a discrete entity called the "Western Hemisphere." Representations of this hemisphere endowed it with territorial integrity and well-guarded "traditions of liberty." It thus made sense, in the face of pervasive linguistic, ethnic, and religious diversity; significant political differences; and vast economic disparities, to talk about a unified Western Hemisphere characterized by common values and aspirations. After all, the "principle of the territorial integrity of the Western Hemisphere has been woven into the history, the life, and the thought of all the people of the Americas" (Stevenson, 1962a: 731). The Western Hemisphere, according to Kennedy, was "a hemisphere whose own revolution has given birth to the most powerful forces of the modern age—the search for the freedom and self-fulfillment of man" (1961h: 355).

Second, the construction of the Western Hemisphere and the relations entailed in the Monroe Doctrine prohibited extracontinental powers from entering into the affairs of that hemisphere. The Soviet missile deployment flagrantly disregarded the No Trespassing signs posted on the hemisphere since the Monroe Doctrine. It was not only true by definition that totalitarian states and international communism were inherently aggressive, but the location of the Soviet or communist intrusion rendered this aggression even less palatable. Since the Western Hemisphere shared in the American tradition of liberty and in its free way of life, successful Soviet and communist intervention into this hemisphere would strike a severe blow against global freedom.

Finally, the territorial integrity and the values of the Western

Hemisphere had long been considered a U.S. responsibility. This "cohesive" and "progressive" hemisphere, that is, had traditionally been, and still emphatically was, squarely in the U.S. sphere of influence. Communist aggression against any Latin American nation, including the Soviet missile deployment in Cuba, challenged traditional U.S. dominance of the region. As Hans Morgenthau argued in November 1962, "the transformation of Cuba into a Soviet military base" was "detrimental to the political position of the United States in the Western Hemisphere in that it challenges American influence in an area which has traditionally been regarded an American sphere of influence" (1962: 9). Similarly, Zbigniew Brzezinski lamented that "the presence of Communism in Cuba undermines the American claim that the Western Hemisphere is immune to Communist penetration and that the United States has the capability to exclude Communism from this hemisphere. It thus forces the United States to back down from a traditionally proclaimed position and imposes upon it a humiliation which is bound to have international implications" (1962: 7). The missile deployment thus threatened not only the values and institutions of the Western Hemisphere and the integrity of that hemisphere in the face of alien interference, but U.S. credibility would be undercut as well if the United States failed to respond to Soviet and communist aggression in its traditional sphere of influence. This, in turn, would have serious adverse consequences, not only in the context of the protective relationship that the United States enjoyed with the countries of the Western Hemisphere, but also in the broader context of the cold war and the global battle with international communism. The Soviet missile deployment therefore simply could not be tolerated because U.S. credibility was at stake.

The American Family

The representation of Latin America and the Caribbean as parts of a discernable and indeed self-evident Western Hemisphere that was a legitimate arena of U.S. concern was buttressed by a common metaphor that subsumed all states in that hemisphere into the "American family." The metaphor of the American family and its extensions, themselves pervasive elements of the U.S. security imaginary, provide additional insights into the construction of the Cuban missile crisis and the attendant U.S. national interest.

The American family metaphor appeared quite frequently in discussions of U.S. policy toward Latin America in the years just prior to the missile crisis. For instance, Senator Mansfield had declared in 1960 that "the Soviet Union shall not . . . meddle *in the family affairs* of the Americas" (1960: 93, emphasis added). Similarly, the State Department announced in 1961 that "in recent years *the American family of nations* has moved steadily toward the conclusion that the safety and welfare of all the American Republics will be best protected by the establishment and guarantee within each republic of what the OAS Charter calls 'the essential rights of man'" (1961b: 34, emphasis added). In his speech to the United Nations on October 23, 1962, Stevenson insisted that "the crucial fact" to be faced in the Cuban missile crisis was that "Cuba has given the Soviet Union a bridgehead and staging area in this hemisphere, that it has invited an extra-continental, anti-democratic and expansionist power *into the bosom of the American family,* that it has made itself an accomplice in the Communist enterprise of world dominion" (1962a: 731, emphasis added).

Not surprisingly, this American family was assumed to share a common set of American values, a set of "ideals" that "we [Americans] share with all mankind" (Kennedy, 1961f: 399). On this assumption, despite the cultural, linguistic, ethnic, religious, political, and economic diversity among the peoples of the Americas, Kennedy could argue quite sensibly that the American republics shared the "determination to advance the values of *American civilization.* For this world of ours is not merely an accident of geography. Our continents are bound together by *a common history*—the endless exploration of new frontiers. Our nations are the product of *a common struggle*—the revolt from colonial rule. And our people share *a common heritage*—the quest for dignity and freedom of man" (1961b: 396, emphasis added). In promoting the Alliance for Progress, he could also invoke a common "American revolution" fought in the name of these same values: "Let us once again awaken *our American revolution* until it guides the struggles of people everywhere—not with an imperialism of force or fear but the rule of courage and freedom and hope for the future of man" (401, emphasis added). After all, as Adolf Berle explained, "*The American world* was the first to throw off the shackles of empire. Until half a century ago a dozen empires ruled the world—except the Western Hemisphere" (1961: 619, emphasis added). The American family was thus assumed to share the values of anticolonialism, human dignity, and freedom. Moreover, Rubottom claimed that, in common with the people of the United States, Latin Americans "set the highest value on freedom, and . . . believe that this freedom is best assured by the effective exercise of representative democracy." In fact, it was assumed that "peoples in the American Republics aspire to societies in which the individual free man can, through the ballot box, have a voice in his destiny" (Rubottom, 1960: 3). In 1961, in an interview with *Izvestia,* Kennedy could therefore describe "our dispute with Cuba" as centered on the fact that "until the present government of Cuba will allow free and honest elections, in our opinion, it cannot claim to represent the majority of the people" (1961k: 743). Latin Americans were thus constructed not only as sharing with the people of the United States a broad set of values but also as partaking of their commitment to the specific institutions of representative, electoral democracy. In fact, "representative democracy" was treated as the "accepted inter-American principle" (Stebbins, 1960: 349). Furthermore, Latin Americans also "believe in economic as well as in political freedom and, in the last analysis, reject the regimentation which all totalitarian ideologies seek to impose upon them" (Rubottom, 1960: 4). That is, Latin Americans were assumed to share an American commitment to economic as well as political freedom, to the liberal economics of the market and its accompanying institutions. Because all members of the American family shared the same aspirations for freedom, and specifically for economic and political freedom defined in terms of liberal economic and political institutional arrangements, communist ideology was pronounced "utterly contrary to *our way of life in the Americas*" (Rubottom, 1958: 1, emphasis added). As a result, "all of the nations of this hemisphere have traditionally presented" a common front "against totalitarian dictatorships in the Old World" (Rubottom, 1960: 2), including their reincarnation in the form of Soviet or communist despotism. After all, no "rational person would prefer tyranny to tolerance or dictatorship to democracy" (Rusk, 1962a: 890). And because all members of the American family strove for the same objectives and were faced by the same threat to their aspirations, Eisenhower could argue that, just as in all families, the "important consideration is that every member of the American family of nations should feel responsible for promoting the welfare of all" (1960f: 571).

The pervasiveness of the "American family" metaphor in the U.S. security imaginary also made sensible references to the states of Latin America as the "brother" or "sister Republics" of the United States.[18] After all, as Kennedy had said, "all who fight for freedom—particularly in this hemisphere—are *our brothers*" (in "Life in the newsfronts of the world," 1961: 56, emphasis added). This extension of the American family metaphor helped to set the context for the missile crisis. For example, a State Department document on U.S. relations with Cuba claimed that "the nations of the hemisphere, including the United States, have made repeated attempts to dissuade Cuba from thus turning its back on its *brother Republics.*" Despite the betrayal of the Cuban revolution by "Dr. Castro," it continued, "the people of Cuba remain *our brothers*" (U.S. Department of State, 1961b: 29, emphasis added). In 1961 Rusk argued that "within the United Nations, the Cuban delegation has abandoned *its brethren of the hemisphere* to play the smirking sycophant for the Communist bloc" (1962a: 892, emphasis added). Similarly, during the missile crisis itself, a letter that Stevenson proposed to read at the United Nations claimed that the United States "cannot tolerate Soviet-Cuban aggression against us or *our sister republics*" (read by Kennedy from Stevenson's draft, October 27: 40, emphasis added; see also Stebbins, 1962: 301).

As these examples indicate, the American family metaphor and its extensions served to reinforce the putative solidarity and integrity of the Western Hemisphere by representing the American republics as united in a common family enterprise guided by their shared belief in the virtues of freedom, representative democracy, and liberal market economics. The American family metaphor also had a number of further implications. First, problems in the Western Hemisphere, including the social, political, and economic dislocations and the attendant upheavals suffered by its member states, were a family affair, to be dealt with by family members and in accordance with the standards of the American way of life and the principles of the Inter-American System. Second and conversely, outside interference, and particularly the interference of an alien and totalitarian dictatorship, was unacceptable, as was the communist infiltration of Cuba. When faced with a common challenge to their common values, it was up to each family member to protect the others and to prevent the encroachment of tyranny, dictatorship, or totalitarianism into the common

"American home." It was therefore the responsibility of each family member to promote the development within each of these societies of the requisite liberal political and economic institutions. Appropriate solutions to these problems were liberal ones; communist solutions were alien to the American way of life. Third, as "the most powerful and oldest free nation in this hemisphere," it was the "responsibility" of the United States both "to ourselves and to the Americas to provide . . . initiative" and to "breathe new life into the premises and inject new energy into the institutions of inter-American action" (Mansfield, 1960: 96). The preeminent role of the United States, the "most powerful and oldest free nation" in the Western Hemisphere, conferred onto it the responsibility for dealing with the communist intrusion into Cuba. The United States bore a special responsibility not only because of the commitments embodied in the Monroe Doctrine and its extensions and successors but also because "the United States is important to all Latin America . . . as a bastion of freedom" (Eisenhower, 1960d: 469). As Eisenhower argued in 1960, "our [U.S.] interest in *our sister Republics* is of long standing and of deep affection." As a result, "I shall reaffirm to *our sister republics* that we [the United States] are steadfast in our purpose to work with them hand in hand in promoting the security and well-being of all peoples in this hemisphere" (1960b: 460, emphasis added). Representing the Latin American states, including Cuba, as the brothers or sisters of the United States in the American family thus further reinforced the U.S. obligation to protect the other American states from outside aggression.[19] The American family metaphor thus brought with it warrants for liberal rather than communist policies, for hemispheric rather than alien assistance or intervention, and, in particular, for a leading U.S. role in Latin America.

Finally, the Cuban problem and the Cuban missile crisis were of great import to the United States because of the proximity of this particular site of communist aggression to the borders of the United States itself. This was demonstrated by and entailed in the extension of the American family metaphor to an implicit "American home." In this elaboration of the family metaphor, Latin American states, including Cuba in particular, were represented as the backyard, front yard, or doorstep of the United States.[20] In wielding the Cuban problem to criticize the Eisenhower administration, presidential hopeful Senator John Kennedy had charged that it is "a critical situation to find so dangerous and malignant an enemy *on our very doorstep* only eight minutes by jet from Florida. The American people want to know how this was permitted to happen, how the Iron Curtain could have advanced *to our very front yard*" (1960a: 20, emphasis added). In 1961, in supporting U.S. economic assistance to Latin America in a speech before Congress, Senator William Fulbright argued that "with Castro *on our doorstep*" the American people would support such aid (1961: 74, emphasis added). In this image, the Cuban missile crisis was a further attempt by the Soviet Union and the international communist conspiracy to invade the American home. As Douglas Dillon reiterated in 1989, the missile crisis "was something that they had started *in our back yard*" (in Blight and Welch, 1990: 100, emphasis added). (Even Castro had a place in the American home—as a "household pest" [Stebbins, 1963: 275]!)

The representation of Cuba as part of the American home appeared, if in a slightly different form, in a letter sent by President Kennedy to Bertrand Russell. During the missile crisis, Russell had sent letters to Kennedy and to Khrushchev appealing for a peaceful resolution to the crisis. In response to these appeals, Kennedy wrote, "While your messages are critical of the United States, they make no mention of your concern for the introduction of secret Soviet missiles into Cuba. *I think your attention might well be directed to the burglars rather than to those who have caught the burglars*" (in Abel, 1966: 144, emphasis added). Stevenson used the same burglar metaphor in his exchange with the Soviet ambassador, Valerian Zorin, at the United Nations on October 25:

> We are here today and have been this week for one single reason—because the Soviet Union secretly introduced this menacing offensive military buildup into the island of Cuba while assuring the world that nothing was further from their thoughts. The argument, in its essence, of the Soviet Union is that it was not the Soviet Union which created this threat to peace by secretly installing these weapons in Cuba but that it was the United States which created this crisis by discovering and reporting these installations. *This is the first time, I confess, that I have ever heard it said that the crime is not the burglar but the discovery of the burglar.* (Stevenson, 1962b: 735, emphasis added)

This metaphor of course only makes sense in the context of an understanding of Cuba, and of Latin America more broadly, as part of the

American home occupied by members of the American family. In accordance with the Monroe Doctrine, it implies that foreign involvement in the Western Hemisphere is illegitimate, indeed unlawful, and that it amounts to a violation of the sanctity of the American home. The use of this metaphor in the context of the missile crisis conjured up an image in which the Soviet Union had surreptitiously and illicitly intruded onto private property and needed, therefore, to be ejected without delay. Because these charges were leveled by representatives of the United States, they also implied that the invaded property in fact belonged to, or at least was the responsibility of, the United States.[21] It was therefore the rightful task of the United States to effect the ejection of the burglar from the American home.

While the extended metaphor of the American family made sensible and legitimated U.S. intervention in Latin America and Cuba, it simultaneously ruled out the understandings of the events of October 1962 advanced in the narratives of the Caribbean and October crises. Because any communist intervention into or involvement in Cuba constituted external interference in the family affairs of the Americas, the Soviet missile deployment, despite the explanation offered in the story of the Caribbean crisis, could not be understood as defensive. The family metaphor thus further marginalized the already (seemingly) improbable Soviet claim to have been defending Cuba. In any case, such defense was unnecessary. Since they were the acts of the state bearing primary responsibility for Western Hemispheric integrity, the most highly developed model of the free way of life in the Americas and a sister or brother to the American republics and the Cuban people, U.S. actions toward Cuba could not be understood as aggression. Instead, they were attempts to protect the integrity and the virtue of the American family. The claim that the United States was violating Cuban sovereignty, a claim that Castro had made continuously since long before October 1962 and that was located at the heart of the October crisis, was ruled out as well. After all, the affairs of Cuba were family affairs and therefore by definition of legitimate concern and relevance to all members of the American family. The burglar metaphor also denied to the Cubans the right to choose their own house guests. By constructing Cuba as an extension of the American home, this metaphor in effect denied Cuban sovereignty through its incorporation of Cuba into an imagined American family.

The United States and Latin America

By representing the narrower setting of the events of October 1962 for U.S. decision makers and for later producers and consumers of the Cuban missile crisis myth, the prevailing understanding of the Western Hemisphere and of U.S.–Latin American relations contributed to the production of the crisis itself. The invocation of standard objects such as the "Western Hemisphere" and the "American family" and of the quasi-causal arguments entailed within them, including that the United States bore the primary responsibility for the protection and development of that hemisphere, provided a more detailed representation of the situation that the United States faced in October 1962. This narrower context helped further to refine the meaning of the Soviet missile deployment: Not only did it constitute an aggressive intrusion by the international communist movement run from the Kremlin into the free world, but this intrusion violated both the long-established territorial integrity of the Western Hemisphere and the sanctity of the American family and challenged the predominant role of the United States in protecting the American home and managing its family affairs. This meaning, in turn, implied a particular U.S. national interest. It required, in the short run, that the United States act forcefully and without delay to eject the burglar from the American home by securing the removal of the missiles. It required, in the longer run, that the United States counteract the "seduction" (Alba, 1960: 4) of a sister republic. At the same time, it reinforced the marginalization of the Soviet claim to have been defending Cuba against aggression by the United States. Once the situation was constructed as one in which alien, despotic forces were threatening the hemisphere and undermining the American family, interpreting the Soviet missile deployment as the defense of Cuba did not seem sensible. Nor did it make sense to challenge the U.S. construction of its national interest and the resultant quarantine as violations of Cuban sovereignty. The United States, itself a member of the American family, was merely defending that family against dangerous outside interference.

5

Constructing the Cuban Missile Crisis:
The Problem of Cuba

During the 1960s and even up to the present, the United States has frequently discussed Cuba in such terms as to suggest it is a superpower. The tone is hostile, but you always give us credit for far more capabilities than we in fact have. You flatter us. We often wonder why?
— UNNAMED CUBAN OFFICIAL, QUOTED BY WAYNE S. SMITH,
    FOREWORD TO CARLA ANNE ROBBINS, THE CUBAN THREAT

CASTRO AND THE COLD WAR IN CUBA

Before 1958, the United States had not been "particularly interested in Cuba affairs" (Robert C. Hill, in Morley, 1987: 61) largely because U.S.-Cuban relations were proceeding quite smoothly according to well-established and accepted patterns. Nor did the Cuban civil war or insurrection initially cause excessive distress. In 1958, for example, it was still thought that "the insurgents" led by Castro "were plainly neither Communists nor under Communist influence" (Stebbins, 1959: 356).[1] Instead, it appeared that the "main strength" of Cuba's revolutionary movement was "drawn from the rising Cuban middle class. Washington thus saw no reason to depart from its traditional nonintervention policy."[2] In 1959, the revolution itself was still viewed with some tolerance. In that year, as Richard Stebbins has argued, Cuba's revolution was still depicted, in surprisingly positive terms, as a "civil war" in which "a cruel and corrupt dictatorship was driven from power by a group of idealistic and inexperienced young men whose personal heroism and, in many cases, excellent intentions were to prove seriously inadequate to the task of governing a modern nation, even with the virtually unanimous support which they at first enjoyed" (1960: 352). Nonetheless, by late 1959 U.S. observers had begun to detect ominous signs in Cuba. "From the point of view of the United States and of the larger interests of the inter-American community," Stebbins continued,

> the original promise of the Cuban revolution was vitiated as time went on by three principal features: an understandable but certainly exaggerated mistrust and hostility toward the United States; an alarming complaisance toward the activities of local Communist elements, . . . and a proclaimed determination not only to carry out a thoroughgoing social revolution in Cuba itself but to work for the speedy elimination of the remaining political dictatorships in the Caribbean and throughout Latin America. These strongly marked characteristics were enough to convert what originally had seemed a heartening victory for democracy in Latin America into an alarming portent whose disruptive implications extended throughout the inter-American family. (352–353)

By 1960, the standard U.S. history of the Cuban Revolution had been substantially rewritten. It was now typically maintained that "the revolutionary government established by Fidel Castro in Cuba at the beginning of 1959 had early revealed signs of Communist infiltration as well as virulent animosity toward the United States" (Stebbins, 1961: 292). Furthermore, "the attempt of the Soviet Government to take the Cuban revolution under its direct protection" brought the cold war "for the first time into the heart of the Americas" and established "a Communist bridgehead ninety miles from the United States" (Stebbins, 1961: 292). By allowing this "Communist infiltration" into Cuba, Cuba's revolutionary leaders had "expressly repudiate[d] the traditional concept of representative democracy" and had began to show "less interest in reforming the existing political and economic system than in promoting a thoroughgoing social revolution—a revolution which, moreover, was not to be confined to Cuba but, in their view, was ultimately destined to be extended to the rest of Latin America" (294). Because Cuba had reestablished diplomatic relations with the Soviet Union, it had also become "easy to picture the Communist network that could develop throughout the Americas around the nucleus of a Soviet embassy in

Havana" (305). By 1960, then, the Cuban leadership was understood to be "walking hand in hand with the Sino-Soviet bloc" (Christian Herter [then secretary of state], in Stebbins, 1961: 314) and the Cuban revolution to have been transformed into the "Cuban- and Communist-inspired threat of 'Fidelismo'" (Stebbins, 1961: 331).[3] By 1960, in short, "the Cuban problem" had arrived (298).[4]

A more complete analysis of the construction of the myth of the Cuban missile crisis and of the U.S. national interest in that crisis requires that we examine the prevailing understanding of Cuba and of this so-called Cuban problem. Though Cuba was largely absent as an actor both from the ExComm deliberations and from the myth of the missile crisis, the characteristics articulated to the objects "Cuba," "Castroism," the "Cuban Revolution," and the "Cuban people," as well as the nature of U.S.-Cuban relations as these came to be represented in the U.S. security imaginary in the years after the Cuban Revolution, further flesh out the meaning of the missile crisis and the attendant U.S. national interest.

Constructing the Cuban Problem

At the time of the missile crisis, Cuba had for a number of years presented the United States with an irritating problem. This so-called Cuban problem arose not long after the Cuban Revolution and, as even McNamara has admitted, the U.S. administration was "hysterical about Castro" by the time of the Bay of Pigs (in U.S. Senate Select Committee to Study Governmental Operations with respect to Intelligence Activities, 1975: 157). The official U.S. story of the deterioration of U.S.-Cuban relations after the Cuban Revolution and of the origins of the Cuban problem places the onus both on the new revolutionary Cuban government and on the bipolar cold war struggle between "communism" and "freedom." In a State Department description of the course of these relations, for example, Cuban actions toward the United States were depicted as follows:

> Elements of the Castro movement were engaged in anti-American activities even during the revolution against Batista. Soon after it came to power in 1959, the Castro government turned away from its previous promises, permitted Communist influence to grow, attacked and persecuted its own supporters in Cuba who expressed opposition to communism, arbitrarily seized U.S. properties, and made a series of baseless charges against the United States. It ignored, rejected, or

imposed impossible conditions on repeated U.S. offers to cooperate and negotiate. In 1960 Cuba established close political, economic, and military relationships with the Sino-Soviet Bloc, while increasing the pace and vehemence of its measures and attacks against the United States. (U.S. Department of State Bureau of Public Affairs, 1962: 1–2)

The next paragraph then recounts the U.S. response to these alleged Cuban provocations, implying that all of these U.S. actions *followed* both Cuban hostility toward the United States and communist influence in Cuba:

> In mid-1960 the United States and its allies initiated a series of measures *as a deliberate response* to Communist efforts to establish a beachhead for subversion in this hemisphere. The United States prohibited the further import of Cuban sugar into this country. Exports, except for certain foods and medicines, were prohibited soon afterward. In February 1962, the President made the embargo substantially complete, extending the import prohibition to indirect as well as direct purchases. (2, emphasis added)

This apparently straightforward narrative clearly implies that Cuban actions and communist influence precipitated U.S. hostility toward Cuba. These events can be represented differently, however, with correspondingly different conclusions about the genesis of the Cuban problem.

An alternative narrative might highlight the flip-flopping of hostile actions between the United States and Cuba, not only portraying a chain of escalatory disagreements (rather than unilateral Cuban or communist hostility) but also indicating that much of the responsibility for this escalation rested with the United States (rather than with Cuba or communism). Such a narrative might begin with calls in the U.S. House and Senate, already heard in the spring of 1959, for the overthrow of the Castro regime and for economic sanctions against Cuba (Robbins, 1983: 72, 81). Particularly insulting to Cubans was the *New York Daily News*'s call for the restoration of the Platt Amendment, which would permit U.S. military intervention in Cuba (Thomas, 1971: 1076). It could then be pointed out that in January 1960 Congress had been asked to approve presidential control over the U.S. sugar quota in order to give the administration a lever to use against the new Castro government (Kenworthy, 1960a: 8).[5] In February 1960, because it feared an imminent cut in its sugar quota, the Cuban government signed a trade agreement with the Soviet Union, arranging to barter sugar for oil (Schwartz, 1960: 6). (It could also be noted that even the Batista government had, in the 1950s, looked to the Soviet Union as an alternative market for Cuban sugar [Robbins, 1983: 17].) In mid-June, calls for the United States to "really do something" about "the Cuban situation" increased (Senator George Smathers [D–Florida], in Kenworthy, 1960b: 6).[6] In late June, American-owned oil refineries in Cuba refused, with U.S. government encouragement, to refine Soviet crude oil (Benjamin, 1990: 194). In response, and amid additional fears that its U.S. sugar market was about to disappear, Cuba nationalized the Texas Company (Texaco) petroleum refinery on June 29 (Phillips, 1960a: 1) and the refinery of Esso (Cuba) Inc. on July 1 (Szulc, 1960: 1). As expected, Eisenhower completely eliminated the Cuban sugar quota on July 6. On July 9 Khrushchev then announced Soviet willingness to use force to protect Cuba from armed U.S. intervention (Khrushchev, 1960a), and he informed the Cuban government on July 10 that the Soviet Union would increase its purchases of Cuban sugar to make up for the U.S. cut (Phillips, 1960b). As Philip Bonsal, former U.S. ambassador to Cuba, has explained, "Russia came to Castro's rescue only after the United States had taken steps designed to overthrow him" (1971: 192). This alternative narrative, in short, not only highlights the pivotal U.S. role in escalating tensions with Cuba but also makes it look as though "Washington actually wanted to precipitate a crisis" (Robbins, 1983: 95).

The transformation between 1959 and 1960 of the official U.S. narrative of the genesis of the Cuban problem and the corresponding assignment of blame for the deterioration of U.S.-Cuban relations to Cuba and "international Communism" were clearly not unrelated to the 1960 presidential campaign. In response to Republican charges that a Democratic administration would be "soft on Communism," presidential candidate John Kennedy went to sometimes quite extravagant lengths to demonstrate that he understood the danger posed to the United States by the "Communist orientation" of the Castro government. "For the first time in the history of the United States," he proclaimed on August 26, 1960, "an enemy stands poised at the throat of the United States. There is no doubt of the Communist orientation of the Castro government. They are our enemy and will do anything to contribute to our downfall. Not only as a satellite of the Soviet Union in the future but also [as] they attempt to spread their revolution through all of Latin America" (1960d: 79). On November 7, 1960, he again insisted that the "big problem" of the new administration "would be to contain Castro, to prevent him spreading his influence throughout all of Latin America." If that were not accomplished, if "Castro should spread his power, then our security would be directly threatened" (94–95).

The vilification of Castro and of the Cuban Revolution continued throughout the Kennedy administration (and, of course, beyond).[7] The Castro regime came to be considered "a clear and present danger" to the "authentic and autonomous revolution of the Americas" because the "Cuba of Castro," a State Department publication asserted in 1961, "offers the Western Hemisphere a new experience—the experience of a modern totalitarian state" (U.S. Department of State, 1961b: 2, 16). This "totalitarian" Cuban state posed a threat to the Americas because, as Stevenson had argued in the United Nations after the Bay of Pigs debacle, the "problem created in the Western Hemisphere by the Cuban revolution . . . is that every effort is being made to use Cuba as a base to force totalitarian ideology into other parts of the Americas" (1961: 673). Similarly, in early 1962 the State Department reiterated that the "grave and urgent challenge" posed to the Western Hemisphere "results from the fact that the Castro regime has betrayed its own revolution by delivering it into the hands of powers alien to the hemisphere and by transforming it into an instrument deliberately intended to suppress the hope of the Cuban people for a return to representative democracy and to subvert established governments of other American Republics" (U.S. Department of State, 1962: 130).

These statements contain two of the central issues that defined the Cuban problem. First, allowing an alien power to interfere in the region ran counter to the integrity of the Western Hemisphere, to the American values of the American family. As Senator Mansfield argued in 1960, "What is at stake is larger than Cuba and Castro." In fact, he continued,

> what is at stake is hemispheric solidarity and . . . the highly fruitful commercial and other contacts which this solidarity has yielded over the years.
>
> If the national attitude of this country could be expressed on Cuba . . . there would be a firmness which I am sure is shared by

other American states that the Soviet Union shall not fish in the trou-
bled waters of the Caribbean or meddle in the family affairs of the
Americas, or un-nerve us by waving its missiles. (1960: 93)

The Cuban problem, that is, undermined the long-standing and
hard-won integrity of the Western Hemisphere and of the American
family. The Castro regime had forced a breach into the traditional
solidarity of the hemisphere and threatened to undermine the traditional U.S. hegemonic position there. "Another Cuba," Schlesinger
warned in 1961, and "the game would be up through a good deal of
Latin America" (in Paterson, 1989: 127).

Second, Cuba now provided a base for further Soviet and communist subversion of, or aggression against, the American republics.
Just as international communism was typically represented as directly connected, through a global conspiracy, to the Kremlin, so too
Castro and the Cuban government came to be understood as tools of
the Soviet Union. In 1960, in response to Khrushchev's public pledge
to support the revolutionary Cuban government, Eisenhower argued
that the "close ties that have developed between the Soviet and
Cuban governments . . . shows [sic] the clear intention to establish
Cuba in a role serving Soviet purposes in this hemisphere" (1960e:
567). Adolf Berle, then chairman of the Task Force on Latin America,
similarly lamented the "seizure of the Castro regime by the Sino-
Soviet bloc" (1961: 618). Viewed through the lenses of the U.S. security imaginary, then, Cuba came to be understood as "a new satellite" established by "the Russians," situated "only 90 miles from
American shores" (Kennedy, 1960d: 91) and governed by "Khrushchev's chief puppet in the Caribbean" ("Summary of editorial comment," 1961: 10). Castro and his allegedly communist revolution
came to be represented as a Trojan horse inside of which Soviet and
communist influence had surreptitiously been smuggled into Cuba
and into the Western Hemisphere more generally. Extending this
metaphor to include the additional infiltration of nuclear weapons,
Richard Stebbins claimed in his analysis of the Cuban missile crisis
that both the governments and the peoples of Latin America "were
profoundly shaken by the realization that the [Cuban] regime so
many of them had idolized had been playing the role of a Soviet
'Trojan horse' and exposing them to a genuine, if still limited, risk of
nuclear annihilation" (1963: 307).

Though Cuba has persistently been portrayed as a Soviet satellite, as having been taken over by the Soviets through an international communist conspiracy, Carla Anne Robbins has noted that "the fitful course of the early Cuban-Soviet alliance is evidence that Moscow was unaware of any such conspiracy" (1983: 74). In other words, different interpretations of Soviet-Cuban relations are possible. According to Robbins, "Moscow first approached the Cuban Revolution with a great deal of caution" (91) and avoided contact with the Castro regime for over a year. The first Soviet overture toward Cuba came thirteen months after the revolution, when Anastas Mikoyan led a Soviet trade delegation to Cuba. The mission resulted in a trade agreement in which the Soviet Union agreed to purchase Cuban sugar and to extend credit to enable Cuba to purchase industrial equipment and petroleum (92). Moreover, just as the United States only slowly and reluctantly recognized the Sino-Soviet split, so too it never recognized that Cuba and the Soviet Union might have different interests and pursue divergent foreign policies. The notion that Cuba was a *Soviet* base for the subversion of the hemisphere persisted throughout the cold war. During the 1960s, however, Cuba in fact pursued a foreign policy increasingly at odds with that of the Soviet Union. Castro criticized the Soviet policy of coexistence with the West, advocating instead a policy of "proletarian internationalism." He disregarded the Soviet focus on East-West conflict, attempting instead to place North-South conflict at the center of socialist foreign policy. And he explicitly challenged Soviet leadership of the socialist bloc, seeking quite overtly to gain the leadership of the nonaligned nations and of socialist movements in the so-called Third World (Robbins, 1983: chapters 2, 4).

Nonetheless, once it had been established within the U.S. security imaginary that this new Cuban satellite was governed by a "Soviet puppet," it also made sense to claim, as the State Department insisted in 1961, that "under Castro Cuba has already become a base and staging area for revolutionary activity throughout the continent" (1961b: 25). As a result, at the time of the missile crisis Kennedy was absolutely determined to prevent additional revolutions in Latin America or the Caribbean that might give the Soviet Union another bridgehead in the Western Hemisphere. After all, aggressive totalitarian regimes are never content with one small victory. Since successful totalitarian aggression would, by definition, be followed by further aggression, allowing the Soviets to retain one such "bridgehead" a mere "ninety miles from the United States" (Stebbins, 1961: 292) would undoubtedly spur them on in their ambition to establish another. Indeed, according to the U.S. administration and other observers, Cuba had become "an action base from which teams of Communists, backed by the Soviet Union and Communist China, are seeking to turn the Caribbean Sea into a Communist lake" ("Cuba's Latin goal behind U.S. break," 1961: 6). Because of the connections presumed to link together all elements of the global communist conspiracy, that is, Soviet involvement in Cuba was assumed to herald the arrival of teams of Communists whose goal would be the further expansion of communism and of Soviet influence. As a result, throughout the 1960s it was believed that Cuban communist agents were

> fomenting revolution in almost every Latin American country, leading guerrilla operations in Argentina, plotting political assassinations in Colombia, shipping arms to Venezuela, and inciting student riots in Puerto Rico. Cuban-based guerrilla training schools were said to be graduating thousands of Latin American subversives each year who were then sent back to their homelands to lead Cuban-style revolutions. (Robbins, 1983: 3)[8]

The Cuban missile crisis was constructed in this context. Representations of the Soviet missile deployment, because they drew on the resources of the U.S. security imaginary, depicted it as an instance of general communist, not simply Soviet, penetration of the hemisphere, which raised the odds, particularly if the penetration were successful, that other communist interventions would follow. Rusk could therefore argue that the missile crisis highlighted the problem of "the growing intervention of the international Communist movement in this hemisphere" (1962c: 721).

This second aspect of the Cuban problem, that it provided a base for continued Soviet and communist subversion of and aggression against other Caribbean and Latin American states, posed a particular danger because of the economic, social, and political troubles pervading Latin America at the time. These troubles ranged "from minority rule in many of the countries, an impoverished people with substandards [sic] of living and education, generally poor communications facilities, one- or two-crop economies, and inadequate distribution of wealth, to the basically unsolved problem of integrating large Indian populations into the modern social structure." Furthermore, these problems generated "unrest" which in turn was "complicated by internal economic crises and the rise of nationalism, all of which have provided fertile ground for the Communists and other extremists, who are all too ready to resort to violence" (U.S. Information Agency, 1961: 90). The exploitation of these conditions by "Communists and other extremists" meant that the intrusion of the international communist movement into the Western Hemisphere was unlikely to remain confined to Cuba alone. Instead, the international communist conspiracy directed from the Kremlin threatened to spread from Cuba to the rest of Latin America not only because that was the intended goal of the Communist conspiracy but because Latin America provided such fertile ground for the spread of revolution.

The danger that communism would spread from Cuba to other Latin American states was enhanced by the Cuban provision of a model for social and economic development, a model that responded to Latin American conditions. As one commentator put it,

> The Cuban revolution has had reverberations throughout Latin America. Castro and his rebels have caught the imagination of the humble people who, in many countries, wish they could destroy their own military cliques as Castro destroyed Cuba's. Vast numbers of these common people also wish to effect similar land reforms and other programs of the kind Castro has inaugurated since coming to power. (Alexander, 1960: 4–5)

Castro and the Cuban Revolution, in other words, provided an attractive model for social change. The depressed economic conditions in "poor, underdeveloped areas" such as "some of the Americas" meant that these areas "offer fertile fields for Communist economic coercion" (Cabell, 1959: 751). Indeed,

> the Soviets—and in fact, the entire Sino-Soviet bloc—are attempting to pass themselves off as the foremost examples of crash economic progress. They are out to get the credit for filling the immediate desires of these newly developing areas. But—and this is the big hooker—while they are at it, the Communists not only try to assume control of the resources of these countries but also attempt to control the minds and souls of the peoples in the areas. The Communists want nations to become increasingly dependent economically upon the Communist Bloc. The stage is then set for ultimate Communist takeover. (751)

Conditions in Latin America thus provided the Soviet Union with an opportunity for economic imperialism, in part through the model of the Cuban Revolution.

Finally, economic and social conditions in Latin America, and their exploitation by "Communists" and other "extremists," meant as well that the U.S. position as leader in the hemisphere was in jeopardy. Economic difficulties in particular made it "profitable for agitators to try to create the popular image of Uncle Sam as an exploiter of the downtrodden masses, and to give a distasteful connotation to the 'Yanqui'" (U.S. Information Agency, 1961: 90). The task of the United States, then, both in order to prevent communist expansion and in order to retain its leadership position, was "to compete with Fidel Castro," and indirectly with the Soviet Union, "for the allegiance of a continent in revolutionary ferment" (Schlesinger, 1965: 760).

The Alliance for Progress provided a long-term strategy to overcome these dangerous conditions, to undermine the appeal both of the Cuban model of revolutionary social change and of Soviet trade and economic assistance, and to bolster U.S. prominence in the region. It was, in short, designed (at least in part) to provide for the "containment of Castro" (Schlesinger, 1965: 783) and the Cuban Revolution and, thereby, for the containment of Soviet influence in the Western Hemisphere. As Senator Fulbright argued in 1961,

> Although Latin America now has the best group of governments it has ever had, most of them are still heavily influenced by the traditional elite classes who give only lipservice, if that, to social reform. They do not really have it in their hearts to promote land reform and to revise tax structures. We must, of course, continue to deal with these governments. We must attempt, however, to make the most conservative groups see that their survival—the continued independence of their own nations from the domination of Moscow—depends upon their willingness to come to grips with the needs and demands of their own people. (1961: 76)

By inducing conservative Latin American governments to promote evolutionary social and economic change, the Alliance for Progress would warn Castro "that he could no longer count on the Latin American states falling to Marxist revolution of their own weight" (Schlesinger 1965: 759). Nonetheless, Schlesinger cautioned, "the *Fidelistas* and their communist allies were redoubling their efforts to disrupt the democratic effort and seize the energies of change for themselves." As a result, "the struggle for the future of Latin America was well joined—and the outcome thus far indeterminate" (1965: 759).

To enhance the chances for success in this struggle, the evolutionary model of development offered by the Alliance for Progress was represented as a *revolutionary* alternative to the Cuban-Soviet development model. U.S. officials explicitly appropriated the terminology of revolution the better to legitimize U.S. policy and to undercut the appeal of Castroism and of Soviet trade and economic assistance in Latin America. At a special meeting of the OAS in 1961, for example, Dillon attempted to sell the alliance by invoking José Martí, the father of Cuban revolution: "It was a great American—José Martí," Dillon pronounced, "who reminded us that 'We Americans are one in origin, in hope and in danger.' We meet today in fulfillment of that concept—brought together by our common origin, fired by our common hopes, determined to conquer our common dangers" (1961: 408, emphasis added). (The invocation of Martí in this context, of course, completely ignored the fact that Martí had become a firm opponent of the United States and of U.S. policy toward Cuba and the rest of Latin America [Pérez, 1990: 78–81]. What Martí called "*nuestra América*" [our America] was Latin America— that is, an America with a distinct Hispanic heritage and separate from North America—and he considered an aggressive and imperialist United States to be chief among "our common [Latin American] dangers" [Martí, 1953: 231–234].)[9] Nonetheless, in charting "the future course of our hemisphere" at Punte del Este, Dillon invoked not only the common heritage and values of the American family on which that course should be based, but he also invoked their common spirit of revolution. Having proclaimed that the American states faced "a revolutionary task," he continued,

> But we are no strangers to revolution. From the shores of the Americas almost 200 years ago went forth the call to freedom and national independence which today guides men's actions in all the turbulent continents of the world.
>
> It was our hemisphere which first proved that men could rule themselves, that colonial shackles could be cast off, and that governments could be the instruments of man's liberty.
>
> This was the spirit of our revolution and of the revolutions it has inspired. It is the spirit which has shaped our hemisphere. It is the

spirit of our continuing struggle against the despotism which is as ancient as the Pharaohs, no matter what new form it may assume; and it is that spirit—the legacy of Artigas and San Martín, of Bolívar and Washington, of O'Higgins and José Bonifacto—which guides our actions here today. (1961: 408–409)[10]

The task for the United States in Latin America in the early 1960s, then, was to provide an alternative model for economic development that could tap this revolutionary ferment, contain Castroism and the Cuban model of revolutionary change, thereby contain Soviet and communist expansion into the Western Hemisphere, and simultaneously maintain the U.S. position of preeminence in the region (e.g., Kennedy, 1961c).

These two central concerns encompassed in the Cuban problem—the interference by an alien power in the solidarity of the Western Hemisphere and the transformation of Cuba into a base for Soviet and communist aggression and subversion into the rest of Latin America—also brought with them a third: the Cuban problem, and especially the Cuban missile crisis, threatened U.S. prestige. The third component of the Cuban problem was the challenge it presented not only to the unique role enjoyed by the United States in the Western Hemisphere but to the global credibility of the United States. This challenge, of course, became particularly acute during the Cuban missile crisis itself. As Hans Morgenthau argued in November 1962, "Cuba is being transformed into a Soviet military base . . . [which] affects the interests of the United States adversely." Specifically, it was "detrimental to the political position of the United States in the Western Hemisphere in that it challenges American influence in an area which has traditionally been regarded an American sphere of influence." As a result, he continued, "The Soviet presence in Cuba . . . affects the prestige of the United States as a great power" (1962: 9). Zbigniew Brzezinski offered the same argument, insisting that

> insofar as long-range considerations are concerned, the presence of Communism in Cuba undermines the American claim that the Western Hemisphere is immune to Communist penetration and that the United States has the capability to exclude Communism from this hemisphere. It thus forces the United States to back down from a traditionally proclaimed position and imposes upon it a humiliation which is bound to have international implications. (1962: 7)

The Cuban problem in general and the missile crisis in particular, that is, were not only understood to threaten the Western Hemisphere, the American family, and the U.S. role in the region, but were also understood to challenge the status of the United States as a global superpower. The missiles that the Soviets deployed in Cuba, then, added insult to injury by publicly exposing the threat that the Soviet Union, international communism, and the Cuban problem posed to U.S. claims to hemispheric leadership, to its leadership of the free world, and to its superpower status.

These various facets of the Cuban problem help to explain the contemporary U.S. construction of the Cuban missile crisis and of the attendant U.S. national interest. In particular, they help to explain why the United States could not simply ignore the Soviet missiles installed in Cuba in 1962. Even if both their real similarity to the extraterritorial missile installations of the United States and their irrelevance to the strategic balance had been recognized explicitly, the missiles still could not have been permitted to remain in Cuba. The reason is simple: The Soviet missile deployment symbolized, and was firmly embedded in, the longer-standing Cuban problem. This Cuban problem brought with it a whole host of objects of U.S. security that needed to be protected (such as the solidarity of the Western Hemisphere, the common values of the American family, and U.S. leadership), revealed other objects that posed security threats (such as Soviet puppets, Trojan horses, and the international communist conspiracy), and generated quasi-causal arguments (such as the inevitable expansion of communist subversion and aggression and the need for quick and decisive action to prevent that expansion) that helped to define for U.S. decision makers what the Cuban missile crisis was about. In short, as former White House and State Department official Richard N. Goodwin remarked, "the entire history of the Cold War, its positions and assumptions, converged upon the 'problem of Cuba'" (in Paterson, 1989: 125) and thus upon the missiles themselves.

The Cuban problem was therefore central to the definition of the U.S. national interest in the Cuban missile crisis. Allowing the Soviets to deploy and retain the missiles in Cuba would have appeared to limit the ability of the United States to curtail the communist subversion of the American family and of American civilization. It would thus have undercut the unique position of the United States in the Western Hemisphere established by the Monroe Doctrine and its extensions. Having insisted on the importance of the integrity and solidarity of the Western Hemisphere to its own and to global security, the United States could not accept their subversion. Furthermore, and perhaps most important, by signaling U.S. acquiescence in its own humiliation, it would have undermined U.S. credibility and prestige as a superpower. The failure of the United States successfully to oppose the blatant communist intrusion of nuclear missiles into its own long-established sphere of influence would have weakened its credibility as the defender of freedom in the global battle with international communism. Since it was axiomatic for the United States that freedom was "indivisible" (Eisenhower, 1959b: 30), the defeat of freedom in Cuba threatened the continued existence of freedom throughout the globe. This was true for (at least) two reasons. First, if the communists were successful in Cuba, they would be encouraged to pursue further aggression and subversion in Latin America and elsewhere, that is, to take additional "slices off the salami." Second, if the communists were successful in Cuba, the humiliation of the United States would hamper the performance of its leading role in defending global freedom. Faced with such dire consequences if the Soviet missiles were permitted to remain in Cuba, the solution to the Cuban missile crisis was obvious: The missiles simply had to go.

Fidelista Viruses and Revolutionary Beards

Despite the image of a forcible Soviet or communist seizure of Cuba implied in the Trojan horse metaphor and articulated overtly in U.S. discussions of Cuba, the close relationship between the Cuban government and the Soviet Union was not understood as having been brought about solely by Soviet coercion. As Kennedy had argued, the Cuban government under Castro "makes itself a willing accomplice to the Communist objectives in this hemisphere" (1961i: 580). That Cuba had willingly become a servant of the Soviet Union informed the U.S. representation of the Cuban missile crisis as well. For example, in his speech to the U.N. Security Council on October 23, 1962, Stevenson argued that

> the threat lies in *the submission* of the Castro regime to the will of an
> aggressive foreign power. . . . The foremost objection of the states of
> the Americas to the Castro regime . . . is because he has aided and

abetted an invasion of this hemisphere. . . . The crucial fact is that Cuba *has given* the Soviet Union a bridgehead and staging area in this hemisphere, . . . that *it has made itself an accomplice* in the Communist enterprise of world domination. (1962a: 730–731, emphasis added)

Rusk also argued that the "Castro regime" had "*surrendered* the Cuban national heritage" to "Soviet power" (1962c: 721, emphasis added). In short, Castro, as I discuss in more detail later, had betrayed the Cuban Revolution. Ascribing complicity in Soviet expansion to Castro and the Cuban regime meant that Castro had not simply been coerced into the Soviet bloc. Nor had he been duped. Instead, it was implied, Castro and other members of Cuba's revolutionary regime were themselves malevolent; they had willingly and knowingly invited an alien and despotic form of government into the American home. This portrait of malevolence manifests itself perhaps most starkly in the extension of various disease and contagion metaphors to Castro and to Castroism or Fidelism.[11]

A common set of tropes in the postwar U.S. security imaginary represented communism as a disease, infection, or infestation. Already in the "long telegram," for example, Kennan had described "world communism" as a "malignant parasite which feeds only on diseased tissue" (1946: 63). J. Howard McGrath, Truman's attorney general, warned in 1950 that each communist "carries in himself the germs of death for society" (in Theoharis, 1974: 279). And John Cabot, assistant secretary of state for inter-American affairs in the Eisenhower administration, remarked in the mid-1950s that "we should not assume that the anti-bodies which exist in the Latin American body politic will always repel the intrusion of the Communist virus. Indeed, in Guatemala they have not done so" (in Immerman, 1982: 132).

True to this model, Castroism or Fidelism and the threat that they posed to the Western Hemisphere were also described using variants of the "communism as disease" or "communism as bodily affliction" metaphors. Echoing the standard representation of communism in Latin America as "a cancerous threat to the national life of each of the 21 American Republics" (Rubottom, 1958: 14), Vice President Nixon, during the 1960 presidential campaign, described Castro's regime as "an intolerable cancer." The goal of U.S. policy toward Cuba, he continued (mixing his disease metaphors), must therefore be "to quarantine the Castro regime" (in Robbins, 1983: 97) to prevent the spread of the disease to other Latin American states. Later, in defending increased U.S. economic aid to Latin America, Senator Fulbright described the Castro government as "a running abscess in the Caribbean" (1961: 77). Benito Nardone, the former president of Uruguay, wielded the same metaphor, characterizing "Castroism" as a "Communist abscess." The task for the Americas was therefore "to isolate the Communist abscess, then cut it out" (1961: 92), lest it infect the remaining states in Central and South America. In October 1962, in a statement to the House Select Committee on Export Control, George Ball defended the U.S. trade embargo against Cuba as "directed toward nullifying Cuba's usefulness as a source of infection for international communism" (1962: 591). Virtually the identical words were used in the story of the Cuban missile crisis as told by the Department of Defense, which explained that the "U.S. policy of isolating Cuba economically, a policy in which our allies have increasingly cooperated, has been aimed at nullifying Cuba's usefulness as a source of Communist infection in Latin America" (U.S. Department of Defense Armed Forces Information and Education, 1962: 3). In discussing the Cuban problem faced by the United States in 1962, one analyst used a slightly different metaphor, asserting that "some way of drawing the Cuban tooth" must be found "before it infected the whole American body" (Stebbins, 1963: 272). A disease metaphor also appeared in U.S. justifications of the Alliance for Progress. "The virus of Fidelismo," it was argued in this context, "had naturally made much greater inroads among the Spanish-speaking peoples of the hemisphere" (Stebbins, 1962: 297). Because of pervasive economic stagnation and social unrest, the peoples of Latin America were "susceptible to Communist and pro-Cuban influences" (298). Given the causes of this susceptibility, the Alliance for Progress was "the best and perhaps the only long-range antidote to the Fidelist-Communist virus" (343).

These metaphors of disease and other bodily afflictions, standard fare within the U.S. security imaginary, both portray Fidelism or Castroism as a particular kind of object and entail certain warrants for action. According to this view, Castroism and communism did not simply offer a system of rule different from, and alien to, that to which the American family aspired. Instead, they presented a mortal danger to its health. The immediacy of the danger to the other American states was highlighted through the metaphors of contagious diseases: In particular, the communist virus or infection in Cuba, this metaphor implied, could quite easily spread to other Caribbean and Latin American countries. It is this notion of contagion that provides the warrant for action entailed in these metaphors. Whether the infection was caused by a virus, an abscess, an infected tooth, or a cancer, action was necessary to prevent its spread to healthy portions of the American body politic. A contagious or malignant disease cannot simply be allowed to run its course; instead, treatment is required. When the infection was represented as a virus, for example, it was argued that the United States must "take action" to "quarantine the regime of Premier Fidel Castro" ("U.S. is seeking to isolate Castro," 1961: 1). Constructing Castroism in this way helped to legitimate certain U.S. policies, including, for example, the imposition of an arms or trade embargo. When the infection was contained in an abscess or a decaying tooth, then the abscess had to be cut out or the tooth drawn. Sometimes, in other words, the measures required to ensure the safety of the healthy were quite drastic. Representing Castro and the Cuban regime as an abscess or an infected tooth thus legitimated rather drastic U.S. measures, including the attempt to assassinate Castro and other Cuban leaders, the attempt forcibly to overthrow the Cuban regime, and attempts to instigate an internal rebellion that would, like an antibody, eradicate the infection from the inside.[12] In short, the pervasive and repetitious portrayal of Castro, Castroism, and the Cuban regime as a virus or other contagious disease that posed a threat of infection to the remainder of the American family both constructed the Cuban problem in more detail as dangerous and malevolent and rendered it palatable to seek and to implement a wide range of measures, some quite draconian, against Castro and the Cuban regime.

The alien and malevolent character of the Cuban regime was further reinforced through apparently quite irrelevant descriptions of "Dr. Castro and his lieutenants" (Stebbins, 1960: 353)[13] as bearded. The U.S. Information Agency, for example, described Castro as "a bearded, unkempt Cuban revolutionary" who functioned "as a symbol and rallying point for violence in the area" (U.S. Information Agency, 1961: 89). Ernesto (Che) Guevara, one of Castro's "gang," was also described as exercising, or at least attempting to exercise, his "bearded charms" in "influential circles in South America" (Stebbins, 1962: 332). Similarly, *Life* magazine described Castro as "a bearded student of law on a small island" who, shockingly, had managed to "menace an entire hemisphere" ("The menacing push of Castroism," 1961: 82). As a result of the Cuban missile crisis, Clare Boothe Luce asserted in 1963, Castro had been "bumped from the rank of the bearded secular savior of South America, to that of a minor Communist prophet" (1963: 297). As noted earlier, Cuba became a central issue in the 1960 presidential election. Campaigning in the South, vice-presidential candidate Lyndon Johnson "said he knew what to do" about Castro and the Cuban problem: "First he'd take that Castro fellow and wash him. (Cheers.) *And then shave him.* (Cheers.) And then spank him. (Wild cheers.)" (as reported in Halberstam, 1972: 28–29, emphasis added).

The frequent references to the beards sported by Castro and his compatriots were not as irrelevant as they might at first appear. Instead, these descriptions, like the contagion metaphors, rendered "Castro and his gang" (Kennedy, 1960a: 20) unpalatable by conjuring up a set of unpleasant and even threatening associations, especially among middle-class Americans in the early 1960s. For instance, given prevailing standards of acceptable physical appearance, their beardedness connoted unkemptness which, in turn, indicated a general lack of respect for, or a desire to flout, middle-class conventions. This lack of respect for conventional niceties, in turn, implied a lack of responsibility and an unwillingness to act in an accepted civilized fashion.[14] After all, as George Ball reminded the ExComm on October 16, Castro was "obviously erratic and foolish" (in May and Zelikow, 1997: 100). Perhaps the most salient fear was that these bearded revolutionaries, with their uncivilized ways, would completely undermine the very fiber of middle-class—that is, capitalist—society in Cuba (and ultimately, if they were successful, in the rest of Latin America) by nationalizing private property. The use of such descriptions was therefore neither accidental nor irrelevant. U.S. policy makers had been preoccupied with the potential in Latin America for the nationalization of American-owned economic assets. Fears about the nationalization of private property had loomed large for the United States after the "liberation" of Cuba from Spain (Pérez, 1990: chapters 4, 5). It had been a major reason for U.S. sponsorship of the coup that overthrew the constitutionally elected government of Jacobo Arbenz in Guatemala in 1954 (e.g., Immerman, 1982; Schlesinger and Kinzer, 1982). It reemerged as a major issue between the United States and Cuba in May 1959. With the adoption by the Cuban government of the Agrarian Reform Law (Robbins, 1983: 86–91), the issue of the nationalization of and compensation for American-owned economic assets in Cuba—first land holdings and then, in particular, the telephone and electric power companies—had become an important arena of disagreement between the Eisenhower administration and the Cuban revolutionary government. As Rubottom argued in 1960, a major U.S. concern in Latin America was "radical economic transformation in which the private property of the local population as well as foreigners would be seized without compensation and the economy subjugated completely to the control of the state" (Rubottom, 1960: 5). Such actions were unacceptable to the United States because they clearly threatened the capitalist institutions central to the free way of life that the United States was committed to defend. If the nationalization of foreign property was not resisted in Cuba, it was feared, such a policy might prove increasingly attractive to other Latin American states as well. Persistently describing the Cuban revolutionaries as "bearded" reinforced the belief that they were indeed dangerous radicals who posed a serious threat to the free and civilized way of life of the Americas.

I have stressed this relatively minor trope of beardedness for two reasons. First, it indicates that even seemingly trivial descriptions, particularly when they are often repeated, can have significant effects in the construction of meaning. In this case, the repeated mention of Cuban beards helped to construct Castro, the Cuban regime, and the Cuban Revolution as threatening to civilization and, specifically, to the civilized American way of life and its institutions. At the same time, it elided at least one alternative understanding: that the Cuban Revolution was an indigenous attempt to enhance the well-being of the Cuban population by ending its neocolonial economic dependence on the United States.

Second, Castro's beardedness is a good example of the conventional—that is, the contingent and constructed—character of the articulations of the U.S. security imaginary. It provides a particularly good example because Castro and his compatriots were also described as "bearded" within the imaginary of revolutionary Cuba. In this alternative imaginary, however, *barbudos* (bearded ones) "were symbols of the revolution" (Franqui, 1985: 13).[15] The beard represented the hardships that the Cuban revolutionaries had willingly endured while struggling to rid Cuba of Batista; it therefore conferred onto its wearer revolutionary status and legitimacy. The significance of the beard was highlighted in the following anecdote told by Carlos Franqui: Franqui reports that after the revolution he shaved off his beard, whereupon he "ran into Fidel in the National Palace." When Castro saw him without his beard, "he exploded" and asked, "How could you cut off your beard?" Franqui flippantly answered, "The barber did it for me." Castro was apparently not amused, and he replied: "You can't do it. It's a symbol of the revolution. It doesn't belong to you. It belongs to the revolution" (14). Whether or not this story is apocryphal, it does make clear that in the Cuban revolutionary lexicon the "beard" was of great symbolic importance. As Castro told a meeting of the National Press Club in New York in April 1959: "When we finish our jobs we will cut off our beards" (in Robbins, 1983: 83). In contrast to the negative association the beard held within the U.S. security imaginary, its associations in the Cuban revolutionary imaginary were positive. Since it connoted the dedication of the revolutionary and his willingness to suffer hardships for the sake of the revolution, it was valorized in a way diametrically opposed to its articulation within the U.S. security imaginary.[16] (The positive symbolism of the beard in revolutionary Cuban discourse apparently did not go unnoticed by at least some members of the U.S. state and in fact formed the basis for one of the more bizarre, and hilarious, CIA plots against Castro. This plot involved "waiting until Castro left his shoes outside a hotel door to be polished, and then dusting them with thallium salts—a powerful depilatory—so that his hair would fall out." Without his beard, CIA planners apparently thought, "Castro would have neither charisma nor popular support"! Unfortunately for the CIA, Castro canceled the trip during which this "assault on his follicles" was to take place, and the plan was never implemented [Blight, Allyn, and Welch, 1993: 436, note 4; see also Wyden, 1979: 40].)

In addition to the consequences already mentioned, both the metaphor of Fidelism as a communist virus or other disease and the representation of the Cuban revolutionaries as bearded had a further effect on the understanding, within the U.S. security imaginary, of the Cuban missile crisis. Both of these representations reinforced the irrelevance of Cuba as a state or actor, rather than merely as a physical space, to U.S. discussions of the Cuban missile crisis. As I discuss in more detail in the next section, these representations helped to constitute the Castro regime as illegitimate, thus vitiating any need for the United States, during the Cuban missile crisis, to take seriously either the desires and demands expressed by Castro or the sovereignty of the Cuban state. After all, a responsible leader, such as the United States, does not have to be concerned about the preferences of a virus or of an uncivilized bearded revolutionary.

Dr. Castro Betrays the Cuban People

Finally, the construction of the Cuban problem and of the Cuban missile crisis rested heavily on the argument that "Castro and his gang have betrayed the ideals of" the Cuban Revolution, which had initially "reflected the aspirations of the Cuban people" for "individual liberty and free elections" (Kennedy, 1960a: 20), for a "better way of life," and for "the full opportunity to improve their status" on the basis of "free and democratic institutions" (U.S. Department of State, 1960: 3). Indeed, as one historian has pointed out, "the 'revolution betrayed' argument was advanced early and repeated often" and became "the linchpin of the North American propaganda campaign against Cuba" (Pérez, 1990: 249).[17] "The leaders of the revolutionary regime," it was typically argued, "betrayed their own revolution" when they "delivered that revolution into the hands of powers alien to the hemisphere" (U.S. Department of State, 1961b: 1). In response to Cuban charges of U.S. involvement in the Bay of Pigs, for example, Stevenson had attacked the Castro regime, arguing, among other things, that "Dr. Castro chose to embark on a systematic betrayal" of the pledges of the Cuban Revolution and thus "presided over a methodical and shameless corruption of his own revolution" (1961: 670). Even at the outset of a purportedly objective "Chronology of Important Events in United States–Cuban Relations, 1957–1962" prepared by the State Department, it was asserted that, whereas the "U.S. Government attempt[ed] to get along with the Castro regime," the Cuban government persistently demonstrated both "hostility toward the United States and betrayal of the Cuban revolution to international communism" (in U.S. Senate Committee on the Judiciary, 1961b: 896). During the Cuban missile crisis, Rusk explained to the OAS that "this new Soviet intervention means a further tightening of the enslavement of the Cuban people by the Soviet power to which the Castro regime has surrendered the Cuban national heritage" (1962c: 721). And in his public announcement of the Cuban missile crisis, Kennedy charged that Cuba's "nationalist revolution" had been "betrayed" and that Cuba had fallen "under foreign domination." Its leaders were "no longer Cuban leaders inspired by Cuban ideals." Instead, they were "puppets and agents of an international conspiracy" that had turned Cuba against its "friends and neighbors" (1962c: 10).

In contrast to the malevolence ascribed to the Cuban government through these and related representations, expressly positive characteristics were (sometimes)[18] ascribed to the Cuban population. The "Cuban people" were often positioned in stark contrast to the "Castro regime." As a result, the Castro regime was portrayed as without the support of the Cuban people, who continued to share the aspirations of the American family. After all, Castro had "deliberately deceived the Cuban people until he was finally in power and then betrayed their trust by turning Cuba over to the Communists" (U.S. Department of State Bureau of Public Affairs, 1962: 1).

The image of the revolution betrayed accorded with the standard representation in the U.S. security imaginary of the populations of communist-governed countries as enslaved or held captive by, and thus as necessarily opposed to, their puppet governments, who actually served the oriental despots of the Kremlin. According to NSC 68, for example, "the Kremlin's objectives . . . is [sic] the total subjective submission of the peoples now under its control. The concentration camp is the prototype of the society which these policies are designed to achieve" (U.S. National Security Council, 1950: 393). The countries under Soviet control were therefore persistently characterized as being held captive (e.g., U.S. Congress, 1959) by the Soviet Union and "international communism." This enslaved condition was represented as characteristic of all of the "oppressed totalitariat of the Soviet world" (U.S. National Security Council, 1950: 395). Accordingly, then, the United States should oppose communist regimes but should not "make us enemies of the people instead of the evil men who have enslaved them" (392).

In 1960, in a policy statement on Cuba, Eisenhower followed this advice when he described Cuba as "a country with whose people the people of the United States have enjoyed and expect to continue to enjoy a firm and mutually beneficial friendship." He added that the United States was confident that the Cuban people had "the ability . . . to recognize and defeat the intrigues of international communism" (1960a: 135–136). In announcing the severance of U.S. diplomatic relations with Cuba on January 3, 1961, Eisenhower again reassured "the Cuban people" that "our [U.S.] friendship" for them "is not affected." Instead, he continued, "it is my hope and my conviction that in the not too distant future it will be possible for the historic friendship between us once again to find its reflection in normal relations of every sort. Meanwhile, our sympathy goes out to the people of Cuba now suffering under the yoke of a dictator" (1961: 891). In 1962, Rusk argued before the foreign ministers of the OAS that "we have no quarrel with the people of Cuba. As this week we have welcomed a free Dominican Republic back into the inter-American community, so we looked forward to the day when a free and progressive government will flourish in Havana, and the Cuban people can join with us in the common undertakings of the hemisphere" (1962a: 892). In statements such as these, then, the Cuban people are expressly constructed as distinct from the Cuban regime. They are constructed as well, in contrast to their "bearded" leaders, as sharing the same aspirations as all other members of the American family. And because they share the same values and aspirations, they are constructed as the object of U.S. friendship and of legitimate U.S. concern.

Since the Castro regime had betrayed the Cuban people, it followed not only that the Cuban people could be treated as distinct from that regime but that the people themselves were unhappy with and disaffected from it. In a report on Operation Mongoose, Brigadier General Edward Lansdale wrote that "there is evidence that the repressive measures of the Communists, together with disappointments in Castro's economic dependency on the Communist formula, have resulted in an anti-regime atmosphere among the Cuban people which makes a resistance program a distinct and present possibility." Furthermore, he added, the "Cuban people feel helpless and are losing hope fast" (1962: 23). In 1962 Rusk was asked by a reporter, "Is it our [U.S.] information, sir, that considerable anti-Castro sentiment exists in Cuba?" Rusk replied in the affirmative:

I think that that is very definitely our impression and that this is growing, because of the ruthlessness of the regime and the great severity of the regime on the people and their economy and their traditional way of life. I think we know that the Castro regime has great organized support. It has the accouterments of a police state, but it also has underneath it what has happened in so many dictatorships of that sort—deep resentment on the part of the people themselves. (1962b: 597)

To support the distinction between the Castro regime and the Cuban people, the relations between them were consistently represented as antagonistic. This characterization reappeared in full force during the Cuban missile crisis. For example, toward the end of his October 22 speech, which was unusually widely broadcast to "insure maximum Cuban audience for the President's words" (U.S. Information Agency, 1962: 4), Kennedy addressed the "captive" Cuban population directly, saying,

I want to say a few words to the *captive people of Cuba,* to whom this speech is being directly carried by special radio facilities. I speak to you as a friend, as one who knows of your deep attachment to your fatherland, as one who shares *your aspirations for liberty and justice for all.* . . . . I have no doubt that *most Cubans today look forward to the time when they will be truly free*—free from foreign domination, free to choose their own leaders, free to select their own system, free to own their own land, free to speak and write and worship without fear or degradation. And then shall Cuba be welcomed back to the society of free nations and to the associations of this hemisphere. (1962c: 10–11, emphasis added)

In October 1962, immediately after the missile crisis, the State Department again assured the American public that

though it is hard to judge accurately, it is estimated that Castro retains the positive support of only about 20 percent of the population—mostly people under 25 years of age and bureaucrats committed to the success of the revolution. Disaffection is growing steadily, as is shown by the number of disillusioned Cubans fleeing the country and by increasing instances of spontaneous uprisings, anti-government sabotage, and widespread passive resistance. Disaffection is even beginning to grow among those under 25, as well as among the older Cubans. (U.S. Department of State Bureau of Public Affairs, 1962: 4)

Though the opposition of the Cuban people to the Castro regime was treated in the security imaginary as an axiomatic truth—after all, it followed from the assumptions that all people, especially those in the Western Hemisphere, shared the same American aspirations and values and that the Cuban regime, like all totalitarian despotisms, oppressed its population and denied them the fulfillment of these aspirations—it was, in fact, debatable. In early 1961, for example, after the United States broke diplomatic relations with Cuba, a "group of American lawyers said that the Cuban revolution 'has the overwhelming support of the Cuban people'" (Phillips, 1961a: 6). Even Philip Bonsal, former U.S. ambassador to Cuba, has acknowledged that the U.S. perception of popular opposition to the Cuban government was overly influenced by "'our largely anti-Castro informers'" (in Pérez, 1990: 248). According to some commentators, then, the Castro government enjoyed considerable popular support.

Paradoxically, U.S. policy contributed significantly to that support. Jonathan Kwitny, for example, has argued that the "animosity of the United States" formed "the mortar that binds the bricks of the Cuban revolution" (1984: 242). The Bay of Pigs was a significant ingredient in that mortar. At Playa Girón, "Cuba won what most Cubans regard as the most heroic military victory in their history—maybe even in all of Latin American history. The little island nation of about 6 million people . . . overwhelmed and wiped out an invasion force sent by the world's mightiest country." Indeed, "they have watched Goliath attack and get beat. Now Cuba isn't just *any* little guy; it's David, victorious, and the people love it. It has galvanized them as nothing else could have" (219, 242, emphasis in the original). In August 1961, according to a famous report in *Harper's Magazine,* at a farewell party for delegates to the Alliance of Progress conference at Punte del Este, Che Guevara actually asked White House assistant Richard Goodwin to thank Kennedy for the Bay of Pigs invasion. Before the Bay of Pigs, Guevara is reported to have explained, "Castro had held a tenuous grip on the Cuban revolution, with the economy in chaos and numerous internal factions plotting against him. But the invasion, Guevara said jovially, had assured Castro's hold on the country. It had made him even more of a hero, as the man who had defended Cuba against the greatest power in the world" (Branch and Crile, 1975: 61).[19] The U.S. trade embargo, designed in part to foment popular unrest against the Castro government by creating economic hardships, may also have had unexpected and unintended results. Known in Cuba as *el bloqueo* (the blockade), it was resented, at least by many Cubans, for making life for Cubans more difficult (Kwitny, 1984: 264). That resentment was directed not at the Cuban regime but at the United States. As Louis Pérez has argued more generally, "the defense of the [Cuban] revolution became synonymous with the defense of national sovereignty. And once the question of sovereignty was invoked, a deep wellspring of national sentiment was tapped in behalf of the revolution" (1990: 247).[20]

Other repressive or unfashionable measures undertaken by the Cuban government have also been understood by Cubans as responses to U.S. policy and may also have buttressed the domestic reputation of the government that the United States was attempting to topple. As David Detzer has noted, "The CIA's . . . strategy of how to deal with Cuba was to weaken the reputation of Castro's regime. If existence in Cuba turned sour, they believed, Fidel's prestige would inevitably decline. Eventually dissatisfaction would increase to the point where a revolt would occur. Washington's objective, therefore, was to make life unpleasant in Cuba. It devised ingenious ways of doing so" (1979: 34). In addition to a variety of quite bizarre plots to assassinate Castro and other Cuban leaders—that is, to cut out the abscess of Castroism—these ingenious measures included numerous attempts at economic sabotage. For example, CIA agents contaminated Cuban supplies of sugar, Cuba's major export, in the hope that other countries would thereby be discouraged from buying it. They burned fields of sugar cane and sugar warehouses and blew up chemical plants, railroads, and oil refineries (Branch and Crile, 1975: 57–60). They opened boxes of machinery bound for Cuba to "chip off a gear lock on a machine" (unnamed CIA official, in Branch and Crile, 1975, 52). They put "invisible, untraceable chemicals into lubricating fluids" so that diesel engine parts would wear out "faster than they could get replacements." "One of our more sophisticated operations," an unidentified CIA official later explained,

was convincing a ball-bearing manufacturer in Frankfurt, Germany, to produce a shipment of ball bearings off center. Another was to get a manufacturer to do the same with some balanced wheel gears. You're talking about big money when you ask a manufacturer to go along with you on that kind of project because he has to reset his whole mold. And he is probably going to worry about the effect on future business. You might have to pay him several hundred thousand dollars or more. (in Branch and Crile, 1975: 52)

In short, the same CIA official recalled, "We were doing almost anything you could dream up" to sabotage the already fragile Cuban economy (52).[21] All of these tricks were designed to impede Cuban economic activity, thereby making life in Cuba unpleasant and undercutting the legitimacy of the Castro regime with the Cuban people. As Kwitny has reported, however, the Cuban people may not have been fooled by these and other U.S. machinations. Indeed, "people all over Cuba," he noted,

> are fond of pointing out that the Committees for Defense of the Revolution weren't started until five months *after* the Bay of Pigs; that Cuba didn't expropriate U.S.-owned oil refineries until *after* the refinery owners refused to handle oil that Cuba bought from the U.S.S.R. at bargain rates; that Cuba didn't tie its sugar sales to Soviet purchases until *after* the U.S. cut its import quota in reprisal against Cuban policies; and that the U.S. broke relations with Cuba, not the other way around. (1984: 267–268, emphasis in the original)

Many Cubans, in other words, interpreted the hardships and repression in Cuba as the result of U.S. rather than of Cuban actions. Such evidence to the contrary notwithstanding, however, within the U.S. security imaginary the Cuban people were persistently constructed as standing in opposition to the Castro regime. By repeatedly reasserting this opposition, by reinforcing the image of this opposition with a stream of reports on the number of disgruntled Cuban émigrés fleeing to the United States, and by pointing to parallels between the "enslaved Cuban people" and the "oppressed totalitariat" of the Soviet world, the possibility that the Cuban people might support the Cuban regime and oppose U.S. interference was rendered implausible.

At least two significant implications are entailed in this oppositional construction of the Cuban people and the Cuban regime. First, this representation entails the quasi-causal argument that the Cuban regime, rather than reflecting the legitimate aspirations of the people, was instead run by Communists connected through the international communist movement to the Kremlin. It denied that the

Cuban government represented the real wishes of the people and implied instead both that the Cuban leadership was largely a collection of treacherous, malevolent Communists and that the Cuban people were enslaved. This argument, of course, meant that the government that emerged from the Cuban Revolution was illegitimate in the eyes of the Cuban people. It could therefore also be considered illegitimate by the rest of the free world and did not need to be considered representative of the Cuban nation. As a result, Castro's charges during the October crisis, that the United States had violated Cuban sovereignty, could be dismissed. An illegitimate government, after all, should not be allowed to conceal or protect its nefarious doings behind the screen of sovereignty.

Second, the opposition between the Cuban people and the Cuban regime entails a warrant for action. In its leadership of the global battle against world communism, in its defense of freedom, and in its familial role as a leading member of the American family, the United States was obligated both to assist the Cuban people to throw off their chains and to facilitate the realization of their true aspirations. As Senator Mansfield argued in 1960, in the face of acts that "grossly outrage the conscience of the Americas," the "doctrine of non-intervention" is "not adequate to the need" (1960: 99). An illegitimate and malevolent Cuban regime that oppressed its own population was just such a gross outrage. As a result, the actions taken by the United States with respect to Cuba prior to the missile crisis were not aggression against a legitimate state, as had repeatedly been charged by the Soviet Union and Cuba. They were, instead, attempts to defend the legitimate aspirations of the Cuban people for individual liberty and free elections against a malevolent dictatorship under the foreign domination of the Kremlin and its global communist conspiracy. Charges of U.S. aggression against Cuba—such as were leveled in the stories of the Caribbean and October crises— were thus deflected, or rendered unintelligible, by representing Cuba as without a legitimate national government that could truly exercise sovereignty.

THE UNITED STATES AND CUBA

The general representation of the Cuban problem and the more specific renderings of Castro, the Cuban regime, the Cuban Revolution, and the Cuban people further defined for U.S. state officials the nature of the situation they faced in October 1962 and so contributed to the production of the Cuban missile crisis itself. In fact, as Paterson has suggested,

> The origins of the missile crisis . . . derived largely from United States–Cuban tensions. To stress only the global dimension of Soviet-American competition, as is commonly done, is like saying that a basketball game can be played without a court. Cuba was the court. To slight the local or regional sources of the conflict is to miss a central point: Nikita Khrushchev would never have had the opportunity to begin his dangerous missile game if Kennedy had not been attempting to expunge Castro and his revolution from the hemisphere. (1989: 140–141)

The invocation of objects such as the "Trojan horse" of Soviet and "communist" "aggression" and of quasi-causal arguments such as "Dr. Castro's betrayal of the Cuban people" provided a more detailed representation of the situation faced by the United States in October 1962.

This construction of Cuba and U.S.-Cuban relations contributed to the creation of a particular understanding of the Cuban missile crisis and the U.S. national interest, most notably by ruling out alternative interpretations. For example, with the Cuban regime and the Cuban people represented as antagonists, the Cuban missile crisis could not be understood as the product of U.S. aggression against Cuba, with the result that Soviet claims to be defending Cuba and the invocation by the Cuban government of its right to self-defense were literally rendered meaningless. After all, there was nothing to defend against. By contrasting the malignant Castro regime with the legitimate aspirations of the Cuban people for freedom, what might have been understood as U.S. aggression against Cuba—such as closing U.S. markets to Cuban sugar, breaking diplomatic relations with Cuba, promoting a trade embargo against Cuba, and sponsoring the Bay of Pigs invasion—were transformed instead into attempts to assist the Cuban people to liberate themselves from the yoke of a dictator. This, of course, coincided with the image, made commonsensical by the U.S. security imaginary, of the United States as a nation that defends freedom and national independence against foreign aggression and communist subversion.

In addition, the alternative understanding typically presented by

Castro—that as a sovereign state the Cuban government had the right to ask a friendly state for military assistance and that the U.S. response was a violation of Cuban sovereignty—was also rendered nonsensical in two ways. First, since Castro and the Cuban regime were in fact Soviet puppets—and bearded, infectious puppets at that—they were not a legitimate Cuban government. Their illegitimacy, in turn, meant that they could not claim sovereignty for their decisions and actions. Second, since the Cuban regime clearly oppressed the Cuban people, it could not claim to represent the Cuban nation. In fact, the construction of the object the "Castro regime" implicitly represents the Cuban government as defending itself not from U.S. aggression but ultimately from a possible revolt by those Cuban people whose aspirations for freedom it had betrayed. Again, then, it could not claim to be truly sovereign and therefore could not successfully assert its sovereignty in the face of U.S. objections. The illegitimacy of the Castro regime meant that its desires and its protestations were irrelevant. They could thus safely be, and indeed should have been, disregarded. In both of these ways, the representation of the Cuban problem helps to explain why Cuba was virtually invisible both during the Cuban missile crisis and in the subsequent mythical retelling of the events of October 1962.

6

Identity and National Interests: The United States as the Subject of the Cuban Missile Crisis

The mere existence of an alternative mode of being, the presence of which exemplifies that different identities are possible and thus denaturalizes the claim of a particular identity to be the *true identity, is sometimes enough to produce the understanding of a threat.*

— DAVID CAMPBELL, WRITING SECURITY

THE U.S. SECURITY IMAGINARY AND U.S. IDENTITY

At the center of the vision of the world constructed through the U.S. security imaginary is a particular understanding of the object or, more accurately, the subject "the United States." A now classic story from the ExComm meetings nicely illustrates the importance of U.S. identity to the construction of the U.S. national interest in the Cuban missile crisis:[1] During debate over the possibility of launching an unannounced air strike against the missile bases in Cuba, Robert Kennedy is reported to have written a note in which he claimed that "I now know how Tojo felt when he was planning Pearl Harbor" (in Schlesinger, 1965: 803). Later in the discussion, Schlesinger reported, Robert Kennedy insisted that

> he did not believe that, with all the memory of Pearl Harbor and all the responsibility we would have to bear in the world afterward, the President of the United States could possibly order such an operation. *For 175 years we had not been that kind of country. Sunday-morning surprise blows on small nations were not in our tradition.*

Thousands of Cubans would be killed without warning, and hundreds of Russians too. We were fighting for something more than survival, and *a sneak attack would constitute a betrayal of our heritage and our ideals.* (806–807, emphasis added)

On October 18, George Ball reiterated this sentiment: "Mr. President," he said,

I think that it's easy, sitting here, to underestimate the kind of sense of a funk that you have in the allied countries within—even perhaps in Latin America, if we act without warning, without giving Khrushchev some way out. Even though it may be illusory, I think we still have to do it [give some warning], because I think that the impact on the opinion and the reaction would be very much different than a course of action where we strike without warning, that's like Pearl Harbor. It's the kind of conduct that one might expect of the Soviet Union. *It is not the conduct that one expects of the United States.* (in May and Zelikow, 1997: 143)

As Robert Kennedy put it shortly thereafter, "it's the whole question of . . . what kind of a country we are" (in May and Zelikow, 1997: 149). More accurately, perhaps, the use of the Pearl Harbor analogy underscored for U.S. decision makers what kind of subject the United States was *not*—that is, it was not a country whose values and traditions would countenance an unannounced "sneak attack"—and, as a result, certain policy options were effectively foreclosed. The surprise air strike against Cuba was shelved, at least in the short term.

The identity of "the United States," and specific arguments about what sort of subject "the United States" was or was not, were not, however, used simply to score debating points during policy discussions among U.S. state officials. Rather, that identity was always central to the postwar U.S. security imaginary and so to U.S. analyses of international politics, to U.S. foreign policy, and to U.S. national interests. One primary function of any social imaginary is to define an identity, to define "the being of the group and of the collectivity" (Castoriadis, 1987: 147). According to Castoriadis, "every human being defines himself or herself and is defined for others in relation to an 'us.' But this 'us,' this group, this society—what is it, who is it? It is, first of all, a symbol, the insignias of existence that every tribe, every city, every society has always ascribed to itself. Above all it is, of course, a name" (147–148). In the case of a security imaginary in particular, the central identity being defined is that of the subject being secured. For the postwar U.S. security imaginary, this subject was the United States. It was this identity or subject position—constructed under the name "the United States"—that tied the various objects and quasi-causal arguments discussed in preceding chapters together into a more or less coherent vision of the world of international politics. The U.S. subject position, in other words, was the linchpin of the U.S. security imaginary, it resided at the heart of the so-called Cuban missile crisis, and it was central to the definition of U.S. national interests in that crisis. At the same time, through the process of interpellation, this U.S. identity legitimized U.S. policy decisions and helped to ensure their reception as common sense. U.S. identity, that is, made sense of the orthodox U.S. representation of the Cuban missile crisis and so of the U.S. national interest in that crisis. Four constitutive features of U.S. identity—U.S. leadership, its defense of freedom, its need for strength, and its persistent credibility problem—were particularly salient to the postwar U.S. security imaginary and so to the representation of the Cuban missile crisis.

The Burdens of Leadership

Since World War II, the U.S. position as leader and the attendant responsibilities and obligations have simply been taken for granted. The United States has consistently been represented as the leader of the West and the free world, as the global champion of freedom and democracy. This U.S. leadership role was forcefully asserted in NSC 68: "The absence of order among nations," its authors argued, "is becoming less and less tolerable" and "this fact imposes upon us [the United States], in our own [U.S.] interests, the responsibility of world leadership" (U.S. National Security Council, 1950: 390). Two assumptions were typically adduced to support the claim to U.S. leadership. First, it was treated as axiomatic that the United States had won World War II and that this victory imposed upon it the awesome responsibility of creating "half a world, the free half" in its image (Acheson, 1969a: "Apologia pro libre hoc"). In 1945 Truman had already announced that "whether we like it or not, we must all recognize that the victory which we have won has placed upon the American people the continued burden of responsibility for world leadership" (1945: 549). As a result of the successful outcome of

World War II, that is, the United States had been forced, however reluctantly, to shoulder the burden of global leadership. Second, the exceptional character of the United States also saddled it with this burden. The uniqueness of the United States resided in its free society, which provided the rest of the world with an outstanding model of the way in which free institutions and the free way of life could develop and flourish. This uniqueness, in turn, conferred upon the United States the "right to the moral leadership of this planet" (Kennedy, in Lundestad, 1989: 527). Indeed, as the authors of NSC 68 argued, the United States had the obligation to "demonstrate power, confidence and a sense of moral and political direction" so that these same qualities could blossom around the world (U.S. National Security Council, 1950: 404). In short, then, as Kennedy concisely put it in 1961, "our [U.S.] strength as well as our [U.S.] convictions have impressed upon this nation the role of leader in freedom's cause" (1961f: 396).

The representation of the United States as world leader in freedom's cause entailed a number of significant consequences for U.S. identity. First, the notion of "leadership" clearly provided a warrant for action. It is expected, quite simply, that a leader *will act*. Leaders who fail to act, who remain passive, hesitate, or dawdle, forsake their leadership position. Second, a leader is expected both to determine when action is required and to suggest the correct course of action. To do so, of course, a leader must define both when action is required and what classes of action are appropriate and inappropriate under the circumstances. In particular, a leader must identify threats and then propose ways to counter them. These tasks confer on a leader the "right to moral leadership," the "right" to set the standards against which threats and appropriate policy responses are measured. Third, the leader is not only permitted to fulfill these functions but is, indeed, obligated to do so. The leadership role, in other words, carries with it not only rights and privileges but duties and obligations; it carries with it what Truman called the "burden of responsibility." Just as the "white man's burden" had imposed upon the British the obligation to bring Anglo-Saxon civilization to the backward and often barbaric "natives" residing within its empire, so global leadership conferred upon the U.S. the burden of preserving and promoting freedom, democracy, and order. In the context of the cold war, bearing the burden of leadership responsibility meant, of course, that the United States was obligated to defend democracy, freedom, national independence, and order from the inevitable assaults of totalitarian despotism and the international communist conspiracy. Furthermore, as discussed in chapter 4, the United States had a traditional and special obligation, articulated in the Monroe Doctrine and its extensions, to establish, preserve, and promote freedom in the Western Hemisphere. This obligation, reinforced through the American family metaphor, was especially salient during the Cuban missile crisis. As Rusk argued in the ExComm, in the face of the Soviet missile deployment in Cuba, the United States had an "obligation to do what has to be done" (Rusk, October 16: 173).

These three corollaries of leadership brought with them a fourth. Since U.S. leadership entailed obligations or burdens of responsibility, U.S. decisions and actions could be understood as, at least in part, disinterested. The rhetoric of "*burdens* of responsibility" implies that these obligations, which are (at least in part) voluntarily assumed as the unavoidable concomitant of leadership, constitute an encumbrance and a cost to the leader. When the United States engaged in global leadership, then, it was acting in part altruistically rather than strictly for its own gain. The altruism implied in the representation of U.S. leadership responsibilities as burdens is captured in the notion of U.S. commitments. Within the security imaginary, what might otherwise be understood as U.S. intervention has typically been described in terms of commitments: In virtue of its leadership, the United States contracted commitments to defend freedom and national independence, to protect its allies in NATO, SEATO, ANZUS, and the OAS, and to counter communist aggression in, for instance, Korea, Ma-tsu and Quemoy, Laos, South Vietnam, Guatemala, and, of course, Cuba. One implication of the term "commitment" is that these obligations are partially other-regarding: Commitments are pledges or promises that their maker is bound to honor, even if they bring with them significant costs.[2]

Distinctions between U.S. commitments and the self-interested actions of other states pervaded U.S. discussions both of the cold war with international communism and of the Cuban missile crisis. They construct the United States as an objective, largely disinterested and other-regarding subject. For example, in a discussion of the global struggle with international communism in which the missile crisis took place, Sorensen claimed that in "situations in the new and developing nations which Khrushchev somewhat hypocritically called 'wars of liberation,'" such as in the Congo, Laos, and South Vietnam, the "extent of *U.S. commitment* and of *Communist power involvement* differed from one to the other" (1965: 634, emphasis added). Attributing "power involvements" to "Communists" and "commitment" to the United States implied that Communists were engaged in aggression for the sake of self-interested gain, in particular imperial expansion, whereas the United States was merely fulfilling, in an other-regarding fashion, the burdens of a leader.

The implications of this distinction are clear: Commitments made by leaders such as the United States are legitimate; the power involvements of Communists are not. As Eisenhower proclaimed in response to Khrushchev's promise in 1960 to assist Cuba against future U.S. aggression,

> The Inter-American system has declared itself . . . beginning with the Rio Treaty, as opposed to any such [Soviet] *interference.* We are *committed* to uphold those agreements. I affirm in the most emphatic terms that the United States will not be deterred from *its responsibilities* by the *threats* Mr. Khrushchev is making. Nor will the United States, in conformity with its *treaty obligations,* permit the establishment of a regime dominated by international Communism in the Western Hemisphere. (1960e: 568, emphasis added)

Here Soviet involvement with Cuba was constituted as "interference" and its assurance to Cuba was constituted as "threats"; U.S. assurances to its allies, treaty partners, and sister republics, on the other hand, were constructed as commitments, "responsibilities," and "obligations." The rhetoric of the burdens of leadership borne by the United States thus reinforces the understanding of the United States as a subject that acts defensively, not aggressively.

According to this logic, U.S. leadership and its burdens of responsibility help to make sense of the claims, made throughout the missile crisis, that U.S. extraterritorial missile deployments were (necessarily) defensive and not to be compared with the (necessarily) offensive missile installations that the Soviet Union had established in Cuba. The Soviet missile deployments were undertaken secretly and treacherously by a despotic totalitarian regime and they were thus, by definition, aggressive and illegitimate. Indeed, they were a "provocation" that challenged U.S. leadership and an example of "attempted nuclear blackmail" (Sorensen, 1965: 700, 706). U.S. missiles in Turkey, on the other hand, had been installed as part of a U.S. commitment to defend its NATO allies against communist, and specifically Soviet, aggression. As Kennedy reminded his audience on October 22, "our own [U.S.] strategic missiles have never been transferred to the territory of any other nation under a cloak of secrecy and deception" (1962c: 5). Their deployment was therefore legitimate. In consequence, the U.S. and NATO missiles were not to be compared to the Soviet missiles in Cuba—the symmetry between them was merely "superficial" (Welch and Blight, 1987–88: 13)— and could not be used, during the Cuban missile crisis, to justify in-action on the part of the free world's leader. The do-nothing response to the Soviet missile deployment in Cuba was ruled out by the various corollaries of the assumption of U.S. leadership.

Fifth and finally, during the Cuban missile crisis the construction of the United States as the hemispheric and global leader with both a moral obligation and formal commitments to defend freedom elided any view of U.S. actions as intervention in the affairs of a sovereign Cuba. It also obscured what might have been understood as the domination of Cuba entailed in the U.S. response to the Soviet missile deployment, in the U.S. demand that the missiles and other military resources be removed, and in the U.S. assumption of the right to keep Cuba under surveillance to assure that these U.S. demands had been met. These alternative understandings were ruled out by transforming into common sense the claim, made during the missile crisis, that U.S. history, "unlike that of the Soviets since the end of World War II, demonstrates that we have no desire to dominate or conquer any other nation or impose our system upon its people" (Kennedy, 1962c: 5). Because of the construction of the United States as a leader, this claim made sense, even in the face of the many overt military and covert U.S. interventions around the world between 1945 and 1962.[3]

General C. P. Cabell, deputy director of the CIA, provided an argument in 1959 that parallels the U.S. understanding of the difference between the extraterritorial missile deployments of the United States and the U.S.S.R. and helps to explain the U.S. understanding of the Cuban problem. Trading on two different notions of bases, he argued that the Communists "have developed a network of subversive bases in all major countries of the world. From these bases they are now operating an offensive designed to cut down and overthrow the democratic institutions and governments of the host and neighboring countries. They are operating from these subversive bases without permission of the host country." These communist bases "represent an inherent part of the Communist scheme and . . . are on the attack with every means at their disposal." He then argued that "in spite of this fact, the Communists clamor about American military bases abroad." However, as Cabell made clear, the two kinds of bases were in no way comparable for, as everyone knew, unlike the bases of the Communists, "Our [U.S.] bases are defensive." U.S. military bases abroad "are there with the permission of the duly constituted governments of the areas." Furthermore, "Their presence, in many cases, strengthens the economy of the countries in which they are located and certainly strengthens the defenses of these countries" (1959: 752). Whereas Soviet or communist bases are by definition designed for aggression and subversion, U.S. bases, quite altruistically, provide services for others; specifically, they strengthen both the economies and the defenses of those states privileged by their presence.

At the heart of the U.S. security imaginary, then, was a U.S. identity defined in part by the burdens of leadership it had shouldered. Defining the United States as the leader of the free world provided warrants for and legitimized the prominent, indeed unilateral, U.S. role in deciding that the Soviet missiles in Cuba were a threat, in defining the nature of the threat that they posed, in determining the range of appropriate policy responses (in this case military action over diplomacy or inaction), and even in unilaterally implementing the specific policy that it claimed most clearly served the interests of the free world, the American family, and the betrayed people of Cuba. Given this U.S. identity, it is hardly surprising that "leadership" in the Cuban missile crisis was considered "inevitably" to have fallen "in large degree on the United States" (Stevenson, 1962a: 728). Because of its self-styled leadership in ordering the postwar world and in defining and defending the freedom and the independence of nations in the Western Hemisphere, it was true by assumption that the United States legitimately bore the responsibility for managing the missile crisis—for imposing a meaning on the Soviet missiles in Cuba, for determining the appropriate course of action in response to those missiles, and for implementing that policy decision.

Though the implications of ascribing to the United States the identity of "global leader" are easily discovered, it is not yet clear from this discussion why "our strength" and "our convictions" should, as Kennedy argued they did, "have impressed upon" the United States these global leadership responsibilities to begin with (1961f: 396). After all, these same virtues might have prompted an inward turn in which U.S. strength was used to protect its territorial integrity, the better to foster the internal development of its liberal convictions and its liberal domestic institutions. That is, U.S. strength and U.S. convictions might have led to what Hunt has called an "introverted" rather than to an "extroverted" vision of U.S. "national greatness" (1987: chapter 2). In the postwar era, the transformation of U.S. strength and U.S. convictions into an extroverted vision of U.S. national greatness in which the United States came necessarily to inhabit the role of *global* leadership was legitimized through the more specific meanings articulated to U.S. "convictions," particularly its commitment to freedom.

"The Land of the Free . . ."

Central to the identity of the United States, and the major reason for its leadership role, was its articulation to freedom. Within the security imaginary, the United States was represented as unique; it was an exceptional society because of its unprecedented development of liberty. It was a society in which the virtue of freedom and its attendant institutions—in particular, representative or liberal democracy and a liberal market economy—had been more elaborately and more successfully developed than in any other. Its tradition of freedom and liberty meant that it had a "sense of moral and political direction" (U.S. National Security Council, 1950: 404), which conferred on it a leadership role. The United States thus could and should serve as a model or guide (a standard denotation of leader) to all those who aspired to a similar life.

The U.S. identity as the model, and indeed the patron, of freedom was constituted both in explicit claims made about the United States and in the oppositions in which this U.S. identity was contrasted with others. In the first case, the United States was explicitly defined as the patron of freedom. For example, Kennedy asserted in 1961 that "our nation is on the side of man's desire to be free, and the desire of nations to be independent" (1961e: 369). "We stand for freedom," he asserted (1961f: 396), and "we stand, as we have always stood from our earliest beginnings, for the independence and equality of all nations" (397). Similarly, Wymberley Coerr, then deputy assistant secretary for inter-American affairs, asserted in 1961 that

> our objective toward the nations of Latin America is simple: We want the friendship of their governments and peoples. . . . We seek no satellites. We control no fifth columns or traitorous domestic parties with which to convert independent nations into satellites. We cherish the independence of the nations in this hemisphere as the key to their friendship for us, recognizing that it would suffer from undue exertions of our influence and that under Soviet domination it would die. (U.S. Department of State, 1961a: 1)

As this example already begins to indicate, in the second case the U.S. identity was defined in opposition to its enemies. The prevailing representation of the Soviet and communist adversaries of the United States contributed significantly to the production of U.S. identity. By defining its adversary as a totalitarian regime that enslaved its subject populations, for instance, it was implied that the United States, in contrast, was a democratic state that acted to free rather than enslave others. By defining its adversary, on the model of "Red Fascism," as a totalitarian regime that engaged in persistent secret treachery, the United States was constructed as engaged in open rather than secret diplomacy, as forthright and trustworthy rather than treacherous, and as using force only defensively. The security imaginary, then, identified the United States as an accomplished free nation, as the model of freedom, free institutions, and the free way of life, by explicitly assigning these virtues to the United States and by contrasting it with adversaries characterized by the corresponding vices.

It was not only true that the United States could serve as a model or guide to other societies in search of freedom. In addition, it was assumed that in order for the United States both to preserve its own unique freedoms and successfully to serve as a guide to others, it must "foster a world environment in which the American system can survive and flourish" (U.S. National Security Council, 1950: 401). This meant that the protection of its own exceptional free society required that it guarantee a suitable world order. That the need to protect its own free society required the United States to protect freedom globally stemmed from the axiom that freedom is indivisible:

A threat to freedom anywhere is a threat to freedom everywhere. In 1950, for example, Truman justified U.S. participation in the Korean War on these grounds: "We cannot hope to maintain our own freedom," he argued, "if freedom elsewhere is wiped out" (1950a: 610). In 1959, during the Berlin crisis, Eisenhower assured West Berliners that "we recognize that *freedom is indivisible*. Wherever in the world freedom is destroyed, by that much is every free nation hurt" (1959b: 30, emphasis added). As a result, as Kennedy asserted, "every time a country, regardless of how far away it may be from our own borders—every time that country passes behind the Iron Curtain the security of the United States is thereby endangered" (1963: 727). The indivisibility of freedom obligated the United States to "promot[e] a world order" (Kennan, in Gaddis, 1982: 27) in which freedom could flourish. In addition to its own exceptional status as the model of freedom, then, U.S. identity required that the United States promote freedom anywhere and everywhere. "Exporting democracy" to Latin America and elsewhere thus came to be seen as "a legitimate and significant goal of U.S. foreign policy" (Lowenthal, 1991: vii).

The quasi-causal "indivisibility of freedom" argument and its implications for U.S. leadership played a significant role in the orthodox U.S. representation of the Cuban missile crisis. In addressing the continued danger presented by the Castro regime in Cuba, for example, Kennedy argued in the aftermath of the Bay of Pigs disaster that "we intend to profit from this lesson. . . . We intend to intensify our efforts for a struggle in many ways more difficult than war. . . . *I am determined upon our system's survival and success*, regardless of the cost and regardless of the peril!" (1961d: 306, emphasis added). The "survival and success" of the U.S. "system" were at stake in Cuba not, as Kennedy himself admitted, because "a nation of Cuba's size" (305) was a direct threat to the United States. Instead, the U.S. system's "survival and success" were at stake in Cuba because it served as "a base for subverting the survival of other free nations throughout the hemisphere." As a result, Kennedy argued, "It is not primarily our interest or our security but theirs which is now, today, in the great peril. It is for their sake as well as our own that we must show our will." In short, "the real issue" in Cuba was "the survival of freedom in this hemisphere itself" (305). Because freedom is indivisible, a threat to freedom anywhere, even in "a nation of Cuba's size," was a threat to freedom everywhere, including the entire Western Hemisphere and the United States itself. The Cuban problem, then, posed a threat to the very identity of the United States: It threatened its status as the patron of global freedom, and it ultimately threatened the United States itself as the model of a free society. The quasi-causal argument asserting the indivisibility of freedom rendered Castro's regime, and communism anywhere in the Western Hemisphere, nonnegotiable.

The United States could sensibly be represented as the patron of freedom outside its own borders not only because of the indivisibility of freedom but also because it was a fundamental tenet of the U.S. security imaginary that others shared with the United States its commitment to freedom, defined according to the liberal U.S. model. If the peoples of other nations were not fortunate enough to enjoy the same freedoms and the same free institutions, it could readily be assumed that they aspired to do so. This was particularly true of the American republics, whose peoples were represented as sharing a common heritage and common values with the United States (see chapter 4). Latin Americans were assumed to "set the highest value on freedom," to "believe that this freedom is best assured by the effective exercise of representative democracy" (Rubottom, 1960: 3), and to believe in and aspire to liberal economic institutions, that is, to "economic as well as political freedom" (4). In short, they shared "the values of American civilization" (Kennedy, 1961b: 396). The Cuban people (see chapter 5) were also assumed to share these "aspirations for liberty and justice for all" (Kennedy, 1962c: 10). On the assumption that the values that the United States labeled freedom and liberty and the desire for institutions of representative democracy and a liberal market economy were common to all Americans, Eisenhower argued in 1960 that "the key" to U.S. policy in Latin America, as elsewhere, was "the right to choose," because "human beings everywhere, simply as an inalienable right of birth, should have freedom to choose their guiding philosophy, their form of government, their methods of progress" (1960c: 220). U.S. leadership in defense of freedom therefore required, as had been institutionalized in the Monroe Doctrine and its successors, that the United States oppose what it considered "intervention in the internal affairs of an American state," defined as any situation in which "any power, whether by invasion, coercion or subversion, succeeded in denying freedom of choice to the people of any of our sister republics" (220;

see also Eisenhower, 1960d: 468). Since it could safely be assumed that all peoples, and especially those in the American family, aspired to the same liberal values and institutions, the establishment of communist institutions, such as those purportedly being developed in Cuba after the revolution, was an explicit and obvious denial of this inalienable right to choose. On the assumption of shared American values, it was literally unthinkable that the Cuban people might themselves freely choose an alternative definition of freedom or alternative institutional arrangements. It was thus on the basis of this quasi-causal argument—that, since all peoples shared the same American values and the same aspirations, communist institutions were necessarily illegitimate and, where they existed, had been imposed against the will of the people—that U.S. leadership and its responsibility for establishing and maintaining a suitable world order were seen not to clash with the principle of nonintervention. U.S. support for anti-Castro forces, its attempts to isolate Cuba economically and diplomatically, and, finally, its stance during the missile crisis could have been understood as illegitimate intervention in Cuban affairs. They were instead narrated as consistent both with global U.S. leadership in protecting freedom and national independence and with the legitimate aspirations of the Cuban people themselves.

". . . and the Home of the Brave"

A third constitutive feature of U.S. identity defined it as "the home of the brave." This representation attributed to the United States the twin virtues of strength, or physical capabilities, and will, or moral courage and resolve, thus constituting the United States as an emphatically masculine identity. U.S. bravery, or the possession of both strength and will, were, of course, also important sources of U.S. leadership. As Kennedy had said, it is not only "our [U.S.] convictions" but also "our [U.S.] strength" that "impose" upon the United States its leadership position (1961f: 396). U.S. strength helped to create and justify U.S. leadership quite simply because strength was needed to combat the totalitarian adversary. As General Eisenhower explained in 1945, "A weakling, particularly a rich and opulent weakling, seeking peaceable solution of a difficulty, is likely to invite contempt; but the same plea from the strong is listened to most respectfully" (1945: 109). During World War II, the United States had in fact demonstrated that it was strong, and in the aftermath of

World War II no other state had been left with comparable strength. The stage was thus set for U.S. leadership. But strength itself was not enough. In addition, the will, or the moral courage, to use that strength was needed as well. Again, the U.S. commitment to its allies in World War II had demonstrated that the U.S. possessed the courage to use its strength in the defense of freedom.

Having acquired this leadership role, the United States had, for at least two reasons, explicitly to maintain both its strength and its will. First, they were required because of the indivisibility of freedom. If an attack on freedom anywhere is an attack on freedom everywhere, then the United States, with its leadership responsibilities, had to be prepared to meet any such attack. Second, both strength and will were required because of the specific character of the totalitarian aggressor. Its penchant for salami-slicing tactics and the related danger of appeasement meant that strength and courage were necessities; weakness would only invite further aggression. In 1961, in the midst of the global U.S. battle with international communism that provided the setting for the Cuban missile crisis, Kennedy reiterated the importance of strength and courage:

> The message of Cuba, of Laos, of the rising din of Communist voices in Asia and Latin America—these messages are all the same. *The complacent, the self-indulgent, the soft societies* are about to be swept away with the debris of history. Only *the strong,* only the industrious, only *the determined,* only *the courageous,* only the visionary who determine the real nature of our struggle can possibly survive. (1961d: 306, emphasis added)

Similarly, later in 1961 during the conflict with the Soviet Union over West Berlin, Kennedy again argued that the United States had to demonstrate both strength and will: "We need the capability of placing in any critical area at the appropriate time a force which, combined with those of our allies, is large enough to make clear our determination and our ability to defend our rights at all costs—and to meet all levels of aggressor pressure with whatever levels of force are required" (1961g: 535). As noted earlier, this argument was prominent during the missile crisis as well. Stevenson argued before the United Nations on October 23 that "if we do not stand firm here, our adversaries may think that we will stand firm nowhere—and we guarantee a heightening of the world civil war to new levels of intensity and danger" (1962a: 733). Even a small slice off the salami, in other words, required that the United States, bearing the burdens of leadership, show both strength and resolve. Having shouldered the burden of leadership, that is, the nature of freedom (specifically, its indivisibility) and the nature of totalitarianism (specifically, its insatiable aggressiveness) required that the United States continuously demonstrate both its strength and its will. U.S. identity, then, was not only masculine but aggressively macho. The fear of appearing weak—whether of arms or of will—loomed large, since weakness, a feminine characteristic, would excite not the requisite respect but only contempt. U.S. identity was thus constructed not only in opposition to the external other of secretive and duplicitous totalitarians but also in opposition to an internal, feminine other defined as weak, soft, complacent, and self-indulgent. As a result, the United States not only had to be strong, courageous, determined, and firm, it also had repeatedly to reenact these characteristics.

Though strength and will were always central constitutive features of this masculinized U.S. identity, the rhetoric of strength was unusually prominent just before the Cuban missile crisis and in some ways set the tone for that crisis. This was in part a consequence of the Bay of Pigs, which had become "a virtual synonym for international humiliation" (Branch and Crile, 1975: 49). Because of the misadventure at the Bay of Pigs, the Republican senatorial and congressional campaign committees had already announced that Cuba would be "the dominant issue of the 1962 campaign" (Sorensen, 1965: 670). In the course of that campaign, William P. Miller, the chairman of the Republican National Committee, took a poke at Kennedy's "most sensitive spot" (Nathan, 1975: 263), the Bay of Pigs and U.S.-Cuban relations, arguing that "if we were asked to state the issue in one word, that word would be Cuba—symbol of the tragic irresolution of the Administration" ("Notes of the month," 1962: 453). As a result of the administration's humiliation at the Bay of Pigs and the attendant charges of irresolution, the situation was such that "while outside [of the White House] everyone spoke of Camelot," the word "most bandied about inside the Kennedy Administration was *tough*" (Branch and Crile, 1975: 60, emphasis in the original). Within the context of domestic U.S. politics, the toughness of Kennedy and of his Democratic administration thus became a dominant theme. Furthermore, Kennedy had also been particularly concerned over his image in Khrushchev's eyes. Since the Bay of Pigs, as Detzer described it, "if Khrushchev thought him timid, Kennedy worried, Russia might become more aggressive. And if that happened, the United States might have to go to war. As with legendary gunfighters, so long as a President had a reputation for toughness, he might avoid serious conflict. The opposite also seemed to be true. His inaction during the Bay of Pigs, Kennedy thought, might lead to trouble" (1979: 33). This preoccupation with toughness was captured in the cowboy metaphor that was apparently common among the clandestine forces employed by the Kennedy administration to overthrow Castro or, at least, to destabilize the Castro regime. In describing the role played by paramilitary forces in the CIA intrigues against Cuba and Castro, Ray Cline, then CIA deputy director for intelligence, noted, "You need to understand the national consensus of the 1950s and '60s, when we believed the world was a tough place filled with actual threats of subversion by other countries. The Russians had cowboys around everywhere, and that meant we had to get ourselves a lot of cowboys if we wanted to play the game. You've got to have cowboys" (in Branch and Crile, 1975: 57).

Although the Kennedy administration seems to have had a particular obsession with appearing tough, it should be emphasized that this preoccupation with toughness had already been established as an outstanding feature of the postwar U.S. security imaginary. As Nathan has pointed out, "The missile crisis illuminates a feature of the American character that came to be considered a requisite personality trait of the cold war." This requisite personality trait was "toughness" (1975: 267). The rhetoric of U.S. strength or toughness thus much preceded the Cuban missile crisis and the Kennedy administration. In 1958, for example, John Lodge had argued that strength was necessary because, as the world had learned through Munich and its aftermath, "peace is in sober truth a product of strength, war is a derivative of weakness" (1958: 68). In 1960 Eisenhower proclaimed that it was "America's might" that served as "an anchor of free-world security" (1960b: 462). In his inaugural address, Kennedy had sounded the same theme with the following famous words: "Let every nation know, whether it wishes us well or ill, that we shall pay any price, bear any burden, meet any hardship, support any friend, oppose any foe to assure the survival and the success of liberty. . . . We dare not tempt them with weakness. For only when our arms are sufficient, beyond all doubt, can we be certain that they will never be employed" (1961a: 13–14). This "persistent national preoccupation with military preparedness" (Klare, 1989: 141), with toughness, strength, and will, was thus a characteristic feature of the postwar U.S. subject position.

The persistent concern for U.S. toughness, strength, and will, both prior to and within the Kennedy administration, contributed significantly to the U.S. interpretation of the Cuban missile crisis and the U.S. national interest. During the early ExComm discussions it quickly became clear that the United States could not afford to allow Cuba to be seen as its equal. Allowing the Soviet missiles to remain in Cuba, Kennedy said on October 16, "makes them [the Cubans] look like they're coequal with us [the United States] and that . . ." And Dillon concluded for him, that "we're scared of the Cubans" (October 16: 186). Such a perception would be intolerable because the continuation of U.S. leadership required the maintenance of U.S. strength and the perception of U.S. resolve. According to Alsop and Bartlett's analysis of the missile crisis, Khrushchev had set a "trap" for the United States. "The objective of the trap was both political and strategic. If the trap had been successful, our missile warning system would have been by-passed and the whole strategic balance overturned. But the President and most of his advisors put the main emphasis on the political objective. 'If they'd got away with this one,' says one member of ExComm, 'we'd have been a paper tiger, a second-class power.'" (1962: 18). The Cuban missile crisis, that is, raised questions about U.S. strength, toughness, and will and thus challenged both the global and the hemispheric leadership of the United States by threatening to reduce the United States to, or to expose it as, a "paper tiger." I. F. Stone's description of the missile crisis reiterates this theme. According to Stone, "The question was whether, with the whole world looking on, Kennedy would let Khrushchev get away with it. The world's first thermonuclear confrontation turned out to be a kind of ordeal by combat between two men to see which one would back down first" (1966: 12). A central aspect of the missile crisis, then, was the macho test of wills, of toughness, between Kennedy and Khrushchev and between the states they represented. To preserve its leadership, the United States had to win this test of toughness. In a perhaps extreme but nonetheless telling display of this preoccupation with toughness, Dean Rusk, in an excess of machismo, reportedly said on October 18, "If we don't do this we go down with a whimper. Maybe it's better to go down with a bang" (in Abel, 1966: 70). It was not possible, according to this view, simply to ignore the Soviet missile deployment, for to do so would have put U.S. toughness in doubt, undermined the U.S. leadership position, and thus transformed the United States into a second-class power, a paper tiger.

The U.S. identity required the maintenance of strength and courage, but it also implied that this strength should worry only aggressive, totalitarian states. After all, "no other country fears a strong America." In fact, "no decent preparations of our own will be regarded suspiciously by others," because, as Eisenhower said, "we are trusted" (1945: 109). Unlike the despotic totalitarian regimes whose growing strength necessarily signals aggressive intentions, U.S. strength would be used for beneficent purposes: for the defense of freedom and national independence and for the preservation of the American way of life. As Kennedy explained explicitly during the Berlin crisis, "we make our proposals today, while building up our defenses over Berlin . . . because . . . *we are compelled against our will to rearm*" (1961j: 621, emphasis added). That is, U.S. military might was defensive rather than offensive and was expanded only under compulsion. That no one without aggressive intentions need fear the United States was implied in the distinction, already discussed above, between U.S. commitments and Soviet power involvements or threats. As Eisenhower warned Khrushchev in 1960, the United States was "committed to uphold" the agreements of the Inter-American System and would not be "deterred from its responsibilities" by Soviet "threats" or Soviet "interference" (1960e: 568). That no one need fear U.S. strength was implied as well in the distinction between U.S. and communist overseas bases. The communist ones were "subversive bases" and were "operating an offensive designed to cut down and overthrow the democratic institutions and governments" (Cabell, 1959: 752). Those of the United States, on the other hand, were "defensive." Their presence posed no threat but instead "strengthen[ed] the economy" and "certainly strengthen[ed] the defense" of the countries in which they were established (752). Finally, there was no need for others to fear U.S. economic strength because U.S. foreign economic assistance, such as that provided through the Marshall Plan or the Alliance for Progress, was designed and intended to foster the independence and freedom of its recipients. "Our assistance," Kennedy explained to the Inter-American Economic and Social Council of the OAS, "is only the first step in our continuing and expanding effort to help build a better life for the people of the hemisphere" (1961h: 355). Soviet economic assistance, on the other hand, was designed "to assume control of the resources" of the recipient countries and, even worse, "to control the minds and souls of the peoples in the areas" (Cabell, 1959: 751). After all, these totalitarian despots "want nations to become increasingly dependent economically upon the Communist bloc. The stage is then set for ultimate Communist takeover" (751). In short, though U.S. strength and the courage to use it simultaneously contributed to its leadership identity and were necessary for the United States successfully to exercise its leadership, they were unthreatening to most states because they were used in an other-regarding fashion to promote shared rather than selfish projects. The invocation of this particular aspect of U.S. identity disallowed the persistent Cuban claims that U.S. actions toward Cuba before, during, and after the missile crisis violated Cuban sovereignty and should be understood as hostile, aggressive intervention. Only Soviet or communist strength was used for such purposes. The United States, in contrast, obviously used its leadership, its strength, and its courage to protect the freedom of the hemisphere, the legitimate aspirations of the Cuban people, and ultimately, of course, the United States itself from a hostile, extracontinental invasion.

The Bane of Credibility

The defining characteristics of the U.S. identity—its leadership, its commitment to freedom, and its need for strength—produced for the United States a pervasive and inescapable credibility problem. Claims to U.S. leadership, assertions of its willingness to defend global freedom, and avowals of its strength and courage all involved a combination of promises and threats. To be of any use, these promises and threats had to be believed. But the very nature of the promises and threats rendered their believability suspect. As a result, each of these facets of U.S. identity generated both a need for the United States to be credible and, simultaneously, serious doubts about that credibility.

U.S. leadership generated a credibility problem because that leadership needed constantly to be reproduced and reenacted. Understood initially to have been earned through U.S. success in World War II, U.S. leadership required that the United States periodically demonstrate both its ability to guide and protect its allies and followers and its ability to counter threats by actual and potential opponents. That is, U.S. leadership had continually to be renewed, the confidence of its allies had continually to be justified, and the reliability of its threats against its adversaries had continually to be reaffirmed. These needs led the United States to make additional specific promises or commitments and specific threats, such as Kennedy's announcements that to preserve freedom in the Western Hemisphere the United States would not tolerate offensive weapons in Cuba (Kennedy 1962a, 1962b), in order to show that it indeed deserved and was living up to its position of leadership. But these additional commitments generated more credibility problems because they created additional points at which U.S. credibility could be challenged. As Gabriel Kolko has argued, the "essentially open-ended undertakings inherent in its desire to sustain the confidence of its allies and the fear of its putative enemies has caused the United States to stake its role in the world on controlling events in relatively minor places" (1980: 293). In short, the need for credibility prompted the United States to make additional commitments, which in turn became potential sites for threats to U.S. credibility.

This problem with U.S. credibility was in part the result of the putative indivisibility of freedom. As the authors of NSC 68 put it, "The assault on free institutions is world-wide," and as a result, "a defeat of free institutions anywhere is a defeat everywhere" (U.S. National Security Council, 1950: 389). A failure by the United States to respond to Soviet or communist aggression, no matter how far away from the United States or how small the nation under attack, would be a threat to the U.S. claim to be protecting freedom globally and hence a challenge to its credibility. Furthermore, on the basis of the standard quasi-causal argument entailed in the Munich analogy and the concomitant dangers of appeasement, weakness on the part of the free world, and especially on the part of its leader, was understood to breed aggression. Firmness was thus needed to halt or to contain that aggression. To demonstrate its credibility as a leader and successfully to promote and protect freedom through strength, the United States needed to show firmness or resolve. Should the dominoes begin to fall in earnest, should the Fidelista virus begin to spread throughout the free world, or even through the Western

Hemisphere, global freedom and the free society so painstakingly nurtured in the United States would be in danger both because its indivisibility would have been compromised and because appeasement would lead to further aggression. The United States would be seen as a paper tiger and its leadership would correspondingly be undercut.

Since U.S. leadership, its defense of freedom, and its possession of strength and resolve defined U.S. identity, the problem of credibility generated by each of these constitutive features became central to that identity as well. That is, "the United States" became a subject that had to be demonstrably credible. It is not surprising, then, that U.S. credibility was a central issue in the construction of the Cuban problem. In chastising the Kennedy administration for allowing Castro and communism to survive in Cuba after the abortive Bay of Pigs invasion, Barry Goldwater harped on the threat that Castro and the Cuban relationship to the Soviet Union posed for U.S. credibility. The persistence of a Soviet "showcase" in Cuba, he argued,

> is not only a danger to the United States; it *is also a disgrace and an affront which diminishes the respect with which we are held by the rest of the world* in direct ratio to the length of time we permit it to go unchallenged. I suggest that if the American people are concerned about *this Nation's prestige throughout the world,* let them look to Cuba as well as to Laos. Let them ask how *our commitments* to the United Nations and the Organization of American States make up for the extension of slavery and subversion in the Western Hemisphere. Let them ask whether we still adhere, in any slight degree to the spirit of the Monroe Doctrine, or *whether we have surrendered all of our national interests to the collective consideration of other powers.* In the matter of Cuba, we have moved with an *astounding timidity and indecision.* We have been mesmerized by the intellectual theory of nonintervention while Castro goes on shouting insults, confiscating our property, jailing our citizens and courting the deadliest enemy this world has ever known. *Our posture before the world is one of a paralyzed, confused giant who is only vaguely aware of the danger confronting him—a giant possessed of all the strength necessary to meet the danger but unable to decide whether to use it.* (1961: 422, emphasis added)

And this credibility problem was particularly salient during the Cuban missile crisis. Kennedy highlighted the problem of U.S. credibility in his speech to the U.S. public on October 22 when he proclaimed that the Soviet missile deployment could not be accepted by the United States "if our [U.S.] courage and our [U.S.] commitments are ever to be trusted again by either friend or foe" (1962c: 6). Having said that the United States would not tolerate offensive Soviet weapons in Cuba, accepting the Soviet missile deployment would have undercut U.S. credibility. This, in turn, would have threatened the identity of the United States *as* the legitimate leader of the free world. In the aftermath of the crisis, Kennedy again invoked the importance of U.S. credibility, explaining that the Soviet missiles had been unacceptable because their continued presence in Cuba would have appeared to change the balance of power (1962d: 898). The credibility of U.S. leadership could have been undermined by even the appearance of a change in the power relations between the United States and the Soviet Union. Had the United States allowed the missiles to remain in Cuba, the United States might have been perceived as a paper tiger unable or unwilling to honor its promises or to make good on its threats.

The logic of credibility, of course, is fundamentally circular and ultimately self-defeating. For the United States to demonstrate its continued credibility as the tough leader in the fight for freedom, extensive commitments were required. However, these commitments, such as had been made with respect to the importance of Cuba, the nonnegotiability of Castroism, and the intolerability of any Soviet missile deployment in Cuba, immediately became additional targets at which threats by the adversary could be launched. A failure to respond to those threats would again challenge U.S. credibility. As a result of the particular construction of its identity, the United States became embroiled in a continuous and ultimately futile (because necessarily unsuccessful) search for absolute credibility. That is, the identity constructed for the United States in the security imaginary— as the tough and resolute leader in freedom's cause—was fundamentally *precarious*. It was by its very nature continually under attack and therefore had constantly to be reasserted and reinforced. Each time it was reinforced, however, a new target at which attacks could be launched was created. As a result, the overarching U.S. national interest became precisely maintaining its credibility. As Abram Chayes, legal adviser to the Kennedy administration, explained on November 3, 1962, "the primary elements in the confrontation of the last weeks [that is, the Cuban missile crisis] have been the ability and the will of the United States to deploy the necessary force in the area to establish and enforce the quarantine, and the mobilization of friends and allies—in the hemisphere, in Europe, and elsewhere in the world—in support of our action" (1962: 763). In other words, the central issue involved in the Cuban missile crisis was the "ability" and "will" of the United States (that is, its strength and its resolve) both to deploy force and to mobilize (that is, to lead) its friends and allies. The most important U.S. national interest in the Cuban missile crisis, in short, was maintaining or living up to the identity constructed for the United States out of the U.S. security imaginary. Senator Richard Russell (D–Georgia), chairman of the Armed Services Committee, voiced these sentiments in no uncertain terms during the October 22 meeting at which Kennedy briefed congressional leaders on the crisis: "It seems to me that we are at a crossroads," Russell informed the president. "We're either a first-class power or we're not" (in May and Zelikow, 1997: 258). In arguing against the blockade and for a military strike against Cuba, Russell further insisted that "we've got to take a chance somewhere, sometime, if we're going to retain our position as a great world power" (265). The "obviousness" of the U.S. national interest in the Cuban missile crisis—that is, securing the removal of the Soviet missiles from Cuba—was therefore due, in large part, to the fact that the Soviet missile deployment issued an unacceptable challenge to the already precarious identity of the United States.

THE LOGIC OF IDENTITY AND THE CUBAN MISSILE CRISIS

At the heart of the Cuban missile crisis, then, resides a discursively constructed subject—the United States—with a particular, discursively constituted identity. The Cuban missile crisis was produced in representations of the Soviet missile deployment in Cuba as a serious threat to the well-established cold war identity of the United States. At the same time, this crisis provided the United States with the opportunity to reassert that identity, to attempt, yet again, to secure its always-precarious self.

Foreign policy problems, and especially acute problems, or "crises," are political acts, not facts; they are social constructions forged by state officials in the course of producing and reproducing state identity.[4] Although foreign policy problems, including acute crises, are typically understood to issue from outside of the state and at least potentially to disrupt its normal functioning, such problems are in fact internal to the functioning of states. More specifically, they are inextricably intertwined with state identity in two complementary ways: First, state identity enables the construction of foreign policy problems; second and conversely, such problems enable state identity.

That state identity enables foreign policy problems is the less problematical claim. After all, problems must be problems *for* some subject and, in the context of an international politics defined around states, that subject is typically, although not necessarily, the state.[5] The argument is quite straightforward. A problem can only be recognized by asking, *For whom* is this situation a problem? In the case of foreign policy problems, the "whom" is generally a very particular subject—the anthropomorphized state subject residing at the heart of the state's security imaginary. The Cuban missile crisis, as this chapter has shown, was an acute problem, a crisis, for the subject "the United States." Similarly, the Caribbean crisis and October crisis (see chapter 1) were acute problems for the subjects "the Soviet Union" and "Cuba," respectively. Defining a foreign policy problem thus depends, at least in part, on the identity of the state provided in its security imaginary.

But foreign policy problems also enable state identity. Such problems are an important means, although certainly not the only one, for the production and reproduction of state identity. Paradoxically, though serious foreign policy problems are understood to be extraordinary events that threaten states and that state officials therefore want either to avoid altogether or to manage successfully, they actually benefit states in at least two ways.[6] First, they facilitate the internal consolidation of state power. As has been well established elsewhere, problems, and crises in particular, provide opportunities that can facilitate the building of state machineries (e.g., Tilly, 1985; Skocpol, 1979; Barnett, 1992), opportunities during which the control exercised by a state over its population can be enhanced (e.g., Ayoob, 1983–84) and during which the relations of power within the state itself can be refined and elaborated (e.g., Bostdorff, 1994; Schlesinger, 1973). Second, and more central to the argument being advanced here, foreign policy problems allow for the articulation and rearticulation of relations of identity/difference as a means of both constituting and securing state identity.[7]

This latter claim, of course, rests on a specific understanding of state identity. In particular, it rests on a conception of state identity as always produced in a relationship with difference. As William Connolly has argued, identity is always "established in relation to a series of differences that have become socially recognized. These differences are essential to its being. If they did not coexist as differences, it [identity] would not exist in its distinctness and solidity" (1991: 64). Identity and difference are mutually constitutive: There is always a politics of identity through which identity and difference are defined in tandem. Furthermore, this indispensable politics of identity sometimes, and in international politics usually, involves a further politics of othering "by which established identities protect themselves through the conversion of difference into otherness" (159). The "maintenance of one identity (or field of identities)," especially in international politics, "involves the conversion of some differences into otherness, into evil, or one of its numerous surrogates. Identity requires difference in order to be, and it converts difference into otherness in order to secure its own self-certainty" (64). The process of securing an identity—of fixing, or establishing the certainty of, an identity—is thus often accomplished by transforming mere difference into otherness. When transformed into otherness, difference comes to be defined, for instance, as evil (for example, the Soviet Union and communism), as debased or backward (for example, the Third World), as inferior (for example, the soft and feminine), or as mad (for example, rogue dictators)—in short, as in some way dangerous. Identity, or the self, is threatened "not merely by *actions* that the other might take to injure or defeat the true identity but by the very visibility of its mode of *being* as other" (66, emphasis in the original). The very existence of a different identity defined as other, that is, threatens the stability and certainty of the self. That is, if identity is fixed by othering, as it was in the postwar U.S. security imaginary, the identity of the self becomes fundamentally insecure.

Difference and otherness thus stand in a "double relation" to self-identity: "They constitute it and they threaten it" (67). State identities, like all identities, are therefore always potentially precarious:[8] Difference constitutes identity (for example, "they," the Soviet Union, are not like "us," the United States); in order to secure that identity, difference is often transformed into otherness ("they," the Soviet Union, are secretive, duplicitous, and aggressive); and this very otherness, *in* its otherness, threatens identity ("their" aggressiveness and duplicity threatens "our" freedom). It is for this reason that foreign policy problems and state identity are mutually constituting. When state identity is created through othering, it is always in fact precarious and thus needs to be stabilized or reproduced. Foreign policy problems, and especially acute crises like the Cuban missile crisis, present important opportunities for the (re)production—sometimes successful, sometimes not, sometimes only partially so—of such precarious state identities.

During the Cuban missile crisis, U.S. leadership—defined in opposition to aggressive totalitarian others, secretive and duplicitous communist others, and soft and weak feminine others—conferred onto the United States the task of defining the situation in October 1962, of determining the appropriate course of action, and of implementing the chosen policy, quarantine. This identity also defined the U.S. national interest as requiring the removal of the Soviet missiles from Cuba because their remaining in Cuba in the face of explicit and public U.S. objections would have presented an unacceptable challenge to the already precarious leadership identity of the United States. The identification of the United States with freedom allowed the United States legitimately to define Soviet involvement and the Soviet missile deployment in Cuba as contrary to the interest of the Cuban people in freedom. As a result, the Cuban government's objections to U.S. actions were disallowed. The importance to the U.S. identity of strength and resolve meant that the United States had to see to the removal of the missiles to maintain its credibility as both global and hemispheric leader. Finally, the pervasive problem of U.S. credibility central to U.S. identity meant that the need to enforce the removal of the missiles was obvious. The failure to do so would undermine the very *identity* of the United States *as* the global leader, *as* the patron of freedom, and *as* the strongest and most resolute state in the free world. In other words, the way in which U.S. decision makers understood the Cuban missile crisis, and the reason why the U.S. national interest in that crisis seemed so obvious both to them and to subsequent commentators, cannot be explained without understanding the identity of the United States that sat at the heart of the postwar U.S. security imaginary. It was the identity of the United States, and the precariousness of that identity, that made the national interest so obvious to U.S. decision makers and U.S. observers alike. The Cuban missile crisis, in turn, provided U.S. state officials with the opportunity to reproduce U.S. identity performatively. In representing the missile crisis in a particular way, in deploying U.S. military force and acting out U.S. resolve, the already precarious identity of the United States as the global leader in freedom's cause was (temporarily) reasserted and reinscribed.[9]

7

National Interests and Common Sense

Common sense . . . is the diffuse, unco-ordinated features of a generic form of thought common to a particular period and a particular popular environment.

— ANTONIO GRAMSCI, SELECTIONS
FROM THE PRISON NOTEBOOKS

COMMON SENSE AND THE CUBAN PROBLEM

As Benedict Anderson said of the French Revolution, its apparently self-evident "it-ness" (1991: 81) was in fact the product of an extended process of social construction. The same is true of the Cuban missile crisis. The events of October 1962, whether in their representation in the popular myth or in U.S. state officials' understanding of them, were not simply apprehended objectively by participants, by later analysts, or by other observers. They were not, as the realist injunction has it, "problems of international politics" that decision makers could see "as they are" (Morgenthau, 1951: 7). Instead, the self-evident "it-ness" of the missile crisis was constructed, quite laboriously and sometimes quite deliberately, out of and through the postwar U.S. security imaginary. The representation of the problems confronting the United States in October 1962 and the attendant U.S. national interest were constructed by U.S. state officials and traditional intellectuals through the postwar U.S. security imaginary. And because this imaginary was widely shared, the corresponding myth

225

of the Cuban missile crisis also came to be accepted as the common-sense understanding of these events among a broader public, including many academic analysts.

The dual processes of articulation and interpellation through which the national interest is constructed, that is, at the same time produce common sense. By "common sense" I mean what Gramsci called the "diffuse, unco-ordinated features of a generic form of thought" (1971b: 330, note) that provide our "categories of practical consciousness" (Hall, 1986a: 30). Social constructions become common sense when they have successfully defined the relation of meaning to reality as one of representation. That is, they become common sense when particular representations of reality are treated as if they neutrally or transparently represent the real. Common sense thus entails the reification or naturalization of constructed representations of the world, thereby obscuring their constructed nature and their ideological effects. It is therefore the "moment of extreme ideological closure" (Hall, 1985: 105) when social constructions appear as natural. As a result, common sense sets the limits on the possible; it "becomes the horizon of the taken-for-granted: What the world is and how it works, for all practical purposes" (Hall, 1988: 44). It is through the dual processes of articulation and interpellation, then, that the naturalness of particular representations is created and the corresponding exclusion of other representations is effected.

According to McGeorge Bundy, what "made it so clear to Kennedy and to Congress in September and October [of 1962] that they should take a firm and flat stand against Soviet nuclear weapons in Cuba" was ultimately "a visceral feeling that it was intolerable for the United States to accept on nearby land of the Western Hemisphere Soviet weapons that could wreak instant havoc on the American homeland" (1988: 412–413). Bundy thus explained the obviousness of the U.S. national interest during the Cuban missile crisis as the result of a "strong national conviction" (413). This "strong national conviction," this "visceral feeling" about the U.S. national interest in the Cuban missile crisis, resulted from a socially and discursively constructed common sense. It was the product of the postwar U.S. security imaginary and of the well-developed template it provided for representing the world of international politics and the place of the United States in it. Indeed, the constant, numbing repetition of the same stock phrases and descriptions points to the tremendous constructive labor involved in producing the "thing" that became known as the Cuban missile crisis. This constant repetition—by drawing on and reinforcing the same contingent representations of objects, of threats, and of the relations among them—contributed to the reception of these representations as common sense, as real objects, threats, and relations that could simply and objectively be perceived. It thus defined the taken-for-granted of international politics and U.S. foreign policy. Other objects and arguments could find no comfortable place within the horizons of this taken-for-granted.

The constant, numbing repetition of the *same* stock phrases points as well to the astonishing poverty of concepts available within the postwar U.S. security imaginary for understanding international politics and U.S. national interests. That imaginary circumscribed a remarkably limited set of possible objects and quasi-causal arguments with which to represent events in international politics. According to this view, virtually all human beings either shared a commitment to or aspired to the same American values and institutions. Virtually all discomfiting events were understood to be brought about by external enemies with nefarious and often devious plans of aggression or subversion that threatened the free way of life either in the United States or elsewhere in the already free or potentially free world. Virtually all of these discomfiting events somehow threatened U.S. credibility. The United States had therefore to respond with vigor to reassert the credibility of its global and hemispheric leadership. The cold war world of international politics, in short, was produced by and reinforced the precariousness of U.S. identity.

The narrowness of the taken-for-granted defined by the U.S. security imaginary helps to explain the commonsense understanding, discussed in chapter 1, of the events of October 1962 as the Cuban missile crisis. It also helps to explain the silences, discussed in chapter 2, that characterized the ExComm discussions of these events. It explains why the Soviet claim to have been defending Cuba has routinely been dismissed as "laughable" within the myth of the missile crisis and why the Soviet explanation was never taken seriously in the repeated discussions of Soviet motives among ExComm participants. The Soviet claims to be defending Cuba were ignored because, within the U.S. security imaginary, it was perfectly reasonable to argue that the *Soviet* missile deployment constituted aggression against the Western Hemisphere and that the United States had an obligation to defend against such aggression. However, it was not reasonable, or even intelligible, within that imaginary to say "The *United States* is engaging in aggression against Cuba, and the Soviet Union must therefore defend Cuba against the United States." Such a statement was quite patently nonsense; it was ruled out, it was rendered unintelligible, by the security imaginary.

The commonsense understanding of the events of October 1962 also explains why Cuba rarely appears as an actor in the story of the Cuban missile crisis and why Cuban sovereignty was not considered by U.S. state officials in their analyses of appropriate U.S. policy responses. The security imaginary allowed for statements of the form "we [the United States] will enforce *our right*" to conduct surveillance over Cuba (Rusk, October 16: 172, emphasis added) and "we [the United States] do have to enforce *our right* to overfly and to have a look" (Rusk, October 27: 86, emphasis added). It did not, in contrast, allow for statements of the form "Cuba has the right to defend itself, as it sees fit, against aggression from the United States." Although U.S. airborne surveillance of Cuba, not to mention the blockade itself, could easily have been interpreted as a violation of Cuban sovereignty and thus as a contravention of international law, such considerations were not seriously entertained. After all, a communist puppet government that permitted its people to be subjected to foreign domination had no such rights, least of all in the Western Hemisphere with its long-standing tradition of liberty. At the same time, the United States, as the leader in freedom's cause, had the legitimate obligation, it bore the burden, of defending the hemisphere from external aggression.

The commonsense understanding of the events of October 1962 explains as well why the argument that the Soviet missiles were strategically irrelevant is absent from the missile crisis myth and why it received short shrift in the ExComm deliberations. In the face of Republican attacks on Kennedy's Democratic administration, and given the threat to the Western Hemisphere and to the credibility of the United States in the global battle with Soviet-directed international communism, the irrelevance of the missiles to the strategic balance was itself irrelevant to the problem faced by the United States. Ultimately, in fact, it was not the missiles that were at issue in the Cuban missile crisis. Instead, the missiles were an abbreviated, if vivid and particularly frightening, metaphor for the U.S.-Soviet conflict, for the global battle between international communism and freedom, and for the multidimensional Cuban problem in the Western Hemisphere. In short, the missiles quickly came to symbolize the pervasive threats faced by that always precarious identity, "the United States." To maintain this identity, to maintain U.S. credibility as the tough leader in the fight for freedom, this symbol of Soviet and communist aggression and subversion could not be allowed to remain in the U.S. backyard.

Finally, and most important, the commonsense understanding of the situation faced by the United States in October 1962 helps to explain the final and central silence that characterizes both the myth of the missile crisis and U.S. decision making during that crisis. That is, by helping to account for both these silences and the prevailing representations of the events of October 1962, it helps to explain the failure of both U.S. decision makers and subsequent analysts to question or even to discuss the "obvious" U.S. national interest in securing the removal of the Soviet missiles from Cuba. Having narrated the situation facing the United States in a manner consistent with the narrow horizons of the postwar U.S. security imaginary, no other national interest was conceivable.

The particular identity constructed for the United States through the postwar U.S. security imaginary simultaneously rendered the problem of Soviet missiles in Cuba and the attendant U.S. national interest both sensible and legitimate. The commonsense status and the legitimacy of the U.S. national interest arose from the fact that the identity "the United States" occupied the subject position from which the U.S. security imaginary was spoken. That is, statements made from within this imaginary entailed the identity that the imaginary created for the United States: statements from within the imaginary made sense *if* one occupied the subject position of the United States. As a result, such statements invited their audience (during the missile crisis this especially included U.S. decision makers, the U.S. public, and the peoples and governments of Latin America) to identify with, to imagine themselves in the position of, the United States. They invited members of their audience, for example, to imagine themselves as a powerful yet concerned family member who—because they were committed to the solidarity of the Western Hemisphere, to the integrity and virtue of the American family and its common values, to democracy and diversity, and to the disavowal of secrecy and treachery—was in a uniquely responsible position that both enabled and obliged them to challenge the global threat posed by totalitarianism and the hemispheric threat posed by the Soviet Trojan horse and by the communist infiltration of Cuba. In so doing, the conclusions drawn from the quasi-causal arguments made sense and were legitimized. The audience was interpellated as a democratic subject that, as the champion of freedom and national independence, indeed defended the free way of life around the world. The audience was interpellated as open and honest people who would not secretly connive to disturb the established order and threaten world peace. Instead, as open and honest individuals they wished to preserve peace, order, freedom, and the independence of nations. The audience was simultaneously interpellated as tough leaders in the global fight for freedom, leaders who recognized that totalitarian aggression must be met with a firm and resolute response.

The interpellation of the audience into the U.S. subject position, in other words, produced a "we." Through this shifty shifter, U.S. identity became the identity of the individual speaker or hearer of the statements, the representations, crafted out of the resources provided by the U.S. security imaginary. The typical response to the invitation issued by this ambiguous "we" was therefore one of recognition: "Yes, 'we' are like *this* (that is, a tough leader, democratic, and in favor of freedom) and not like *that* (that is, alien, despotic, and aggressive)." Once this identification had been produced, then the description of the world provided, the logic of the quasi-causal arguments presented, and the warrants for action drawn from these descriptions and arguments were rendered plausible and persuasive. Since "we" are democratic and not despotic or totalitarian, since totalitarian conformity threatens democratic diversity and alien invasions threaten the American family, and since "we" are the leader of the free world, "we" must respond with firmness to this totalitarian aggression.

The same processes of articulation and interpellation that made sensible and legitimized the U.S. national interest and U.S. actions during the Cuban missile crisis pushed alternative understandings of that crisis beyond the boundaries of the intelligible. Since "we" are not aggressive and hostile, it is not conceivable that "we" could have precipitated the Cuban missile crisis, and certainly not through "our" aggression against Cuba. After all, "we" stand for freedom and national independence and so are neither unreasonably hostile nor prone to aggressive actions. In conjunction with the characteristic objects and quasi-causal arguments used to describe the situation faced by the United States in the Cuban missile crisis, the identity constructed for the United States—as the strong and credible leader in the defense of freedom—and the interpellation of the audience into this subject position helped to produce a persuasive logic that defined the Soviet missiles as unacceptable and both required and legitimized a forceful U.S. policy in pursuit of their removal.

COMMON SENSE AND CONTINUITY:
THE CUBAN PROBLEM AFTER THE COLD WAR

The production of the Cuban missile crisis and of the U.S. national interest in securing the removal of the Soviet missiles from Cuba was enabled by the identity constructed for the United States through the postwar U.S. security imaginary. Despite the so-called end of the cold war and of the postwar era, this U.S. identity, as well as the identity of Cuba and the attendant character of U.S.-Cuban relations, have largely persisted, albeit in slightly rearticulated form. As a result, U.S. policy toward Cuba in the late 1980s and through much of the 1990s has not responded significantly to changes in the global distribution of power that characterize the post–cold war era. Nor has it responded noticeably to changes in administration. Despite the exhaustion of the threats represented by the United States as emanating from the Soviet Union and the international communist movement and as channeled against the Western Hemisphere through Cuba, the Cuban problem remains and the United States persists in its hostile and aggressive policies toward Cuba.

Recent U.S. constructions of Cuba still draw, in significant ways, on the cold war representations of the Cuban problem as these constituted U.S. interests in and policy toward Cuba during the cold war, but some of the details of that Cuban problem have been rearticulated. The construction of Cuba as a "communist totalitarian dictatorship" (U.S. Congress, 1996: section 205:b:1) on the model of "Red Fascism" (see chapter 4) has continued after the cold war. For example, on an episode of the PBS series *Frontline* ("Castro: The Last Communist," 1992), Castro and Cuba were implicitly articulated to fascism and thus to totalitarianism through the association of Castro with Benito Mussolini. The episode emphasized that Castro had learned his oratorical techniques by studying Mussolini. To sharpen this point, visual images of Castro and Mussolini were alternated to show the similarities in the mannerisms that accompanied their public pronouncements. The effect was to create an association of Castro to Italian fascism and thus to standard images of totalitarianism (see Saco, 1992: 138–139, note 54). This "totalitarian" Cuban regime, it is further argued, "has deprived the Cuban people of any peaceful means to improve their condition" (U.S. Congress, 1996: section 2:6) and "utilizes torture in various forms . . . as well as execution, exile, confiscation, political imprisonment, and other forms of terror and repression, as means of retaining power" (section 2:15).

As was the case throughout the cold war, this totalitarian Cuban government continues to be represented as aiding revolution and subversion in Central America and Africa. In addition, it has been accused of drug trafficking and supporting international terrorism (e.g., Reagan, 1986; U.S. Congress, 1996). Under the Reagan administration, for example, Cuba was not represented merely as supporting home-grown revolutions in Nicaragua and elsewhere; instead, it was reconstructed as "the main cause of violence and instability in Central America" (Reagan, 1986: 22–23; see also "National Bipartisan Commission on Central America," 1984: 107–108). More recently, Cuba has also been charged with "harbor[ing] fugitives from justice in the United States" and with "threaten[ing] international peace and security by engaging in acts of armed subversion or terrorism such as the training and supplying of groups dedicated to international violence" (U.S. Congress, 1996: section 2:13, 14). If the United States was "hysterical about Castro" by 1961, as McNamara has since argued (in U.S. Senate Select Committee to Study Governmental Operations with respect to Intelligence Activities, 1975: 157), this hysteria seems to have survived the end of the cold war.

During the cold war, Cuba was constructed as a Soviet minion and a projection of the Soviet threat into the Western Hemisphere (see chapter 5). As recently as 1991, Radio Martí transmissions were still representing Cuba in these terms. According to one "testimonial" segment from July 2, 1991, for example, the Cuban Revolution of 1959 obtained for the Soviet Union "its first beachhead in American territory" and "brought forth a profound ideological and economic dependence" on "the Russian empire." With the disintegration of the "Soviet bloc," and the presumed global renunciation of communism that the demise of the Soviet bloc has come to signify,

Cuban communism was reconstructed as a phenomenon that will not survive much longer: "Castroism, while it may seem long to us, is a passing accident. As things are today, it is dead. Although the cadaver is not yet mindful of its own lifelessness, people, it is a cadaver" (Roberto Valero, in a Radio Martí Program, July 2, 1991).[1] Popular U.S. news programs have reproduced these constructs: On January 21, 1992, for instance, PBS's *MacNeil/Lehrer Newshour* offered a segment on Cuba entitled "Focus—Numbered Days?" and on February 11, 1992, PBS's *Frontline* aired "Castro: The last communist." The key rearticulation in U.S. constructions of Cuba and Castro, then, is from Cuban communism as a Soviet-led international communist threat to Cuban communism as dead or, at least, dying. This rearticulation has persisted through the Clinton administrations. In response to a question, asked at a May 1993 public address, as to why the United States continues its embargo against Cuba, Secretary of State Warren Christopher declared that the embargo would help spur necessary democratic change in Cuba and that what warranted continued U.S. pressure on Cuba was the fact that "Castro is a relic of the past" (Christopher, 1993). And Stuart Eizenstat, the president's and the secretary of state's "Special Representative for the Promotion of Democracy in Cuba" (Clinton, 1996b), has repeatedly claimed that "Cuba remains an anachronism in our Western Hemisphere. It is the only totalitarian dictatorship out of 35 countries. There are 34 democracies; a whole wave of democratic movement in Latin America, which has been so positive, has failed only in Cuba. . . . there is no reason why the Cuban people do not deserve the same sorts of freedoms that others enjoy" (Eizenstat, 1996b; see also 1996a).

Recapitulating the well-worn U.S. appropriation of the rhetoric of revolution in promoting the Alliance for Progress, the concepts of "revolution" and "change" in contemporary U.S. discussions of the Cuban problem have been disarticulated from the socialism of the Cuban system and rearticulated to so-called pro-democracy movements in Eastern Europe (e.g., Bush, 1991a: 1233). In the process, the discourse of the Cuban problem persists, but the nature of the problem has been redefined slightly: The problem is now Castro's intransigence in the face of the failure or death of communism. Nonetheless, this representation continues to draw heavily both on the standard notion of the universal aspirations for U.S. values such as freedom and democracy (see chapter 5)—rearticulated as aspirations for pro-democratic change that have emerged, or reemerged, in the post–cold war era—and on the ubiquitous distinction between Castro and the Cuban people (see chapter 5). Months after the fall of the Berlin Wall, for instance, Bush drew on this reconstruction, asserting that "Fidel Castro should be celebrating along with other countries the demise of the Berlin Wall. Instead, Castro is criticizing Gorbachev for being not true to a communist revolution. He's out of step. He's swimming against the tide. He is a symbol, the lone holdout of a Marxist totalitarianism that has failed all around the world. And he ought to be better to his people than that" (Bush, 1991b: 64). Similarly, after the dismantling of the Soviet Union, Bush stated simply that "Castro's vision of the future is to cling to a failed past. His determination to keep Cuba an antidemocratic Communist state dooms the Cuban people to a predetermined fate" (Bush, 1992b: 905).

Despite these minor rearticulations, U.S. policy toward Cuba actually became more, rather than less, aggressive during the 1990s. The end of systemic superpower competition has not been matched by a cessation of U.S. anti-Castro policy. Instead, the United States has strengthened its policy of isolating Cuba and of spurring "democratic change" in Cuba by passing the Cuban Democracy Act in 1992 and the Cuban Liberty and Democratic Solidarity (Libertad) Act of 1996, better know as the Helms-Burton Act. The Cuban Democracy Act revitalized the thirty-two-year-old embargo against Cuba in order to "promote a peaceful transition to democracy in Cuba through the application of appropriate pressures on the Cuban Government and support for the Cuban people" (U.S. Senate, 1992). The Helms-Burton Act was designed, among other things, "to seek international sanctions against the Castro government in Cuba" and "to plan for support of a transition government leading to a democratically elected government in Cuba" (U.S. Congress, 1996). This act, Clinton pronounced, "reaffirms our common goal of promoting a peaceful transition to democracy in Cuba by tightening the existing embargo while reaching out to the Cuban people" and signals "our continued commitment to stand by the Cuban people in their peaceful struggle for freedom" (Clinton, 1996a).

The defense of the Cuban Democracy Act offered by Representative Robert G. Torricelli (D–New Jersey) is instructive. Though his defense focused less directly on questions of U.S. security, it continued to emphasize "democratic freedoms" and "the Cuban people's suffering" and added a heightened concern for "human rights." In its effort to persuade Castro to change, the bill blends "carrots and sticks" by permitting donations of food, medicine, and medical supplies "to a Cuban government that recognizes human rights and basic democratic freedoms" and by providing improved telephone and mail service between the United States and Cuba. "But," Torricelli continued, "the bill tightens a United States embargo that was slowly eroding to make it more effective." The point of the bill is to send a clear message to Castro that, despite the collapse of their Soviet sponsor and of the international communist movement, U.S. policy will not change until Castro himself initiates liberal-democratic reforms—reforms constructed as both morally defensible and historically unavoidable. After all, as had been assumed in the cold war representation of the Cuban problem, it was obvious that "Mr. Castro remains the base cause of the Cuban people's suffering." Furthermore, according to Torricelli, "most of our trading partners . . . are disillusioned by their failed attempts to persuade President Fidel Castro to embrace minimal reforms" (Torricelli, 1992).[2] According to this view, then, the tighter sanctions established in the bill reflect the normative imperatives of an international community concerned with human rights violations and the lack of democratic freedoms in Cuba. Both the Bush and the Clinton administrations have expressed the same arguments. "The Castro dictatorship cannot and will not survive the wave of democracy that has swept over the world," Bush declared (1992b: 905), because "Castro is on his own" (1992a: 676). And despite concerns that the Clinton administration might "go soft" on Cuba (Whitefield, 1993), it continues to understand U.S.-Cuban relations in the terms of this rearticulated Cuban problem: "I support the embargo against Cuba," Clinton reaffirmed in 1994, "and I believe that it should stand until there is some real movement toward freedom and democracy in Cuba" (letter to the author and Diana Saco, January 22, 1994).

The Helms-Burton Act was also defended and explained in terms surprisingly similar to the cold war representation of the Cuban problem. According to Stuart Eizenstat, "This Act is a reasonable statute which seeks to promote democracy in Cuba and to protect the property rights of thousands of American citizens whose property was confiscated without compensation by the Castro regime" (Eizenstat, 1997). As the act itself says, "The Cuban people deserve to be assisted in a decisive manner to end the tyranny that has oppressed them for 36 years, and the continued failure to do so constitutes ethically improper conduct by the international community" (U.S. Congress, 1996: section 2:27). Given the U.S. leadership identity, of course, this means that the United States has a "commitment to help bring freedom and prosperity to the people of Cuba" (Eizenstat, 1996a). The international community should join the U.S. in this project, Clinton asserted, "so the people of Cuba can enjoy the freedom and prosperity they deserve."[3] "The Cuban people have lived under tyranny for too long," Clinton continued, and so "We must sustain our efforts to hasten the arrival of democracy in Cuba. . . . We will not be satisfied until that day arrives" (Clinton, 1997). After all, as we know from decades of representations of the Cuban problem, "the Cuban people deserve our help in rejoining the family of democracies in the Americas" (Eizenstat, 1996c). Similarly, in explaining U.S. policy under the Helms-Burton Act to the Permanent Council of the OAS, U.S. Ambassador Harriet Babbitt insisted that "we should not lose sight of the basic cause of the problem—and that is the nature of the Cuban regime, the sole defiant exception to our hemispheric consensus in support and defense of democracy, of open societies and of integrated, free market economies" (Babbitt, 1996). As these brief snippets indicate, the problem of Cuba remains the totalitarian and despotic nature of its governing regime, its failure to satisfy the aspirations of the Cuban people for liberal democracy and a capitalist economic system, and its flagrant violation of the shared values of the American family.

As the policies articulated in, and the defenses of, the Cuban Democracy Act and the Helms-Burton Act indicate, this slightly revamped representation of a continuing Cuban problem reaffirms U.S. leadership identity and thus U.S. prominence in the promotion of a peaceful transition toward democracy in Cuba. Warrants for this leadership role continue to be drawn from the established U.S. identity as the defender of the free world. This U.S. leadership identity, thrust upon the United States by its victory in World War II (see chapter 6), continues to be grounded in the U.S. status as "the first and most powerful democracy in the world" (e.g., "Enfoque," Radio Martí Program, July 1, 1991). In defending increased cultural and academic exchanges to Cuba, Jeffrey Davidow, acting assistant secretary of state for inter-American affairs, argued in 1996 that such programs "will increase the Cuban people's exposure to American ideas and ideals in a focused way. . . . Those ideas will spread, and they will bring Cuba into its rightful place in our hemispheric family of democratic nations" (Davidow, 1996). The unchanged U.S. identity as both the leader in defense of freedom and democracy and as the unique model of the ideal free society continues to underpin the U.S. representation of the Cuban problem and provides a warrant for U.S. action. It implies that the United States can and should take a leadership role in supporting pro-democratic movements wherever they emerge and in promoting democracy in those places, like Cuba, where spontaneous pro-democracy movements by the people are possible, given current social and economic hardships, but systematically repressed (e.g., Samuel Huntington, interview on "Enfoque," Radio Martí Program, July 1, 1991). This U.S. identity helps to make sensible the persistent U.S. refrain in the 1990s that the U.S.-led international community should isolate Castro and help to spur the transition to democracy in Cuba: "We urge all democratic governments to join us. No nation should help bankroll this [Cuban] dictatorship" (Bush, 1992a).

In short, despite the end of the cold war, no real change in U.S. policy toward Cuba has taken place. The United States has continued through the representation of the Cuban problem to construct both its own identity and Cuba's in such a way that both U.S. hostility toward Cuba and its violation of Cuban sovereignty are perpetuated while, simultaneously, the persistence of this hostility and aggression are rendered both sensible and laudable. The Helms-Burton Act is explicitly designed to alter the domestic institutions and structure of Cuban society. For example, Clinton explained the appointment of a "Special Representative for the Promotion of Democracy in Cuba" as a means "to build international support for increasing pressure on Cuba to open up politically and economically; encouraging forces for change on the island; better targeting foreign assistance in ways that advance democratic goals; and promoting business practices that will bring democracy to the Cuban workplace" (Clinton, 1996b). All of these changes, without which the U.S. embargo will not be called off, require that Cuba change its internal institutional arrangements. Once again the United States is seeking to dictate

Cuba's domestic politics and in so doing is shamelessly violating Cuban sovereignty. The rationale? U.S. leadership in the global search for democracy and freedom.

U.S. political leaders have tried valiantly to interpellate U.S. allies, particularly in Europe, into this representation in order to secure their consent to U.S. policy. Most generally, the defense of the Helms-Burton Act has rested on the attempt to interpellate "freedom loving people's everywhere" (Eizenstat, 1997) into the representations of U.S. policy toward Cuba. More specifically, Eizenstat in particular has attempted to interpellate Europeans as U.S. partners in the pursuit of democracy. "The U.S. has been a partner of our European allies for five decades," Eizenstat avowed,

> since the end of World War II, to protect freedom and democracy in Europe, and more recently working with our European allies to assist Central and Eastern European countries and those of the former Soviet Union to make the transition from the communist past to free regimes. . . . We call on our European allies to work with us and to join us to do more to help bring democratic change to the only totalitarian regime in the hemisphere of which we're a part. We're asking them [the Europeans] to do no more than we have done with them in Europe. (Eizenstat, 1996a)

On another occasion Eizenstat argued, even more aggressively, that "just as we've spent 50 years spending tens of billions of dollars working for Europe, to promote freedom and democracy on this continent, and to this very day have 25,000 troops in Bosnia, and over 100,000 committed to NATO, it's not too much to ask Europe to work with us to promote democracy in the only repressive regime in the hemisphere in which we live" (1996b). These interpellations, based in part on a shared commitment to democracy, in part on a shared history in World War II and through the cold war, and in part on guilt and a somewhat petulant U.S. demand for gratitude, attempt to secure European consent to U.S. Cuban policy by hailing the Europeans into the U.S. representation of the Cuban problem, thus rendering it commonsensical.

Nonetheless, the common sense of the Cuban problem seems to be eroding somewhat, perhaps indicating that the postwar U.S. security imaginary is no longer interpellating at least parts of its intended audience as it did in the past. For example, despite Torricelli's and others' claims that the Cuban Democracy Act reflects the concerns of the international community, it was soundly criticized by many countries, including U.S. allies. Since the mechanisms specified by the Cuban Democracy Act for tightening the embargo—for example, sanctioning foreign subsidiaries of U.S. companies trading with Cuba and prohibiting ships trading with Cuba from docking in U.S. ports for six months—effectively subject foreign subsidiaries and shipping companies to U.S. policy on Cuba, a number of U.S. trading partners, including Canada, Great Britain, and Mexico, have argued that the bill infringes on their sovereignty (Scott, 1992; Wolf, 1992). In fact, on November 24, 1992, the U.N. General Assembly voted 59 to 3 to demand that the United States lift the embargo against Cuba. Only Romania and Israel voted with the United States, while a staggering seventy-one countries abstained (Meisler, 1992). In June 1994, nineteen Latin American nations, plus Spain and Portugal, called for "the elimination of unilateral economic and trade boycotts" of Cuba ("Castro dons civies for Latin conference," 1994), while Canada restored economic aid to Cuba ("Canada is restoring aid to Cuban regime," 1994). The Helms-Burton Act, of course, also generated strong opposition from many U.S. allies and trading partners, including the Rio Group, the European Union, and the OAS. Canadian officials lobbied actively to block the act, and the nationally circulated *Globe and Mail* editorialized that "once again, the U.S. Congress and the president are building a steamroller to peel a potato" (quoted in Crary, 1994). Not a resoundingly successful interpellation! Even within the United States, the common sense on Cuba seems to be breaking down, or at least to be more open to question than it was in the past. A recent poll in Dade County, Florida, home of a significant portion of the Cuban-American community, for example, indicated that there now exists "a wide and healthy plurality of views on a number of issues," including current United States policy toward Cuba. According to this poll, 48 percent of respondents now favored establishing a national dialogue with Cuba, while 45 percent opposed such a dialogue. And 60 percent favored U.S. companies doing business with Cuba, while only 38 percent were opposed ("Time to change a static Cuba policy," 1997).

The growing plurality of plausible articulations of the Cuban problem in the contemporary period points to the open-ended nature of the politics of representation, to the contingent and ultimately contestable nature of common sense. Ongoing ideological labor is being carried out on all sides in such a way as to render sensible competing actions by the United States (for example, allowing U.S. companies to do business in Cuba, or not). In a "post–cold war" world of capitalist triumphalism, of liberal democracies and free markets, the orthodox common sense of the Cuban problem is being questioned and, at least for some, rearticulated.

COMMON SENSE AND THE STUDY OF WORLD POLITICS

In essence, common sense is created by implying an empiricist epistemology—and in particular by implying a referential theory of language and meaning in which words and concepts refer unproblematically to their empirical referents. The common sense of the U.S. national interest in the Cuban missile crisis was reinforced by both the U.S. cultural commitment to a pragmatic and empiricist conception of knowledge and, importantly, by the prevalence of this epistemology within the academic study of international politics. The belief that the representations constructed out of the U.S. security imaginary during the cold war were in fact real representations rather than social constructions was reinforced in particular by the predominance of realism, broadly understood, in the study of international relations and especially in the analysis of the national interest. As Justin Rosenberg argued, realism "continues to have a disorganizing effect on its critics" because it "has been able to organize them into certain familiar areas of contestation which reinforce its own dominance" (1990: 298).

By taking the state, anarchy, and sovereignty as given, as the horizon of the taken-for-granted of international politics, realism has set the terms of debate over the understanding and explanation of international politics and foreign policy. By emphasizing its commitment to "is" over "ought," it obscures the "ought" implicit in its own representations of the world and of the national interest. It simultaneously relegates most, if not all, critical arguments to the category of an idealism that does not comprehend the realities of power and therefore cannot contribute to the rational analysis and formulation of foreign policy. Realism's conception of a unitary, discrete sovereign state also interpellates individuals into realist ideology because "it sits easily with the popular nationalist identification with the 'home' state which comprises most individuals' participation in the international system" (Rosenberg, 1990: 297–298). The postwar U.S. security imaginary had exactly the same effect during the Cuban missile crisis. By authoritatively defining the real, it removed from critical analysis and political debate what was in fact a set of socially constructed representations with profound ideological effects. It thus led to the reception of one particular representation (that of the Cuban missile crisis) as the real and to one particular U.S. national interest (that of securing the removal of the Soviet missiles from Cuba) as common sense.

One of the ways in which realism disorganizes its opponents is by drawing a sharp distinction between the real, which is the purview of realism and of serious analysis, and common sense. Realism, on its own evaluation, provides a way to cut through common sense, propaganda, ideology, and the like in order to reveal the hard truths, the realities, of world politics. But according to the argument that I have made here, this distinction between common sense and the real is fundamentally false. Common sense is not separate from but is in fact constitutive of reality. Rather than being rejected, then, perhaps common sense should instead form one of the more important starting points for the analysis of world politics. As I have sought to demonstrate in this book, such a starting point can throw significant new light onto even such well-studied topics as the Cuban missile crisis, and by implication onto international crises in general.

Recognizing the constitutive character of common sense, in turn, opens up a variety of other possible domains of inquiry that have often been overlooked in our attempts better to understand world politics. One such domain, I would argue, is popular culture. Students of international relations have rarely descended from the heights of interstate interaction to analyze the everyday cultural conditions that make particular state actions possible and that render them sensible to wider publics. But as I have suggested, these mundane cultural conditions are integral to rather than irrelevant for state action. It matters deeply that U.S. state actors are able to interpret and to define world politics in ways that at least significant portions of the U.S. population, and other audiences, find plausible and persuasive. The reproduction of common sense, and specifically of the grounds upon which particular representations are constructed and make sense, however, cannot be restricted to the representational practices of state actors. On the contrary, those representations are made sensible in no small part precisely because they fit with the constructions of the world and its workings into which diverse populations are hailed in their everyday lives. Representing world politics is not an unusual or extraordinary activity; rather, it is a relentlessly mundane and commonplace one. A key site at which that representation takes place, then, is in popular culture, in the everyday practices of meaning making that structure the quotidien. Perhaps it is time we devoted a little less attention to the doings of state actors and instead devoted a little more to the "silent" masses in whose name they claim to speak.

Notes

INTRODUCTION

1. For a recent survey of criticisms of the concept, see W. D. Clinton, 1994: chapters 2, 4.

2. National interests belong to a specific class of social facts—that of interests more generally—that are of special importance to the modern explanation of social phenomena. The notion of interest, as William Connolly has argued, "is one of those concepts that connects descriptive and explanatory statements to normative judgement" because reference to interests "carries . . . into political discourse" the presumption "that people [or states] ought to be able to do what they choose or want to do unless overriding considerations intervene," since "the sort of wants" designated by the term "are exactly those deemed to be somehow important, persistent, basic or fundamental to politics" (1983: 46).

3. More recently, it has been argued that there are "two faces of state action," one international and one domestic, and that additional state interests should be deduced from the location of the state in domestic society (Mastanduno, Lake, and Ikenberry, 1989: 461). Though this analysis adds state interests related to the "second image" (Waltz, 1959)—that is, literal characteristics of the state—to the traditional realist model, these interests are still treated as given and as deducible from structures rather than as socially constructed.

4. This limitation was, of course, touted as an advantage by Kenneth Waltz, who argued that an "elegant" systemic theory of international politics would explain "what pressures are exerted and what possibilities are

posed by systems of different structure," but could not, and should not strive to, explain "just how, and how effectively, the units of a system [that is, states] will respond to those pressures and possibilities" (1979: 71).

5. At least two recent literatures—on the role of ideas (e.g., Goldstein, 1988, 1989, 1993; Goldstein and Keohane, 1993) and of epistemic communities (e.g., Haas, 1992)—might be thought to provide a more substantive account of national interests. Though both provide a "progressive problem shift" (Lakatos, 1970) within realist theory by tackling the issue of policy indeterminacy, they do not actually address the question of the national interest. Instead, they consider the problem of policy alternatives *within* the confines of a single national interest without providing any information on the origins of those interests.

6. To see that two realists can come to dramatically opposed conclusions about the national interest, one need only examine Hans Morgenthau's (1969: 129) and Henry Kissinger's (1969: 130) conflicting prescriptions concerning U.S. involvement in Vietnam.

7. A variation on this problem also undermines the otherwise useful discussion of the national interest by W. D. Clinton (1994). Despite his welcome emphasis on argumentation and "good reasons," Clinton grounds his analysis in an objective notion of the "common good" that particular national interests approximate more or less well (chapter 3, esp. 51–55).

8. An excellent overview of the relevant literatures can be found in George, 1994.

9. See also Haggard, 1991.

10. It is to avoid the pervasive anthropomorphization of the state that I use the more traditional term "national interest" rather than "state interest." Anthropomorphizing the state helps to obscure the importance of domestic processes in the construction of national interests, of state action, and thus of outcomes of international politics. Of course, the term "national interest" also brings with it unwanted baggage, specifically, the ideas that what is in the interests of the state is also in the interests of the nation to which it is ostensibly attached and that there is a single interest that can be attributed to all members of a putatively national community. My continued use of the term "national interest" should not be read to entail either of these connotations.

11. Wendt does argue that first- and second-image "determinants of state identity"—that is, individual and state-level characteristics—are important, but he brackets these in order to "clarify the 'logic' of anarchy" (1992: 396) and so provides no tools with which to investigate these other determinants.

12. Furthermore, once one recognizes that interests and identities are constructed, there is no theoretical reason to assume that the process of construction occurs only, or even most importantly, at the interstate level.

Unless one makes a prior analytical or substantive commitment to a state-centric analysis, it makes more sense to assume that this constructive process occurs in many places, and especially in the domestic context from which the linguistic and cultural resources of state officials are drawn.

13. This argument is not meant to reproduce the traditional distinction between unit-level, or domestic, politics and system-level, or international, politics as alternative sources or loci of explanation. I would want, with others (e.g., Walker, 1993), to reject these as distinct levels of analysis and instead to understand the distinction itself as a discursive strategy that allocates power and helps to construct a particular (realist) world.

14. I draw loosely on and adapt Cornelius Castoriadis's (1987) notion of a "social imaginary" *(l'imaginaire social)*. This notion is much more encompassing than the security imaginary I discuss here, since the social imaginary provides for "the orientation of a society" (Tomlinson, 1991: 157) as a whole. Security imaginaries, in contrast, can be thought of as what Castoriadis called a "peripheral imaginary" which is itself rooted in the "central" imaginary of a society (1987: 131) but provides, more narrowly, a vision of the world of international politics and the place of a state within it. For good introductions to Castoriadis's notion of the social imaginary, see Tomlinson, 1991: 154–163, or Thompson, 1984: chapter 1. For a discussion of a security imaginary similar to mine, see Muppidi, 1999.

15. It is not just the content of interests, national or otherwise, that are constructed. The very notion that interest motivates action and so should be referred to in explanations of behavior and social outcomes is itself a relative novelty. It was only with liberalism and the rise of capitalism that interest first came to be understood as the motivating force driving the actions of individuals. That interest as a general category, regardless of its content, should be of central importance to social analysis is thus itself a social construction rather than a natural fact. The laborious ideological process of establishing the primacy of interests is detailed by Albert Hirschman (1977) in his description of the victory, accompanying the "triumph" of capitalism, of the "interests" over the "passions" as the motivation for human action.

16. For a detailed analysis of the U.S. construction of the Cuban problem, see Weldes and Saco, 1996.

17. For extensive discussions of the logic of these arguments see Weldes, 1993. Critical analyses of the Munich analogy and the dangers of appeasement can be found in Lanyi, 1963; Rystad, 1981–1982; Richardson, 1988; and Beck, 1989. The domino theory is discussed in Ross, 1978; Slater, 1987; and Jervis and Snyder, 1991.

18. Claiming that these quasi-causal arguments may not be empirically valid or accurate neither undermines nor contradicts the claim that such arguments are constructions, since these empirical claims may be false on their

own terms—that is, even if one treats such constructions as given. For example, even if we accept the construction of some states as dominoes, the domino theory turns out to be false. As Jerome Slater (1987) has argued, in no case has the logic of the theory, that one small state's collapse would precipitate the collapse of others, been fulfilled.

19. This is roughly the sequence of collapse envisioned by Dwight D. Eisenhower in his famous articulation of the "'falling domino' principle" (1954). Others saw the sequence of falling dominoes (or rotting apples or some other such metaphor) somewhat differently, but always with the same net effect: The United States must step in to stop the collapse (or rot, or whatever). See, for example, Bullitt, 1948; Acheson, 1969b; U.S. Senate Committee on Foreign Relations, 1947.

20. The idea that the Cuban missile crisis was an outstanding example of crisis decision making and crisis management was for many years virtual dogma in the study of crises (e.g., Sorensen, 1965; Abel, 1966; Hilsman, 1967; Allison, 1971: 39; Kennedy, 1971; Janis, 1983). As Stuart Thorson and Donald Sylvan have pointed out, this positive, not to say ecstatic, evaluation of U.S. decision making during the Cuban missile crisis was due to "the apparently benign ending of the crisis" (1982: 540). If one questions either how benign that ending actually was, as do some revisionist historians of the missile crisis (e.g., Nathan, 1975, 1992; Bernstein, 1979; Thompson, 1992), or the need for these events to have been understood as a crisis to begin with, as I attempt to do here, then the canonical status of the missile crisis as a precedent for excellent decision making begins to be undermined. Other critiques of this ostensibly dazzling display of diplomacy can be found in Stone, 1966; Steel, 1969; Bernstein, 1980; and Costigliola, 1995.

1. REPRESENTING MISSILES IN CUBA

1. The existence of at least three different crises in October of 1962 has generally passed unnoticed by American scholars and commentators. Recent exceptions are Allyn, Blight, and Welch, 1992, which notes the existence of these three divergent crises and provides brief outlines of each that emphasize some of the differences between them; Blight, Allyn, and Welch, 1993; and Scott and Smith, 1994.

2. On October 14, Richard Heyser flew his U-2 over western Cuba, taking the reconnaissance photographs that confirmed the presence of missile sites in San Cristóbal. October 16, on which President Kennedy was informed of the missiles, has traditionally been designated as the beginning of the Cuban missile crisis. Although the Cuban missile crisis is almost always defined in terms of the thirteen days from October 16 through October 28, it is occasionally dated from October 13, the day on which the possibility of

Soviet missiles was taken seriously enough to warrant ordering a U-2 over-flight of Cuba; see, for example, Farnsworth, 1988: 195. For a dramatic rendering of the "private" phase of the missile crisis up to Kennedy's speech on October 22, see Knebel, 1962.

3. Kennedy was referring to an official TASS statement of September 12, which read, "The government of the Soviet Union has authorized TASS to state also that there is no need for the Soviet Union to set up in any other country—Cuba, for instance—the weapons it has for repelling aggression, for a retaliatory blow. The explosive power of our nuclear weapons is so great and the Soviet Union has such powerful missiles for delivering these nuclear warheads that there is no need to seek sites for them somewhere beyond the boundaries of the Soviet Union" ("TASS statement on aid to Cuba," 1962: 14).

4. Most official U.S. government publications on, as well as scholarly treatments of, the Cuban missile crisis include a map that depicts the 1,200-mile range of the medium-range ballistic missiles (MRBMs) deployed in Cuba and the 2,000-mile range of the intermediate-range ballistic missiles (IRBMs) still to be deployed when the United States discovered the missiles.

5. In response to the U.S. request, the OAS passed a resolution that required "the immediate dismantling and withdrawal from Cuba of all missiles and other weapons with any offensive capability" (Organization of American States, 1962: 723).

6. This Joint Resolution had resolved that "the United States is determined (a) to prevent by whatever means may be necessary, including the use of arms, the Marxist-Leninist regime in Cuba from extending, by force or the threat of force, its aggressive or subversive activities to any part of this hemisphere; (b) to prevent in Cuba the creation or use of an externally supported military capability endangering the security of the United States" (U.S. Congress, 1962: 373). Similarly, on September 4, Kennedy had asserted that the introduction by the Soviet Union of "offensive ground-to-ground missiles" or of "other significant offensive capabilities" into Cuba would raise "the gravest issues" (Kennedy, 1962a: 2). On September 13 he had reiterated this warning, arguing that "if at any time the Communist build-up in Cuba were to endanger or interfere with our security in any way, including our base at Guantánamo, our passage to the Panama Canal, our missile and space activities at Cape Canaveral, or the lives of American citizens in this country, or if Cuba should ever attempt to export its aggressive purposes by force or the threat of force against any nation in this hemisphere, or become an offensive military base of significant capacity for the Soviet Union, then this country will do whatever must be done to protect its own security and that of its allies" (1962b: 674).

7. Robert Divine described the resolution of the crisis as follows: "At

the last minute, *Khrushchev accepted* the graceful way out that Kennedy had left him, withdrawing the missiles in return for an American pledge not to invade Cuba" (1971: 4, emphasis added). In *On the Brink* James Blight and David Welch describe the resolution in similar terms: "The United States and the Soviet Union seemed to be on the brink of war," they argued. "The next morning, *Khrushchev gave in*" (1990: 4, emphasis added). Though the orthodox story of the Cuban missile crisis typically portrays the Kremlin as having accepted U.S. terms, as having given in, the proposals accepted by the U.S.S.R. were in fact those initially made by Khrushchev in his letter of October 26 (in Pope, 1982: 37–49).

8. Although this metaphor has come to refer to the U.S. victory over the Soviets in the missile crisis as a whole, it was coined earlier in the crisis, when Soviet ships first turned back from the U.S. quarantine zone. At that point Dean Rusk is alleged to have said to McGeorge Bundy that "we're eyeball to eyeball and I think the other fellow just blinked" (reported in Abel, 1966: 153).

9. The idea that the Cuban missile crisis was John F. Kennedy's "finest hour" was prominent in early accounts (e.g., Abel, 1966; Schlesinger, 1965; Kennedy, 1971; Sorensen, 1965). Though the missile crisis is typically portrayed as having spanned only thirteen days, culminating in its dramatic resolution on October 28, it was not actually resolved that easily. Instead, "sticky issues soon emerged," including Castro's refusal to allow on-site inspections of the dismantling of the missiles, his refusal to allow the removal of Soviet IL-28 bombers from Cuba, his refusal to allow the withdrawal of Soviet troops stationed in Cuba, the potential construction of a Soviet submarine base in Cuba, and the refusal by the United States to give a public guarantee that it would not invade Cuba (Bernstein, 1979: 8). In fact, the United States "never issued any public or official statement of a commitment not to invade Cuba after the highly conditional statement by President Kennedy of November 20, 1962—the conditions of which (an international inspection in Cuba to verify the continuing absence of offensive arms) had not been met" (Garthoff, 1987: 94). Indeed, the "understanding" reached between the United States and the Soviet Union during October and November 1962 "was not really consummated until August of 1970, and not confirmed publicly until October of that year" (97).

10. Because Americans tend to be less familiar with the Soviet and Cuban narratives, I present them in somewhat greater detail. Relatively concise, although slightly divergent, accounts of the Caribbean crisis can be found in Khrushchev, 1970: 540–558; 1962a; 1962b; in Anatolii Gromyko, 1971: 161–226; and in the Soviet contributions to Blight and Welch, 1990 and to Allyn, Blight, and Welch, 1992. Anatolii A. Gromyko's account of the Caribbean crisis in *Die 1036 Tage* highlights in particular

the Soviet understanding of U.S. actions as imperialist, expansionist, and designed to protect U.S. capital against the encroachment of socialism (1970: 265–266).

11. Anatolii A. Gromyko wrote: "Vor allem ist ihnen zu entnehmen, daß die USA-Regierung auch während der Präsidentenzeit Kennedys bereit war, zur alten und *konterrevolutionären Politik des 'großen Knüppels'* zu greifen, wie sie Anfang des Jahrhunderts schon Präsident Theodore Roosevelt praktiziert hatte [Most important, one must infer that the U.S. government was prepared, also during Kennedy's presidency, to resort to the old *counterrevolutionary politics of the 'big stick'* that President Theodore Roosevelt had already practiced at the beginning of the century]" (1970: 299, emphasis added).

12. The official TASS statement pointed out that "The Soviet Union, like the other Socialist countries, has stretched forth the hand of aid to the Cuban people because we understand Cuba's situation particularly well. After the October Revolution, when the young Soviet state was in capitalist encirclement and the peoples of our country suffered tremendous difficulties caused by the postwar devastation, the United States, instead of giving assistance, undertook armed intervention against the Soviet Republic. American troops landed in Murmansk, Archangel and the Far East, British troops landed in Archangel and occupied Baku, French troops landed in Odessa and Japanese in the Maritime Territory. The imperialist powers set up counterrevolutionary armies under the leadership of Kolchak, Yudenich, Denikin and Wrangel, mobilized and armed the entire counterrevolutionary gang, this scum. . . . Now the United States of America wants to repeat against little heroic Cuba all that it once did against our country" ("TASS statement on aid to Cuba," 1962: 13). Similarly, in the aftermath of the Bay of Pigs, it was charged in *Pravda* that "the U.S. ruling circles are mortally afraid that Cuba, building its own independent life, will become an example to other countries of Latin America. And, with the hands of American hirelings, traitors to the Cuban people, the U.S.A. is trying to deprive the Cubans of the right to decide their own fate, just as the U.S.A. previously took this right from the people of Guatemala" ("Rooseveltian policies," 1961: 6).

13. By this time the decision to deploy the missiles had already been made, or had at least been contemplated. According to Sergei Mikoyan, the idea of deploying missiles in Cuba was first raised in April 1962 (in Blight and Welch, 1990: 238).

14. The dual purpose of the missile deployment was stressed by numerous Soviet participants in the Moscow Conference, including Dimitri Volkogonov (in Allyn, Blight, and Welch, 1992: 29, 53), Fyodor M. Burlatsky (45–46), and Georgy Shakhnazarov (68).

15. The protection of Cuba from U.S. aggression was highlighted by

Khrushchev not only in his memoirs but also at the time of the crisis in his letter to Kennedy of October 26 (in Pope, 1982: 39–41).

16. As Rafael Hernández explained at the Moscow Conference in 1989, the Cubans call this event the "October crisis," and not the "Caribbean crisis" or the "missile crisis" because "there had already been an April crisis, a May crisis, and one in September" of 1962 (in Allyn, Blight, and Welch, 1992: 173). For a detailed analysis (but one that still bears pervasive markers of its U.S. origins) of Castro's more recent narration of the October crisis at the Havana Conference of 1992, see Blight, Allyn, and Welch, 1993: esp. chapter 4.

17. Playa Girón is the beach at the Bahia de Cochinos, or Bay of Pigs. In 1992, Castro singled out the Bay of Pigs as providing the antecedents of the October crisis, arguing that "in Girón, we find the antecedents of the October Crisis because there is no doubt that, for Kennedy, it meant a severe political blow. He was embittered by this event. He was very upset. And afterwards the issue of Cuba had a special meaning for him. This was reflected in the relations between the two countries" (1992: 332).

18. In Havana, on April 28, 1961, just after the Bay of Pigs, President Dorticós read a note, signed by himself and Castro, that revealed Cuban fears of an imminent U.S. attack. Part of that note, read to the foreign diplomatic core, stated that "the conduct of Government circles of the United States, ostensible acts of war preparations against our country and information in the American press concerning consultations and explorations carried out by the State Department of that country with Latin American chancelleries asking aid for a direct armed attack against our country show the intention of the Government of the United States to carry out that attack" (in Phillips, 1961b: 3).

19. Dorticós also cited the Joint Resolution issued by the U.S. Congress in 1962 (see note 6). As Dorticós said, this resolution was understood in Cuba to signal the "prior sanction" by Congress "to the use of arms, to armed aggression against our country, in order to prevent in our territory the creation or use of a military capability endangering the security of the United States" (1962: 373).

20. That the Cubans (and the Soviets) were expecting a U.S. attack on Cuba is made quite clear in a variety of Cuban (and Soviet) contributions to the Moscow Conference proceedings (Allyn, Blight, and Welch, 1992).

21. The claim that Soviet missiles were stationed in Cuba to protect Cuba from U.S. invasion has been reiterated by Castro innumerable times. In a speech he gave on July 26, 1980, for example, he again stated, "Mercenary invasions, pirate attacks, plans for direct aggression. Wasn't all that what led to nuclear missiles being stationed in Cuba? Why did we agree to that? Simply to counter U.S. plans of direct aggression against Cuba" (1980: 328).

22. In 1992 Castro presented a slightly different argument in which the primary reason for the missile deployment shifted from the defense of Cuba to the strategic situation. Claiming that the Cubans "did not have any doubts" about the missile installation, he explained that "first of all, when the issue of the missiles was first brought up, we thought it was something beneficial to the consolidation of the defensive power of the entire socialist bloc, that it would contribute to this. We did not want to concentrate on our [Cuba's] problems. Subsequently, it represented our defense. Subsequently. . . . In all truth and summarizing, we, from the beginning, saw it as a strategic operation" (1992: 333). At the Moscow Conference, Emilio Aragonés (a member of the Cuban Secretariat, the Cuban decision-making body, during the October crisis) also argued that the deployment of the missiles was undertaken "not so much to defend Cuba as to change the correlation of forces between capitalism and socialism" (in Allyn, Blight, and Welch, 1992: 51; see also 123–124). Given the argument that an improved strategic situation for the Soviet Union would help to protect Cuba from a U.S. attack, these two arguments are not in fact so different.

23. On this Castro clearly differed with Khrushchev. In the same speech, Castro proceeded to point out that "in contrast, to tell the truth, Khrushchev went along with the game of categorizing the weapons. He turned it into something intentional. Since he did not have any intention of using the weapons in an offensive operation, he believed that it was the intention that defined the nature of the weapons. But it was very clear that Kennedy did not understand it that way. Kennedy did not understand the issue of intentions but rather the issue of type of weapons, whether they were strategic weapons or not. That was the issue [for Kennedy]" (1992: 337).

24. Sorensen points out that this quote is often misinterpreted to mean that Kennedy thought the chances of a nuclear war stood at "between one in three and even." The correct interpretation, Sorensen maintains, is that Kennedy assigned these odds to the chance that "the Soviets would go all the way to war against the United States" (in Blight and Welch, 1990: 87). Despite Sorensen's caveat, this quote is nonetheless typically understood to mean that the world had come closer than ever before to nuclear war.

25. In Blight and Welch's *On the Brink*, Albert Carnesale recognizes that the installation of the missiles cannot, by itself, have initiated the crisis. After all, as he argued, the crisis was caused by the United States as well "because of the way it reacted to the missiles in Cuba" (in Blight and Welch, 1990: 104). This recognition is not part of the standard story of the Cuban missile crisis. Another exception is David Detzer's *The Brink* (1979). He begins his study of the missile crisis with a chapter on Cuba and a second on U.S.-Cuban relations prior to the crisis. In the latter, he details U.S. aggression, both overt and covert, against Cuba and the Castro government. Again,

setting the missile crisis in the context of U.S. aggression, thus making it seem less like a bolt from the blue, is not part of the myth of the Cuban missile crisis.

26. Most accounts of the Cuban missile crisis insist on this short, thirteen-day time span. Robert Kennedy's *Thirteen Days* (1971) is the most obvious example. Elie Abel's early account in *The Missile Crisis* (1966) is divided into chapters that are simply entitled "Sunday, October 14" through "Sunday, October 28" (which add up to a still short fifteen days). Graham Allison's famous *Essence of Decision* (1971) begins with a calendar of October 1962 on which the sixteenth through the twenty-eighth are highlighted. Even in Blight and Welch's more recent analysis, the missile crisis is described as "those thirteen dramatic days in October 1962" (1990: 22). This same time span was emphasized in two recent television documentaries honoring the thirtieth anniversary of the missile crisis. Each was organized, quite typically and yet also quite dramatically, around the same sequence of thirteen days conventionally associated with the Cuban missile crisis (see "The missiles of October," 1992, and "The Cuban missile crisis," 1992; the original version of the latter documentary was part of the PBS series *War and Peace in the Nuclear Age*). Both of these recent documentaries, although they include some of the Soviet material presented at the Cambridge Conference, in no way challenge the orthodox U.S. story of the Cuban missile crisis. The same dramatic framing device, this time specifying a fourteen-day duration, appeared in a recent article in *USA Today*, in which the author claimed that "the crisis . . . began on October 15, 1962, when US spy planes spotted Soviet missiles on Cuba" and ended "on October 28 with the Soviet leader backing down" (Raitberger, 1997: 10A). In *On the Brink*, the precise time frame that should be assigned to the missile crisis is questioned explicitly only once, by Scott D. Sagan. But the only alternative he offers extends the end of the crisis into November, when the Soviet IL-28 bombers were finally removed from Cuba as well (in Blight and Welch, 1990: 62, 73), an extension that is then rejected by Sorensen (in Blight and Welch, 1990: 73).

It is interesting that on October 29, Kennedy's tapes capture him ordering a president's commemorative "for the Executive Committee of the National Security Council who've been involved in this matter." He described what he wanted as "something that would have the month of October on it. And the 10 days—would have a line drawn around the calendar days; yeah, it would be a calendar. . . . It's about 12, about 12. The days with the line drawn around it. Let's see, Tuesday, Thursday, October—what is it? That's the 29th, I would say, so it would be the 28th" (in May and Zelikow, 1997: 660–661). According to May and Zelikow, the commemorative was prepared by Tiffany's in silver for about thirty U.S. state officials (661).

27. Allison did not, of course, mean this in quite the same way that I do.

All three of his conceptual frameworks—the rational actor, organizational process, and governmental (bureaucratic) politics models—analyze a set of events as interpreted from *within* the confines of the U.S. security imaginary: They all begin with the orthodox portrait of the event—the Cuban missile crisis—sketched above.

28. The importance and role of narrative in historiography has been stressed by many philosophers and historians, including, for example, Danto, 1985; Gallie, 1964; LaCapra, 1985; and White, 1978, 1987.

2. THE VIEW FROM THE EXCOMM

1. In this chapter I focus on what became the dominant view of the crisis for Kennedy, his advisers, and other U.S. state officials. There were certainly disagreements among these individuals, some of which I mention below. For an interesting look at the crisis from the point of view of different personalities, including John F. Kennedy, Robert Kennedy, Dean Acheson, and Adlai Stevenson, see White, 1996.

Among those who participated in the ExComm meetings were President John F. Kennedy and Vice President Lyndon B. Johnson, and, in alphabetical order, Undersecretary of State George Ball, Special Assistant to the President for National Security Affairs McGeorge Bundy, Deputy Director of the CIA General Marshall Carter, Secretary of the Treasury Douglas Dillon, Deputy Secretary of Defense Roswell Gilpatric, Deputy Undersecretary of State U. Alexis Johnson, Attorney General Robert F. Kennedy, Assistant Secretary of State for Latin America Edwin Martin, Secretary of Defense Robert McNamara, Director John McCone of the CIA, Assistant Secretary of Defense Paul H. Nitze, Secretary of State Dean Rusk, Presidential Press Secretary Pierre Salinger, Presidential Counsel Theodore Sorensen, Chairman General Maxwell Taylor of the Joint Chiefs of Staff, and Special Adviser for Soviet Affairs Llewellyn Thompson.

2. The transcripts of the ExComm meeting of October 16 are published in "White House tapes and minutes," 1985, and will hereafter be cited as October 16. Extensive excerpts from the transcripts of the ExComm's October 27 meeting are published in "October 27, 1962," 1987–88, and will be cited as October 27. Complete transcripts can be found in May and Zelikow's *The Kennedy Tapes* (1997).

3. The Hawk's Cay Conference, held in the Florida Keys on March 5–8, 1987, was organized by James G. Blight and sponsored by Harvard University's Project on Avoiding Nuclear War. It brought together former members of the ExComm and a set of U.S. scholars noted for their work on the missile crisis. Excerpts are transcribed in Blight and Welch, 1990.

4. The United States was understood to be threatened not only by the

missile deployment itself but by the crisis that those missiles sparked. The crisis (as distinct from the missile deployment that provoked it) threatened the United States directly because of the possibility of escalation to a general war or even to a nuclear war. It also threatened West Berlin and Turkey, which, as NATO allies and part of the free world, were objects of U.S. national interests, because they might be attacked by the Soviet Union in the event that the crisis escalated (see, for example, the discussions by John F. Kennedy [on October 19, in May and Zelikow, 1997: 176–177], by McGeorge Bundy [October 27: 52], or between President Kennedy and Prime Minister Harold Macmillan [on October 22, in May and Zelikow, 1997: 283–284]). I do not discuss these potential threats to the United States and to other objects of U.S. security generated within the crisis because I am interested in the production of that crisis to begin with.

5. This ostensible physical threat to the United States has consistently been emphasized in both official government and scholarly discussions of the Cuban missile crisis through the endless reproduction of maps showing the range and potential target areas of the Soviet missiles in Cuba. These maps, of course, neither show the range and target areas of the missiles that the United States had deployed around the Soviet Union nor explain what incentive the Soviet Union might have had to use those missiles in launching a nuclear attack against the United States.

6. Revised estimates indicate that in 1962 the Soviet Union actually had fewer than fifty operational ICBMs. For example, in 1987, Garthoff claimed that at the time of the missile crisis the Soviet arsenal had included only forty-four ICBMs (in Blight and Welch, 1990: 31).

7. By the mid-1950s, Khrushchev's de-Stalinization project had led to upheavals in Eastern Europe, first in Poland and then, in 1956, in Hungary. Roughly simultaneously, the United States and Britain became embroiled in a conflict with Egypt over the funding of the Aswan Dam and other contentious issues. In response, in April 1956, Gamal Abdel Nasser seized the Suez Canal by nationalizing the Universal Suez Canal Company, which had been controlled by the British. In October, after Israel attacked Egypt, Britain and France did as well. What Kennedy called "the Egyptian and the Hungary thing," also known as the "Suez-Hungary combination," refers to the fact that "the confrontation in the Middle East provided Khrushchev with the perfect opportunity for counteraction. As Anglo-French columns moved into the Canal area on November 4 and 5, Russian tanks crushed the Hungarian uprising" (LaFeber, 1985: 188; see also May and Zelikow, 1997: 17).

8. The Turkish missile trade is one of the few serious discrepancies between the public myth of the Cuban missile crisis and the understanding of the situation developed within the ExComm. It does not appear as part of the public story because the early sources for that myth vehemently, and

falsely, denied that such a trade had ever been considered. Theodore Sorensen, for one, asserted that "the President had no intention of destroying the Alliance by backing down. . . . He decided to treat the latest Khrushchev message [of October 27] as propaganda and to concentrate on the Friday night letter" (1965: 714). In *Thirteen Days,* Robert Kennedy gave the same impression. On October 27 he reportedly told Soviet ambassador Anatolii Dobrynin that "there could be no quid pro quo or any arrangement" exchanging the Jupiter missiles in Turkey for Soviet missiles in Cuba (1971: 86). (Theodore Sorensen has since admitted that he falsified Robert Kennedy's account of the Turkish missile deal in order "to disguise the fact that the President had authorized a secret assurance to Khrushchev that the Jupiter missiles would be removed from Turkey" [Scott and Smith, 1994: 669].) Finally, Arthur Schlesinger emphatically argued that "the notion of trading the Cuban and Turkish bases had been much discussed in England; Walter Lippmann and others had urged it in the United States. But Kennedy regarded the idea as unacceptable, and the swap was promptly rejected" (1965: 827). See also Hilsman, 1967: 203.

The inaccuracy of these claims was finally exposed in the so-called Rusk revelation. At Hawk's Cay, Dean Rusk shocked the participants when he disclosed that President Kennedy had instructed him on October 27 "to open up a channel to the United Nations through which a public trade of missiles—SS-4s and SS-5s in Cuba for NATO Jupiters in Turkey—might have been consummated" (in Blight and Welch, 1990: 114). See also Lukas, 1987, and Pace, 1987. In contrast to the popular missile crisis myth, "the withdrawal of the Jupiter missiles from Turkey in the spring of 1963 was indeed part of a private deal that led to the withdrawal of Soviet missiles from Cuba in November, 1962" (Allyn, Blight, and Welch, 1989–90: 165).

9. In this context it is also worth pointing to the rather remarkable claim made by Sorensen at the Hawk's Cay Conference: "Let me say," he asserted, "that the line between offensive and defensive weapons was drawn in September, and it was not drawn in a way which was intended to leave the Soviets any ambiguity to play with. I believe the President drew the line precisely where he thought the Soviets were not and would not be; that is to say, *if we had known that the Soviets were putting forty missiles in Cuba, we might under this hypothesis have drawn the line at one hundred, and said with great fanfare that we would absolutely not tolerate the presence of more than one hundred missiles in Cuba. . . . I am suggesting that one reason the line was drawn at zero was because we simply thought the Soviets weren't going to deploy any there anyway*" (in Blight and Welch, 1990: 43, emphasis added). If this argument is accurate, it further reinforces the claim that concern to safeguard U.S. and administration credibility, rather than fears of the missiles themselves, powerfully motivated U.S. decision makers

in their response to the Soviet missile deployment. (But cf. Blight and Welch, 1990: 363–364, note 45.)

10. Domestic politics were also highlighted by Steel, 1969, and Stone, 1966. For an argument that Cuba played a less-important role in the 1960 campaign, see Beck, 1984.

11. According to Sorensen, the ExComm initially considered six options: (1) "Do nothing," (2) "Bring diplomatic pressures and warnings to bear on the Soviets," (3) "Undertake a secret approach to Castro," (4) "Initiate indirect military action by means of a blockade," (5) "Conduct an air strike," and (6) "Launch an invasion" (1965: 682). Most of the ExComm deliberations, however, revolved around a blockade and an air strike, the latter often combined with an invasion of Cuba.

12. The terms "hawk" and "dove" are usually attributed to Stewart Alsop and Charles Bartlett in their report on the missile crisis in the *Saturday Evening Post* (1962: 20), although May and Zelikow suggest that, since the source for this article was John F. Kennedy, the terms may actually have been coined by him (May and Zelikow, 1997: 202, note 15). The hawks, among whom are generally counted Dean Acheson, Douglas Dillon, McGeorge Bundy, John McCone, Paul Nitze, and Maxwell Taylor, preferred immediate and decisive military action in the form of an air strike against the missile bases. The doves, including Robert Kennedy, Robert McNamara, Dean Rusk, Theodore Sorensen, and Llewellyn Thompson, favored a naval blockade. Though the hawks/doves distinction is important in addressing some questions about the Cuban missile crisis, it is not relevant to the argument I am making. My interest lies precisely in those assumptions that all of the decision makers, whether hawks or doves, shared and that led them to agree from the outset that the missiles had to be removed. Furthermore, I do not agree with Blight and Welch that the hawks and doves faced "incommensurable crises" (1990: 201). As their own careful comparison shows, the two positions are comparable and the relative merits of each can be assessed. Blight and Welch themselves conclude that "the doves exhibited the more prudent and realistic approach to coping with uncertainty, and thereby advocated wiser courses of action" (220).

13. As Abram Chayes, State Department legal adviser during the missile crisis, pointed out, a fourth option, the "buy 'em out" strategy, was in fact discussed extensively, especially on October 27. In this strategy the United States would trade the missiles in Turkey for those in Cuba. "This one gets talked about much less than the others," Chayes argued in 1989, "because of the power of the Munich stigma and because it sounds a lot less courageous. But in fact we did, in part, buy 'em out, and the President seems to have been willing to go even further than he did in this direction if need be. . . . I have a distinct recollection of a meeting on Saturday. . . . somebody

polled the group on whether we thought we were going to get out of this thing without trading the Jupiters . . . and not a single person thought we were!" (in Blight and Welch, 1990: 102–103). I do not discuss the "buy 'em out" option here because it did not become important until after the receipt of Khrushchev's letter of October 27. The crisis was then resolved, at least for the United States and the Soviet Union, on the twenty-eighth. Until the receipt of Khrushchev's proposal, the focus in the ExComm had been on military strategies for securing the removal of the missiles.

14. The various difficulties raised by the air strike are discussed in most treatments of the Cuban missile crisis. See, for example, Allison, 1971: 58–61, and Sorensen, 1965: 684–685.

15. For a searing criticism of Robert Kennedy's Pearl Harbor analogy, see Acheson, 1969b: 76. For more on the importance of the Pearl Harbor analogy to the missile crisis, see May and Zelikow, 1997: 3–4.

16. A list of the difficulties that a blockade would create is provided in Sorensen, 1965: 687–688.

17. Discussions of the merits of a blockade can be found in Kennedy, 1971: 15–17; Allison, 1971: 60–61, 202–203; Abel, 1966: 81; and Sorensen, 1965: 805–806, passim.

18. This is not to imply that other military options, such as an air strike, were no longer considered once the blockade had been decided upon, since one of the benefits of the blockade option was that it left room for escalation. As the crisis again escalated, the wisdom and utility of various additional measures, including an invasion of Cuba, were debated as well. In particular, air strikes and an invasion were again seriously discussed on October 27 after the news reached the ExComm that low-flying U.S. surveillance aircraft had been fired upon. The alternatives, under the eleventh-hour conditions of Black Saturday, were starkly laid out by McNamara: "I think we ought to either do one of two things. . . . we're either going to return that fire, tomorrow, but in a limited fashion against the things that fired against us, or against their air defenses, or, alternatively, if we *don't* return the fire tomorrow, we ought to go in the next day with [words unclear] sorties. One or the other" (October 27: 65, emphasis and brackets in the original). Shortly thereafter, when the ExComm members were informed that a U-2 had actually been shot down over Cuba, taking direct action became even more imperative. McNamara was again the one to lay the options out explicitly: "I think we can defer an air attack on Cuba until Wednesday or Thursday, but *only* if we continue our surveillance and—and—uh—fire against anything that fires against the surveillance aircraft, and only if we maintain a tight blockade in this interim period. If we're willing to do these two things, I think we can defer the air attack until Wednesday or Thursday" (October 27: 66, emphasis in the original). The decision to implement air strikes was

deferred while the ExComm awaited the ultimately successful outcome of the Trollope ploy.

19. The exhaustiveness of the ExComm deliberations has been a prominent part of the myth of the Cuban missile crisis. Arthur Schlesinger, for example, claimed that the decision to initiate the blockade was based on an "exceedingly vigorous and intensive debate" and that "major alternatives received strong, even vehement, expression" (1973: 173). Abel makes a similar claim. "That first day's crisis discussions," he asserted, "amounted, in Dean Rusk's phrase, to 'boxing the compass.' The entire spectrum of possible American responses was reviewed" (1966: 50). This aspect of the myth was invoked as recently as the Tower Commission Report on the Iran-Contra affair. In their discussion of the proper role for the National Security Council, the authors of the report hold up the ExComm as an exemplary case: "President Kennedy, for example, did not have adequate consultation before entering upon the Bay of Pigs invasion, one of his greatest failures. He remedied this in time for the Cuban missile crisis, one of his greatest successes" (Tower, Muskie, and Scowcroft, 1987: 89). Critics, on the other hand, have argued that the discussions by the ExComm were in fact much too limited (e.g., Yarmolinsky, 1970–71; Lippmann, 1963; Steel, 1969; Stone, 1966; Walton, 1972). Acheson, 1969b, also casts doubt on the exhaustiveness of the deliberations, although from a hawkish point of view favoring an air strike.

20. David Welch is one of the few analysts even to note this absence (1989: 433). However, he does not pursue its significance for the U.S. narration of the Cuban missile crisis or the construction of the U.S. national interest.

21. That Soviet motives revolved around the strategic balance has also been maintained in much of the secondary literature on the missile crisis. Examples include Alsop and Bartlett, 1962: 18; Horelick and Rush, 1966: 141, 153–154; Tatu, 1969: 230–231; Kahan and Long, 1972: 564–590; and Garthoff, 1988: 65–66.

22. In the transcript the speaker is tentatively identified as George Ball. See also Brzezinski, 1962: 7–8; Horelick and Rush, 1966: 142; and Cline, 1988: 194, 196.

23. Lists of such hypotheses can be found in Blight and Welch, 1990: 116–117; Allison, 1971: 43–56; Hilsman, 1967: 201–202; Medland, 1988: 36; and Sorensen, 1965: 676–678. The issue of Soviet domestic politics was raised at the Moscow Conference by William Taubman (in Allyn, Blight, and Welch, 1992: 122). Sergo Mikoyan responded that "there was no direct connection of those difficulties in agriculture, or others in our country, with the decision to defend Cuba" (in Allyn, Blight, and Welch, 1992: 139).

24. It is interesting to note in this context that Paul Huth and Bruce

Russett (1984) do not include the Soviet missile deployment as an instance of attempted extended deterrence. (Thanks to David Welch for this point.) With increased access to information about the missile crisis, and perhaps with the waning of the cold war, however, the dominant story of the Cuban missile crisis is finally being transformed, particularly in the increasing acceptance of the defense-of-Cuba argument. For example, Allyn, Blight, and Welch have recently argued that "the Soviet decision to deploy medium- and intermediate-range ballistic missiles (MRBMs and IRBMs) in Cuba appears to have been a response to three main concerns: *first, the perceived need to deter an American invasion of Cuba and prevent the destruction of the Cuban revolution*; second, the perceived need to redress the gross imbalance in deliverable strategic nuclear weapons that favored the United States; and third, the desire, born of national pride and prestige, to counter American deployments of nuclear weapons on the Soviet periphery, by exercise of the Soviet Union's 'equal right' to deploy its own nuclear missiles on territory adjacent to the United States. According to recent Soviet testimony, the first and second appear to have been the most important motivations, though there is disagreement on the proper assignments of weight to each" (1989–90: 138–139, emphasis added). Other recent accounts that take the defense-of-Cuba argument more seriously include Paterson, 1990: 249–256; Bernstein, 1990; Hershberg, 1990; and Lebow and Stein, 1994.

25. Arthur Schlesinger also denigrated the Soviet claim to be defending Cuba when he described the Soviet accusation, made in September 1962, that the United States was "preparing for aggression against Cuba" as "truculent," implying that the Soviets were acting belligerently rather than defensively (1965: 799). Alsop and Bartlett similarly cast doubt on Khrushchev's defensive claims when they argued that Khrushchev "piously maintained" that his intentions "were purely defensive" (1962: 16).

26. This is consistent with their focus on the question of Soviet motives in *On the Brink,* but it is a bit difficult to reconcile with their own claims of a Soviet defensive motivation in Allyn, Blight, and Welch, 1989–90: 138–139; see note 4 in this chapter.

27. I am not arguing that the Soviet account is necessarily true, that Khrushchev "really did" deploy the missiles in defense of Cuba. Instead, I am attempting to show merely that the Soviet and Cuban claims to have been acting to defend Cuba were plausible, given prior U.S. actions against Cuba and contemporary U.S. military plans and covert operations, and that taking these claims seriously might have altered the understanding of U.S. national interests.

28. Blight and Welch organized a second conference, held in Cambridge, Massachusetts, in October 1987. At this conference Soviet representatives

joined the U.S. participants to discuss the events of October 1962. Some of the proceedings are transcribed in their *On the Brink* (1990).

29. Even at this conference, which seems finally to have convinced at least Robert McNamara that the Soviets and Cubans might really have anticipated a U.S. invasion, the defense-of-Cuba hypothesis was not initially taken seriously. Each time the Soviet representatives claimed that the Soviet Union or Khrushchev had been attempting to defend Cuba, the U.S. participants responded with questions about what they clearly believed was the real issue: Soviet perceptions of the strategic balance between the United States and the Soviet Union. Only late in the conference, after considerable argument by the Soviet participants, was the Soviet claim to have been defending Cuba addressed by the Americans (Blight and Welch, 1990: chapter 5, esp. 239–244).

30. McNamara had clearly changed his view. The statement, quoted in the text, made at the Moscow Conference in January 1989, is even stronger than his already unusual statement of two years earlier. "We should recognize," he had argued early on at Hawk's Cay, "that we didn't then (and we don't today) give much thought to how Moscow will read what we are doing. We'd carried out the Bay of Pigs operation never intending to use American military force—but the Kremlin didn't know that. We were running covert operations against Castro. We'd convinced them we were actively trying to overthrow the Cuban regime. We never had put adequate emphasis on how the Soviets were interpreting our actions and how they might respond" (in Blight and Welch, 1990: 29). Not all U.S. analysts, observers, or former participants have been convinced by these Soviet arguments and revelations, however. An example is Ray S. Cline, CIA deputy director for intelligence from 1962 to 1966. In a response to the Cambridge Conference, he has asserted that "Mikhail Gorbachev's team of official intellectuals is engaged in a program of historical revisionism serving Moscow's interests" (1988: 190).

31. Except for the president, these men were all members of the Special Group (Augmented) that was created to deal with the problem of Cuba (see Schlesinger, 1978: 477, note).

32. In his discussion, Bundy does not mention the rest of the history of U.S. aggression against Cuba in 1960 and 1961, from the oil embargo and the elimination of the Cuban sugar quota to the suspension of diplomatic relations. Though Bundy clearly recognized some of the difficulties attendant upon the failure of U.S. decision makers to consider Soviet perceptions of U.S. actions, and though that failure is critical to an understanding of the Cuban missile crisis, he nevertheless devotes only a very short discussion to this issue, turning, as is typical, to a discussion of the strategic balance (1988: 416–420, passim).

33. At least according to Scott Armstrong, however, the Moscow Conference put Cuba "back into the Cuban missile crisis for Americans in a very definitive way here, in some sense" (in Allyn, Blight, and Welch, 1992: 193); see also Armstrong and Brenner, 1987.

34. Although the resolution of the crisis is conventionally portrayed as having allowed Khrushchev to save face, this is itself a dubious claim. As Stephen R. Shalom has argued, by rejecting the Jupiter missile trade that Khrushchev made in a public offer to resolve the crisis, the United States was in effect "insisting that Moscow accept a public humiliation" (1988: 75). A private commitment either not to invade Cuba or to remove the Jupiter missiles from Turkey would not "mitigate Khrushchev's humiliation, since humiliation is by its nature public" (76). Moreover, when the resolution of the crisis dragged into November because the United States insisted that the Soviets remove their IL-28 aircraft from Cuba, Khrushchev was again humiliated. As the issue became acute, "Khrushchev suggested a face-saving way out. If the U.S. would lift the blockade, he would quietly remove the bombers shortly thereafter. But Washington, having placed itself in Khrushchev's shoes, decided the shoes needed tightening. They rejected his proposal. Khrushchev would have to be humiliated again and publicly antagonize his Cuban ally" (78).

35. This reference to Castro occurs in a discussion of conservative reaction to Kennedy's handling of the missile crisis. "For some in the Pentagon and the CIA," Bundy pointed out, "the removal of Castro was not only an end of great value in itself—a view which the President strongly shared—but one whose achievement could now be justified by his complicity in creating this clear and present danger" to U.S. national interests (1988: 397). According to these conservative critics, the removal of the missiles should not have been the only U.S. objective in the missile crisis. Instead, the Kennedy administration should have used the opportunity to rid itself of Castro's government once and for all.

36. Two notable exceptions are the 1989 Moscow Conference, to which the Soviet organizers invited Cuban participants (see Allyn, Blight, and Welch, 1992), and the 1992 Havana Conference, which focused on the Cuban role in and story of these events (excerpts in Blight, Allyn, and Welch, 1993).

37. Interestingly, this contribution was deleted from the second edition of Divine's book (1988).

38. There are, of course, exceptions. Morley, 1987, for example, takes U.S. aggression against Cuba seriously and pays more attention than is usual to Cuban politics and Cuban interests.

39. Interestingly, although many of the participants in the crisis agreed that the missiles were of little strategic value, even after twenty-five years, at

the Hawk's Cay and Moscow Conferences, the effects of the Soviet missile deployment on the strategic balance received considerable and animated attention (see Blight and Welch, 1990: 26–37, 230–252; Allyn, Blight, and Welch, 1992).

40. Marc Trachtenberg, in his introduction to the transcript of the October 16 meeting, in "White House tapes and minutes," points out that the idea that the missiles might have had no effect on the strategic balance did not receive the attention one might expect (1985: 169). However, like most other analysts of the Cuban missile crisis, he fails to pursue this insight to ask *why* this issue was ignored.

41. The question marks indicate the transcriber's uncertainty as to the identity of the speakers.

42. For a contrary argument, see Garthoff, who argues that "the management and the resolution of the crisis from both sides was even more haphazard than was originally realized. . . . Indeed, in the missile crisis both the United States and the Soviet Union were groping almost blindly for a bottom-line basis for compromise that would serve the interests of both" (1988: 77).

43. Albert and Roberta Wohlstetter were similarly complementary (1965: 18–19); see also note 19 in this chapter.

44. Janis claimed that "whether the President was right or wrong in setting up his objective is not relevant to a discussion of group decision making" (1972: 142). This claim rests on an inappropriate distinction between ends and means, between substantive and procedural rationality. As a result, it inappropriately shields from critical analysis the question of the rationality of the ends, of the national interests, pursued by the United States during the Cuban missile crisis.

45. These are among the issues that Welch and Blight claimed could be satisfactorily answered with the release of the transcripts from October 16 and 27 (1987–88: 5–29).

3. CONSTRUCTING NATIONAL INTERESTS

1. For an opposing argument that associates Jefferson with U.S. expansionism, particularly into Indian lands, see Drinnon, 1990. Whether or not Jefferson's vision was really introverted or extroverted is not important to my argument. The fact remains that introverted arguments existed that could have been articulated to the vision of U.S. greatness.

2. For an example of such an investigation, in which a formal analysis, albeit one that slights power, is provided of the range of interpretive possibilities available for U.S. state officials in their construction of the Korean War, see Milliken, 1994.

3. The fictional character of these nodal or central subject positions is

captured well by Castoriadis, who argues that "central significations are not significations 'of' something—nor are they, except in a second-order sense, significations 'attached' or 'related' to something. They constitute that which, for a given society, brings into being the co-belonging of objects, acts and individuals which, in appearance, are most heterogeneous. They have no 'referent'; they institute a mode of being of things and of individuals which relate to them. . . . They are presentified-figured through the totality of the explicit institutions of society and the organization of the world as such and of the social world which these institutions serve to instrument. They condition and orient social doing and representing, in and through which they continue as they are themselves altered" (1987: 364).

4. The anthropomorphization of the state in much current U.S. international relations theorizing is thus no accident, nor is it peculiar to international relations scholarship. Instead, it reflects the anthropomorphization of the state that animates the language of the U.S. national interest used by U.S. state officials (and others) in the practice of U.S. foreign policy. The habit of anthropomorphizing the state in U.S. international relations theory thus reproduces state officials' views of the world, thereby both legitimizing U.S. state policy and helping to fix attention onto the issues of "problem-solving" rather than of critical theory (see Cox, 1981).

5. The importance of state identity and processes of state identity construction, especially for the United States, are discussed in detail by David Campbell (e.g., 1992, 1994).

6. From a realist perspective, of course, this seems obvious. But it is not. The central object of the national interest, even within the United States, does not have to be "the United States." As many critics of the concept of national security have emphasized, the object to be protected by policies in the national interest can be both larger and smaller than the state. Larger objects might be global, such as some notion of human rights or the environment. Smaller objects might be individuals, in particular their economic, ecological, and personal security interests. See, for example, Barnet, 1988; Buzan, 1983; and Matthews, 1989.

7. I am not implying that all individuals are successfully interpellated into the dominant representations. For a fascinating account of individuals who came to refuse what were once firm interpellations into the U.S. nuclear strategic discourse, see Everett, 1989. However, for a variety of reasons, many or most individuals are in fact successfully interpellated into the dominant discourse. Why particular individuals resist interpellation whereas others do not may have a variety of explanations, from peculiarities of individual socialization and education to individual psychology to the presence of alternative discourses that these individuals find more persuasive. Though this is an interesting question for further research, addressing it is beyond

the scope of this project. For a provocative take on this issue, see Smith, 1988.

8. One reason that imaginaries are not merely false—in the sense either of "false consciousness" or of mere dogma or rationalization—is precisely that they account for individuals' self-understandings. As Eagleton says, "in order to be truly effective," an ideology or, in my terms, an imaginary "must make at least some minimal sense of people's experience, must conform to some degree with what they know of social reality from their practical interaction with it" (1991: 14). If our everyday understanding or knowledge of the world were not in significant respects practical, we could not successfully negotiate that world. An imaginary therefore "can't be false in any simple sense," as Hall pointed out. After all, "practical bourgeois men," functioning with a liberal imaginary, do in fact "seem capable enough of making profit, working the system, sustaining its relations, exploiting labor, without benefit of a more sophisticated or 'truer' understanding of what they are involved in" (Hall, 1986a: 30).

9. The use of "we" to mean "the United States," and specifically actions taken by the U.S. state, is pervasive in U.S. culture. It can be observed in public forums such as newspaper editorials and television interviews in which journalists, politicians, and "ordinary" folk routinely refer to the United States as "we." In discussion with colleagues about this phenomenon, it has become apparent that university students are also widely prone to the use of this locution. An interesting research question concerns the extent to which this intimate identification—or successful interpellation—of individual citizens with the state and state policy is unique to the United States. On the basis of anecdotal evidence provided by friends and colleagues from diverse cultural backgrounds, including in particular Canada, New Zealand, and India, this intimacy looks to be a peculiarly American phenomenon or, at least, to be more prevalent in the United States than elsewhere. If this is true, then the interpellation of individuals into the security imaginary of other states either is accomplished through other processes or is not accomplished as successfully as it appears to be in the United States.

10. The importance of these institutions to the formulation of foreign policy and their interconnections with the state's national security apparatus are well documented. See, among others, Hoffman, 1977; Lyons and Morton, 1965; Smith, 1966; Kolko, 1969; Shoup and Minter, 1977; Berman, 1983; Herman and O'Sullivan, 1989; and Dalby, 1990.

11. I am using the term here as defined by Hall, whose conception of "organic" and "traditional" intellectuals is, I think, slightly different from Gramsci's. In any case, Hall has defined "traditional intellectuals" as those who "align themselves with existing dispositions of social and intellectual forces" and whose intellectual labors are thus intended to serve the status

quo, whereas "organic intellectuals" are those who "align themselves with emerging popular forces and seek to elaborate new currents of ideas" (1986b: 21–22). The intellectuals housed in the intellectual apparatuses I am discussing are traditional intellectuals in the sense that they have aligned themselves "with existing dispositions of social and intellectual forces" in helping to produce, reproduce, and legitimate the security imaginary.

12. Individual national security analysts, including nuclear strategists, diplomatic historians, and foreign policy analysts, move quite easily from university to think tank, to private foundation, and to the apparatus of the national security state. Prominent examples include Bernard Brody, Zbigniew Brzezinski, Herbert Feis, Louis Halle, Samuel Huntington, Walter Kaufmann, George Kennan, Jeane Kirkpatrick, Henry Kissinger, Hans Morgenthau, Joseph S. Nye, Walt Rostow, Arthur Schlesinger Jr., and Adam Yarmolinsky. All of these individuals have followed career paths that have crisscrossed this network of ideological, intellectual, and national security apparatuses (e.g., Kaplan, 1983; Melanson, 1983; Lundestad, 1989).

13. I deviate here from Foucault's terminology. Foucault used the terms "discursive" and "non-discursive" practices where I follow Laclau and Mouffe (1987: 82–84) in using the terms "linguistic" and "nonlinguistic."

14. The rhetorical character of much cold war historiography, as well as its complicity with U.S. foreign policy, is discussed by, among others, Melanson, 1983; Lundestad, 1989; and Cumings, 1993. For a fascinating analysis of the role played by the same cold war rhetoric in a legal context, specifically in the construction of the Rosenberg trial and the subsequent execution of Julius and Ethel Rosenberg, see Carmichael, 1993.

15. This is true not only of cynical, manipulative uses of language and of decorative, literary uses of language but of self-consciously scientific uses of language as well. That the language of economics, generally assumed to be one of the more scientific of the social sciences, is highly rhetorical has been argued persuasively by Donald McCloskey (1985, 1990). The role of rhetoric in various human sciences is addressed in Nelson, Megill, and McCloskey, 1987. Even the rhetoric of mathematics has come under scrutiny (e.g., Kline, 1980; Davis and Hersh, 1981).

4. CONSTRUCTING THE CUBAN MISSILE CRISIS: COLD WAR REPRESENTATIONS

1. Similar rhetorical constructions have been highlighted by Wayne Brockriede and Robert Scott, who asserted that "above all, the Cuban missile crisis reveals men caught up . . . completely in events shaped by words and in part shaping words" (1970: 116). However, the conclusion they drew from their analysis of the missile crisis as a "complex persuasive campaign" (79) is

that "although rhetoric did not lead to a complete resolution of fundamental problems, it played an important role: *it kept the Cold War cold*" (116, emphasis added). They reached this conclusion because of their focus on the "restraint" that they argued characterized the public utterances of U.S. decision makers during the missile crisis. (On U.S. restraint and Kennedy's "limited goals," see also Lippmann, 1963: 55–58.) What they did not recognize, however, is the role that this "rhetoric," a constitutive component of the U.S. security imaginary, first played in generating the crisis itself.

2. On containment, see, for example, Kennan, 1947; U.S. National Security Council, 1950; and Gaddis, 1982.

3. According to Allen Dulles, the tactics of "salami slicing" had been outlined by Mátyás Rákosi, former general secretary of the Hungarian Communist Party, whom Dulles described as "the former overlord of Hungary." Dulles explained that "some years ago, in describing how communism conquered that once charming and inherently anti-Communist society, he [Rákosi] said it was a matter of applying 'salami tactics'—that is, of slicing the political sausage piece by piece until the whole was lost before the progressive loss of the separate parts had been noticed" (1962: 746).

4. Interestingly, Stevenson was himself accused of advocating appeasement after allegedly proposing during the missile crisis that the United States publicly announce a willingness to neutralize the threat from Cuba by trading the Soviet missiles in Cuba for U.S. missiles in Turkey (Alsop and Bartlett, 1962: 20). For a critique of this view of Stevenson's role, see Schlesinger, 1965: 835–838.

5. The "deception theme" is highlighted by Brockriede and Scott as well. They argue, for instance, that in Kennedy's speech of October 22 "the detailed account of Soviet duplicity . . . put the mildness of American response in brighter relief, [and] probably gave the administration an advantage in communicating with friendly nations and neutrals" (1970: 84). This analysis is fine, as far as it goes. But it implicitly represents the U.S. response as mild *in fact* and neglects the possibility that the U.S. response was *constructed as* mild by the rhetoric itself. After all, from a perspective emphasizing Cuban sovereignty, the U.S. quarantine of Cuba, far from being mild, was an unjustified and indeed illegal act of war. In addition, they ignore the fact that the course chosen by the U.S. administration could be and has been interpreted not as responding mildly but, rather, as setting the Soviet Union up for humiliation. See, for example, Nathan, 1975: 268, and Steel, 1969: 18.

6. According to Kennan and as became part of the security imaginary, this goal, not in fact achieved through Stalin's infamous pact with Hitler, was finally attained through Soviet military gains at the conclusion of World War II. Kennan, however, went on to claim that "this program was intended not only to increase the physical military strength of Russia. It was intended

to prevent the formation in Central and Eastern Europe of any power or coalition of powers capable of challenging Russian security" (1967: 520). This second part of Kennan's argument, which interpreted Soviet actions as at least in part defensive, did not become part of the U.S. security imaginary. Instead, within that imaginary, the establishment of an Eastern Europe of regimes friendly to the Soviet Union came to symbolize its inherently expansive and aggressive character.

7. Contrasting images of the oriental coexisted within the U.S. social imaginary. In general, "Orientals" were depicted as "inscrutable and somnolent." But this generic image has at least two variants. In addition to the negative image of subhuman cunning, there is a more positive image as well. As Hunt argues, "An observer developing that image [of the Oriental] in a favorable direction might hold them up as a people of promise, on the verge of shaking off a stagnant cultural tradition and improving their position in the hierarchy of race. Viewed in this light, they would appear admirably trustworthy, clean, and industrious" (1987: 69). U.S. images of "the Oriental," as with images of "the Latino" and "the Indian," thus had at least two variants: "a positive one, appropriate to happy times when paternalism and benevolence were in season, and a negative one, suited to those tense periods when abuse or aggrandizement became the order of the day" (1987: 69). Within the security imaginary, the specific image of the oriental articulated to the Kremlin was, of course, the expressly negative one.

8. It is perhaps for this reason that Kennedy referred to his Soviet experts during the missile crisis as "demonologists" (in May and Zelikow, 1997: 107; see also Ball, in May and Zelikow, 1997: 110).

9. According to the testimony of a Cuban representative to the Moscow Conference of 1989, Emilio Aragonés (a member of the Cuban Secretariat during the October crisis), the Cubans wanted a public agreement between Cuba and the Soviet Union concerning the missile deployment. As Aragonés put it, "this was our opinion, that a pact had to be signed and publicized and that the emplacement of missiles in Cuba should not be a surreptitious action, but rather something done in accordance with an official pact between two nations." He then explained that "Khrushchev said no" because he "wanted to buy time" (in Allyn, Blight, and Welch, 1992: 52). Moreover, according to Jorge Risquet (head of the Cuban delegation to the Moscow Conference), a military accord between the two states did in fact exist: The "accord was drafted, it was initialed in the Soviet Union by Raul Castro and [Rodion] Malinovsky, and it was brought to Cuba by [Aleksandr] Alekseev. In Cuba, comrade Fidel Castro revised it, in order to add a political introduction explaining why it was a military accord, so that the document could be made public. He sent it to the Soviet Union with [Emilio] Aragonés and Che Guevara. In the Soviet Union they agreed to the revisions and it was

thought that it would be signed publicly between Nikita Khrushchev and Fidel Castro, during a visit by Khrushchev that was planned for November in Havana; but the accord took effect as soon as it was initialed" (71). Not making the accord public was, in Risquet's view, a major foreign policy blunder by Khrushchev.

10. The use of the initial capital in the word "Communism" was quite common in the United States throughout the cold war (and beyond). Because only proper names are capitalized in English, this usage reinforces the idea that there exists an unproblematic and self-evident object—an identifiable, intentional actor—called "Communism." It thus helps to make sensible the claims about "Communist aggression," "Communist invasions," "Communist penetrations," or "Communist subversions" by constituting a monolithic and conspiratorial subject prone to nefarious practices.

11. The evil nature of this conspiracy was again highlighted in an article taken from the *Miami Tablet* of March 11, 1961, and entered into the official record of the Hearings on the Latin American Conference on National Sovereignty. In this article it was claimed that "Cuban children as young as 4 years old are being shipped to the Soviet Union for indoctrination in Communist beliefs and techniques, according to reports reaching here [Miami]. The purpose is to train the children as elite 'shock troops' to be returned as adults to Cuba and other Latin American countries for infiltration and subversion" (U.S. Senate Committee on the Judiciary, 1961a: 10).

12. In Theodore Sorensen's *Kennedy*, the chapter that precedes his discussion of the Cuban missile crisis is entitled "The Continuing Crises." It places the Cuban problem squarely into the context of the global containment of communist expansion (1965: 634–666).

13. Even before the missile crisis, the Cuban problem had persistently been portrayed by the United States as a hemispheric rather than a bilateral issue (see, for example, Stebbins, 1962: 306, 311). Exactly the same argument about the scope of the Cuban problem had been made the year before by Adlai Stevenson in the course of his attempt to convince the United Nations that the United States was not involved in the Bay of Pigs invasion. "Let me make it clear," he argued, "that we do not regard the Cuban problem as a problem between Cuba and the United States. The challenge is not to the United States but to the hemisphere and its duly constituted body, the Organization of American States" (1961: 671). Similarly, in response to Cuba's President Dorticós's announcement to diplomats in Havana on April 27, 1961, that the Cuban government was willing to discuss its differences with Washington (in Phillips, 1961b: 1), State Department spokesman Lincoln White replied, "We have repeatedly said that the basic problem in Cuba is communism in this hemisphere. Trade and economic measures may be subject to negotiations, but communism in this hemisphere is not negotiable."

In this context he went on to stress that the Cuban problem was "a multilateral problem, not a bilateral problem" that could be discussed or negotiated between the United States and Cuba alone (in Phillips, 1961b: 1).

14. Presumably, van Alstyne is treating the northern and southern hemispheres as "real" hemispheres, in contrast to the "imaginary" "western hemisphere," both because the equator provides a clearly identifiable and agreed upon demarcation line between them and because clear differences between these two hemispheres, such as the reversal of seasons, can be pointed to. Whether or not the northern and southern hemispheres are in fact somehow more "real" than the Western Hemisphere is an interesting question, but one that lies outside the scope of this project.

15. The principle of interventionism embodied in the Monroe Doctrine and the Roosevelt Corollary was explicitly applied to Cuba with the Platt Amendment. Article 3 of that amendment, enacted by the U.S. Congress in 1901, read: "The Government of Cuba consents that the United States may exercise the right to intervene for the preservation of Cuban independence, the maintenance of a government adequate for the protection of life, property, and individual liberty, and for the discharging the obligations with respect to Cuba imposed by the Treaty of Paris on the United States, now to be assumed and undertaken by the Government of Cuba" (in Wright, 1959: 57). In response to persistent U.S. pressure, the Cuban constitutional convention finally accepted the Platt Amendment as an appendix to its own 1901 Constitution. As Louis Pérez has put it, the Platt Amendment was "an adequate if imperfect substitute for annexation" that "served to transform the substance of Cuban sovereignty into an extension of the U.S. national system" (1990: 109). Under the auspices of the Platt Amendment, the U.S. military occupied all or parts of Cuba from 1906 to 1909, in 1912, and again from 1916 to 1921 (Atkins, 1989: 303). The Platt Amendment was declared null and void by the Cuban Provisional Government in 1933 and formally abrogated in 1934 as part of President Franklin D. Roosevelt's Good Neighbor Policy.

16. U.S. anticommunism or anti-Bolshevism of course preceded the postwar era, even with respect to Latin America. As Hunt has pointed out, "Forces dedicated to 'Soviet subversion' also seemed to stalk the Americas through the twenties and thirties, especially in Cuba and Mexico, stirring up political unrest and anti-Yanqui sentiment and threatening the United States with 'a communist seizure of power' right in its backyard" (1987: 139). Indeed, during the 1920s and the 1930s anti-Bolshevism shaped not only U.S. relations with the Soviet Union and central Europe but its relations with Latin America and southern Europe as well. In particular, "American policy makers employed the Bolshevik Revolution during the interwar years as a framework for understanding other revolutionary and

reformist phenomena," and as a result they "all too often . . . misinterpreted indigenous movements for social change as manifestations of a Comintern conspiracy" (Little, 1983: 377, 380).

17. As Richard Stebbins has argued, despite long-standing U.S. concerns over "Bolshevism" and "communism" in Latin America, the region did not play a prominent role in U.S. foreign policy in the early years of the cold war (1959: 351). However, the combined influence of the establishment of a supposedly communist-influenced regime in Guatemala in 1954; Vice President Richard Nixon's unexpectedly humiliating trip to Peru and Venezuela in 1958, which "gave the United States the rudest surprise since Sputnik" (350); and, most important, the Cuban Revolution in 1959 forcibly brought the importance of the Western Hemisphere to the attention of U.S. decision makers and shifted Latin America to a more central space in the concerns of cold war U.S. foreign policy.

18. The United States was sometimes also constructed, if more implicitly, as the "father" of the American family. For example, Theodore Roosevelt's Corollary maintained that "continued *misconduct or disturbance* in a Latin American country might force the United States to intervene" ("Monroe Doctrine guards West," 1960: 3), which could be read as portraying the Latin American states as potentially naughty children over whom the father needed to exercise continued vigilance and occasional discipline. I do not pursue this extension of the American family metaphor here. Lest it be thought that this is too far-fetched, however, I should like briefly to quote Michael Hunt's discussion of U.S. cartoon depictions of Cuba at the turn of the century. He notes that Americans discovered during the so-called Spanish American War that many Cubans were in fact quite dark skinned and argues that this "quickly transformed the cartoon Cuban into *a petulant child* whose place on the racial hierarchy was made clear by his stereotypical black features and his minstrel drawl. This picture of *Cuban infantilism* helped Americans to ignore the protests of *this obviously immature and turbulent people* against outside intervention and control, and it provided justification for a policy of keeping them in an appropriately dependent relationship to the United States. . . . an *infantile and often negroid Latin,* provided *the justification for Uncle Sam's tutelage and stern discipline*" (1987: 62).

19. The metaphor of the Latin American states as sister republics specifically had a related extension as well. If the Latin American states were sisters in the American family, then the communist threat amounted to their "seduction" (Alba, 1960: 4). The invocation of this particular metaphor brought with it the quasi-causal argument that, given the opportunity, the Communists would seduce these sister republics away from both their American family and from the path of virtue, that is, from the straight and narrow pursuit of the shared values of American civilization. As the defender of these values,

it was the familial obligation of the United States to prevent the seduction of its sisters by the Soviet Union or the international communist movement. As Hunt said of earlier depictions of Latin Americans, including Cubans, as "a fair-skinned and comely seniorita," representations of the Latin American states as the sisters of the United States provided a warrant for "Uncle Sam" to "rush in and sweep the Latin lady off her feet, save her . . . from some sinister intruder from outside the hemisphere, and introduce her to the kind of civilized life she deserved" (1987: 59–60). This argument implied as well that U.S. and OAS actions taken against the Castro regime, such as the trade embargo and later the quarantine that ended the missile crisis, were not violations of Cuban sovereignty. They were instead the fulfillment of a familial obligation, undertaken to rescue a sister republic from the blandishments of her shameless communist seducer.

20. Though the Latin American states are all members of the American family, they do not actually live *in* the American home. Instead, they perch rather precariously on its doorstep, in its backyard, or in its front yard, thus reinforcing a hierarchy of states in which the United States rules the roost.

21. The quasi-causal argument involved in this particular metaphor is related to the notion that Cuba had been "lost" to communism, as if it had been a possession of the United States that had gone missing. (The metaphor of countries lost to communism, as if they had at one time been U.S. possessions, was of course a staple of the U.S. security imaginary.) During the 1960 presidential campaign, for instance, Kennedy charged that the Eisenhower administration had lost Cuba (see, for example, the discussion in Meyer and Szulc, 1962). The same argument was put forward in a report submitted to the Senate Judiciary Committee's Subcommittee on Internal Security: "Right now [the end of 1960], *one key country—Cuba—is lost.* Cuba is dominated and directed by Communist leaders as faithful to Moscow and Peiping as any of their European satellites. Cuba under Castro is no longer a peaceful tropical island but an advance landing strip of the Soviet Union and Communist China *at our very doorstep.* It is the Communist takeoff field for the penetration and subjugation of Mexico, Central America, Panama, and the nearby areas of South America" (Hill, 1961: 809, emphasis added).

5. CONSTRUCTING THE CUBAN MISSILE CRISIS: THE PROBLEM OF CUBA

1. An important secondary source that helps to illuminate the construction of the Cuban missile crisis is the series *The United States in World Affairs* published by Harper and Row for the Council on Foreign Relations. This is a useful source of "official" U.S. history because, as Michio Kaku and Daniel Axelrod have noted, "in selecting his Cabinet, Kennedy relied heavily

on the advice of [Robert] Lovett, one of the most powerful and influential figures in what Arthur J. Schlesinger Jr. called the 'American Establishment,' that loose old boys' network of about a hundred senior government officials and Wall Street bankers centered around the Council on Foreign Relations" (1987: 136). McGeorge Bundy, Robert McNamara, and Dean Rusk, for example, were all associated with the council, and it was the council that sponsored this yearly study of U.S. foreign relations.

2. That the long-standing and accepted U.S. policy toward Cuba was in fact one of persistent *intervention* rather than nonintervention is forcefully and convincingly argued in Pérez, 1990.

3. The U.S. claim that many of the Cuban leaders were Communists came in part from the testimony of Major Díaz Lanz, the exiled head of Castro's air forces, before a hearing of the Senate Internal Security Subcommittee in July 1959. Lanz provided a list of "known Communists" in powerful positions in the Cuban government, a list that included Fidel Castro and his brother Raúl; Che Guevara; Armando Hart, Cuba's minister of education; and David Salvador, the leader of the Cuban labor movement. As Carla Anne Robbins has pointed out, "subsequent research has proved most of Díaz Lanz's charges to be without basis." In fact, "most of the 'known Communists' on his list were members of the July 26th Movement and not the PSP [Partido Socialista Popular, or Cuban Communist Party]. Some, like David Salvador, were known to be committed anti-Communists and were later purged from the regime for that reason" (1983: 89).

4. For some, the Cuban problem had arrived even earlier. Immediately after his Washington meeting with Castro in April 1959, for instance, Vice President Nixon wrote a memo to the White House, the State Department, and the CIA "suggesting that Cuban exiles be trained and armed as a reserve force in case Washington saw the need to remove Castro from power" (Robbins, 1983: 85). In March 1960, Eisenhower ordered the CIA to begin a clandestine program to train Cuban exiles for an invasion of Cuba.

5. Congress granted Eisenhower this power on July 5; on July 6 he cut the Cuban sugar quota to zero. Using sugar as a tool to punish the Castro government became the subject of a lively debate: Those opposing this strategy included both domestic U.S. sugar producers, who worried about presidential rather than congressional control over the sugar quota (Blair, 1960: 24), and those who thought such a move might strengthen Castro in Cuba ("Cuban sugar quota," 1960: 46).

6. Smathers was not alone in fanning the flames of hostility against Cuba. On the same day, as Kenworthy reported, Representative Daniel Flood (D–Pennsylvania) argued that "Cuba is more of a satellite country of Russia today than Poland and certainly more than Yugoslavia," Lyndon Johnson (D–Texas) charged that Cuba might be the next place chosen by

Khrushchev to "increase cold war tensions," and Senator Hubert Humphrey (D–Minnesota) asserted that Castro's upcoming visit to Moscow was "another effort on the part of the Russians to put their imprint on Latin America" (Kenworthy, 1960b: 6).

7. The persistence of the Cuban problem into the post–cold war era is discussed in Weldes and Saco, 1996.

8. As Robbins also notes, however, "most of the allegations raised against Cuba during the 1960s proved to be either spurious or vastly exaggerated. While the Castro Government was ideologically committed to the export of revolution, it never had the military means or the support of its allies necessary to mount a major campaign" (1983: 4). For example, although the U.S. government estimated that Cuba was training between 1,000 and 2,500 "Latin American radicals" a year during the 1960s—for a total of between 10,000 and 25,000 Cuban-trained revolutionaries—it turned out that no more than 2,500 Latin Americans were trained during the entire period from 1961 through 1969 (53). Moreover, the United States had, of course, anticipated the Cubans by over a decade. The Army Caribbean School in Panama (renamed the United States Army School of the Americas in 1963), was founded on February 1, 1949. Part of its mission was to help to strengthen the "internal security" capabilities of Latin American militaries. From 1949 through 1964, according to Willard Barber and Neale Ronning, 16,343 officers and enlisted men from twenty Latin American countries (including 291 from Cuba) graduated from this Spanish-language U.S. counterinsurgency training program (1966: 145).

9. For a fuller analysis of the appropriation of Martí in U.S. foreign policy discourse, see Saco, 1992: 86–100.

10. As Michael Hunt has suggested, the only revolutions acceptable to the United States are those that meet "stringent standards" that are themselves culled from the experience of the American Revolution. According to this view, "Revolution was a solemn affair, to be conducted with a minimum of disorder, led by respectable citizens, harnessed to moderate political goals, and happily concluded only after a balanced constitution, essential to safeguarding human and property rights, was securely in place" (1987: 116). The Alliance for Progress, which did not challenge the continued operation or the expansion of the free way of life and its institutional manifestation in the free market, was to provide for a revolution of this American type.

11. The system of rule implemented by the Cuban government under Castro has typically been personalized by calling it "Castroism" or "Fidelism." For example, Robert D. Crassweller argued in 1971 that "Castroism was a form of personal power, familiar in Latin American tradition and unique only in the wondrous magnetism upon which that power was based and in the missionary and proselytizing zeal that was its bridge to the larger Latin

American scene" (1971: 22). The personalization of Castroism contributed to the typical distinction, which I discuss in the next section, between "the Cuban regime" and "the Cuban people."

12. For an interesting discussion of the development of similar metaphors, such as *der Jüdische Parasit* (the Jewish parasite), within European, and specifically German, culture, see Bein, 1965. Classic examples of the extreme consequences that can follow from such metaphors can be found throughout the writing of Nazi propagandist Alfred Rosenberg, including his *Der Mythus des 20. Jahrhunderts* (1935).

13. The Cuban government was (and is) rarely given a dignified designation. Just as the Soviet government was typically referred to as "the Kremlin," so the Cuban government was generally called "the Cuban regime" or "the Castro regime." In addition, it was variously described as "Castro and his gang" (Kennedy, 1960a: 20), as "Dr. Castro and his lieutenants" (Stebbins, 1960: 353; 1961: 326), and as "Dr. Castro and his associates" (Stebbins, 1961: 335). Frequent references to "*Dr.* Castro" seem to draw on a kind of anti-intellectualism in which the title "Doctor" conjures up images not of the healer or learned scholar but of mad scientists like Dr. Frankenstein and Dr. Strangelove.

14. Castro was typically presented as in some way uncivilized. For instance, in 1961 *Life* ran a series of articles on "The crisis in our hemisphere." Part 1 of the series began with a close-up of Castro's face that focused on his eyes. The caption under the photograph read, in part: "The messianic eyes of Fidel Castro, hypnotic and hungry for power, summon up a new and nightmarish danger for the U.S." ("The crisis in our hemisphere," 1961: 81). Castro was then described as "a spell-binding master politician whose ambition to become a world figure amounts almost to insanity" ("The menacing push of Castroism," 1961: 82). This particularly lurid description was not so different from the representations of the Fidelista virus provided by U.S. decision makers or in Stebbins's *The United States in World Affairs* series. Like the use of "beardedness" as a description, this focus on Castro as power hungry and insane brought with it associations to wildness, to an inability or an unwillingness to conform to the ways of American civilization or to the dictates of the American way of life.

15. I am grateful to Diana Saco for pointing out to me the importance of beardedness in Cuban revolutionary discourse.

16. Such different interpretations of the "same" sign or linguistic element are not unusual. As Terry Eagleton has pointed out, a particular linguistic element or sign can be "pulled this way and that" by competing social groups. It can be "inscribed from within with a multiplicity of ideological 'accents'" (1991: 195).

17. This argument was popularized by Theodore Draper (1962, 1965).

18. I add the qualifier "sometimes" because this is only true when "the Cuban people" are set in contrast to "the Cuban regime." Many of the constructions prominent within the security imaginary draw on a racist ideology in which various "races" are organized hierarchically. In this hierarchy, Latinos, including Cubans, are not highly ranked. Instead, they are situated "midway up the hierarchy of race," falling somewhere between the Latin peoples of Europe and the black Africans at the bottom (Hunt, 1987: 58). At the time of the Spanish-American War, for example, Cubans were depicted as "hapless victims" of Spanish colonialism. Cartoon representations of Cubans at the time "played on the theme of womanhood outraged." The prevalent image was of an often white "feminine Cuba . . . ravaged and desperate for rescue from her Spanish master" (61). As Hunt noted, however, "closer contact" with the Cuban people "impressed on Americans the fact that many Cubans were swarthy, even black." As a result, cartoon images of the Cuban changed to an image of "a petulant child whose place on the racial hierarchy was made clear by his stereotypical black features and his minstrel drawl" (62).

This image of the Cuban as infantile and incompetent continued in the postwar era. Two remarkably explicit examples appear in the ExComm transcripts. On October 19, General Taylor noted that "by logic we ought to be able to say that we can deter these missiles as well as the Soviet missiles, the ones from the Soviet Union. I think the thing that worries us, however, is these being potentially under the control of Castro. Castro would be quite a different fellow [unclear] missiles than Khrushchev. I don't think that's the case now, . . . But there's always the risk of their falling into Cuban hands" (in May and Zelikow, 1997: 184). And on October 27, in discussing the shooting down of Major Anderson's U-2 over Cuba, Alexis Johnson expressed the opinion that it would be "a very different thing" if the plane had been shot down by Cubans rather than by Russians: "*You could have an undisciplined anti-aircraft—Cuban anti-aircraft outfit fire, but to have a SAM-site and a Russian crew fire is not any accident*" (October 27: 71, emphasis added). In other words, though the Soviet (or Russian) crews may have served a dangerous totalitarian government, they were at least capable (after all, they are white, even if also Slavs). Their actions might have been provocative, dangerous, and outright cruel, but they were also controlled and intended, not accidental. The "natives," on the other hand, were undisciplined, probably incapable of fully understanding modern technology, including modern weapons, and more likely than the Russians to be irresponsible and incompetent. If the Cubans controlled the nuclear missiles, that would be an additional worry; if they launched the SAM attack on Major Anderson's U-2, it could well have been an irresponsible accident. Similarly, Robbins has argued that one of the reasons that Washington asked the U.S. oil companies to refuse to refine the Soviet petroleum in 1959 was that they expected this action to "force the Cuban economy and the Castro Government to collapse." The reason for this optimistic assessment, she continued, was that the Americans "did not think the Cubans could run the refineries by themselves" (1983: 95).

19. According to this same report, "Goodwin, by his own account, acknowledged the backhanded compliment and asked Guevara to return the favor by invading the U.S. Naval Base at Guantánamo, Cuba. This would give Kennedy a pretext for openly using America's overwhelming military force, releasing him from the clandestine restrictions of the secret war." Guevara apparently smiled at this response but declined, saying that "Castro would never be so stupid" (Branch and Crile, 1975: 61).

20. Nor was Cuban hostility toward the United States something new. Instead, it had its origins in 1898 when the United States, during the so-called Spanish-American War, interfered in the Cuban War for Independence. As Robbins has put it, "American troops were supposedly sent to help Cuban patriots expel their colonial masters. But once the Americans landed, it was almost impossible to get them to go home" (1983: 16). U.S. actions, then, had already generated considerable Cuban hostility toward the United States by the turn of the century. Repeated U.S. intervention in Cuba under the auspices of the Platt Amendment kept that hostility alive.

21. A pervasive racism against "natives," whether American or otherwise, is evident in these CIA projects against Castro and Cuba. In a manner reminiscent of the "Indian scalping" of earlier American history, William (Rip) Robertson, who ran paramilitary operations against Cuba for the CIA, told Ramon Orozco, one of his commandos, "'I'll give you $50 if you bring me back an ear'" from a raid on Cuba. When Orozco brought back two ears, Robertson reportedly "laughed," told Orozco he was "crazy," and paid him $100 (in Branch and Crile, 1975: 58). As Richard Drinnon has pointed out, the very name of these clandestine programs, Operation *Mongoose*, "hinted that its targets were rodentlike natives" (1990: 438).

6. IDENTITY AND NATIONAL INTERESTS

1. The importance of questions of state identity, and the inadequacy of realism's treatment of state identity as both fixed and uniform across states, has been demonstrated in a variety of recent arguments, including Campbell, 1992, 1994; Doty, 1993, 1996; Weldes, 1996; and Wendt, 1992.

2. One might note as well that this notion of costly global obligations borne by the United States has been so inculcated in public consciousness that it has created a recent backlash wherein a significant number of U.S.

citizens criticize U.S. foreign policy for "helping" other countries rather than focusing on domestic concerns. I would like to thank Jack Blanton for pointing out this connection.

3. It also made sense despite explicit attempts by the United States in the immediate aftermath of World War II to export democracy, that is, to *impose* democracy, on countries such as Japan and Germany. As one proponent of the U.S. policy of "exporting democracy" put it: In these countries, "Washington's first aim was to 'democratize' these conquered, warlike countries, a political goal explicitly tied to changes in their socioeconomic order" (Smith, 1991: 74). The effort to change the socioeconomic order of conquered countries was democratization rather than intervention or aggression because, unlike a despot, a leader by definition assists and guides its allies or followers; it does not dominate or impose itself upon them. After all, the leader's assistance and guidance is already a burden undertaken out of both a sense of duty or moral obligation and a specific promise to live up to its leadership commitments.

4. As a result, of course, any particular representation of a foreign policy problem or crisis can be contested. As was demonstrated in chapter 1, the orthodox U.S. construction of the Cuban missile crisis was immediately and forcefully disputed, although with little success in the United States, by both the Soviet narrative of the Caribbean crisis and the Cuban story of the October crisis.

5. Sometimes, of course, the subject of a foreign policy problem or crisis is other than the state. For Robert McNamara, for example, the Cuban missile crisis was less a crisis for the United States in general than for the Kennedy administration in particular. As McNamara argued on October 16 in the ExComm, it was "a domestic, political problem" (October 16: 192). At stake was the administration's credibility with its domestic public in the face of its own repeated claims that it would not tolerate the stationing of Soviet offensive weapons in Cuba.

6. As is reflected in the title of his recent book on crisis outcomes, *Danger and Opportunity* (1995), Eric Herring recognizes that crises present both "dangers and opportunities" to state officials, but he defines both dangers and opportunities solely in terms of given state interests rather than in terms of discursively constituted state identity (1–3).

7. I am particularly grateful to Lisa Disch and Michael Shapiro for encouraging me to pursue this second aspect of the relationship between crisis and state identity in Weldes, 1997.

8. This process of othering, although it has been a hallmark of postwar U.S. foreign policy, need not occur, and state identities are therefore only potentially, but not always in fact, precarious. Whether or not a particular state identity is in fact insecure depends on the presence of a politics of othering such as I have described in this and preceding chapters.

9. The importance of the identity of the United States to the understanding of the Cuban missile crisis and to the construction of the U.S. national interest by U.S. state officials can also be seen by examining the
primary lesson attributed to the Cuban missile crisis. One of the most significant consequences of the missile crisis, as Nathan has pointed out, is that
"force and toughness became enshrined" as tools of U.S. foreign policy
(1975: 269). According to the orthodox view of the Cuban missile crisis, its
outcome was a triumph of toughness, strength, and will. (For some of its
conservative detractors, of course, U.S. policy was not firm enough and the
United States should have used the opportunity of the missile crisis to get rid
of Castro once and for all [e.g., Luce, 1963].) As Alsop and Bartlett reported
shortly after the crisis had been resolved, " 'Once or twice,' an ExComm
member recalls, 'the President lost his temper on minor matters. But he never
lost his nerve.' This must be counted a huge intangible plus. A President's
nerve is the essential factor when the two great nuclear powers are 'eyeball
to eyeball' " (1962: 20). Similarly, in the famous words of Arthur Schlesinger
Jr., the missile crisis displayed "to the whole world" the "ripening of an
American leadership unsurpassed in the responsible management of power.
From the moment of challenge the American President never had a doubt
about the need for a hard response. . . . It was this combination of toughness
and restraint, of will, nerve and wisdom, so brilliantly controlled, so matchlessly calibrated, that dazzled the world" (1965: 840–841). The identity of
the United States as the tough leader in the global fight for freedom thus
came to be seen as the central lesson of the Cuban missile crisis. As a consequence, that crisis had a significant impact on the future conduct of U.S. foreign policy. As Nathan has forcefully argued, "Tragically and ironically, the
'lessons' of the Cuban missile crisis—that success in international crisis was
largely a matter of national guts; that the opponent would yield to superior
force; that presidential control of force can be 'suitable,' 'selective,' 'swift,'
'effective,' and 'responsive' to civilian authority; and that crisis management and execution are too dangerous and events move too rapidly for anything but the tightest secrecy—all these inferences contributed to President
Johnson's decision to use American power against Hanoi in 1965. . . . Even
the language of the Gulf of Tonkin Resolution was almost identical to that
which Kennedy's legal advisors had drawn up for the OAS in October
1962." Thus, though the Cuban missile crisis may have changed the international environment in some important respects, it also "riveted American
expectations to the necessities of the diplomacy of violence" (Nathan, 1975:
280–281). On this reading, the missile crisis was an unfortunate triumph of
"guts" (Nathan, 1975) and "military solutions" (Yarmolinsky, 1970–71)
over compromise and diplomacy.

7. NATIONAL INTERESTS AND COMMON SENSE

1. All translations from Radio Martí are by Diana Saco. For more detail, see Saco, 1992.

2. This claim is false, as I argue later in the text.

3. The Helms-Burton Act emphasized the "decline of at least 60 percent in the last 5 years" in the Cuban economy and claims that "the welfare and health of the Cuban people have substantially deteriorated" in part "as a result of this economic decline" (U.S. Congress, 1996: section 2:1, 2). Not surprisingly, but with amazing hypocrisy, it attributes this decline to a variety of factors—"(A) the end of its subsidization by the former Soviet Union of between 5 billion and 6 billion dollars annually; (B) 36 years of communist tyranny and economic mismanagement by the Castro government; (C) the extreme decline in trade between Cuba and the countries of the former Soviet bloc; and (D) the stated policy of the Russian government and the countries of the former Soviet bloc to conduct economic relations with Cuba on strictly economic terms"—but never mentions the devastating effects produced by thirty-six years of U.S. embargo (U.S. Congress, 1996: section 2:1)

References

Abel, Elie. 1966. *The Missile Crisis.* Philadelphia: J. B. Lippincott.

Acheson, Dean. 1969a. *Present at the Creation: My Years in the State Department.* New York: W. W. Norton.

———. 1969b. "Homage to plain dumb luck: Dean Acheson's version of Robert F. Kennedy's version of the Cuban missile affair." *Esquire,* February, 76–77, 44, 46.

Alba, Victor. 1960. "'Fidelism' for export." *New Leader,* September 5, 3–4.

Alexander, Robert J. 1960. "Cuba and the sugar quota: U.S. economic reprisals against Castro government would harm good-neighbor policy." *New Leader,* March 21, 3–5.

Allison, Graham T. 1971. *Essence of Decision: Explaining the Cuban Missile Crisis.* Boston: Little, Brown.

Allyn, Bruce J., James G. Blight, and David A. Welch. 1989–90. "Essence of revision: Moscow, Havana, and the Cuban missile crisis." *International Security* 14(3): 136–172.

Allyn, Bruce J., James G. Blight, and David A. Welch, eds. 1992. *Back to the Brink: Proceedings of the Moscow Conference on the Cuban Missile Crisis, January 27–28, 1989.* Lanham, MD: University Press of America.

Alsop, Stewart, and Charles Bartlett. 1962. "In time of crisis." *Saturday Evening Post,* December 8, 16–20.

Althusser, Louis. 1971 [1970]. "Ideology and the ideological state apparatuses: Notes toward an investigation." In his *Lenin and Philosophy and Other Essays,* translated by B. Brewster, 127–186. New York: Monthly Review Press.

Anderson, Benedict. 1991 [1983]. *Imagined Communities: Reflections on the Origin and Spread of Nationalism.* Rev. ed. London: Verso.

Armstrong, Scott, and Philip Brenner. 1987. "Putting Cuban and crisis back in the Cuban missile crisis." *Los Angeles Times,* November 1, part 5, 3. Reprinted in Philip Brenner, William M. LeoGrande, Donna Rich, and Daniel Siegel, eds., *The Cuba Reader: The Making of a Revolutionary Society,* 336–339. New York: Grove Press, 1989.

Atkins, G. Pope. 1989. *Latin America in the International Political System.* Boulder, CO: Westview Press.

Ayoob, Mohammed. 1983–84. "Security in the Third World: The worm about to turn." *International Affairs* 60(1): 41–51.

Babbitt, Harriet. 1996. "Statement to the OAS Permanent Council on the Cuban Liberty and Democratic Solidarity Act," September 11. Online. Available: http://usiahq.usis.usemb.se/topical/econ/libertad/libbaoas.htm [December 27, 1997].

Ball, George. 1962. "Trading relations between the free world and Cuba." Statement before the House Select Committee on Export Control, October 3. *Department of State Bulletin,* October 22, 591–595.

Barber, Willard F., and C. Neale Ronning. 1966. *Internal Security and Military Power: Counterinsurgency and Civic Action in Latin America.* Columbus: Ohio State University Press.

Barnet, Richard J. 1988. "Rethinking national strategy." *New Yorker,* March 21, 104–114.

Barnett, Michael. 1992. *Confronting the Costs of War: Military Power, State, and Society in Egypt and Israel.* Princeton: Princeton University Press.

Beck, Kent M. 1984. "Necessary lies, hidden truths: Cuba in the 1960 campaign." *Diplomatic History* 8(1): 37–59.

Beck, Robert J. 1989. "Munich's lessons reconsidered." *International Security* 14(2): 161–191.

Bein, Alexander. 1965. "Der Jüdische Parasit: Bemerkungen zur Semantik der Judenfrage." *Vierteljahreshefte für Zeitgeschichte* 13(2): 121–149.

Benjamin, Jules R. 1990. *The United States and the Origins of the Cuban Revolution: An Empire of Liberty in an Age of National Liberation.* Princeton: Princeton University Press.

Berle, Adolf A. 1961. "The Inter-American System and the program for economic and social progress." Address to the Association of the Bar of the City of New York, April 12. *Department of State Bulletin,* May 1, 617–621.

Berman, Edward H. 1983. *The Influence of the Carnegie, Ford, and Rockefeller Foundations on American Foreign Policy: The Ideology of Philanthropy,* Albany: State University of New York Press.

Bernstein, Barton J. 1979. "Bombers, inspection, and the no invasion pledge:

Kennedy and ending the missile crisis." *Foreign Service Journal* 56(7): 8–12.

———. 1980. "The Cuban missile crisis: Trading the Jupiter's in Turkey?" *Political Science Quarterly* 95(1): 97–125.

———. 1990. "Commentary: Reconsidering Khrushchev's gambit: Defending the Soviet Union and Cuba." *Diplomatic History* 14(2): 231–239.

Blair, William M. 1960. "U.S. weighs move on Cuba's sugar." *New York Times,* January 9, 24.

Blight, James G. 1989. *The Shattered Crystal Ball: Fear and Learning in the Cuban Missile Crisis.* Savage, MD: Rowman and Littlefield.

Blight, James G., Bruce J. Allyn, and David A. Welch. 1993. *Cuba on the Brink: Castro, the Missile Crisis, and the Soviet Collapse.* New York: Pantheon Books.

Blight, James G., Joseph S. Nye Jr., and David A. Welch. 1987. "The Cuban missile crisis revisited." *Foreign Affairs* 66(1): 170–188.

Blight, James G., and David A. Welch. 1990. *On the Brink: Americans and Soviets Reexamine the Cuban Missile Crisis.* 2nd ed. New York: Noonday Press.

Bohlen, Charles E. 1973. *Witness to History, 1929–1969.* New York: W. W. Norton.

Bonsal, Philip W. 1971. *Cuba, Castro, and the United States.* Pittsburgh: University of Pittsburgh Press.

Borovsky, V. 1961. "Alliance against progress." *Pravda,* August 7. Reprinted in *Current Digest of the Soviet Press* 13(32) (September 6): 23.

Bostdorff, Denise M. 1994. *The Presidency and the Rhetoric of Foreign Crises.* Columbia: University of South Carolina Press.

Branch, Taylor, and George Crile III. 1975. "The Kennedy vendetta: How the CIA waged a silent war against Cuba." *Harper's Magazine,* August, 49–63.

Brockriede, Wayne, and Robert L. Scott. 1970. *Moments in the Rhetoric of the Cold War.* New York: Random House.

Brown, Wendy. 1988. *Manhood and Politics: A Feminist Reading of Political Theory.* Totowa, NJ: Rowman and Littlefield.

Brzezinski, Zbigniew. 1962. "Cuba in Soviet strategy." *New Republic,* November 3, 7–8.

Bullitt, William C. 1948. "How we won the war and lost the peace." Parts 1 and 2. *Life,* August 30, 83–97; September 6, 86–103.

Bundy, McGeorge. 1988. *Danger and Survival: Choices about the Bomb in the First Fifty Years.* New York: Random House.

Bush, George. 1991a. "Remarks at the Beacon Council Annual Meeting in Miami Florida," September 30. *Public Papers of the Presidents: George Bush, 1991,* 1223. Washington, DC: Government Printing Office.

————. 1991b. *Bush on Cuba: Selected Statements by the President,* Washington, DC: Cuban American National Foundation.

————. 1992a. "Statement on actions to support democracy in Cuba," April 18. *Weekly Compilation of Presidential Documents,* April 27, 676.

————. 1992b. "Statement on the 90th anniversary of Cuban independence," May 20. *Weekly Compilation of Presidential Documents,* May 25, 905.

Buzan, Barry. 1983. *People, States, and Fear: The National Security Problem in International Relations.* Chapel Hill: University of North Carolina Press.

Cabell, C. P. 1959. "The nature of the communist threat: The triple threat attack on the West." Address to the National Security Commission, Committee Meeting of the American Legion, Minneapolis, Minnesota, August 21. *Vital Speeches of the Day,* October 1, 751–754.

Campbell, David. 1992. *Writing Security: United States Foreign Policy and the Politics of Identity.* Minneapolis: University of Minnesota Press.

————. 1994. "Foreign policy and identity: Japanese 'other'/American 'self.'" In Stephen J. Rosow, Naeem Inayatullah, and Mark Rupert, eds., *The Global Economy as Political Space,* 147–169. Boulder, CO: Lynne Rienner.

"Canada is restoring aid to Cuban regime." 1994. *(Cleveland) Plain Dealer,* June 21, 6A.

Carmichael, Virginia. 1993. *Framing History: The Rosenberg Story and the Cold War.* Minneapolis: University of Minnesota Press.

Castoriadis, Cornelius. 1987 [1975]. *The Imaginary Institution of Society.* Translated by Kathleen Blamey. Cambridge: MIT Press.

Castro, Fidel. 1962a. "Text of Castro statement," October 28. *New York Times,* October 29, 19.

————. 1962b. "Excerpts from Premier Fidel Castro's broadcast," November 1. *New York Times,* November 2, 14.

————. 1976. "Angola: African Girón." Speech in Havana's Karl Marx Theater, April 19. Reprinted in Michael Taber, ed., *Fidel Castro Speeches: Cuba's Internationalist Foreign Policy, 1975–1980,* 86–97. New York: Pathfinder Press, 1981.

————. 1980. "There is only one road to liberation: That of Cuba, that of Grenada, that of Nicaragua." Speech at a rally at Ciego de Avila, Cuba, July 26. Reprinted in Michael Taber, ed., *Fidel Castro Speeches: Cuba's Internationalist Foreign Policy, 1975–1980,* 316–338. New York: Pathfinder Press, 1981.

————. 1992. "Foreign Broadcast Information Service Transcript of Fidel Castro's remarks at the Havana Conference on the Cuban missile crisis," January 11. Reprinted in Laurence Chang and Peter Kornbluh, eds., *The Cuban Missile Crisis, 1962: A National Security Archive Documents Reader,* 330–345. New York: New Press.

"Castro: The last communist." 1992. *Frontline*. Public Broadcasting Service, February 11.

"Castro dons civies for Latin conference." 1994. *New York Times,* June 6, A3.

Chayes, Abram. 1962. "The legal case for U.S. action in Cuba." Address at Harvard Law School, November 3. *Department of State Bulletin,* November 19, 763–765.

Christopher, Warren. 1993. Public address, Ted Mann Concert Hall, University of Minnesota, Minneapolis, May 23.

Churchill, Winston. 1946. "Mr. Churchill's address calling for a united effort for world peace." Speech in Fulton, Missouri, March 5. *New York Times,* March 6, 4.

Cline, Ray S. 1988. "Commentary: The Cuban missile crisis." *Foreign Affairs* 68(4): 190–196.

Clinton, W. David. 1986. "The national interest: Normative foundations." *Review of Politics* 48(4): 495–519.

———. 1994. *The Two Faces of National Interest*. Baton Rouge: Louisiana State University Press.

Clinton, William Jefferson. 1994. Letter to Jutta Weldes and Diana Saco, January 22.

———. 1996a. "Statement by President Clinton upon signing the Cuban Liberty and Democratic Solidarity Act," March 12. Online. Available: http://usiahq.usis.usemb.se/topical/econ/libertad/libpres1.htm [December 27, 1997].

———. 1996b. "Statement by President Clinton appointing Stuart Eizenstat as Special Envoy," August 16. Online. Available: http://usiahq.usis.usemb.se/topical/econ/libertad/libpres3.htm [December 27, 1997].

———. 1997. "Statement by President Clinton concerning implementation of the Cuban Liberty and Democratic Solidarity Act," January 3. Online. Available: http://usiahq.usis.usemb.se/topical/econ/libertad/libpres4.htm [December 27, 1997].

Connolly, William E. 1983. *The Terms of Political Discourse*. 2nd edition. Princeton: Princeton University Press.

———. 1991. *Identity/Difference: Democratic Negotiations of Political Paradox*. Ithaca, NY: Cornell University Press.

Costigliola, Frank. 1995. "Kennedy, the European allies, and the failure to consult." *Political Science Quarterly* 110(1): 105–123.

Cox, Robert. 1981. "Social forces, states, and world orders: Beyond international relations theory." *Millennium: Journal of International Studies* 10(2): 1–30.

Crary, David. 1994. "Canada irked by U.S. sanctions on Cuba." *(Cleveland) Plain Dealer,* March 2, 9A.

Crassweller, Robert D. 1971. *Cuba and the U.S.: The Tangled Relationship.* New York: Foreign Policy Association.

"The crisis in our hemisphere." 1961. *Life,* June 2, 81.

"The Cuban missile crisis: At the brink." 1992. Documentary, produced by Zvi Dor-Ner for WGBH, Boston, and Central Independent Television, England, October.

"Cuban sugar quota." 1960. *New York Times,* January 12, 46.

"Cuba's Latin goal behind U.S. break." 1961. *New York Times,* January 4, 6.

Cumings, Bruce. 1993. "'Revising postrevisionism'; or, The poverty of theory in diplomatic history." *Diplomatic History* 17(4): 539–569.

Dalby, Simon. 1990. *Creating the Second Cold War: The Discourse of Politics.* London: Pinter.

Danto, Arthur C. 1985. *Narration and Knowledge, Including the Integral Text of "Analytical Philosophy of History."* New York: Columbia University Press.

Davidow, Jeffrey. 1996. "Opening statement of Jeffrey Davidow, acting assistant secretary of state for Inter-American Affairs, before the Senate Foreign Relations Committee," July 30. Online. Available: http://usiahq. usis.usemb.se/topical/econ/libertad/libdavid.htm [December 27, 1997].

Davis, Philip J., and Reuben Hersh. 1981. *The Mathematical Experience.* Boston: Houghton Mifflin.

Detzer, David. 1979. *The Brink: Cuban Missile Crisis, 1962.* New York: Thomas Y. Crowell.

Dillon, Douglas. 1961. "Address by Secretary of the Treasury Douglas Dillon." Address to the Inter-American Economic and Social Conference, Punta del Este, Uruguay, August 7. In Richard P. Stebbins and Elaine P. Adam, eds., *Documents on American Foreign Relations, 1961,* 408–416. New York: Harper and Brothers, for the Council on Foreign Relations, 1962.

Divine, Robert A., ed. 1971. *The Cuban Missile Crisis.* Chicago: Quadrangle Books.

———. 1988. *The Cuban Missile Crisis.* 2nd ed. New York: Markus Wiener.

"Doctrine alive, U.S. says." 1960. *New York Times,* July 13, 3.

Dorticós, Osvaldo. 1962. Address by President Osvaldo Dorticós to the United Nations General Assembly, October 8. United Nations, General Assembly, Seventeenth Session, *Plenary Meetings.* Vol. 2, October 5–November 20, 369–376. New York: United Nations.

Doty, Roxanne Lynn. 1993. "Foreign policy as social construction: A post-positivist analysis of U.S. counterinsurgency policy in the Philippines." *International Studies Quarterly* 37(3): 297–320.

———. 1996. *Imperial Encounters.* Minneapolis: University of Minnesota Press.

Draper, Theodore. 1962. *Castro's Revolution: Myths and Realities*. New York: Praeger.

———. 1965. *Castroism: Theory and Practice*. New York: Praeger.

Drinnon, Richard. 1990 [1980]. *Facing West: The Metaphysics of Indian-Hating and Empire Building*. New York: Schocken Books.

Dulles, Allen W. 1962. "An analysis of communist techniques for conquest." Address to the American Bar Association, San Francisco, August 9. *Vital Speeches of the Day*, October 1, 743–747.

Dulles, John Foster. 1954. "Events in Guatemala." Radio and television address, June 30. *Vital Speeches of the Day*, July 15, 591–592.

Eagleton, Terry. 1991. *Ideology: An Introduction*. London: Verso.

Eisenhower, Dwight D. 1945. "National strength is a necessity: No country fears a strong America." Address to the American Legion National Commanders, Chicago, Illinois, November 20. *Vital Speeches of the Day*, December 1, 108–110.

———. 1954. "The president's news conference of April 7, 1954." In *Public Papers of the Presidents: Dwight D. Eisenhower, 1954*, 381–390. Washington, DC: Government Printing Office, 1960.

———. 1958. "Statement by the president following the landing of United States Marines in Beirut," July 15. *Public Papers of the Presidents: Dwight D. Eisenhower, 1958*, 553–557. Washington, DC: Government Printing Office, 1959.

———. 1959a. "Message of the president on the Mutual Security Program for Fiscal Year 1960," March 13. In Paul E. Zinner, ed., *Documents on American Foreign Relations, 1959*, 93–110. New York: Harper and Brothers, for the Council on Foreign Relations, 1960.

———. 1959b. "Security in the free world." Radio and television address to the nation by the president, March 16. In Paul E. Zinner, ed., *Documents on American Foreign Relations, 1959*, 24–34. New York: Harper and Brothers, for the Council on Foreign Relations, 1960.

———. 1960a. "Statement by the president restating United States policy toward Cuba," January 26. *Public Papers of the Presidents: Dwight D. Eisenhower, 1960–61*, 134–136. Washington, DC: Government Printing Office, 1961.

———. 1960b. "The president's pre-departure broadcast," Washington, February 21. In Richard P. Stebbins and Elaine P. Adam, eds., *Documents on American Foreign Relations, 1960*, 460–464. New York: Harper and Brothers, for the Council on Foreign Relations, 1961.

———. 1960c. "Address before a joint session of the Congress of Brazil," February 24. *Public Papers of the Presidents: Dwight D. Eisenhower, 1960–61*, 216–221. Washington, DC: Government Printing Office, 1961.

———. 1960d. "Report by the president to the nation," March 8. In

Richard P. Stebbins and Elaine P. Adam, eds., *Documents on American Foreign Relations, 1960, 466–470.* New York: Harper and Brothers, for the Council on Foreign Relations, 1961.

———. 1960e. "Statement by the president concerning Premier Khrushchev's announcement of support for the Castro regime in Cuba," July 9. *Public Papers of the Presidents: Dwight D. Eisenhower, 1960–61,* 567–568. Washington, DC: Government Printing Office, 1962.

———. 1960f. "The president's news conference at Newport, Rhode Island," July 11. *Public Papers of the Presidents: Dwight D. Eisenhower, 1960–61,* 568–575. Washington, DC: Government Printing Office, 1962.

———. 1960g. "The president's news conference," August 24. *Public Papers of the Presidents: Dwight D. Eisenhower, 1960–61, 647–658.* Washington, DC: Government Printing Office, 1962.

———. 1961. "Statement by the president on terminating diplomatic relations with Cuba," January 3. *Public Papers of the Presidents: Dwight D. Eisenhower, 1960–61, 891.* Washington, DC: Government Printing Office, 1962.

Eizenstat, Stuart. 1996a. "Statement and remarks to the press by Stuart E. Eizenstat," August 16. Online. Available: http://usiahq.usis.usemb.se/topical/econ/libertad/libserem.htm [December 27, 1997].

———. 1996b. "Morning news briefing by special representative Stuart Eizenstat on the Cuban Liberty and Democratic Solidarity Act," September 4. Online. Available: http://usiahq.usis.usemb.se/topical/econ/libertad/libsepc1.htm [December 27, 1997].

———. 1996c. "Speech given in Paris by special representative Stuart Eizenstat on the Cuban Liberty and Democratic Solidarity Act," October 25. Online. Available: http://usiahq.usis.usemb.se/topical/econ/libertad/libsesp1.htm [December 27, 1997].

———. 1997. "Briefing given in Washington by special Representative Stuart Eizenstat on Helms-Burton waiver," January 3. Online. Available: http://usiahq.usis.usemb.se/topical/econ/libertad/waiver.htm [December 27, 1997].

Everett, Melissa. 1989. *Breaking Ranks.* Philadelphia: New Society.

Farnsworth, David N. 1988. *International Relations: An Introduction.* Chicago: Nelson-Hall.

Fay, Brian. 1975. *Social Theory and Political Practice.* London: George Allen and Unwin.

"Focus: Numbered Days?" 1992. *MacNeil/Lehrer Newshour,* Public Broadcasting Service, January 21.

Foucault, Michel. 1977. *Discipline and Punish: The Birth of the Prison.* Translated by Alan Sheridan. New York: Vintage Books.

Franqui, Carlos. 1985 [1981]. *Family Portrait with Fidel: A Memoir.* Translated by Alfred MacAdam. New York: Vintage Books.

Fulbright, J. William. 1961. "Senator Fulbright's defense of H.R. 6518." Reprinted in *Inter-American Economic Affairs* 15(1): 72–78.

Gaddis, John Lewis. 1974. "Was the Truman Doctrine a real turning point?" *Foreign Affairs* 52(2): 386–402.

———. 1982. *Strategies of Containment: A Critical Appraisal of Postwar American National Security Policy.* New York: Oxford University Press.

Gallie, W. B. 1964. *Philosophy and the Historical Understanding.* New York: Schocken Books.

Garthoff, Raymond L. 1962. "The military significance of the Soviet missile bases in Cuba." Memorandum, October 27. Reprinted as Document D in his *Reflections on the Cuban Missile Crisis,* rev. ed., 202–203. Washington, DC: Brookings Institution, 1989.

———. 1987. *Reflections on the Cuban Missile Crisis.* Washington, DC: Brookings Institution.

———. 1988. "Cuban missile crisis: The Soviet story." *Foreign Policy* 72 (Fall): 61–80.

George, Alexander, David K. Hall, and William E. Simons. 1971. *The Limits of Coercive Diplomacy: Laos, Cuba, Vietnam.* Boston: Little, Brown.

George, Jim. 1989. "International relations and the search for thinking space: Another view of the Third Debate." *International Studies Quarterly* 33(3): 269–279.

———. 1994. *Discourse of Global Politics: A Critical (Re)Introduction to International Relations.* Boulder, CO: Lynne Rienner.

Goldstein, Judith. 1988. "Ideas, institutions, and trade policy." *International Organization* 42(1): 179–217.

———. 1989. "The impact of ideas on trade policy." *International Organization* 43(1): 31–71.

———. 1993. *Ideas, Interests, and American Trade Policy.* Ithaca, NY: Cornell University Press.

Goldstein, Judith, and Robert O. Keohane, eds. 1993. *Ideas and Foreign Policy: Beliefs, Institutions, and Political Change.* Ithaca, NY: Cornell University Press.

Goldwater, Barry. 1961. "Tragic situation in Cuba." Address to the Seventieth Continental Congress, National Society of the Daughters of the American Revolution, Washington, DC, April 17. *Vital Speeches of the Day,* May 1, 419–423.

Gramsci, Antonio. 1971a. *The Modern Prince.* New York: International.

———. 1971b. *Selections from the Prison Notebooks.* Edited and translated by Quintin Hoare and Geoffrey Nowell Smith. New York: International.

Greiner, Berndt. 1990. "The Cuban missile crisis reconsidered: The Soviet view. An interview with Sergo Mikoyan." *Diplomatic History* 14(2): 205–221.

Gromyko, Anatolii A. 1970. *Die 1036 Tage des Präsidenten Kennedy.* Translated from Russian by Michael Frost. Berlin: Dietz Verlag.

———. 1971. "The Caribbean crisis." Part 1: "The U.S. government's preparation of the Caribbean crisis" and Part 2: "Diplomatic efforts of the USSR to eliminate the crisis." Reprinted in Ronald R. Pope, ed., *Soviet Views on the Cuban Missile Crisis,* 161–226. Lanham, MD: University Press of America, 1982.

Haas, Peter, ed. 1992. "Knowledge, Power, and International Policy Coordination." Special issue of *International Organization* 46(1).

Haggard, Stephen. 1991. "Structuralism and its critics: Recent progress in international relations theory." In Emanuel Adler and Beverly Crawford, eds., *Progress in Postwar International Relations,* 403–437. New York: Columbia University Press.

Halberstam, David. 1972 [1969]. *The Best and the Brightest.* New York: Random House.

Hall, Stuart. 1982. "The rediscovery of 'ideology': Return of the repressed in media studies." In Michael Gurevitch, Tony Bennett, James Curran, and Janet Woollacott, eds., *Culture, Society, and the Media,* 56–90. London: Methuen.

———. 1985. "Signification, representation, ideology: Althusser and the post-structuralist debates." *Critical Studies in Mass Communication* 2(2): 91–114.

———. 1986a. "The problem of ideology: Marxism without guarantees." *Journal of Communication Inquiry* 10(2): 28–44.

———. 1986b. "Gramsci's relevance for the study of race and ethnicity." *Journal of Communication Inquiry* 10(2): 5–27.

———. 1986c. "On postmodernism and articulation: An interview with Stuart Hall." Edited by Lawrence Grossberg. *Journal of Communication Inquiry* 10(2): 45–60.

———. 1988. "The toad in the garden: Thatcherism among the theorists." In Cary Nelson and Lawrence Grossberg, eds., *Marxism and the Interpretation of Culture,* 35–57. Urbana: University of Illinois Press.

Herman, Edward S., and Noam Chomsky. 1988. *Manufacturing Consent: The Political Economy of the Mass Media.* New York: Pantheon Books.

Herman, Edward S., and Gerry O'Sullivan. 1989. *The "Terrorism" Industry: The Experts and Institutions That Shape Our View of Terror.* New York: Pantheon Books.

Herring, Eric. 1995. *Danger and Opportunity: Explaining International Crisis Outcomes.* Manchester, England, and New York: Manchester University Press.

Hershberg, James G. 1990. "Before 'The missiles of October': Did Kennedy plan a military strike against Cuba?" *Diplomatic History* 14(2): 163–198.

Herz, John. 1951. *Political Realism and Political Idealism: A Study in Theories and Realities.* Chicago: University of Chicago Press.

Hill, Robert C. 1961. "Confidential report and suggestions on Latin America." Reprinted in U.S. Senate Committee on the Judiciary, *Communist Threat to the United States through the Caribbean: Hearings before the Subcommittee to Investigate the Administration of the Internal Security Act and Other Internal Security Laws,* 809–814. 87th Cong., Part 13, March 29, April 26, June 1, and July 27. Washington, DC: Government Printing Office, 1962.

Hilsman, Roger. 1967. *To Move a Nation: The Politics of Foreign Policy in the Administration of John F. Kennedy.* Garden City, NY: Doubleday.

Hirschman, Albert O. 1977. *The Passions and the Interests: Political Arguments for Capitalism before Its Triumph.* Princeton: Princeton University Press.

Hitchens, Christopher. 1996. "Minority Report: Out of the Crossfire." *Nation,* March 4, 8.

Hoffmann, Stanley. 1977. "An American social science: International relations." *Daedalus* 106(3): 41–60.

———. 1978. *Primacy or World Order: American Foreign Policy since the Cold War.* New York: McGraw-Hill.

Hollis, Martin, and Steve Smith. 1990. *Explaining and Understanding International Relations.* Oxford: Clarendon Press.

Horelick, Arnold L. 1964. "The Cuban missile crisis: Analysis of Soviet calculation and behavior." *World Politics* 16(3): 363–389.

Horelick, Arnold L., and Myron Rush. 1966. *Strategic Power and Soviet Foreign Policy.* Chicago: University of Chicago Press.

Hunt, Michael H. 1987. *Ideology and U.S. Foreign Policy.* New Haven: Yale University Press.

Huth, Paul, and Bruce Russett. 1984. "What makes deterrence work? Cases from 1900–1980." *World Politics* 36(4): 496–526.

Immerman, Richard H. 1982. *The CIA in Guatemala: The Foreign Policy of Intervention.* Austin: University of Texas Press.

Janis, Irving L. 1972. *Victims of Groupthink: A Psychological Study of Foreign Policy Decisions and Fiascos.* Boston: Houghton Mifflin.

———. 1983. *Groupthink: Psychological Studies of Policy Decisions and Fiascos.* 2nd ed., Boston: Houghton Mifflin.

Jervis, Robert, and Jack Snyder, eds. 1991. *Dominos and Bandwagons: Strategic Beliefs and Great Power Competition in the Eurasian Rimland.* New York: Oxford University Press.

Jessup, John K. 1961. "What we must do to defeat Communism." *Life,* November 10, 38–41, 94–108.

Kabbani, Rana. 1986. *Europe's Myths of Orient.* Bloomington: Indiana University Press.

Kahan, Jerome H., and Anne K. Long. 1972. "The Cuban missile crisis: A study of its strategic context." *Political Science Quarterly* 87(4): 564–590.

Kaku, Michio, and Daniel Axelrod. 1987. *To Win a Nuclear War: The Pentagon's Secret War Plans.* Boston: South End Press.

Kaplan, Fred. 1983. *The Wizards of Armageddon.* New York: Simon and Schuster.

Karnow, Stanley. 1989. *In Our Image: America's Empire in the Philippines.* New York: Ballantine Books.

Kelly, J. 1995. "'Amicable divorce' could turn nasty, experts say." *USA Today,* November 22, 12A.

Kennan, George F. 1946. "Moscow embassy telegram #511: 'The long telegram,'" February 22. Reprinted in Thomas H. Etzold and John Lewis Gaddis, eds., *Containment: Documents on American Policy and Strategy, 1945–1950,* 50–63. New York: Columbia University Press, 1978.

———. 1947. "The sources of Soviet conduct." *Foreign Affairs* 25(4): 566–582. Reprinted in his *American Diplomacy,* expanded ed., 107–128. Chicago: University of Chicago Press, 1984.

———. 1967. *Memoirs, 1925–1950.* Boston: Little, Brown.

Kennedy, John F. 1960a. "Excerpts from Kennedy talk on Cuba," October 6. *New York Times,* October 7, 20.

———. 1960b. "Text of statement by Kennedy on dealing with Castro regime," October 20. *New York Times,* October 21, 18.

———. 1960c. "Transcript of the fourth Kennedy-Nixon debate on the issues of the campaign," October 21. *New York Times,* October 22, 8–9.

———. 1960d. "Senator John F. Kennedy on the Cuban situation: Presidential campaign of 1960." *Inter-American Economic Affairs* 15(3) (1961): 79–95.

———. 1961a. "Inaugural address of President John F. Kennedy," January 20. In Richard P. Stebbins and Elaine P. Adam, eds., *Documents on American Foreign Relations, 1961,* 12–15. New York: Harper and Brothers, for the Council on Foreign Relations, 1962.

———. 1961b. "Address by Kennedy at a White House reception," March 13. In Richard P. Stebbins and Elaine P. Adam, eds., *Documents on American Foreign Relations, 1961,* 395–401. New York: Harper and Brothers, for the Council on Foreign Relations, 1962.

———. 1961c. "Inter-American fund for Social Progress." Message of President Kennedy to the Congress, March 14. In Richard P. Stebbins and Elaine P. Adam, eds., *Documents on American Foreign Relations,*

1961, 401–408. New York: Harper and Brothers, for the Council on Foreign Relations, 1962.

———. 1961d. "Address before the American Society of Newspaper Editors," April 20. *Public Papers of the Presidents: John F. Kennedy, 1961,* 304–306. Washington, DC: Government Printing Office, 1962.

———. 1961e. "Address to the 39th Annual Convention of the National Association of Broadcasters," May 8. *Public Papers of the Presidents: John F. Kennedy, 1961, 367–370.* Washington, DC: Government Printing Office, 1962.

———. 1961f. "Special message to Congress on urgent national needs," May 25. *Public Papers of the Presidents: John F. Kennedy, 1961, 396–406.* Washington, DC: Government Printing Office, 1962.

———. 1961g. "Radio and television report to the American people on the Berlin crisis," July 25. *Public Papers of the Presidents: John F. Kennedy, 1961, 533–540.* Washington, DC: Government Printing Office, 1962.

———. 1961h. "Alliance for Progress, a program for the peoples of the Americas." Message from President Kennedy read to a special meeting of the Economic and Social Council of the OAS, Punta del Este, Uruguay, August 7. *Department of State Bulletin,* August 28, 355–356.

———. 1961i. "The president's news conference of August 30, 1961." *Public Papers of the Presidents: John F. Kennedy, 1961, 572–580.* Washington, DC: Government Printing Office, 1962.

———. 1961j. "Address in New York City before the General Assembly of the United Nations," September 25. *Public Papers of the Presidents: John F. Kennedy, 1961, 618–626.* Washington, DC: Government Printing Office, 1962.

———. 1961k. "Transcript of interview with the president by Aleksei Adzhubei, editor of *Izvestia,*" November 25. *Public Papers of the Presidents: John F. Kennedy, 1961, 741–752.* Washington, DC: Government Printing Office, 1962.

———. 1962a. "Kennedy's Cuba statement," September 4. *New York Times,* September 5, 2.

———. 1962b. "The president's news conference of September 13, 1962." *Public Papers of the Presidents: John F. Kennedy, 1962, 674–681.* Washington, DC: Government Printing Office, 1963.

———. 1962c. *The U.S. Response to Soviet Military Buildup in Cuba.* Report to the People, October 22. Department of State publication 7449, Inter-American Series 80. Washington, DC: Government Printing Office.

———. 1962d. "After two years: A conversation with the president." Television and radio interview, December 17. *Public Papers of the Presidents: John F. Kennedy, 1962, 889–904.* Washington, DC: Government Printing Office, 1963.

———. 1963. "Remarks at the High School Memorial Stadium, Great Falls, Montana," September 26. *Public Papers of the Presidents: John F. Kennedy, 1963*, 727–730. Washington, DC: Government Printing Office, 1964.

Kennedy, Robert F. 1971 [1969]. *Thirteen Days: A Memoir of the Cuban Missile Crisis*. With an afterword by Richard E. Neustadt and Graham T. Allison. New York: W. W. Norton.

Kenworthy, E. W. 1960a. "Senators assail Castro's actions." *New York Times*, January 23, 1.

———. 1960b. "U.S. will indict Cuba before O.A.S." *New York Times*, June 18, 1, 6.

Khrushchev, Nikita. 1960a. "Address by Soviet Premier Khrushchev to a conference of teachers at the Kremlin, July 9, 1960." Reprinted in *Inter-American Efforts to Relieve International Tensions in the Western Hemisphere, 1959–1960*, 215–217. Department of State publication 7409, Inter-American Series 79. Washington, DC: Government Printing Office, 1962.

———. 1960b. "Transcript of Khrushchev's news conference on U.S. plane and other issues," July 12. *New York Times*, July 13, 6–7.

———. 1961a. "Message from N. S. Khrushchev, chairman of the U.S.S.R. Council of Ministers, to U.S. president J. Kennedy," April 23. Reprinted in *Current Digest of the Soviet Press* 13(16) (May 17): 7–9.

———. 1961b. "Message from N. S. Khrushchev, chairman of the U.S.S.R. Council of Ministers, to U.S. president J. Kennedy," April 18. Reprinted in *Current Digest of the Soviet Press* 13(16) (May 17): 4–5.

———. 1962a. "Khrushchev's report on the international situation: I." Report to the U.S.S.R. Supreme Soviet, December 12. Reprinted in *Current Digest of the Soviet Press* 14(51) (January 16, 1963): 3–8.

———. 1962b. "Khrushchev's report on the international situation: II." Report to the U.S.S.R. Supreme Soviet, December 12. Reprinted in *Current Digest of the Soviet Press* 14(52) (January 23, 1963): 3–10.

———. 1970. *Khrushchev Remembers*. With an introduction, commentary, and notes by Edward Crankshaw, translated and edited by Strobe Talbott. New York: Bantam Books.

Kirkpatrick, Jeane. 1989–90. "Beyond the cold war." *Foreign Affairs* 69(1): 1–16.

Kissinger, Henry. 1969. *American Foreign Policy: Three Essays*. New York: W. W. Norton.

Klare, Michael T. 1989. "East-West versus North-South: Dominant and subordinate themes in U.S. military strategy since 1945." In John R. Gillis, ed., *The Militarization of the Western World*, 141–165. New Brunswick, NJ: Rutgers University Press.

Kline, Morris. 1980. *Mathematics: The Loss of Certainty.* New York: Oxford University Press.

Knebel, Fletcher. 1962. "Washington in crisis: 154 hours on the brink of war." *Look,* December 18, 43–44, 49–52, 54.

Koh, Harold Hongju. 1990. *The National Security Constitution: Sharing Power after the Iran-Contra Affair.* New Haven: Yale University Press.

Kolko, Gabriel. 1969. *The Roots of American Foreign Policy: An Analysis of Power and Purpose.* Boston: Beacon Press.

———. 1980. *Confronting the Third World: United States Foreign Policy, 1945–1980.* New York: Pantheon Books.

Kwitny, Jonathan. 1984. *Endless Enemies: The Making of an Unfriendly World.* New York: Congdon and Weed.

LaCapra, Dominick. 1985. *History and Criticism.* Ithaca, NY: Cornell University Press.

Laclau, Ernesto. 1979. *Politics and Ideology in Marxist Theory.* London: Verso.

Laclau, Ernesto, and Chantal Mouffe. 1985. *Hegemony and Socialist Strategy: Towards a Radical Democratic Politics.* London: Verso.

———. 1987. "Post-Marxism without apologies." *New Left Review* 166: 79–106.

LaFeber, Walter. 1984. *Inevitable Revolutions: The United States in Central America.* Expanded ed. New York: W. W. Norton.

———. 1985. *America, Russia, and the Cold War, 1945–1984.* 5th ed. New York: Knopf.

Lakatos, Imre. 1970. "Falsification and the methodology of scientific research programs." In Imre Lakatos and Alan Musgrave, eds., *Criticism and the Growth of Knowledge,* 91–196. Cambridge: Cambridge University Press.

Lansdale, Edward. 1962. "The Cuba Project." February 20. Reprinted in Laurence Chang and Peter Kornbluh, eds., *The Cuban Missile Crisis, 1962: A National Security Archive Documents Reader,* 23–37. New York: New Press, 1992.

Lanyi, George A. 1963. "The problem of appeasement." *World Politics* 15(2): 316–328.

Lazo, Mario. 1968. *Dagger in the Heart: American Policy Failures in Cuba.* New York: Funk and Wagnalls.

Lebow, Richard Ned, and Janice Gross Stein. 1994. *We All Lost the Cold War.* Princeton: Princeton University Press.

"Life in the newsfronts of the world." 1961. *Life,* June 2, 56.

Lippmann, Walter. 1963. "Cuba and the nuclear risk." *Atlantic Monthly,* February, 55–58.

Little, Douglas. 1983. "Antibolshevism and American foreign policy,

1919–1939: The diplomacy of self-delusion." *American Quarterly* 35(4): 376–390.

Lockwood, Lee. 1967. *Castro's Cuba, Cuba's Fidel: An American Journalist's Inside Look at Today's Cuba.* New York: Macmillan.

Lodge, John. 1958. "Peace is a product of strength." Address to the Navy League, October 27. *Vital Speeches of the Day,* November 15, 66–69.

Lowenthal, Abraham, ed. 1991. *Exporting Democracy: The United States and Latin America.* Baltimore: Johns Hopkins University Press.

Luce, Clare Boothe. 1963. "The seventeen year trend to Castro: The art of economic brinkmanship." Address to the Los Angeles World Affairs Council, January 22. *Vital Speeches of the Day,* March 1, 295–299.

Lukas, Anthony M. 1987. "Class reunion: Kennedy's men relive the Cuban missile crisis." *New York Times Magazine,* August 28, 22–27, 51, 58, 61.

Lundestad, Geir. 1989. "Moralism, presentism, exceptionalism, provincialism, and other extravagances in American writings on the early Cold War years." *Diplomatic History* 13(4): 527–545.

Lyons, Gene M., and Louis Morton. 1965. *Schools for Strategy: Education and Research in National Security Affairs.* New York: Praeger.

McCloskey, Donald. 1985. *The Rhetoric of Economics.* Madison: University of Wisconsin Press.

———. 1990. *If You're So Smart: The Narrative of Economic Expertise.* Chicago: University of Chicago Press.

McNamara, Robert. 1962. "The communist design for world conquest." Address to the Fellows of the American Bar Association, Chicago, February 17. *Vital Speeches of the Day,* March 1, 296–299.

Mansfield, Mike. 1960. "New horizons for the Americas." Speech delivered to the Special Session of Congress, August 8. Reprinted in *Inter-American Economic Affairs* 14(2): 89–101.

Martí, José. 1953. "Carta a Manuel Mercado." In *José Martí: Pensamiento Político.* Havana: Municipio de La Habana.

Mastanduno, Michael, David A. Lake, and G. John Ikenberry. 1989. "Toward a realist theory of state action." *International Studies Quarterly* 33(4): 457–474.

Matthews, Jessica Tuchman. 1989. "Redefining security." *Foreign Affairs* 68(2): 162–177.

May, Ernest R., and Philip D. Zelikow, eds. 1997. *The Kennedy Tapes: Inside the White House during the Cuban Missile Crisis.* Cambridge: Belknap Press of Harvard University Press.

Medland, William J. 1988. *The Cuban Missile Crisis of 1962: Needless or Necessary?* New York: Praeger.

Meisler, Stanley. 1992. "U.N. rebuffs U.S. on Cuba embargo." *Los Angeles Times,* November 25, A1.

Melanson, Richard A. 1983. *Writing History and Making Policy: The Cold War, Vietnam, and Revisionism.* Lanham, MD: University Press of America.

"The menacing push of Castroism." 1961. *Life,* June 2, 82–91.

Meyer, Karl E., and Tad Szulc. 1962. *The Cuban Invasion.* New York: Praeger.

Milliken, Jennifer. 1994. "A grammar of state action: US policymakers' social construction of the Korean War." Ph.D. diss., University of Minnesota.

Minutes of the first Operation Mongoose meeting with Attorney General Robert Kennedy. 1961. December 1. Reprinted in Laurence Chang and Peter Kornbluh, eds., *The Cuban Missile Crisis, 1962: A National Security Archive Documents Reader,* 20–22. New York: New Press, 1992.

"The missiles of October: What the world didn't know." 1992. ABC Television documentary.

"Monroe Doctrine guards West." 1960. *New York Times,* July 13, 3.

Morgenthau, Hans J. 1951. *In Defense of the National Interest: A Critical Examination of American Foreign Policy.* New York: Knopf.

———. 1952. "Another 'great debate': The national interest of the United States." *American Political Science Review* 46(4): 961–988.

———. 1962. "Negotiations or war?" *New Republic,* November 3, 9.

———. 1969. *A New Foreign Policy for the United States.* New York: Praeger, for the Council on Foreign Relations.

———. 1970. *Truth and Power: Essays of a Decade, 1960–1970.* New York: Praeger.

———. 1978 [1948]. *Politics among Nations: The Struggle for Power and Peace.* 5th ed., rev. New York: Knopf.

Morley, Morris H. 1987. *Imperial State and Revolution: The United States and Cuba, 1952–1986.* Cambridge: Cambridge University Press.

Morris, Roger. 1977. *Uncertain Greatness: Henry Kissinger and American Foreign Policy.* New York: Harper and Row.

Muppidi, Himadeep. 1999. "Postcoloniality and the production of insecurity: The persistent puzzle of U.S.-Indian Relations." In Jutta Weldes, Mark Laffey, Hugh Gusterson, and Raymond Duvall, eds., *Cultures of Insecurity: States, Communities, and the Production of Danger.* Minneapolis: University of Minnesota Press.

Nardone, Benito. 1961. "A Latin president's battle-tested advice." *Life,* June 2, 92.

Nathan, James A. 1975. "The missile crisis: His finest hour now." *World Politics* 27(2): 256–281.

Nathan, James A., ed. 1992. *The Cuban Missile Crisis Revisited.* New York: St. Martin's Press.

National Bipartisan Commission on Central America (Kissinger Commission). 1984. "Report." Washington, DC: Government Printing Office.

Nelson, John S., Allan Megill, and Donald N. McCloskey, eds. 1987. *The*

Rhetoric of the Human Sciences: Language and Argument in Scholarship and Public Affairs. Madison: University of Wisconsin Press.

Norris, John G. 1961. "No missile gap exists, defense study shows." *Washington Post,* February 7, 1.

"Notes of the month: Cuba. A U.S. election issue." 1962. *The World Today* 18(11): 453–456.

"October 27, 1962: Transcripts of the meeting of the ExComm." 1987–88. Transcribed by McGeorge Bundy, edited by James G. Blight. *International Security* 12(3): 30–92.

Olsen, Arthur J. 1962. "Monroe Doctrine faces challenge." *New York Times,* September 4, 9.

Organization of American States. 1962. "Text of Resolution," October 23. *Department of State Bulletin,* November 12, 722–723.

Pace, Eric. 1987. "Rusk tells a Kennedy secret: Fallback plan in Cuban crisis." *New York Times,* August 28, 1.

Paterson, Thomas G. 1988. *Meeting the Communist Threat: Truman to Reagan.* Oxford: Oxford University Press.

———. 1989. "Fixation with Cuba: The Bay of Pigs, missile crisis, and covert war against Fidel Castro." In Thomas G. Paterson, ed., *Kennedy's Quest for Victory: American Foreign Policy, 1961–1963,* 123–155. New York: Oxford University Press.

———. 1990. "Commentary: The defense-of-Cuba theme and the missile crisis." *Diplomatic History* 14(2): 249–256.

Paterson, Thomas G., and William J. Brophy. 1986. "October missiles and November elections: The Cuban missile crisis and American politics, 1962." *Journal of American History* 73(1): 87–119.

Pérez, Louis A. Jr. 1990. *Cuba and the United States: Ties of Singular Intimacy.* Athens: University of Georgia Press.

Phillips, R. Hart. 1960a. "Castro orders seizure—Also bitterly attacks U.S. sugar bill." *New York Times,* June 30, 1, 4.

———. 1960b. "Khrushchev tells Cuba he will buy sugar U.S. barred." *New York Times,* July 11, 1, 10.

———. 1961a. "U.S. aides start leaving H̄   a." *New York Times,* January 5, 1, 6.

———. 1961b. "Talks asked b   ' *New̲ ̲ork Times,* April 29, 3.

Pope, Ronald R., ed. 1982. *Sov   /iew. · the   ban Missile Crisis: Myth and Reality in Foreign Policy   ·ᴵ·   \МD: University Press of America.

Powaski, Ronald E. 1987. *March   ᴸᴵmageddon: The United States and the Nuclear Arms Race, 1939 to the Present.* New York: Oxford University Press.

Purvis, Trevor, and Alan Hunt. 1993. "Discourse, ideology, discourse, ideology, discourse, ideology . . . ," *The British Journal of Sociology* 44(3): 473–499.

Raitberger, Francois. 1997. "Behind the scenes in '62 missile crisis." *USA Today,* August 15, 10A.

Reagan, Ronald. 1986. *Reagan on Cuba: Selected Statements by the President.* Washington, DC: Cuban-American National Foundation.

Reston, James. 1960. "Cuba's drift to the left." *New York Times,* February 19, 6.

Richardson, J. L. 1988. "New perspectives on appeasement: Some implications for international relations." *World Politics* 40(3): 289–316.

Ringmar, Erik. 1996. *Identity, Interest, and Action: A Cultural Explanation of Sweden's Intervention in the Thirty Years War.* Cambridge: Cambridge University Press.

Robbins, Carla Anne. 1983. *The Cuban Threat.* New York: McGraw-Hill.

"Rooseveltian policies, but the wrong Roosevelt, says Pravda: Attack on Cuba is challenge to all peace-loving peoples. The 'big stick' again." 1961. *Pravda,* April 20. Reprinted in *Current Digest of the Soviet Press,* 13(16) (May 17): 5–7.

Rosenau, James N. 1968. "National interest." In David L. Sills, ed., *International Encyclopedia of the Social Sciences,* vol. 11, 34–40. New York: Macmillan and Free Press.

Rosenberg, Alfred. 1935. *Der Mythus des 20. Jahrhunderts: Eine Wertung der seelisch-geistigen Gestaltenkampfe unserer Zeit.* Munich: Hoheneichen Verlag.

Rosenberg, Justin. 1990. "What's the matter with realism?" *Review of International Studies* 16(4): 285–303.

Ross, Gregory. 1978. "The domino theory." In Alexander de Conde, ed., *Encyclopedia of American Foreign Policy,* vol. 1, 275–280. New York: Charles Scribner's Sons.

Rothstein, Robert L. 1972. "On the costs of realism." *Political Science Quarterly* 87(3): 347–362.

Rubottom, Roy. 1958. *Communism in the Americas.* Department of State publication 6601, Inter-American Series 53. Washington, DC: Government Printing Office.

———. 1960. *International Communism in Latin America.* Department of State publication 7048, Inter-American Series 60. Washington, DC: Government Printing Office.

Rusk, Dean. 1962a. "Address by Hon. Dean Rusk, secretary of state, at the eighth meeting of Consultation of Ministers of Foreign Affairs of the American States," Punta del Este, Uruguay, January 25. Reprinted as Appendix 1, U.S. Senate, Committee on the Judiciary, hearings before the Subcommittee to Investigate the Administration of the Internal Security

Act and other Internal Security Laws, *Communist Threat to the United States through the Caribbean,* part 13, 889–895. March 29, April 26, June 1, and July 27, 1961. Washington, DC: Government Printing Office.

———. 1962b. "Secretary discusses Cuban situation on 'News and Comment' program," September 30. *Department of State Bulletin,* October 22, 595–598.

———. 1962c. "American republics act to halt Soviet threat to hemisphere." Statement to the Council of the Organization of American States, October 23. *Department of State Bulletin,* November 12, 720–722.

Rystad, Göran. 1981–1982. *Prisoners of the Past? The Munich Syndrome and the Makers of American Foreign Policy in the Cold War Era.* Vol. 2. Studier utgivna av Kungl. Humanistiska Vetenskapssamfundet. Lund, Sweden: CWK Gleerup.

Saco, Diana. 1992. "Voices from the distance: Radio Martí and the (pen)insular construction of Cuban identity." Master's thesis, Florida Atlantic University.

Schlesinger, Arthur M. Jr. 1965. *A Thousand Days: John F. Kennedy in the White House.* Boston: Houghton Mifflin.

———. 1973. *The Imperial Presidency.* Boston: Houghton Mifflin.

———. 1978. *Robert Kennedy and His Times.* Boston: Houghton Mifflin.

Schlesinger, Stephen, and Stephen Kinzer. 1982. *Bitter Fruit: The Untold Story of the American Coup in Guatemala.* Garden City, NY: Doubleday.

Schwartz, Harry. 1960. "Soviet will send Cuba vital goods." *New York Times,* February 19, 6.

Schwichtenberg, Cathy. 1984. "*The Love Boat*: The packaging and selling of love, heterosexual romance, and family." *Media, Culture and Society* 6, 301–311.

Scott, David Clark. 1992. "Plan to stiffen Cuba ban annoys U.S. trading allies." *Christian Science Monitor,* June 23, 1.

Scott, Len, and Steve Smith. 1994. "Lessons of October: Historians, political scientists, policy-makers, and the Cuban missile crisis." *International Affairs* 70(4): 659–684.

Shalom, Stephen R. 1988. "The Cuban missile crisis." *Zeta Magazine* 1(16): 69–80.

Shoup, Lawrence H., and William Minter. 1977. *Imperial Brain Trust: The Council on Foreign Relations and United States Foreign Policy.* New York: Monthly Review Press.

Skocpol, Theda. 1979. *States and Social Revolutions.* Cambridge: Cambridge University Press.

Slater, Jerome. 1987. "Dominos in Central America: Will they fall? Does it matter?" *International Security* 12(2): 105–134.

Smith, Bruce L. R. 1966. *The RAND Corporation: Case Study of a Non-Profit Advisory Corporation.* Cambridge: Harvard University Press.

Smith, Paul. 1988. *Discerning the Subject.* Foreword by John Mowitt. Minneapolis: University of Minnesota Press.

Smith, Steve. 1986. "Theories of foreign policy: An historical overview." *Review of International Studies* 12(1): 13–29.

Smith, Tony. 1991. "The Alliance for Progress: The 1960s." In Abraham Lowenthal, ed., *Exporting Democracy: The United States and Latin America,* 71–89. Baltimore: Johns Hopkins University Press.

Smith, Wayne S. 1983. Foreword to Carla Anne Robbins, *The Cuban Threat,* xi–xvi. New York: McGraw-Hill.

Sondermann, Fred A. 1987 [1977]. "The concept of the national interest." In William C. Olson, ed., *The Theory and Practice of International Relations,* 7th ed. 128–136. Englewood Cliffs, NJ: Prentice-Hall.

Sorensen, Theodore C. 1965. *Kennedy.* New York: Harper and Row.

Stebbins, Richard P. 1959. *The United States in World Affairs, 1958.* New York: Harper and Brothers, for the Council on Foreign Relations.

———. 1960. *The United States in World Affairs, 1959.* New York: Harper and Brothers, for the Council on Foreign Relations.

———. 1961. *The United States in World Affairs, 1960.* New York: Harper and Brothers, for the Council on Foreign Relations.

———. 1962. *The United States in World Affairs, 1961.* New York: Harper and Brothers, for the Council on Foreign Relations.

———. 1963. *The United States in World Affairs, 1962.* New York: Harper and Row, for the Council on Foreign Relations.

Steel, Ronald. 1969. "Endgame." Review of Robert F. Kennedy, *Thirteen Days. New York Review of Books,* March 13, 15–22.

Stevenson, Adlai E. 1961. "Statement of April 17." Statement to Committee 1 (Political and Security) of the U.N. General Assembly, April 17. *Department of State Bulletin,* May 8, 668–675.

———. 1962a. "U.N. Security Council hears U.S. charges of Soviet military buildup in Cuba." Statement of October 23. *Department of State Bulletin,* November 12, 723–734.

———. 1962b. "First statement of October 25." Statement to the U.N. Security Council, October 25. *Department of State Bulletin,* November 12, 734–737.

———. 1962c. "Second statement of October 25." Statement to the U.N. Security Council, October 25. *Department of State Bulletin,* November 12, 737–740.

Stevenson, Adlai E., and Valerian A. Zorin. 1962. "Has the U.S.S.R. missiles in Cuba?" Addresses to the U.N. Security Council, October 25. *Vital Speeches of the Day.* November 15, 77–80.

Stone, I. F. 1966. "The brink." Review of Elie Abel, *The Missile Crisis*. *New York Review of Books*, April 14, 12–16.

Sullivan, Ronald J. 1990. "Dealing with the Soviets." In Schuyler Foerster and Edward N. Wright, eds., *American Defense Policy*, 6th ed., 165–187. Baltimore: Johns Hopkins University Press.

"Summary of editorial comment on United States break in relations with Cuba." 1961. *New York Times*, January 5, 10.

Szulc, Tad. 1960. "Last two refineries seized by Castro; oil supplies low." *New York Times*, July 2, 1, 2.

———. 1986. *Fidel: A Critical Portrait*. New York: William Morrow.

"TASS statement on aid to Cuba and U.S. provocations." 1962. *Pravda*, September 12. Reprinted in *Current Digest of the Soviet Press* 14(37) (October 10): 13–15, 25.

Tatu, Michel. 1969. *Power in the Kremlin: From Khrushchev to Kosygin*. Translated by Helen Katel. New York: Viking Press.

"Texts of U.N.-Cuban notes" (October 27). 1962. *New York Times*, October 28, 31.

Theoharis, Athan. 1974. "The politics of scholarship: Liberals, anti-communism, and McCarthyism." In Robert Griffith and Athan Theoharis, eds., *The Specter: Original Essays on the Cold War and the Origins of McCarthyism*, 262–280. New York: Franklin Wartz.

Thomas, Hugh. 1971. *Cuba: The Pursuit of Freedom*. New York: Harper and Row.

Thompson, John B. 1984. *Studies in the Theory of Ideology*. Berkeley: University of California Press.

Thompson, Robert Smith. 1992. *The Missiles of October: The Declassified Story of John F. Kennedy and the Cuban Missile Crisis*. New York: Simon and Schuster.

Thorson, Stuart, and Donald Sylvan. 1982. "Counterfactuals and the Cuban missile crisis." *International Studies Quarterly* 26(4): 539–571.

Tilly, Charles. 1985. "War making and state making as organized crime." In Peter B. Evans, Dietrich Rueschemeyer, and Theda Skocpol, eds., *Bringing the State Back In*, 169–191. Cambridge: Cambridge University Press.

"Time to change a static Cuba policy." 1997. *Miami Herald*, January 22. Online. Available: http://rs9.loc.gov/cgi-bin/query/D?r105:11:./temp/~r105Rut7:: [October 19, 1997].

Tomlinson, John. 1991. *Cultural Imperialism: A Critical Introduction*. Baltimore: Johns Hopkins University Press.

Topping, Seymour. 1960. "Khrushchev vows aid in any move against Guantanamo base." *New York Times*, July 13, 1.

Torricelli, Robert G. 1992. "How to bring about change in Cuba." *New York Times,* August 10, A16.

Tower, John, Edmund Muskie, and Brent Scowcroft. 1987. *The Tower Commission Report.* Introduction by R. W. Apple Jr. New York: Random House and Bantam Books.

Trachtenberg, Marc. 1985. Introduction to "White House tapes and minutes of the Cuban missile crisis: ExCom meetings, October 1962." *International Security* 10(1): 164–170.

Truman, Harry S. 1945. "Special message to the Congress recommending the establishment of a Department of National Defense," December 19. *Public Papers of the Presidents: Harry S Truman, 1945,* 546–560. Washington, DC: Government Printing Office, 1961.

———. 1947. "Message from the president (Truman) to a Joint Session of the Congress," March 12. In Raymond Dennet and Robert K. Turner, eds., *Documents on American Foreign Relations, 1947,* vol. 9, 646–650. Princeton: Princeton University Press, 1948.

———. 1950a. "Radio and television report to the American people on the situation in Korea," September 1. *Public Papers of the Presidents: Harry S Truman, 1950,* 609–614. Washington, DC: Government Printing Office, 1965.

———. 1950b. "Radio address by the president," December 15. In Raymond Dennet and Robert K. Turner, eds., *Documents on American Foreign Relations, 1950,* vol. 12, 15–18. Princeton: Princeton University Press, for the World Peace Foundation, 1951.

———. 1951. "Radio Report to the American People on Korea and on U.S. Policy in the far East," April 11. *Public Papers of the Presidents: Harry S Truman, 1951,* 223–227. Washington, DC: Government Printing Office, 1965.

———. 1955. *Memoirs.* Vol. 1: *Years of Decision.* Garden City, NY: Doubleday.

Tucker, Robert W. 1961. "Political realism and foreign policy." *World Politics* 13(3): 461–470.

Ulam, Adam B. 1971. *The Rivals: America and Russia since World War II.* New York: Viking Press.

U.S. Congress. 1959. *The Captive Nations.* Joint (Senate) resolution, adopted by the Senate July 6 and the House July 8. In Paul E. Zinner, ed., *Documents on American Foreign Relations, 1959,* 206–207. New York: Harper and Brothers, for the Council on Foreign Relations, 1960.

———. 1962. "Joint resolution of the Congress: Public Law 87–733," approved October 3. In Richard P. Stebbins and Elaine P. Adam, eds., *Documents on American Foreign Relations, 1962,* 372–373. New York: Harper and Row, for the Council on Foreign Relations, 1963.

——. 1996. "Cuban Liberty and Democratic Solidarity (Libertad) Act of 1996." Public Law 104–114, 104th Cong. Online. Available: http://usiahq. usis.usemb.se/topical/econ/libertad/libertad.htm [October 16, 1997].

U.S. Department of Defense. 1964. "Annual report of the secretary of defense." *Annual Report for Fiscal Year 1963*, 1–56. Washington, DC: Government Printing Office.

U.S. Department of Defense Armed Forces Information and Education. 1962. "The Cuban crisis." *For Commanders*, 2(10) (October 30).

U.S. Department of Defense Joint Chiefs of Staff. 1962. "Projection of 'consequences of U.S. military intervention in Cuba,'" (prepared for Special Group Augmented), August 8. Reprinted in Laurence Chang and Peter Kornbluh, eds., *The Cuban Missile Crisis, 1962: A National Security Archive Documents Reader*, 48–51. New York: New Press.

U.S. Department of State. 1957. *A Case History of Communist Penetration: Guatemala*. Department of State publication 6465, Inter-American Series 52. Washington, DC: Government Printing Office.

——. 1960. *The Land Problem in Latin America*. Department of State publication 7112, Inter-American Series 62. Washington, DC: Government Printing Office.

——. 1961a. *Forces of Change in Latin America*. Department of State publication 7157, Inter-American Series 64. Washington, DC: Government Printing Office.

——. 1961b. *Cuba*. Department of State Publication 7171, Inter-American Series 66. Washington, DC: Government Printing Office.

——. 1962. "Department reports on Cuban threats to the Western Hemisphere: Summary." *Department of State Bulletin*, January 22, 129–130.

U.S. Department of State Bureau of Public Affairs. 1962. "Developments in the Cuban situation: Questions and answers," *Foreign Affairs Outlines*. Department of State publication 7454, Inter-American Series 81. Washington, DC: Government Printing Office.

U.S. Information Agency. 1961. "United States Information Agency's estimate of the Latin American situation," March 28. Reprinted in *Inter-American Economic Affairs*, 15(2): 88–91.

——. 1962. *Cuban Crisis 1962: USIA in Action*. Washington, DC: Government Printing Office.

"U.S. is seeking to isolate Castro; says Guantanamo treaty stands; derides aggression charge in U.N." 1961. *New York Times*, January 5, 1.

U.S. National Security Council. 1948. NSC 7: "The position of the United States with respect to Soviet-directed world communism," March 30. Reprinted in Thomas H. Etzold and John Lewis Gaddis, eds., *Containment: Documents on American Policy and Strategy, 1945–1950*, 164–169. New York: Columbia University Press, 1978.

————. 1950. NSC 68: "United States objectives and programs for national security," April 14. Reprinted in Thomas H. Etzold and John Lewis Gaddis, eds., *Containment: Documents on American Policy and Strategy, 1945–1950,* 385–442. New York: Columbia University Press, 1978.

U.S. Senate. 1992. *Cuban Democracy Act of 1992.* Report for the 102nd Congress: Bill Text Report for S.2918, 102nd Cong., 2nd Sess. Online. Available: LEGI-SLATE.

U.S. Senate Committee on Foreign Relations. 1947. *Assistance to Greece and Turkey: Hearings before the Committee on Foreign Relations.* 80th Cong., 1st Sess., March 24, 25, 27, and 31. Washington, DC: Government Printing Office.

U.S. Senate Committee on the Judiciary. 1959. *Communist Threat to the United States through the Caribbean: Hearings before the Subcommittee to Investigate the Administration of the Internal Security Act and Other Internal Security Laws,* 141–179. 87th Cong., 1st Sess., Part III, November 5. Washington, DC: Government Printing Office, 1960.

————. 1961a. *Cuban Aftermath—Red Seeds Blow South: Implications for the United States of the Latin American Conference for National Sovereignty and Economic Emancipation and Peace: Hearing before the Subcommittee to Investigate the Administration of the Internal Security Act and Other Internal Security Laws,* 2–20. 87th Cong., 1st Sess., March 16. Washington, DC: Government Printing Office.

————. 1961b. *Communist Threat to the United States through the Caribbean: Hearing before the Subcommittee to Investigate the Administration of the Internal Security Act and Other Internal Security Laws,* Appendix 2: "Chronology of important events in United States-Cuban relations, 1957–1962," 896–906. 87th Cong., Part 13, March 29, April 26, June 1, and July 27, 1961. Washington, DC: Government Printing Office, 1962.

U.S. Senate Select Committee to Study Governmental Operations with respect to Intelligence Activities. 1975. *Alleged Assassination Plots Involving Foreign Leaders: An Interim Report.* 94th Cong., 1st Sess., November 20. Washington, DC: Government Printing Office, 1976.

U.S. Special Group (Augmented). 1962. "Guidelines for Operation Mongoose," March 14. Reprinted in Laurence Chang and Peter Kornbluh, eds., *The Cuban Missile Crisis, 1962: A National Security Archive Documents Reader,* 38–39. New York: New Press, 1992.

"U.S.S.R. government statement in connection with armed invasion of Cuba." 1961. *Pravda,* April 19. Reprinted in *Current Digest of the Soviet Press* 13(16) (May 17): 3–4.

van Alstyne, Richard W. 1971. "The Monroe Doctrine." In Alexander de

Conde, ed., *Encyclopedia of American Foreign Policy.* Vol. 2, 584–596. New York: Charles Scribner's Sons.

Walker, R .B. J. 1993. *Inside/Outside: International Relations as Political Theory.* Cambridge: Cambridge University Press.

Walton, Richard J. 1972. *Cold War and Counterrevolution: The Foreign Policy of John F. Kennedy.* New York: Viking Press.

Waltz, Kenneth. 1959. *Man, the State, and War: A Theoretical Analysis.* New York: Columbia University Press.

———. 1979. *Theory of International Politics.* New York: McGraw-Hill.

Welch, David A. 1989. "Crisis decision making reconsidered." *Journal of Conflict Resolution* 33(3): 430–445.

Welch, David A., and James G. Blight. 1987–88. "The eleventh hour of the Cuban missile crisis: An introduction to the ExComm transcripts." *International Security* 12(3): 5–29.

Weldes, Jutta. 1993. "Constructing national interests: The logic of U.S. national security in the post-war era." Ph.D. diss., University of Minnesota.

———. 1996. "Constructing national interests." *European Journal of International Relations* 2(3): 275–318.

———. 1997. "The cultural construction of crises: U.S. identity and missiles in Cuba," in Jutta Weldes, Mark Laffey, Hugh Gusterson, and Raymond Duvall, eds., *Cultures of Insecurity: States, Communities, and the Production of Danger,* manuscript.

Weldes, Jutta, and Diana Saco. 1996. "Making state action possible: The U.S. and the discursive construction of 'the Cuban Problem,' 1960–1994." *Millennium: Journal of International Studies* 25(2): 361–395.

"We must win the cold war." 1961. Editorial. *Life,* June 2, 64.

Wendt, Alexander. 1987. "The agent-structure problem in international relations theory." *International Organization* 41(3): 335–370.

———. 1992. "Anarchy is what states make of it: The social construction of power politics." *International Organization* 46(2): 391–425.

White, Hayden. 1978. *Tropics of Discourse: Essays in Cultural Criticism.* Baltimore: Johns Hopkins University Press.

———. 1987. *The Content of the Form: Narrative Discourse and Historical Representation.* Baltimore: Johns Hopkins University Press.

"White House tapes and minutes of the Cuban missile crisis: ExCom meetings, October 1962." 1985. Introduction by Marc Trachtenberg. *International Security* 10(1): 164–203.

"White House upholds tenet." 1960. *New York Times,* July 13, 3.

White, Mark J. 1996. *The Cuban Missile Crisis.* New York: New York University Press.

Whitefield, Mimi. 1993. "Cuba not seen as Clinton priority: Some say administration might work to improve ties." *Miami Herald,* January 12, 6A.

Willauer, Whiting. 1961. "The crisis in U.S. interests in the Caribbean." Reprinted in U.S. Senate Committee on the Judiciary, *Communist Threat to the United States through the Caribbean: Hearings before the Subcommittee to Investigate the Administration of the Internal Security Act and Other Internal Security Laws,* 882–887. 87th Cong., Part 13, March 29, April 26, June 1, and July 27. Washington, DC: Government Printing Office, 1962.

Williams, Raymond. 1979. *Politics and Letters: Interviews with New Left Review.* London: New Left Books.

Williams, William Appleman. 1962 [1959]. *The Tragedy of American Diplomacy.* Rev. and enlarged ed. New York: Delta Books.

Wilson, Woodrow. 1918. "Address to Congress," January 8. Reprinted in Thomas A. Bailey, *Woodrow Wilson and the Lost Peace,* 333–334. Chicago: Quadrangle Books, 1944.

Wohlstetter, Albert, and Roberta Wohlstetter. 1965. "Controlling the risks in Cuba." Adelphi paper no. 17. London: Institute of Strategic Studies.

Wolf, Julie. 1992. "Cuba embargo angers EC." *Guardian,* October 9, 15.

Wright, Theodore P. Jr. 1959. "United States electoral intervention in Cuba." *Inter-American Economic Affairs* 13(3): 50–71.

Wyden, Peter. 1979. *Bay of Pigs: The Untold Story.* New York: Simon and Schuster.

Yarmolinsky, Adam. 1970–71. "The military establishment (or how political problems become military problems)." *Foreign Policy* 1 (Winter): 78–97.

Yergin, Daniel. 1977. *Shattered Peace: The Origins of the Cold War and the National Security State.* Boston: Houghton Mifflin.

———. 1990. *Shattered Peace: The Origins of the Cold War.* Updated and rev. ed. New York: Penguin Books.

Index

J<small>UTTA</small> W<small>ELDES</small> is lecturer in international relations at the University of Bristol. Her recent research has focused on U.S. foreign policy, U.S. relations with Cuba, and the role of popular culture in legitimizing U.S. foreign policy. She is the coeditor, with Mark Laffey, Hugh Gusterson, and Raymond Duvall, of *Cultures of Insecurity: States, Communities, and the Production of Danger* (Minnesota, 1999).